Lecture Notes in Computer Scier

Commenced Publication in 1973
Founding and Former Series Editors:
Gerhard Goos, Juris Hartmanis, and Jan van Leeuwen

Sushil Jajodia   Duminda Wijesekera (Eds.)

Data and Applications Security XIX

19th Annual IFIP WG 11.3 Working Conference on
Data and Applications Security
Storrs, CT, USA, August 7-10, 2005
Proceedings

 Springer

Volume Editors

Sushil Jajodia
Duminda Wijesekera
George Mason University
Center for Secure Information Systems
Fairfax, VA 22030, USA
E-mail: {jajodia,dwijesek}@gmu.edu

Library of Congress Control Number: 2005929872

CR Subject Classification (1998): E.3, D.4.6, C.2, F.2.1, J.1, K.6.5

ISSN   0302-9743
ISBN-10   3-540-28138-X Springer Berlin Heidelberg New York
ISBN-13   978-3-540-28138-2 Springer Berlin Heidelberg New York

Springer is a part of Springer Science+Business Media

springeronline.com

© IFIP International Federation for Information Processing 2005
Printed in Germany

Typesetting: Camera-ready by author, data conversion by Scientific Publishing Services, Chennai, India
Printed on acid-free paper   SPIN: 11535706   06/3142   5 4 3 2 1 0

Preface

The 19th Annual IFIP Working Group 11.3 Working Conference on Data and Applications Security was held August 7–10, 2005 at the University of Connecticut in Storrs, Connecticut. The objectives of the working conference were to discuss in depth the current state of the research and practice in data and application security, enable participants to benefit from personal contact with other researchers and expand their knowledge, support the activities of the Working Group, and disseminate the research results.

This volume contains the 24 papers that were presented at the working conference. These papers, which had been selected from 54 submissions, were rigorously reviewed by the Working Group members. The volume is offered both to document progress and to provide researchers with a broad perspective of recent developments in data and application security.

A special note of thanks goes to the many volunteers whose efforts made the working conference a success. We wish to thank Divesh Srivastava for agreeing to deliver the invited talk, Carl Landwehr and David Spooner for organizing the panel, the authors for their worthy contributions, and the referees for their time and effort in reviewing the papers. We are grateful to T. C. Ting for serving as the General Chair, Steven Demurjian and Charles E. Phillips, Jr. for their hard work as Local Arrangements Chairs, and Pierangela Samarati, Working Group Chair, for managing the IFIP approval process. We would also like to acknowledge Sabrina De Capitani di Vimercati for managing the conference's Web site.

Last but certainly not least, our thanks go to Alfred Hofmann, Executive Editor of Springer, for agreeing to include these proceedings in the Lecture Notes in Computer Science series. This is an exciting development since, in parallel to the printed copy, each volume in this series is simultaneously published in the LNCS digital library (www.springerlink.com). As a result, the papers presented at the Working Conference will be available to many more researchers and may serve as sources of inspiration for their research. The expanded availability of these papers should ensure a bright future for our discipline and the working conference.

August 2005   Sushil Jajodia and Duminda Wijesekera

Organization

General Chair   T. C. Ting (University of Connecticut, USA)
Program Chairs   Sushil Jajodia and Duminda Wijesekera
                        (George Mason University, USA)
Organizing Chairs   Steven Demurjian and Charles E. Phillips, Jr.
                        (University of Connecticut, USA)
IFIP WG11.3 Chair   Pierangela Samarati (Università degli Studi di
                        Milano, Italy)

Program Committee

Gail-Joon Ahn	University of North Carolina at Charlotte, USA
Vijay Atluri	Rutgers University, USA
Sabrina De Capitani di Vimercati	Università degli Studi di Milano, Italy
Steve Demurjian	University of Connecticut, USA
Roberto Di Pietro	University of Rome "La Sapienza", Italy
Csilla Farkas	University of South Carolina, USA
Eduardo Fernandez-Medina	Univ. of Castilla-La Mancha, Spain
Simon N. Foley	University College Cork, Ireland
Ehud Gudes	Ben-Gurion University, Israel
Carl Landwehr	National Science Foundation, USA
Tsau Young Lin	San Jose State University, USA
Peng Liu	Pennsylvania State University, USA
Sharad Mehrotra	University of California, Irvine
Ravi Mukkamala	Old Dominion University, USA
Peng Ning	North Carolina State University, USA
Sylvia Osborn	University of Western Ontario, Canada
Brajendra Panda	University of Arkansas, USA
Joon Park	Syracuse University, USA
Charles Phillips	U.S. Military Academy, USA
Indrakshi Ray	Colorado State University, USA
Indrajit Ray	Colorado State University, USA
Pierangela Samarati	University of Milan, USA
Sujeet Shenoi	University of Tulsa, USA
David Spooner	Rennselaer Polytechnic Institute, USA
Bhavani Thuraisingham	University of Texas at Dalla, and The MITRE Corp., USA
T.C. Ting	University of Connecticut, USA
Ting Yu	North Carolina State University, USA

Sponsoring Institutions

Center for Secure Information Systems, George Mason University
Department of Computer Science and Engineering, University of Connecticut
Dipartimento di Tecnologie dell'Informazione, Università degli Studi di Milano

Table of Contents

Streams, Security and Scalability

Theodore Johnson[1], S. Muthukrishnan[2], Oliver Spatscheck[1], and Divesh Srivastava[1]

[1] AT&T Labs–Research
{johnsont, spatsch, divesh}@research.att.com
[2] Rutgers University
muthu@cs.rutgers.edu

Abstract. Network-based attacks, such as DDoS attacks and worms, are threatening the continued utility of the Internet. As the variety and the sophistication of attacks grow, early detection of potential attacks will become crucial in mitigating their impact. We argue that the Gigascope data stream management system has both the functionality and the performance to serve as the foundation for the next generation of network intrusion detection systems.

1 Introduction

The phenomenal success of the Internet has revolutionalized our society, providing us, e.g., the ability to communicate easily with people around the world, and to access and provide a large variety of information-based services. But this success has also enabled hostile agents to use the Internet in many malicious ways (see, e.g., [10,9,36]), and terms like spam, phishing, viruses, worms, DDoS attacks, etc., are now part of the popular lexicon. As network-based attacks increase, the continued utility of the Internet, and of our information infrastructure, critically depends on our ability to rapidly identify these attacks and mitigate their adverse impact.

A variety of tools are now available to help us identify and thwart these attacks, including anti-virus software, firewalls, and network intrusion detection systems (NIDS). Given the difficulty in ensuring that all hosts run the latest version of software, and the limitations of firewalls (e.g., worms have been known to tunnel through firewalls), NIDS are becoming increasingly popular among large enterprises and ISPs. Network intrusion detection systems essentially monitor the traffic entering and/or leaving a protected network, and look for signatures of known types of attacks. In practice, different NIDS use different mechanisms for the flexible specification of attack signatures. Snort [34], e.g., uses open source rules to help detect various attacks (such as port scans) and alert users. Bro [32], e.g., permits a site's security policy to be specified in a high-level language, which is then interpreted by a policy script interpreter.

As the variety and the sophistication of attacks grow, early detection of potential attacks will become crucial in mitigating the subsequent impact of these attacks (see, e.g., [16,23,25,26,29,24,33,38]). Thus, intrusion detection systems would need to become even more sophisticated, in particular for traffic monitored at high speed (Gbit/sec) links, and it becomes imperative for the next generation of NIDS to:

– provide general analysis over headers and contents of elements in network data streams (e.g., IP traffic, BGP update messages) to detect potential attack signatures.

S. Jajodia and D. Wijesekera (Eds.): Data and Applications Security 2005, LNCS 3654, pp. 1–15, 2005.

– provide highly flexible mechanisms for specifying known attack signatures over these network data streams.
– provide efficient (wire-speed) mechanisms for checking these signatures, to identify and mitigate high speed attacks.

In this paper, we explore the utility of a general-purpose data stream management system (see, e.g., [2,1,4,11]), in particular, Gigascope [13,14,15,12,20], for this purpose We argue that Gigascope has both the *functionality* and the *performance* to serve as the foundation for the next generation of network intrusion detection systems.

The rest of this paper is structured as follows. Section 2 presents the main features of Gigascope's query language in an example driven fashion. Section 3 describes a few representative network-based attacks, and illustrates how Gigascope can be used to aid in the detection of these attacks. Finally, Section 4 describes aspects of Gigascope's run-time architecture that enables high performance attack detection.

2   Gigascope

Gigascope is a high-performance data stream management system (DSMS) designed for monitoring of networks with high-speed data streams, which is operationally used within AT&T's IP backbone [13,14,15,12,20]. Gigascope is intended to be adaptable so it can be used as the primary data analysis engine in many settings: traffic analysis, performance monitoring and debugging, protocol analysis and development, router configuration (e.g., BGP monitoring), network attack and intrusion detection, and various ad hoc analyses. In this section, we focus on the query aspects of Gigascope, and defer a discussion of Gigascope's high-performance implementation until Section 4.

Gigascope's query language, GSQL, is a pure stream query language with an SQL-like syntax, i.e., all inputs to a GSQL query are data streams, and the output is a data stream [20,27]. This choice enables the composition of GSQL queries for complex query processing, and simplifies the implementation. Here, we present the main features of GSQL in an example driven fashion. Later, in Section 3, we show how GSQL can be used to detect various network attacks.

2.1   Data Model

Data from an external source arrives in the form of a sequence of data packets at one or more interfaces that Gigascope monitors. These data packets can be IP packets, Netflow packets, BGP updates, etc., and are interpreted by a protocol. The Gigascope run-time system interprets the data packets as a collection of fields using a library of interpretation functions. The schema of a *protocol stream* maps field names to the interpretation functions to invoke [20].

```
PROTOCOL packet {
    uint time get_time (required, increasing);
    ullong timestamp get_timestamp (required, increasing);
    uint caplen get_caplen;
    unit len get_len;
}
```

```
PROTOCOL Ethernet (packet) {
    ullong Eth_src_addr get_eth_src_addr (required);
    ullong Eth_dst_addr get_eth_dst_addr (required);
    ...
}

PROTOCOL IP (Ethernet) {
    uint ipversion get_ip_version;
}

PROTOCOL IPV4 (IP) {
    uint protocol get_ipv4_protocol;
    IP sourceIP get_ipv4_source_ip;
    IP destIP get_ipv4_dest_ip;
    ...
}
```

Network protocols tend to be layered, e.g., an IPV4 packet is delivered via an Ethernet link. As a convenience, the protocol schemas have a mechanism for field inheritance (specified in parentheses). For example, the `Ethernet` protocol contains all the fields of the `packet` protocol, as well as a few others.

2.2   Filters

A *filter* query selects a subset of tuples of its input stream, extracts a set of fields (possibly transforming them), then outputs the transformed tuples in its output stream. The following query extracts a set of fields for detailed analysis from all TCP (`protocol` = 6) packets.

Q_1^s: SELECT   time, timestamp, sourceIP, destIP,
                    source_port, dest_port, len
      FROM   TCP
      WHERE   protocol = 6

Gigascope supports multiple data types (include IP), and multiple operations on these data types. The following query extracts a few fields from the IPV4 tuples whose `sourceIP` matches `128.209.0.0/24`, and names the resulting data stream as `fq` (this can then be referenced in subsequent GSQL queries).

Q_2^s: DEFINE   { query_name fq; }
      SELECT   time, sourceIP, destIP
      FROM   IPV4
      WHERE   sourceIP & IP_VAL'255.255.255.0' = IP_VAL'128.209.0.0'

2.3   User-Defined Functions

While GSQL has a wide variety of built-in operators, there are situations where a user-defined function would be more appropriate. Gigascope permits users to define functions, and reference them in GSQL queries. The following query, for example, uses longest prefix matching on the `sourceIP` address against the local prefix table to extract data about IPV4 packets from local hosts.

Q_1^f: SELECT   time/60, sourceIP
       FROM   IPV4
       WHERE   getlpmid(sourceIP, 'localprefix.tbl') > 0

2.4   Aggregation

The following *aggregation* query counts the number of `IPV4` packets and the sum of their lengths from each source IP address during 60 second epochs.

Q_1^a: SELECT   tb, sourceIP, count(*), sum(len)
       FROM   IPV4
       GROUP BY time/60 as tb, sourceIP

Aggregation can be combined with user-defined functions to create sophisticated analyses. The following aggregation query uses a group variable computed using a user-defined function, to count the number of `IPV4` packets and the sum of their lengths from each local host during 60 second epochs.

Q_2^a: SELECT   tb, localHost, count(*), sum(len)
       FROM   IPV4
       WHERE   getlpmid(sourceIP, 'localprefix.tbl') > 0
       GROUP BY time/60 as tb,
                getlpmid(sourceIP, 'localprefix.tbl') as localHost

2.5   Merges and Joins

A GSQL *merge* query permits the union of streams from multiple sources into a single stream, while preserving the temporal (ordering) properties of one of the (specified) attributes. The input streams must have the same number and types of fields, and the merge fields must be temporal and similarly monotonic (both increasing or both decreasing). For example, the following query can be used to merge data packets from two simplex *physical* (optical) links to obtain a full view of the traffic on a *logical* link. Such merge queries have proven very useful in Gigascope for network data analysis.

Q_1^m: DEFINE   { query_name logicalPktsLink; }
       MERGE   O1.timestamp : O2.timestamp
       FROM   opticalPktsLink1 O1, opticalPktsLink2 O2

A GSQL *join* query supports the join of two data streams, with a temporal join predicate (possibly along with other predicates), and will emit a tuple for every pair of tuples from its sources that satisfy the predicate in the GSQL WHERE clause. The following query, for example, computes the delay between a tcp_syn and a tcp_ack.

Q_1^j: SELECT S.tb, S.sourceIP, S.destIP, S.source_port,
              S.dest_port, (A.timestamp − S.timestamp)
       FROM   tcp_syn S, tcp_ack A
       WHERE   S.sourceIP = A.destIP and S.destIP = A.sourceIP and
              S.source_port = A.dest_port and S.dest_port = A.source_port
              S.tb = A.tb and S.timestamp $<=$ A.timestamp and
              (S.sequence_number + 1) = A.ack_number

Joins can be combined with aggregates for complex GSQL queries.

2.6 User-Defined Aggregation and Sampling

GSQL permits users to define aggregate functions (UDAFs), and reference them in queries, just like regular aggregates [12]. The specification of the UDAF consists of multiple functions: INITIALIZE (which initializes the state of a scratchpad space), IT-ERATE (which inserts a value to the state of the UDAF), OUTPUT (to support multiple return values from the same UDAF computation), and DESTROY (which releases UDAF resources).[1]

For example, using GSQL's UDAF mechanism, approximate quantile streaming algorithms can be coded, and accessed like in the following query, to compute the median value of len for each source IP address and 60 second epoch:

Q_1^u: SELECT tb, sourceIP, count(*), percentile(len,50)
       FROM   IPV4
       GROUP BY time/60 as tb, sourceIP

The UDAF mechanism is useful to obtain point values (e.g., median packet length), but it is cumbersome for obtaining set values, such as in returning a sample of the data stream (e.g., a subset-sums or a reservoir sample). Given the utility of sampling to analyze high-speed streams, GSQL supports a sampling operator that can be specialized by users to implement a wide variety of stream sampling algorithms [21]. The key observation employed is that even though there are many differences between various stream sampling algorithms, they follow a common pattern. First, a number of items are collected from the original data stream according to a certain criterion (possibly with aggregation in the case of duplicates); this is the *insert* phase. Then, if a condition on the sample is triggered (e.g., the sample is too large), the size of the sample is reduced according to another criterion; this is the *compress* phase. This alternation of insert and compress phases can be repeated several times in each epoch. At the end of the epoch, the sample is output; this is the *output* phase. For example, the following query will report the 100 most common source IP addresses within a 60 second epoch.

---

[1] Additional functions are needed to deal with Gigascope's two-level architecture, which we do not discuss further.

Q_2^u: SELECT   tb, sourceIP
         FROM   IPV4
         GROUP BY time/60 as tb, sourceIP
         CLEANING WHEN   local_count(100) = TRUE
         CLEANING BY   count(*) < current_bucket() − first(current_bucket())

2.7 Query Set

Complex analyses are best expressed as combinations of simpler pieces. By permitting GSQL queries to be named, and re-used in the FROM clause of other GSQL queries, a set of inter-related queries, forming a query DAG, can be defined.

3 Attacks

A large variety of network-based attacks have been discussed in the literature, including viruses, worms, DDoS attacks, etc. (see, e.g., [10,9,16,23,25,26,29,24,33,36,38]). Here, we discuss a few representative attacks, and illustrate how Gigascope can be used to aid in the detection of these attacks.

3.1 Denial of Service

A *denial of service* (DoS) attack is characterized by an explicit attempt by attackers to prevent legitimate users of a service from using that service [7]. DoS attacks have been among the most common form of Internet attacks. The basic form of a DoS attack is to consume scarce computer and network resources, such as kernel data structures, CPU time, memory and disk space, and network bandwidth.

Email Bombing: An example DoS attack that attempts to consume system and network resources is Email Bombing, where attackers send excessively many and large e-mail messages to one or more accounts at a specific victim site [8]. When the attacker makes use of a dispersed set of sources to coordinate such an attack, it is referred to as a distributed DoS (DDoS) attack.

Email Bombing can be detected at the victim site if email is sluggish, possibly because the mailer is trying to process too many messages. An alternative way of checking for this possibility is to monitor the SMTP traffic entering a protected network using Gigascope, and check for hosts that show significant deviations in expected traffic at port 25/SMTP. The following simple GSQL query can track the total SMTP traffic for individual destination IP addresses. Deviations can be monitored by comparing recent behavior with more historical trends.

Q_1^{dos}:DEFINE   { query_name smtp_perhost; }
        SELECT   tb, destIP, count(*), sum(len)
        FROM   TCP
        WHERE   protocol = 6 and dest_port = 25
        GROUP BY time/60 as tb, destIP

Note that, since the number of destination IP addresses in a protected network is likely to be limited, the number of groups created by this query would not explode, even under email bombing. This is similar to "semi-streaming" where we maintain statistics per group or entity [31]. Only the count of the number of packets, and the sum of the packet lengths, would increase for victim hosts.

If the number of destination IP addresses in a network is very large, one can use GSQL's sampling mechanism to keep track of the destination IP addresses, e.g., with the largest counts, using a variant of query Q_2^u.

TCP SYN Flood: A more complex attack against network connectivity, by consuming kernel data structures, is the TCP SYN Flood attack [6], which exploits the 3-way handshake used to establish a TCP connection between a sender and a receiver. In a normal scenario, a sender initiates a TCP connection by sending a SYN packet, the receiver responds with a SYN/ACK packet, and the sender completes the 3-way handshake with an ACK packet. After sending the SYN/ACK packet, the receiver allocates connection resources (kernel data structures) to remember the pending connection for a pre-specified amount of time. A TCP SYN Flood attack occurs when an attacker repeatedly sends SYN packets, typically with different source addresses, causing the receiver to deplete its connection resources, preventing service to legitimate users.

In principle, TCP SYN Flood can be identified by correlating the SYN packets with matching ACK packets in the stream of TCP packets, and alarming when too many SYN packets in a specified time interval appear to be unmatched. The GSQL query set for this purpose, Q_2^{dos}, makes use of joins, as shown below. The outer join ensures that output tuples will be computed even when there are no matched SYN packets in an epoch. Note that this is an estimate since in certain loss conditions, and due to epoch boundary issues, we might get approximate results.

Q_2^{dos}:DEFINE { query_name toomany_syn; }
   SELECT A.tb, (A.cnt − M.cnt)
   OUTER_JOIN FROM all_syn_count A, matched_syn_count M
   WHERE A.tb = M.tb

   DEFINE { query_name all_syn_count; }
   SELECT S.tb, count(*) as cnt
   FROM tcp_syn S
   GROUP BY S.tb

   DEFINE { query_name matched_syn_count; }
   SELECT S.tb, count(*) as cnt
   FROM tcp_syn S, tcp_ack A
   WHERE S.sourceIP = A.destIP and S.destIP = A.sourceIP and
     S.source_port = A.dest_port and S.dest_port = A.source_port
     S.tb = A.tb and S.timestamp <= A.timestamp and
     (S.sequence_number + 1) = A.ack_number
   GROUP BY S.tb

Over a high-speed (e.g., 1 Gbit/sec) link, one could see up to 3 million SYN packets per second [29]. In the worst-case, for reasonably large (multi-second) round-trip times, this may require too much memory to compute the join in matched_syn_count. In such cases, one could sample random SYN packets in the incoming stream (see Section 4.3), and check if they are matched (see, e.g., [17]). A sampling algorithm like reservoir sampling [37], which has been instantiated using GSQL's sampling operator, would suffice for this task.

Alternatively, one could simply count the number of SYN packets and the number of ACK packets in specified windows, and declare the possibility of an attack if there are more of the former than of the latter (as advocated by [38]). The query in Gigascope for this approach is shown below.

Q_2^{dos}:DEFINE   { query_name toomany_syn; }
  SELECT   A.tb, (S.cnt − A.cnt)
  OUTER_JOIN FROM all_syn_count S, all_ack_count A
  WHERE   S.tb = A.tb and (S.cnt − A.cnt) > 0

  DEFINE   { query_name all_syn_count; }
  SELECT   S.tb, count(*) as cnt
  FROM   tcp_syn S
  GROUP BY S.tb

  DEFINE   { query_name all_ack_count; }
  SELECT   A.tb, count(*) as cnt
  FROM   tcp_ack A
  GROUP BY A.tb

3.2 Worms and Viruses

A *worm* is self-propagating malicious code [9]. Unlike a *virus*, which requires a user to do something (such as opening an infected email attachment) for its negative impact, a worm exploits vulnerabilities in the underlying operating system to inflict its damage, and to replicate and propagate by itself. They have been widely discussed in the popular press, because of the significant damage they have caused to the productivity and infrastructure of users.

Viruses rely on user action for their propagation, and hence tend to spread slowly. However, the highly automated nature of worms, along with the relatively widespread nature of the vulnerabilities they exploit allows a large number of systems to be quickly compromised. For example, the Code Red worm exploited a vulnerability in Microsoft IIS servers, and infected more than 250,000 systems in about 9 hours on July 19, 2001. As another example, the Slammer worm exploited a vulnerability in Microsoft's SQL Server 2000 code, and affected nearly 100,000 hosts in 10 minutes on January 25, 2003. Some worms include built-in DoS attack payloads, while others have web site defacement payloads (e.g., Code Red). But, often, their biggest impact is in the collateral damage they cause as they rapidly propagate through the Internet.

Known Worms: Worms can be identified by their payload, and their specific mechanism of propagation. For example, activity of the `Slammer` worm is identifiable in a network by the presence of 376-byte `UDP` packets, destined for port 1434/`UDP` of SQL Server, using the following query.

Q_1^{wv}: DEFINE   { query_name slammer_worm; }
     SELECT   tb, destIP, count(*)
     FROM   UDP
     WHERE   protocol = 17 and dest_port = 1434 and total_ipv4_length = 376
     GROUP BY time/60 as tb, destIP

A number of such header profiles have been identified by detailed traffic analysis [28], and can be encoded directly as GSQL queries.

Unknown Worms: Since worms are self-replicating, ongoing worm propagation should be reflected in the presence of higher than expected *string similarity* among the payloads of network packets. This similarity is due to the unchanging portions of the worm packet payload, which is expected to be present even in polymorphic worms. This intuition has been exploited by various systems like EarlyBird [33] and Autograph [25], which use the frequency of substrings in packet payloads to generate signatures of sources of content similarity (which in turn are indicative of potential worms). A GSQL query akin to Q_2^u could be used to compute heavy hitters on the substring counts of the payload, for this purpose.

Recent work has also examined the utility of the inverse distribution (for a given frequency f, the number of substrings that appear with that frequency) to permit faster detection of potential worms [24]. The following GSQL query can be used for computation of the inverse distribution.

Q_2^{wv}: DEFINE   { query_name inverse_distrib; }
     SELECT   B.tb, B.cnt, COUNT(*) AS invCnt
     FROM   base_distrib B
     GROUP BY B.tb, B.cnt

     DEFINE   { query_name base_distrib; }
     SELECT   C.tb, C.SId, COUNT(*) AS cnt
     FROM   ContentStrings C
     GROUP BY C.tb, C.SId

The cost of this query depends on the number of distinct substrings over all payloads, which is independent of the frequency of worm propagation.

3.3 Probing for Vulnerability

Attacks exploit known vulnerabilities in services. A typical precursor to attacks is the identification of machines that have specific services available, and hence can be potentially exploited. This takes the form of an attacker probing for open ports on a set of host machines (see, e.g., [23,29]).

Ingress Detection: To determine if a port is open, an attacker sends a packet to a host, attempting to connect to the specific port. If the target host is listening on that port, it will respond by opening a connection with the attacker. This implies that during the probing phase, the attacker would not spoof the `sourceIP` address. By monitoring the number of distinct (`destIP, dest_port`) pairs with the same `sourceIP`, one can check for anomalous activity using the following GSQL query.

Q_1^{pv}: SELECT   tb, sourceIP, count_distinct(PACK(destIP, dest_port)) AS cnt
         FROM   TCP
         GROUP BY time/60 as tb, sourceIP

A simpler GSQL query, below, simply tracks the number of distinct targets probed (potentially from different hosts, as would arise in a distributed vulnerability probe), and uses an anomalous increase in this number as an indicator of suspicious activity.

Q_2^{pv}: SELECT   tb, count_distinct(PACK(destIP, dest_port)) AS cnt
         FROM   TCP
         GROUP BY time/60 as tb

Egress Detection: If the target host does not have a listening process on a port, a different kind of response may be generated. For example, a packet sent to such a UDP port may generate an ICMP "port unreachable" response, while a packet sent to such a *TCP* port may generate an RST packet in response. Vulnerability probes (or, port scans) can hence be also identified by monitoring the number of distinct destination addresses generating such responses [29]. This can be easily captured by a variant of Q_2^{pv}, above.

4   Scalability

Gigascope is designed for monitoring very high speed data streams, using inexpensive processors. For example, in [22], non-trivial query sets were run at over 200,000 packets/sec, while using only 38% of one CPU in a two CPU system. To accomplish this goal, Gigascope uses an architecture optimized for its particular applications, incorporating unblocking using timestamps and heartbeats, a two-level architecture, and sophisticated sampling algorithms, each of which are described below.

4.1   Unblocking, Timestamps and Heartbeats

The Gigascope DSMS evaluates queries over potentially infinite streams of tuples. To produce useful output, it must be able to unblock operators such as aggregation, join, and union. In general, this unblocking is done by limiting the scope of output tuples that an input tuple affects. One unblocking mechanism is to define queries over windows of the input stream.

Gigascope's technique for localizing input tuple scope is to require that some fields of the input data streams be identified as behaving like timestamps, e.g., be monotone increasing [14]. The locality of input tuples is determined by analyzing how the query references the timestamp fields. For example, a merge or a join query must relate timestamp fields of both inputs, and an aggregation query must have a timestamp field as one of its group-by variables. For example, suppose that time is labeled as monotone increasing in the TCP stream. Then the tb group-by variable in Query Q_1^q (which counts the packets from each source IP address during 60 second epochs) is inferred also to be monotone increasing. When this variable changes in value, all existing groups and their aggregates are flushed to the operator's output. The values of the group-by variables thus define epochs in which aggregation occurs, with a flush at the end of each epoch.

The timestamp analysis mechanism is quite effective for unblocking operators as long as all input streams make progress. However, if one of the input streams stalls, operators that combine two streams (such as merge, which preserves timestamp order in the output data stream) can stall, possibly leading to a system failure. This can happen, for example, when merging traffic from a gigabit primary link and a backup link (which is used only when the primary link fails, and hence usually carries almost no traffic), for attack analysis. The main problem is that while the presence of tuples in the stream carries temporal information, their absence does not. In such situations, heartbeats or punctuations (see, e.g., [35]) can be used to unblock operators.

Gigascope's punctuation-carrying heartbeats [22] are generated by source query operators by regularly injecting the heartbeat messages carrying temporal update tuples into their output streams. A streaming operator in a subsequent query node in the query DAG emits temporal update tuples whenever it receives a heartbeat from one of its source streams. Thus, the heartbeats propagate throughout the query DAG. [22] discusses detailed implementation issues, and demonstrates the effectiveness of these heartbeats (significant reduction in memory load with a negligible CPU cost), using experiments with join and merge queries over very high-speed data streams.

4.2 Two-Level Architecture

Gigascope has a two-level query architecture, where the *low* level is used for data reduction and the *high* level performs more complex processing [14,12]. This approach is employed for keeping up with high streaming rates in a controlled way. High speed data streams from, e.g., a Network Interface Card (NIC), are placed in a large ring buffer. These streams are called source streams to distinguish them from data streams created by queries. The data volumes of these source streams are far too large to provide a copy to each query on the stream. Instead, the queries are shipped to the streams. If a query Q is to be executed over source stream S, then Gigascope creates a subquery q that directly accesses S, and transforms Q into Q' which is executed over the output from q. In general, one subquery is created for every table variable that aliases a source stream, for every query in the current query set. The subqueries read directly from the ring buffer. Since their output streams are much smaller than the source stream, this *two-level architecture* greatly reduces the amount of copying (simple queries can be evaluated directly on a source stream).

The subqueries (which are called "LFTAs", or low-level queries, in Gigascope) are intended to be fast, lightweight data reduction queries. By deferring expensive processing (expensive functions and predicates, joins, large scale aggregation), the high volume source stream is quickly processed, minimizing buffer requirements. The expensive processing is performed on the output of the low level queries, but this data volume is smaller and easily buffered. Depending on the capabilities of the NIC, we can push some or all of the subquery processing into the NIC itself. In general, the most appropriate strategy depends on the streaming rate as well as the available processing resources. Choosing the best strategy is a complex query optimization problem, that attempts to maximize the amount of data reduction without overburdening the low level processor and thus causing packet drops.

Gigascope uses a large number of optimizations to lower the LFTA processing costs. Low-level operators are compiled into C code that are linked directly to the runtime library to avoid expensive runtime query interpretation. To ensure that aggregation is fast, the low-level aggregation operator uses a fixed-size hash table for maintaining the different groups of a GROUP BY. If a hash table collision occurs, the existing group and its aggregate are ejected (as a tuple), and the new group uses the old group's slot. That is, Gigascope computes a partial aggregate at the low level which is completed at a higher level. The query decomposition of an aggregate query Q is similar to that of subaggregates and superaggregates in data cube computations.

The Gigascope DSMS has many aspects of a real-time system: for example, if the system cannot keep up with the offered load, it will drop tuples. To spread out the processing load over time and thus improve schedulability, Gigascope implements traffic-shaping policies in some of its operators. In particular, the aggregation operator uses a *slow flush* to emit tuples when the aggregation epoch changes. One output tuple is emitted for every input tuple which arrives, until all finished groups have been output (or the epoch changes again, in which case all old groups are flushed immediately).

4.3 Sampling

The complex query set needed to analyze high-speed streams for attacks would often need to rely on approximations, using streaming algorithms, to keep up with their input. Many of these streaming algorithms compute samples (i.e., a small-sized representative of the data suitable for specific queries) in one pass over a high speed data stream. These stream sampling algorithms include generic sampling methods such as fixed-size reservoir sampling [37], as well as methods for estimating specific user-defined aggregates such as heavy hitters [30], distinct counts [18], quantiles [19], and subset-sums [3].

One approach developed in [21] is to develop a single operator that can be specialized to implement a wide variety of stream sampling algorithms. The sampling algorithms that can be implemented as specializations of the sampling operator permit a very simple communication structure, i.e., only between individual samples and the sample summary. The process of sampling is in some ways similar to that of aggregation, since they both collect and output sets of tuples that are representative of the input, while achieving data reduction. This analogy leads to an efficient implementation, based on the use of multiple hash tables, of all specializations of the sampling operator.

An alternative, more flexible, approach to implementing individual stream sampling algorithms in Gigascope is with user-defined aggregate functions (UDAFs). This approach was explored in [12], where both sampling-based UDAFs and sketch-based UDAFs were implemented. The added flexibility of the UDAF approach, even for sampling-based algorithms, is that it permits the specification of algorithms that need "inter-sample communication", especially during the compress phase (such as the quantile algorithm of [19]). Several key performance lessons were identified. First, early data reduction is critical for complex querying of very high speed data streams, and Gigascope's two-level architecture is highly suitable for this purpose. Second, there is often a range of early data reduction strategies to choose from for processing complex aggregates, including use of appropriate subaggregation. The most appropriate strategy depends on the streaming rate as well as the available processing resources; choosing the best strategy is a complex optimization problem, with the goal of maximizing the amount of data reduction without overburdening the low-level query processor.

5 Conclusion

Network-based attacks, such as DDoS attacks, worms, and viruses are now commonplace, and the variety and sophistication of attacks keeps growing over time. Early detection of potential attacks will become crucial in mitigating the subsequent impact of these attacks. Thus, it is imperative for the next generation of NIDS to:

- provide general analysis over headers and contents of elements in network data streams to detect potential attack signatures.
- provide highly flexible mechanisms for specifying known attack signatures over network data streams.
- provide efficient (wire-speed) mechanisms for checking these signatures, to identify and mitigate high speed attacks.

We argue that the Gigascope DSMS has both the functionality and the performance to serve as the foundation for the next generation of network intrusion detection systems. The *functionality* is provided by the expressive, yet high-level, GSQL query language, which supports a rich variety of features including filters, user-defined functions, user-defined aggregation and sampling, and joins. Using example GSQL queries, we have illustrated the utility of these features for discerning and specifying attack signatures. The *performance* is provided by the Gigascope architecture for monitoring very high speed data streams, incorporating features like unblocking using timestamps and heartbeats, a two-level architecture, and sophisticated sampling algorithms.

As network-based attacks evolve, Gigascope will need to evolve as well. Sophisticated cooperation between a distributed set of Gigascope installations will be needed to identify highly distributed attacks on the network infrastructure. Statistical anomaly detection algorithms, both parametric and non-parametric, will need to be expressed in the query language. Sampling and signature computations on the payload, involving reassembly of network packets, will prove useful. We think that Gigascope will be able to meet these challenges.

Acknowledgements

We would like to thank Balachander Krishnamurthy, Morley Mao, Shubho Sen, and Kobus Van der Merwe, for many helpful discussions.

References

1. D. J. Abadi, Y. Ahmad, M. Balazinska, U. Çetintemel, M. Cherniack, J.-H. Hwang, W. Lindner, A. Maskey, A. Rasin, E. Ryvkina, N. Tatbul, Y. Xing, and S. B. Zdonik. The design of the Borealis stream processing engine. In *CIDR*, pages 277–289, 2005. http://www-db.cs.wisc.edu/cidr/papers/P23.pdf.

2. D. J. Abadi, D. Carney, U. Çetintemel, M. Cherniack, C. Convey, S. Lee, M. Stonebraker, N. Tatbul, and S. B. Zdonik. Aurora: A new model and architecture for data stream management. *VLDB J.*, 12(2):120–139, 2003. http://dx.doi.org/10.1007/s00778-003-0095-z.

3. N. Alon, N. G. Duffield, C. Lund, and M. Thorup. Estimating arbitrary subset sums with few probes. In *PODS*, 2005.

4. A. Arasu, B. Babcock, S. Babu, M. Datar, K. Ito, R. Motwani, I. Nishizawa, U. Srivastava, D. Thomas, R. Varma, and J. Widom. Stream: The Stanford stream data manager. *IEEE Data Eng. Bull.*, 26(1):19–26, 2003.

5. V. Atluri, B. Pfitzmann, and P. McDaniel, editors. *Proceedings of the 11th ACM Conference on Computer and Communications Security, CCS 2004, Washington, DC, USA, October 25-29, 2004.* ACM, 2004.

6. CERT. Cert advisory ca-1996-21 TCP SYN flooding and IP spoofing attacks. http://www.cert.org/advisories/CA-1996-21.html, 2000.

7. CERT. Cert coordination center: Denial of service attacks. http://www.cert.org/tech_tips/denial_of_service.html, 2001.

8. CERT. Cert coordination center: Email bombing and spamming. http://www.cert.org/tech_tips/email_bombing_spamming.html, 2002.

9. CERT. Overview of attack trends. http://www.cert.org/archive/pdf/attack_trends.pdf, 2002.

10. CERT. Cert/cc advisories. http://www.cert.org/advisories/, 2004.

11. S. Chandrasekaran, O. Cooper, A. Deshpande, M. J. Franklin, J. M. Hellerstein, W. Hong, S. Krishnamurthy, S. Madden, V. Raman, F. Reiss, and M. A. Shah. TelegraphCQ: Continuous dataflow processing for an uncertain world. In *CIDR*, 2003. http://www-db.cs.wisc.edu/cidr2003/program/p24.pdf.

12. G. Cormode, T. Johnson, F. Korn, S. Muthukrishnan, O. Spatscheck, and D. Srivastava. Holistic UDAFs at streaming speeds. In G. Weikum, A. C. König, and S. Deßloch, editors, *SIGMOD Conference*, pages 35–46. ACM, 2004. http://doi.acm.org/10.1145/1007568.1007575.

13. C. D. Cranor, Y. Gao, T. Johnson, V. Shkapenyuk, and O. Spatscheck. Gigascope: High performance network monitoring with an SQL interface. In M. J. Franklin, B. Moon, and A. Ailamaki, editors, *SIGMOD Conference*, page 623. ACM, 2002. http://doi.acm.org/10.1145/564691.564777.

14. C. D. Cranor, T. Johnson, O. Spatscheck, and V. Shkapenyuk. Gigascope: A stream database for network applications. In A. Y. Halevy, Z. G. Ives, and A. Doan, editors, *SIGMOD Conference*, pages 647–651. ACM, 2003. http://www.acm.org/sigmod/sigmod03/eproceedings/papers/ind03.pdf.

15. C. D. Cranor, T. Johnson, O. Spatscheck, and V. Shkapenyuk. The Gigascope stream database. *IEEE Data Eng. Bull.*, 26(1):27–32, 2003.

16. H. Dreger, A. Feldmann, V. Paxson, and R. Sommer. Operational experiences with high-volume network intrusion detection. In Atluri et al. [5], pages 2–11. http://doi.acm.org/10.1145/1030086.

17. C. Estan and G. Varghese. New directions in traffic measurement and accounting: Focusing on the elephants, ignoring the mice. *ACM Trans. Comput. Syst.*, 21(3):270–313, 2003. http://doi.acm.org/10.1145/859716.859719.

18. P. B. Gibbons. Distinct sampling for highly-accurate answers to distinct values queries and event reports. In P. M. G. Apers, P. Atzeni, S. Ceri, S. Paraboschi, K. Ramamohanarao, and R. T. Snodgrass, editors, *VLDB*, pages 541–550. Morgan Kaufmann, 2001. http://www.vldb.org/conf/2001/P541.pdf.

19. M. Greenwald and S. Khanna. Space-efficient online computation of quantile summaries. In *SIGMOD Conference*, 2001. http://www.acm.org/sigs/sigmod/sigmod01/eproceedings/papers/Research-Greenwald-Khanna.pdf.

20. T. Johnson. GSQL users manual. Accessible from http://www.research.att.com/~johnsont, 2005.

21. T. Johnson, S. Muthukrishnan, and I. Rozenbaum. Sampling algorithms in a stream operator. In *SIGMOD Conference*, 2005.

22. T. Johnson, S. Muthukrishnan, V. Shkapenyuk, and O. Spatscheck. A heartbeat mechanism and its application in Gigascope. In *VLDB Conference*, 2005.

23. J. Jung, V. Paxson, A. W. Berger, and H. Balakrishnan. Fast portscan detection using sequential hypothesis testing. In *IEEE Symposium on Security and Privacy*, pages 211–225. IEEE Computer Society, 2004. http://csdl.computer.org/comp/proceedings/sp/2004/2136/00/21360211abs.htm.

24. V. Karamcheti, D. Geiger, Z. Kedem, and S. Muthukrishnan. Detecting malicious network traffic using inverse distributions of packet contents. In *MineNet*, 2005.

25. H.-A. Kim and B. Karp. Autograph: Toward automated, distributed worm signature detection. In *USENIX Security Symposium*, pages 271–286. USENIX, 2004. http://www.usenix.org/publications/library/proceedings/sec04/tech/kim. html.

26. R. R. Kompella, S. Singh, and G. Varghese. On scalable attack detection in the network. In A. Lombardo and J. F. Kurose, editors, *Internet Measurement Conference*, pages 187–200. ACM, 2004. http://doi.acm.org/10.1145/1028812.

27. N. Koudas and D. Srivastava. Data stream query processing. In *ICDE*, page 1145. IEEE Computer Society, 2005. http://csdl.computer.org/comp/proceedings/icde/2005/2285/00/22851145abs.htm.

28. A. Lakhina, M. Crovella, and C. Diot. Mining anomalies using traffic feature distributions. In *SIGCOMM*, 2005.

29. K. Levchenko, R. Paturi, and G. Varghese. On the difficulty of scalably detecting network attacks. In Atluri et al. [5], pages 12–20. http://doi.acm.org/10.1145/1030087.

30. G. S. Manku and R. Motwani. Approximate frequency counts over data streams. In *VLDB*, pages 346–357, 2002. http://www.vldb.org/conf/2002/S10P03.pdf.

31. S. Muthukrishnan. Data stream algorithms and applications. http://www.cs.rutgers.edu/~muthu/stream-1-1.ps, 2005.

32. V. Paxson. Bro: A system for detecting network intruders in real-time. *Computer Networks*, 31(23-24):2435–2463, 1999. http://dx.doi.org/10.1016/S1389-1286(99)00112-7.

33. S. Singh, C. Estan, G. Varghese, and S. Savage. Automated worm fingerprinting. In *OSDI*, pages 45–60, 2004. http://www.usenix.org/events/osdi04/tech/singh.html.

34. Snort. The de facto standard for intrusion detection. http://www.snort.org.

35. P. A. Tucker, D. Maier, T. Sheard, and L. Fegaras. Exploiting punctuation semantics in continuous data streams. *IEEE Trans. Knowl. Data Eng.*, 15(3):555–568, 2003. http://www.computer.org/tkde/tk2003/k0555abs.htm.

36. US-CERT. Technical cyber security alerts. http://www.us-cert.gov/cas/techalerts/index.html, 2005.

37. J. S. Vitter. Random sampling with a reservoir. *ACM Trans. Math. Softw.*, 11(1):37–57, 1985.

38. H. Wang, D. Zhang, and K. G. Shin. Detecting SYN flooding attacks. In *INFOCOM*, 2002. http://www.ieee-infocom.org/2002/papers/800.pdf.

Towards Privacy-Enhanced Authorization
Policies and Languages

C.A. Ardagna, E. Damiani, S. De Capitani di Vimercati, and P. Samarati

Dipartimento di Tecnologie dell'Informazione,
Università di Milano –26013 Crema - Italy
{ardagna, damiani, decapita, samarati}@dti.unimi.it

Abstract. The protection of privacy in today's global infrastructure requires the combined application solution from technology (technical measures), legislation (law and public policy), and organizational and individual policies and practices. Emerging scenarios of user-service interactions in the digital world are also pushing toward the development of powerful and flexible privacy-enhanced models and languages.

This paper aims at introducing concepts and features that should be investigated to fulfill this demand. In particular, the content of this paper is a result of our ongoing activity in the framework of the PRIME project (*Privacy and Identity Management for Europe*), funded by the European Commission, whose objective is the development of privacy-aware solutions for enforcing security.

1 Introduction

Traditional access control systems are based on regulations (*policies*) that establish who can, or cannot, execute which actions on which resources. However, in today's systems the definition of an access control model is complicated by the need to formally represent complex policies, where access decisions depend on the application of different rules coming, for example, from laws practices, and organizational regulations. Given the complexity of the scenario, these traditional policies are too limiting and do not satisfy all the above requirements. Although recent advancements allow the specifications of policies with reference to generic attributes/properties of the parties and the resources involved, they are not designed for enforcing privacy policies. For instance, privacy issues that are not addressed by traditional approaches include protecting user identities by providing *anonymity*, *pseudonymity*, *unlinkability*, and *unobservability* of users at communication level, system level, or application level. Therefore, the consideration of privacy issues introduces the need for rethinking authorization policies and models and the development of new paradigms for access control and in particular authorization specification and enforcement.

In this paper, we present our recent research work in the context of the PRIME project [12]. Our work deals with three main key aspects:

S. Jajodia and D. Wijesekera (Eds.): Data and Applications Security 2005, LNCS 3654, pp. 16–27, 2005.

– *Resource representation.* Writing access control policies where resources to be protected are pointed at via data identifiers and access conditions are evaluated against their attribute values is not sufficient anymore. Rather, it is important to be able to specify access control requirements about resources in terms of available *metadata* describing them.
– *Context representation.* Distributed environments have increased the amount of context information available at policy evaluation time (e.g., location-based one), and this information is achieving a more and more important role.
– *Subject identity.* Evaluating conditions on the subject requesting access to a resource often means accessing personal information either presented by the requestor as a part of the authentication process or available elsewhere. Identifying subjects raises a number of privacy issues, since electronic transactions (e.g., purchases) require disclosure of a far greater quantity of information than their physical counterparts.

A privacy-enhanced authorization model and language is then described allowing for definition and enforcement of powerful and flexible access restrictions based on generic properties associated with subjects and objects. We also bring forward the idea of exploiting the semantic web to allow the definition of access control rules based on generic assertions defined over concepts in the ontologies that control metadata content and provide abstract subject domain concepts, respectively [16]. These rules are then enforced on resources annotated with metadata regulated by the same ontologies.

The remainder of this paper is organized as follows. Section 2 presents the different types of privacy policies we have identified. Section 3 and Section 4 illustrate our privacy-enhanced model and language, respectively. Section 5 describes a possible representation of expressing our language by using an XML-based syntax. Finally, Section 6 presents our conclusions.

2   Privacy Policies

To address the requirements mentioned in the previous section, different types of policies need to be introduced.

– *Access control policies.* They govern access/release of data/services managed by the party (as in traditional access control) [4].
– *Release policies.* They govern release of properties/credentials/PII of the party and specify under which conditions they can be disclosed [2].
– *Data handling policies.* They define the personal information release will be (or should be) deals with at the receiving party [15].
– *Sanitized policies.* They provide filtering functionalities on the response to be returned to the counterpart to avoid release of sensitive information related to the policy itself.

Access Control Policies. Access control policies define authorization rules concerning access to data/services. Authorizations correspond to traditional (positive) rules usually enforced in access control systems. For instance, an authorization rule can require the proof of majority age and a credit card number (condition) to read (action) a specific set of data (object). Also, an obligation can specify that the credit card number must be deleted at the end of the transaction or that the server must log any request. When an access request is submitted to the party, it is first evaluated against the authorization rules applicable to it. If the conditions for the required access are evaluated to true, access is permitted. If none of the specified conditions that might grant the requested access can be fulfilled, then the access is denied. Finally, if the current information is insufficient to determine whether the access request can be granted or denied, additional information is needed and the client receives an undefined response with a list of requests that she must fulfill to gain the access. For instance, if some of the specified conditions can be fulfilled (e.g., by signing an agreement), then the party prompts the requester with the actions that would result in the required access.

Release Policies. Release policies define the party's preferences regarding the release/disclosure of its Personal Identifiable Information (PII). More precisely, these policies specify to which party, for which purpose/action, and under which conditions/obligations a particular set of PII can be released/disclosed [2]. For instance, a release policy can state that credit card information can be disclosed only in the process of a buy action and upon presentation of a nondisclosure agreement (condition) by the party. The disclosure of PII may only be performed if the release policies are satisfied.

Data Handling Policies. Data handling policies specify how PII is used and processed [15]. More precisely, they should regulate how PII will be used (e.g., information collected through a service will be combined with information collected from other services and used in aggregation for market research purposes), how long PII will be retained (e.g., information will be retained as long as necessary to perform the service), and so on. Clients use these policies to define how her information will be used and processed by the counterpart. In this way, user can manage the information also after its release.

Sanitized Policies. Sanitized policies provide filtering functionalities on the response to be returned to the counterpart to avoid release of sensitive information related to the policy itself (or to the status against which the policy has evaluated). This happens when an *undefined* decision together with a list of alternatives (policies) that must be fulfilled to gain the access to the data/service is returned to the counterpart. For instance, suppose that the policy returned by the access control is "citizenship=EU". The party can decide to return to the user either the policy as it is or a modified policy (obtained by applying the sanitized policies) simply requesting the user to declare its nationality (then protecting the information that access is restricted to EU citizens).

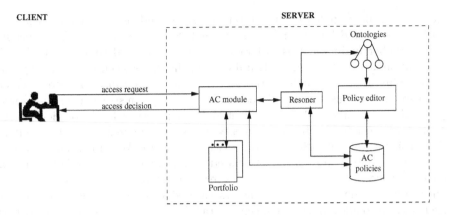

Fig. 1. Architecture

In the following, we deal with access control and release policies: data handling and sanitized policies will be added in future work.

3 Scenario and Basic Elements of the Privacy-Enhanced Model

We consider parties that interact with each other to offer services (see Figure 1). As in a usual client/server interaction, a client asks for a service and a server provides for the service. However, each party can be interchangeably as either a client or a server at different times, with respect to a specific instance of a service request. The access request is processed by the Access Control module (*AC module*). The AC module interacts with the *Reasoner* that takes the access control policies together with the subject, object, and credential ontologies as input and computes the expanded policies including semantically equivalent additional conditions. These conditions, specified in disjunction with the original ones, allow for increasing the original policy's expressive power. The AC module returns to the client a *yes*, *no*, or *undefined* decision. In the latter case, it returns the information about which conditions need to be satisfied for the access to be granted. In this last case, the problem of communicating such conditions to the counterpart arises.

The access control policies are based on generic properties (attributes) associated with the subjects requesting accesses and the resources (data/services) subjects interact with. In the following, we illustrate these basic elements of our model in details.

3.1 Portfolio

The set of properties associated with subjects and objects are represented by means of a *portfolio* [2]. More precisely, a portfolio includes two types of information: *declarations* and *credentials*. A declaration is a statement issued by the party while a credential is a statement issued and signed (i.e., certified) by authorities trusted for making the statement [8]. As an example, the driver license number maintained as a data value at a party and communicated in a negotiation is a declaration. A digital copy of the driver license, released by the public administration to the party, and that the party can submit to a server to prove that it has a driver license or that the administration certifies some properties (e.g., address), is a credential. At a practical level, we view a credential as characterized by two elements: *i)* a signed content, and *ii)* the public digital signature verification key to verify the signature. We can also imagine the existence of (meta)information associated with a credential, outside the signed content. Such information cannot however be trusted as being certified by the authority that signed the credential. In the following, we consider credentials such a mean to allow query for specific data, such as name or address in a driver license, number or expiration date in a credit card. To refer to specific data in a credential we introduce the concept of *credential term*.

Definition 1. A *credential term* is an expression of the form credential_name(*predicate_list*), where credential_name is the name of the credential, and *predicate_list* is a possibly empty list of elements of the form predicate_name(*arguments*).

Intuitively, a credential term can be used to specify a condition on credentials (we will elaborate more on this in Sect. 4). Some examples of credential terms are: driver-license(equal(name, "John Doe")) and identity-card(greater_than(age,18)). The first term denotes the driver-license credential where attribute name should be equal to John. The second term denotes credential identity-card where attribute age should be greater than 18. Declarations and credentials in a portfolio may be organized into a partial order. For instance, an identity-document can be seen as an abstraction for credentials driver-license, passport, and identity-card. Finally, the functionalities offered by a server are defined by a set of services. Intuitively, each service can be seen as an application that clients can execute.

3.2   Ontologies and Abstractions

Our model provides the support for *ontologies* that allow to make generic assertions on subjects and objects [13,14]. More precisely, we use three ontologies: a *subject ontology*, an *object ontology*, and a *credential ontology*. The subject ontology contains terms that can be used to make generic assertions on subjects (e.g., in a medical scenario possible terms are Physician, Patient, assists). The object ontology contains domain-specific terms that are used to describe the resource content such as Video and shows_how. Finally, the credential ontology represent relationships among attributes and credentials (part-of and is-a relationships) to establish what kind of credentials can be provided to fulfill a declaration or credential request. For instance, an ontology can state that attributes birth date and nationality are part_of driver-license, identity-card, and passport. In this way, the reasoning process can point out all the credentials that a user, for example, can provide to prove the satisfaction of a given constraint. To fix ideas and make the discussion clear, suppose that a user can use an on-line car rental service only if she is an European citizen. The access is then allowed if the user can prove her nationality and, according to the credential ontology, this can be done either by showing the `driver-license`, `identity-card`, or `passport`.

Abstractions can also be defined within the domains of users as well as objects. Intuitively, abstractions allow to group together users (objects, resp.) with common characteristics and to refer to the whole group with a name.

4   Privacy-Aware Language

We are now ready to describe the basic constructs of the language used to define the privacy policies and the syntax of the language.

4.1   Basic Elements of the Language

We have identified the following predicates:

- a predicate `declaration` where the argument is a list of predicates of the form `predicate_name(`*arguments*`)`;
- a binary predicate `credential` where the first argument is a credential term (see Definition 1) and the second argument is a public key term. Intuitively, a ground atom `credential(`c, K`)` is evaluated to true if and only if there exists a credential c verifiable with public key K.
- a set of standard binary built-in mathematic predicates, such as `equal()`, `greater_than()`, `lesser_than()`, and so on.
- a set of non predefined predicates that evaluate information stored at the site.

The above predicates constitute the basic literals that can be used in access control and release policies. Note that predicates `declaration` and `credential` have been introduced to distinguish between conditions on data declarations and conditions on credentials (we will elaborate more on this in the following sub-section).

4.2   Policy Components

Syntactically, an access control rule (release rule, resp.) has the following form:

subject WITH *subject-expression* CAN *action* FOR *purpose* ON *object* WITH *object-expression* IF *conditions* FOLLOW *obligations*

where:

- *subject (object)* identifies the subject (object) to which the rule refers;
- *subject-expression (object-expression)* is an expression that allows the reference to a set of subjects (objects) depending on whether they satisfy given conditions that can be evaluated on the user's portfolio (object's profile);

- *action* is the action to which the rule refers (e.g., read, write, and so on)[1]
- *purpose* is the purpose (e.g., `scientific`) to which the rule refers and represents how the data is going to be used by the recipient;
- *conditions* is a boolean expression of generic conditions that an access request to which the rule applies has to satisfy;
- *obligations* is a boolean expression of obligations that the server must follow when manage the information/data/PII.

We now look at the different components in the rule.

Subject Expression. These expressions allow the reference to a set of subjects depending on whether they satisfy given conditions that can be evaluated on the subject's portfolio. Note that the conditions specified through these expressions are very similar to generic conditions. The difference is that while the subject expression is evaluated on the user of the request, generic conditions specify generic constraints that are not evaluated on the requester. More precisely, *a subject expression is a boolean formula of terms of the form*:

- `declaration(`*predicate_list*`)`, where *predicate_list* is a possibly empty list of elements of the form `predicate_name(`*arguments*`)`. Intuitively, a declaration predicate is evaluated to true if each predicate specified in the *predicate_list* is evaluated to true.
- `credential(`*credential_term,K*`)`, where *credential_term* is defined as `credential_name(`*predicate_list*`)` (see Definition 1). Intuitively, a credential predicate is evaluated to true if there exists credential `credential_name` for which each predicate `predicate(`*arguments*`)` in *predicate_list* is evaluated to true and `credential_name` is verifiable with public key K.

Note that the predicates specified as arguments of the `declaration` and `credential` predicates can be: *i)* location-based predicates, *ii)* the standard built-in mathematic predicates, and *iii)* the non predefined predicates that evaluate information stored at the server.

To make it possible to refer to the user of the request being evaluated without the need of introducing variables in the language, we introduce the keyword **user**, whose appearance in a conditional expression is intended to be substituted with the actual parameters of the request in the evaluation at access control time.

Example 1. The following are examples of subject expressions:

- `declaration(equal(`**user**`.name,Bob),greater_than(`**user**`.age,18))` denoting requests made by a user whose name is Bob with `age` greater than 18;
- `credential(passport(equal(`**user**`.job,professor)),`K_1`)` denoting requests made by users who are professors. This property should be certified by showing the `passport` credential verifiable with public key K_1

---

[1] Note that abstractions can also be defined on actions, specializing actions or grouping them in sets.

Object Expression. These expressions allow the reference to a set of objects depending on whether they satisfy given conditions that can be evaluated on the object's profile. Note that the conditions specified through these expressions are very similar to generic conditions. The difference is that while the object expression evaluated on the object (or associated profile) to which the request being processed refers, generic conditions specify generic constraints that are not evaluated on the requested object. More precisely, *an object expression is a boolean formula of terms of the form*:

- `declaration`(*predicate_list*), where *predicate_list* is a possibly empty list of elements of the form `predicate_name`(*arguments*). Intuitively, a declaration predicate is evaluated to true if each predicate specified in the *predicate_list* is evaluated to true.

Note that the predicates specified as arguments of the `declaration` predicate can be: *i)* the standard built-in mathematic predicates, and *ii)* the non predefined predicates that evaluate information stored at the server.

Like for subjects, to make it possible to refer to the object to which the request being processed refers, without need of introducing variables in the language, we introduce the keyword **object**, whose appearance in a conditional expression is intended to be substituted with the actual parameters of the request in the evaluation at access control time.

Example 2. The following are examples of object expressions:

- `declaration(equal(object.creator,user))` denoting all objects created by the requester;
- `declaration(lesser_than(object.creation_date,1971))` denoting all objects created before 1971.

Conditions. We assume that the type of conditions that can be specified in the *conditions* element are only conditions that can be brought to satisfactions at run-time processing of the request. These conditions can be related to agreement acceptance, payment fulfillment, or registration. Conditions can be associated with data at different levels (i.e., attribute, credentials' attributes and credentials) and can be certified or uncertified. More precisely, *conditions are boolean formula of terms of the form*:

- `predicate_name`(*arguments*).

Note that the predicates specified in the *conditions* element can be: *i)* trusted-based conditions stating that, for example, the requester should use a trusted platform, *ii)* the standard built-in mathematic predicates, and *iii)* the non predefined predicates that evaluate information stored at the server.

Example 3. The following is a simple example of condition.

- `fill_in_form(`**user**,*form1)* checks if the requester has filled in form *form1*.

Obligations. They establish how the released PII must be managed by the counterpart. For instance, obligations may state that some data should be deleted after three time accessed, the owner of some data should be notified after every access to the data, some data should be obfuscated or deleted after 3 months, and so on. Obligations can be attached to a particular instance of release data in order to give to the counterpart some rules that must be follow in the PII management.

5 An Example

We now present an example of policy (other examples are omitted here for space constraints) and a possible way of expressing policies by using an XML-based syntax.

We define two namespaces: `xmlns:pol` is the namespace of the policy and `xmlns:ont` is the namespace for the ontology statements. Every policy can contain more than one rule combined through the combine-rule attribute. Each rule has three main components:

- `pol:target` is the target of the policy (subject, object, action, purpose);
- `pol:condition` includes generic conditions (neither related to subject nor object) such as assurance/trust conditions;
- `pol:obligation` includes further steps that the party must take in account when the access is granted.

We now analyze the target component more in details. The target includes the `pol:subject` tag corresponding to the *subject* field described in Section 4. Associated with the subject, there is the subject expression (`pol:subject-expression`) that contains boolean operators (and, or) and a set of constraints (`pol:constraint`). Every constraint has a type and is of the form "*left-value* operator *right-value*". The operator is a matching function, the left-value (`ont:datatype`) have to be a class referencing an ontology structure and the right-value (`ont:instanceref`) can be another class, an instance class, or a literal (e.g., in the rule below the constrain is **user.job** = "doctor"). The object and object expression have the same structure of the subject and subject expression, respectively. Finally, the target includes an action (`pol:action`) and a purpose (`pol:purpose`).

When a request is submitted to the system, the AC module selects all the applicable policies by using the subject, object, action, and purpose specified in the access request and then checks the (expanded) conditions inside the policies to determine the access result (yes/no/undefined).

Example 4. Suppose that an access control policy stated that "A registered user who works as a doctor, can read for research purposes data patientData with the agreement of the patient". This policy is expressed as follows.

registeredUsers WITH declaration (equal(user.work, "doctor")) CAN read FOR
research ON patientDatawithdeclaration (equal(object.patient_agreement,yes))
IF *no-condition* FOLLOW *no-obligation*

```
<pol:policy type="accessControl" combine-rule="first-grant"
 xmlns:pol="http://example.com/policy-namespace"
 xmlns:ont="http://example.com/ontology-namespace">
  <pol:rule>
    <pol:target>
      <pol:subject>registeredUsers</pol:subject>
      <pol:subject-expression>
        <pol:constraint type="declaration">
          <pol:function type="equal">
            <ont:datatype>
              <ont:user/> <ont:job/>
            </ont:datatype>
            <ont:instanceref>
              <ont:user/> <ont:job/>
              <ont:value>doctor</ont:value>
            </ont:instanceref>
          </pol:function>
        </pol:constraint>
      </pol:subject-expression>
      <pol:object>patientData</pol:object>
      <pol:object-expression>
        <pol:constraint type="declaration">
          <pol:function type="equal">
            <ont:datatype>
              <ont:object/> <ont:patient/> <ont:agreement/>
            </ont:datatype>
            <ont:value type="xsd:string">yes</ont:value>
          </pol:function>
        </pol:constraint>
      </pol:object-expression>
      <pol:action>read</pol:action>
      <pol:purpose>research</pol:purpose>
    </pol:target>
    <pol:condition/>
    <pol:obligation> ... </pol:obligation>
  </pol:rule>
  <pol:rule> ... </pol:rule>
</pol:policy>
```

Fig. 2. A simple example of policy

Figure 2 illustrates the policy expressed by using the XML syntax described above. Note that our access control system operates also when the users want to remain anonymous or disclosure only some attributes about themselves, protecting users privacy.

6 Conclusions

This paper has presented the preliminary results of our ongoing activity in the framework of the PRIME project. Issues to be investigated include the filtering and renaming of policies and the addition of obligations. As discussed previously, since access control does not return only a "yes" or "no" access decision, but it returns the information about which conditions need to be satisfied for the access to be granted ("undefined" decision), the problem of communicating such conditions to the counterpart arises. The system should then provide meta-policies for protecting the policy when communication requisites.

Acknowledgments

This work was supported in part by the European Union within the PRIME Project in the FP6/IST Programme under contract IST-2002-507591 and by the Italian MIUR within the KIWI and MAPS projects.

References

1. Bonatti, P., Damiani, E., De Capitani di Vimercati, S., Samarati, P.: A Component-based Architecture for Secure Data Publication. Proc. of the 17th Annual Computer Security Applications Conference (2001), New Orleans, Louisiana.
2. Bonatti, P., Samarati, P.: A Unified Framework for Regulating Access and Information Release on the Web. Journal of Computer Security (2002), vol. 10, 241–272.
3. Ashley, P., Hada, S., Karjoth, G., Powers, C., Schunter, M.: Enterprise Privacy Authorization Language (EPAL 1.1). IBM Research Report (2003), http://www.zurich.ibm.com/security/enterprise-privacy/epal.
4. Samarati, P., De Capitani di Vimercati, S.: Access Control: Policies, Models, and Mechanisms. Foundations of Security Analysis and Design **LNCS 2171** (2001), Springer-Verlag.
5. eXtensible Access Control Markup Language (XACML) Version 1.1. OASIS, 2003, http://www.oasis-open.org/committees/xacml/repository/cs-xacml-specification-1.1.pdf.
6. Ardagna, C.A., Damiani, E., De Capitani di Vimercati, S., Samarati, P.: A Web Service Architecture for Enforcing Access Control Policies. Proc. of the First International Workshop on Views On Designing Complex Architectures (VODCA 2004), Bertinoro, Italy.
7. Ardagna, C.A., Damiani, E., De Capitani di Vimercati, S., Samarati, P.: XML-based Access Control Languages. Information Security Technical Report, (2004), vol. 9.
8. Gladman, B., Ellison, C., Bohm, N.: Digital signatures, certificates and electronic commerce, http://www.clark.net/pub/cme/html/spki.html.
9. Bettini, C., Jajodia, S., Sean Wang, X., Wijesekera, D.: Provisions and Obligations in Policy Management and Security Applications. In Proc. 28th Conf. Very Large Data Bases (VLDB'02), (2002), citeseer.ist.psu.edu/bettini02provisions.html.
10. Park, J., Sandhu, R.: The UCONabc Usage Control Model. ACM Transactions on Information and System Security (TISSEC), (2004), vol. 7, no. 1.
11. World Wide Web Consortium: Semantic Web. http://www.w3.org/2001/sw/.
12. Privacy and Identity Management for Europe (PRIME). http://www.prime-project.eu.org/.

13. Damiani, E., De Capitani di Vimercati, S., Fugazza, C., Samarati, P.: Semantics-aware Privacy and Access Control: Motivation and Preliminary Results. 1st Italian Semantic Web Workshop, (2004), Ancona, Italy.
14. Damiani, E., De Capitani di Vimercati, S., Fugazza, C., Samarati, P.: Extending Policy Languages to the Semantic Web. Proc. of the International Conference on Web Engineering, (2004), Munich, Germany.
15. Cranor, L., Langheinrich, M., Marchiori, M., Presler-Marshall, M., Reagle, J.: The Platform for Privacy Preferences 1.0 (P3P1.0) Specification. http://www.w3.org/TR/P3P/.
16. Ardagna, C.A., Damiani, E., De Capitani di Vimercati, S., Fugazza, C., Samarati, P.: Offline Expansion of XACML Policies Based on P3P Metadata (to appear). ICWE 2005, 5th International Conference on Web Engineering, Sydney, Australia.

Revocation of Obligation and Authorisation
Policy Objects

Andreas Schaad

SAP Research, 805, Av. Dr. Maurice Donat,
06250 Mougins, France
andreas.schaad@sap.com

Abstract. In [Schaad and Moffett, 2002] we have presented our initial inves-
tigations into the delegation of obligations and the concept of review as one
kind of organisational principle to control such delegation activities. This initial work led us to a more detailed and refined analysis of organisational controls [Schaad, 2003], [Schaad and Moffett, 2004] with a particular emphasis on
the notion of general and specific obligations [Schaad, 2004]. In particular, this
distinction allowed us to formally capture how a principal may be related to an
obligation; how obligations relate to roles; and how the delegation of specific and
general obligations may be controlled through the concepts of review and supervision. This paper complements the delegation of obligation and authorisation
policy objects by discussing their revocation, based on the revocation schemes
suggested in [Hagstrom et al., 2001]. In particular, we will investigate how delegated general and specific obligations can be revoked and what effect the presence of roles has on the revocation process. We use the Alloy language and its
automated analysis facilities [Jackson, 2001] to formally support our discussion.

1 Introduction

Organisational control principles, such as those expressed in the separation of duties,
delegation of obligations, supervision and review, support the main business goals and
activities of an organisation. A framework has been presented in [Schaad, 2003] where
organisational control principles can be formally expressed and analysed using the Alloy specification language and its constraint analysis tools [Jackson, 2001]. Specifically
the delegation of obligations and arising review obligations has initially been treated in
[Schaad and Moffett, 2002] and later expanded in [Schaad, 2004]. The delegation of
policy objects must be complemented by their revocation. However, specifying revocation controls may be very complex as, for example, demonstrated in the work of
[Griffiths and Wade, 1976], [Jonscher, 1998] or [Bertino et al., 1997], addressing revocation of permissions in the context of operating and database systems. A more general
framework for revocation has only been proposed recently [Hagstrom et al., 2001]. This
is, however, limited to the revocation of permissions directly assigned to a principal and
does not include a notion of roles. Our paper explores how this revocation framework
can be applied for the revocation of obligation and authorisation policy objects in the
context of our control principle model. Specifically our distinction between general and
specific obligations requires a more detailed discussion of possible revocation schemes.

S. Jajodia and D. Wijesekera (Eds.): Data and Applications Security 2005, LNCS 3654, pp. 28–39, 2005.

The rest of this paper is structured as follows. Section 2 provides a summary of the core static and dynamic concepts of our control principle model, a more detailed formal discussion of which is provided in [Schaad, 2003]. Section 3 will then look at the revocation of policy objects against the dimensions of resilience, propagation and dominance, in particular focusing on the revocation of obligations. Section 4 summarises and concludes this paper.

2   Definition of Policy Objects in the Control Principle Model

Within our control principle model [Schaad, 2003], policy objects are either authorizations or obligations, similar as those defined in Ponder [Damianou et al., 2001]. Principals, or the roles of which principals are a member of, may be subject to these policy objects. In other words, a principal is related to a set of policy objects over the roles he holds or on the basis of a direct assignment. The target of a policy object defines the objects against which the actions of the policy are executed.

Authorisations state what a principal is permitted to do by using the actions defined by the authorisation. Authorisations can be shared between principals through roles or on the basis of direct assignments.

Obligation policies are an abstraction for defining the actions that must be performed by a principal on some target object when some specified event occurs. We extended the object model of [Damianou et al., 2001] and distinguish between general obligations that may be assigned to a role or a principle (e.g. a general obligation to process invoices from supply companies) and their specific instances (e.g. to process the invoice i1 from supplier x1). To support this distinction we require the following four rules to hold (these and are formally defined in [Schaad, 2004]):

1. An obligation instance must always relate to exactly one Principal.
2. An obligation instance has always one general obligation.
3. Every specific obligation a principal holds must be an instance of a general obligation he is a subject of through one of his roles or directly.
4. A general obligation can only have a principal or one of his roles as a subject, but not both.

The s_subject relation captures the assignment of a policy object to an object (which can be a role, principal or other policy object). Using an approach called objectification of state [Jackson, 2001], we can model total order relationships of states, where an expression like (s1.s_subject).p1 would result in all the policy objects principal p1 is a subject of in state s1.

The first rule mentioned above demanding the direct assignment of an obligation instance to a principal would thus translate as follows. Here & is the set intersection operator and Principal the set of principals, while the expression obl.(s.s_subject) yields all the principals subject to an obligation instance obl:

```
fact {all s : State | all obl : ObligationInstance |
one (obl.(s.s_subject) & Principal)}
```

For maintaining a history in such state sequences, we consider the following signature which maintains a DelegationHistory.

```
sig DelegationHistory{
 delegating_principal : Principal,
 receiving_principal : Principal,
 based_on_role : option Role,
 delegated_policy : PolicyObject
}
```

We do not maintain the information about which principal delegated which policy object in the form of an explicit relation, but in an explicit signature with several binary relations. We can do this because we know that, for example, in the context of the delegation of a policy, exactly one principal delegates exactly one policy object to exactly one other principal in between two states. This cardinality is indicated by the absence of the set keyword. The delegating principal may have chosen to delegate on the basis of a direct assignment or over a role as indicated by using the option keyword. Specifically this latter point could not be resolved in a n-ary relation like Principal -> Principal -> Role -> PolicyObject as there is no kind of null value in Alloy that would allow us to express that no role but a direct assignment was used for the delegation. A RevocationHistory and an AccessHistory signature have been defined in a similar way in [2] together with a set of rules, that, e.g. define that for any transition between states there can only be one history entry and other integrity preserving constraints. In essence, we can use Alloy to model sequences of states and define and analyse object access, delegation and revocation activities over such sequences. The history signature is then updated over the lifetime of such a sequence, and maintains, for example, the changes in the s_subject relation when moving from one state to the next as possibly initiated by a delegation activity. This provides all the information needed for supporting revocation activities.

3   Revocation of Policy Objects

In general, revocation of an object is based on its previous delegation and thus requires the following pieces of information [Samarati and Vimercati, 2001]:

– The principals involved in previous delegation(s);
– The time of previous delegation(s);
– The object subject to previous delegation(s)

Our conceptual model provides this information through the defined history signatures and may thus support the various forms of revocation as described in the revocation framework of [Hagstrom et al., 2001].

In this framework different revocation schemes for delegated access rights are classified against the dimensions of resilience, propagation and dominance. Since resilience is based on negative permissions, we do not consider this here, as there is no corresponding concept for the policy objects in our model (unlike Ponder [Damianou et al., 2001] which does provide negative authorisation policies).

The remaining two within our model dimensions may be informally summarised as follows:

1. Propagation distinguishes whether the decision to revoke affects
   - only the principal directly subject to a revocation (local); or
   - also those principals the principal subject to the revocation may have further delegated the object to be revoked to (global).
2. Dominance addresses conflicts that may arise when a principal subject to a revocation has also been delegated the same object from other principals. If such other delegations are independent of the revoker then this is outside the scope of revocation. If, however, such other delegations have been performed by principals who, at some earlier stage, received the object to be revoked via a delegation path stemming from the revoker, then the revoking principal may
   - only revoke with respect to his delegation (weak);
   - revoke all such other delegations that stem from him (strong).

Table 1. Revocation schemes

No	Propagation	Dominance	Name
1	No	No	Weak local revocation
2	No	Yes	Strong local revocation
3	Yes	No	Weak global revocation
4	Yes	Yes	Strong global revocation

Based on these two dimensions, we established 4 different revocation schemes which, due to the absence of the resilience property, are a subset of those described by [Hagstrom et al., 2001]. These are summarised in table 1. We will now investigate how far these schemes can be expressed and integrated with respect to our control principle model and the specific types and characteristics of policy objects. The following two sections will thus discuss the revocation of delegated policy objects along the lines of the above revocation schemes.

3.1   Revoking Delegated Authorisations

Since authorisations are similar to the notion of permissions in [Hagstrom et al., 2001], we will describe the four revocation schemes in terms of a possible delegation scenario. We use function delegate_auth(s1, s2, p1, p2, auth) to state that a principal p1 delegated an authorisation auth to a principal p2 in state s1. Similarly, auth was delegated by p1 to p3 in state s2; by p3 to p2 in state s3; by p2 to p4 in state s4; by p2 to p5 in state s5; and finally by p6 to p4 in state s6. This is summarised in the graph displayed in figure 1 where the nodes stand for the principals, and the arcs are labeled with the respective delegation activity. We assume that in this specific above example the principals always retain the authorisation they delegate. However, it must be noted that in general a principal might decide to drop an authorisation at the time he delegates, which increases the complexity of delegation and revocation schemes as shown in [Schaad, 2003].

A weak local revocation of an authorisation is the simplest case as it does not propagate or dominate any other delegations of the authorisation. For example, if principal p2 revokes auth from principal p5, then p5 will not hold auth anymore. If, however, p1 revokes auth from principal p2, then p2 will continue to hold auth due to the delegation of auth by p3 in state s3.

A strong local revocation will address this later scenario, and if p1 strongly revokes auth from principal p2 locally, then p2 will not continue to hold auth, however, p4 and p5 will. The strong revoke by p1 will only result in p2 losing auth completely, because p3 had been delegated auth by p1 and then delegated it to p1. All delegations of auth to p2 stem from p1. If, for example, p2 strongly revokes auth from p4, then p4 will still hold auth because p2 has no influence on the delegation of auth by p6.

The weak global revocation addresses the revocation of policies which have been delegated more than once through a cascading revocation. Thus, if p1 globally revokes auth from principal p2 then this will result in p5 losing auth, but p2 and p4 will still hold auth due to the delegation of auth by p3 and p6 in s3 and s6 respectively.

Letting p1 revoke auth from principal p2 strongly and globally, auth will then not be held by p2 and p5 anymore, but p4 will still hold it due to the individual delegation by p6.

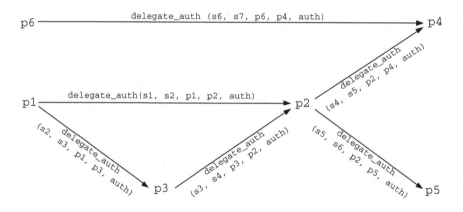

Fig. 1. A delegation scenario for delegating an authorisation auth

3.2   Revoking Delegated Obligations

The delegation of obligations should be complemented by revocation mechanisms as well, and we investigate in the following whether the previously identified four revocation schemes can also be applied in this context. Since we may delegate general and specific obligations as discussed in [Schaad, 2004], their revocation must also be discussed separately.

Revocation of Specific Obligations. We formally required an obligation instance to be assigned to exactly one principal at any time [Schaad, 2004]. It is for this reason that many of the problems we described for the revocation of authorisations cannot occur. We illustrate this with respect to the two applicable dimensions of revocation:

- Dominance does not apply as it is not possible for a principal to have been delegated the same obligation instance from different sources.
- Propagation may apply as a principal is able to delegate a delegated obligation. However, when he delegates he may not retain this obligation.

With respect to the second point, we consider the example of a principal p1 having delegated an obligation instance iob to a principal p2 who in turn delegated it to a principal p3. Should principal p1 now be able to revoke iob directly from p3 or only from p2? We believe that a principal should only be able to revoke a delegated obligation from the principal he delegated it to. The order of revocation thus corresponds to the way the obligation was initially delegated. There may be organisations where a direct revocation of iob from p3 by p1 may be desirable, e.g. a coercive organisation with distinct command structures, where decisions may have to be made rapidly like a hospital or military organisation [Mullins, 1999]. We do, however, not believe that any further argumentation would contribute to the overall goal of this paper.

Revocation of General Obligations. We have argued in [Schaad, 2004] that the delegation of general obligations can be treated almost identically to the delegation of authorisations. Thus, the underlying question here is whether this also applies to the revocation of general obligations. To clarify this, we again look at the revocation of general obligations with respect to the two dimensions of revocation considered in this context:

- Dominance applies since a general obligation may be held by several principals. These may independently delegate this obligation, perhaps to the same principal at different times.
- Propagation applies since a general obligation may be delegated several times between principals.

Considering the first item, the question is whether the revocation of a multiply delegated obligation may override other delegations or not. This has been referred to as strong and weak revocation respectively. We believe that this issue can be addressed like the strong and weak revocation of authorisations, as long as the defined constraints hold. The second item demands to distinguish between local and global revocation. The latter possibly causes a series of cascading revocations if a general obligation has been delegated several times. Again, this can be theoretically treated as in the case of revoking authorisations, but some additional points must be considered.

The delegation of a general obligation may have been followed by the delegation or creation of some instances of that general obligation. This may influence the revocation of a general obligation, because of the constraint that a principal may only hold an obligation instance if he has the corresponding general obligation. So if a general obligation is revoked, then this should result in the revocation of any existing delegated instances for the principal subject to a revocation. A different situation may, however, be where an instance has been created on the basis of a delegated general obligation. The question is whether the revoking principal should be able to revoke an obligation instance he did never hold and subsequently never delegated. One approach may be to demand that the principal holding such instances must first discharge these before a delegated general obligation can be revoked. Another option may be to allow for the delegation of such an instance back to the revoking principal by the principal the general obligation is revoked from. Whatever the decision, we believe that these points present no technical difficulties with respect to the actual revocation activity. A more detailed discussion on organisational aspects of revocation is, however, outside this scope.

3.3 Defining Revocation Mechanisms for the CP Model

Several procedural revocation algorithms exist, as for example defined in the papers of [Griffiths and Wade, 1976], [Jonscher, 1998] or [Fagin, 1978]. However, the definition of a revocation mechanism in a declarative way is a non-trivial task and the only work we are aware of is [Bertino et al., 1997], which is unfortunately strictly tied to their specific authorisation model, and may also be difficult to understand without the possibility of tool supported analysis.

One main underlying design principle of our model is that a declarative specification of delegation and revocation operations should reflect their possible procedural counterparts. This means that they only cause a change to the s_subject relation with respect to the actual objects involved in the delegation and revocation. This has also been defined by a set of framing conditions that support each Alloy function. The strong local and the weak and strong global functions may however also cause changes to the s_subject relation with respect to other objects not explicitly defined when calling a revocation function, since this only describes what the resulting state should look like. We thus argue in the following, that the strong local, and weak and strong global revocation can all be modeled in terms of a series of weak local revocations. This weak local revocation supports revocation of authorisation and obligation policies.

For this reason we only formally outline the function weak_local_revoke() and point to the discussion in [Schaad, 2003]. The three remaining types of revocation are discussed less formally, as they may be understood as a series of weak local revocations.

Weak Local Revocation. Before considering the weak local revocation of a policy object in more detail, we informally recall some possible delegation scenarios that may have an effect on the behaviour of a weak revocation. These scenarios consider whether:

1. A policy object may have been delegated by a principal on the basis of a direct or role-based assignment; or whether
2. The principal a policy object was delegated to may have already been assigned with the object
   - either because he was assigned with the object at the time of system setup or;
   - because of a prior (and not yet revoked) delegation from some other principal.

Depending on the situation, a weak local revocation may behave differently with respect to the changes in the s_subject relation. For example, we consider that a principal p1 delegates an authorisation policy object auth he directly holds to a principal p2 in state s1. In this example, as a result of this delegation p1 loses auth. Principal p2 is also delegated auth by some other principal p3 in state s2. In state s3 principal p1 revokes auth from p2. Because of the delegation by p3 in state s2, p2 must not lose auth. Principal p1 must be assigned with auth again and the revocation of auth from p2 by p1 must be recorded by an update to the revocation history of state s3. A variation of this scenario may be that principal p1 delegated auth in state s1 on the basis of a role he is a member of. This would then mean that when he revokes auth from p2 in s3, the s_subject relation would not change at all. This is because of the delegation by p3 in state s2 and the fact that the initial delegation by p1 in s1 was based on a role, indirectly demanding the retainment of auth by p1 through his role membership. Nevertheless, the revocation would still have to be recorded by an update to the revocation history.

It would not be helpful to provide an exhaustive list of all such possible delegation scenarios here, and the two above examples only reflect in parts the complexity of a weak local revocation within our framework. There are, however, four general properties that need to be evaluated. These concern whether:

- there were multiple delegations of a policy object by and to the same principal;
- whether a role was used for delegation;
- whether there were multiple independent delegations;
- and whether the receiving principal was already subject to the delegated policy object before any delegations.

Based on these two dimensions and more general above properties, we established four different revocation schemes which, due to the absence of the resilience property, are a subset of those described in the revocation framework by [Hagstrom et al., 2001]. This subset is summarised in table 1 and the following four function headers 1-4 outline the behavior and expected return values.

These four functions are now composed to define the weak_local_revoke function 5. For reasons of space we only show the first half of this function. The revoking principal p1 must have delegated a policy object pol to p2 for any revocation to succeed (Precondition). If no role was used for the delegation (Case I) and the delegation was performed on a direct assignment instead, then we check whether there were no delegations of pol to p2 by other principals (Case I.1). This is sufficient as a principal must not delegate the same object twice without an intermediate revocation as defined in the precondition. If Case I.1 holds, then we check whether principal p2 held pol initially or not (Case I.1.a and I.1.b) and update the revocation history and s_subject relation accordingly.

If there were delegations by other principals (Case I.2) then we do not need to check for any initial assignments and just update the revocation history and s_subject relation. The second part of the function checks for the case of a role having been used for the delegation and is not shown here as it is similar in its structure to the first part. The full function and sequence of delegations and revocations we used to test and validate this weak local revocation with can be found in [Schaad, 2003].

Alloy Function 1. *The precondition of revocation. This function evaluates true if a revoking principal* p1 *delegated the policy object* pol *to a principal* p2 *in some state before the current state* cstate *and did not revoke* pol *from* p2 *between that delegation and* cstate.

```
fun revocation_precondition
   (cstate: State, disj p1, p2: Principal, pol: PolicyObject) {...}
```

Alloy Function 2. *A role was used for the delegation. This function evaluates true if a principal* p1 *delegated the policy object* pol *to* p2 *in a state before the current state* cstate *on basis of a role-based assignment to* pol.

```
fun role_was_used_for_del_of_pol
   (cstate: State, disj p1, p2: Principal, pol: PolicyObject) {...}
```

Alloy Function 3. *The object to be revoked was delegated by some other principal. This function evaluates true if some principal* p *other than* p1 *delegated the policy object* pol *to principal* p2 *and did not revoke it before the current state* cstate.

```
fun pol_was_delegated_by_other_p
   (cstate: State, disj p1, p2: Principal, pol: PolicyObject) {...}
```

Alloy Function 4. *The principal* p2 *a policy object* pol *is to be revoked from may have held* pol *even before any prior delegation by the revoking principal* p1. *This function evaluates true if principal* p2 *held* pol *directly in the first state of a state sequence.*

```
fun rev_p_held_pol_initially
   (cstate: State, disj p1, p2: Principal, pol: PolicyObject) {...}
```

Strong Local Revocation. A strong local revocation would be almost identical in its specification. As in the function weak_local_revoke() we would have to check whether a principal was delegated the policy object to be revoked from some other principal. If this is true, like in the example in figure 1, and all delegations of an authorisation policy object auth to a principal p2 stem from principal p1 requesting the revocation, then p2 will not be subject to auth anymore. On the other hand a strong local revoke of auth from p4 by p2 would have no effect on p4's assignment to auth due to the previous delegation of auth to p4 by p6.

These scenarios emphasize again the need for not only keeping track of delegated but revoked policy objects as well. Due to the underlying assumption of our model that only one revocation may happen at a time, such a strong local revocation function cannot be used directly, since it may change several relationships which we cannot keep track of. Nevertheless it may be used to assert that a certain sequence of weak local revocations would suffice for the definition of a strong local revocation. With respect to figure 1 this would mean that a sequence of weak local revocations of auth from p2 by p1 and p3 should be equal to a single strong local revocation of auth from p2 by p1.

Alloy Function 5. *Weak local revocation function composed of functions 1-4.*

```
fun weak_local_revoke (disj s1, s2: State,
                                    disj p1, p2: Principal,
                                    pol: PolicyObject){
//Precondition: p1 has delegated pol to p2 before s1
  revocation_precondition(s1, p1, p2, pol) &&
//Case I: No role was used for this initial delegation
  (!role_was_used_for_del_of_pol(s1, p1, p2, pol) =>
    //Case I.1: No other delegations occurred
    (!pol_was_delegated_by_other_p(s1, p1, p2, pol) =>
      //Case I.1.a: p2 did hold pol initially
      (rev_p_held_pol_initially(s1, p1, p2, pol)    =>
        update_rev_history(s1, p1, p2, pol) &&
        s2.s_subject = s1.s_subject + pol -> p1) &&
      //Case I.1.b: p2 did not hold pol initially
      (!rev_p_held_pol_initially(s1, p1, p2, pol)   =>
        update_rev_history(s1, p1, p2, pol) &&
        s2.s_subject = s1.s_subject + pol -> p1
                                  - pol -> p2)) &&
    //Case I.2: Some other delegation occurred
    (pol_was_delegated_by_other_p(s1, p1, p2, pol)   =>
      update_rev_history(s1, p1, p2, pol) &&
      s2.s_subject = s1.s_subject + pol -> p1)) &&

  ...

//The following second part contains the same cases
//if a role was used for the initial delegation.
  ...

}
```

Weak and Strong Global Revocation. Alloy has only recently started to support re-cursion, an indispensable mechanism to support global revocation as we described it in the previous section. At the time of writing our specification there was no available documentation or examples for the use of recursion. Nevertheless, we felt that at least an outline of how to define global revocation must be provided. The constraint analyser could provide us with a reasonable level of assurance about the working of a global revocation function as defined in [Schaad, 2003].

Weak and strong global revocations are similar in their effects to their local coun-terparts, however, they also consider any possible further delegations of the object to be revoked by the principal this object is revoked from. We have described this in the pre-vious section and only want to point out some specific issues that need to be considered when defining such a global revocation.

Since recursion is required to provide for a global revocation, this means that the weak and strong global revocations functions consist of two parts. In the first part we check whether the object pol had been initially delegated by the revoking principal p1 to p2 as previously outlined. In the second part we then need to check whether there was any further delegation of pol to some other principal p. If this is so, the global revocation function calls itself, now with p2 being the revoking principal and p being the principal pol is revoked from. An example of such a recursive revocation is provided in [Schaad, 2003].

A series of weak local revocations may achieve the same result as weak and strong global revocations, but we did not investigate this any further considering formal proof, as there was not immediate need in the context of this paper.

4 Summary and Conclusion

In this paper we have provided a first possible approach to the revocation of policy objects in the context of our control principle model presented in [Schaad, 2003]. This approach followed the schemes as proposed in [Hagstrom et al., 2001], but due absence of negative authorisations and the specific notion of general and specific obligations and their respective assignment to roles and principals, not all categories of the scheme had to be considered.

We see our work as particularly useful in the context of workflow systems and their security, since our understanding of obligations as event-condition-action rules matches the notion of tasks. Our general obligations then refer to the tasks at the workflow model level, while specific obligations are the occurring instances at execution time of the workflow. The delegation of such tasks may then trigger the delegation of the required permissions.

However, there is remaining work. We need to further analyse the effect of revocation activities on existing review obligations. In particular, we would like to support revocation of an obligation instance by any principal in a delegation chain. Secondly, we specified in our framework that an obligation has a set of supporting authorisations. Although we did not fully investigate this relationship between authorisations and obligations in the context of delegation and revocation activities, we could observe that the delegation and revocation of authorisation objects may violate existing separation of duty properties [Schaad, 2003]. In particular, we could show how dynamic separation properties are "circumvented" by colluding principals with the right to delegate and revoke. This is not a new problem [Harrison et al., 1976] but still requires further analysis from a business process engineering perspective.

Overall, we have now completed the majority of our conceptual work and will look at the implementation of the concepts of delegation, review, evidence, revocation of general and specific obligations and the possible schemes and their practical feasibility in more detail. In fact, the work on collaborative workflows suggested in [Schulz and Orlowska, 2004] will offer interesting perspectives and SAP Research has already implemented collaborative workflow prototypes within which our organisational control principles and delegation and revocation schemes can be implemented. Together with analysis tools such as described in [Rits et al., 2005], we may then achieve a tight match between workflow tasks and the required permissions at application, middleware and database level.

References

Bertino et al., 1997. Bertino, E., Samarati, P., and Jajodia, S. (1997). An Extended Authorization Model for Relational Databases. *IEEE Transactions on Knowledge and Data Engineering*, 9(1):85–101.

Damianou et al., 2001. Damianou, N., Dulay, N., Lupu, E., and Sloman, M. (2001). The Ponder Policy Specification Language. In *Policies for Distributed Systems and Networks*, volume 1995, pages 18–38, Bristol. Springer Lecture Notes in Computer Science.

Fagin, 1978. Fagin, R. (1978). On an Authorization Mechansism. volume 3, pages 310–319.

Griffiths and Wade, 1976. Griffiths, P. and Wade, B. (1976). An Authorization Mechanism for a Relational Database System. *ACM Transactions on Database Systems*, 1(3):243–255.

Hagstrom et al., 2001. Hagstrom, A., Jajodia, S., Parisi-Presicce, F., and Wijesekera, D. (2001). Revocations - A Categorization. In *Computer Security Foundations Workshop*. IEEE Press.

Harrison et al., 1976. Harrison, M., Ruzzo, W., and Ullman, J. (1976). Protection in Operating Systems. *Communications of the ACM*, 19(8):461–471.

Jackson, 2001. Jackson, D. (2001). A Micromodularity Mechanism. In *8th Joint Software Engineering Conference*, Vienna, Austria.

Jonscher, 1998. Jonscher, D. (1998). *Access Control in Object-Oriented Federated Database Systems*. PhD thesis, University of Zurich.

Mullins, 1999. Mullins, L. (1999). *Management and Organisational Behaviour*. Prentice Hall, London, 5th edition.

Rits et al., 2005. Rits, M., De Boe, B., and Schaad, A. (2005). Xact: A bridge between resource management and access control in multi-layered applications. In *ACM Software Engineering Notes of Software Engineering for Secure Systems (ICSE05),*, St. Louis, Missouri, USA.

Samarati and Vimercati, 2001. Samarati, P. and Vimercati, S. (2001). Access Control: Polcies, Models and Mechanisms. In Focardi, R. and Gorrieri, R., editors, *Foundations of Security Analysis and Design*, pages 137–196. Springer Lecture Notes 2171.

Schaad, 2003. Schaad, A. (2003). *A Framework for Organisational Control Principles, PhD Thesis*. Phd, University of York.

Schaad, 2004. Schaad, A. (2004). Delegating organisational obligations - an extended analysis. In *IFIP WG 11.3 Database and Applications Security XVIII*, Sitges, Spain.

Schaad and Moffett, 2002. Schaad, A. and Moffett, J. (2002). Delegation of Obligations. In *3rd International Workshop on Policies for Distributed Systems and Networks (POLICY 2002)*, Monterey, CA.

Schaad and Moffett, 2004. Schaad, A. and Moffett, J. (2004). Separation, review and supervision controls in the context of a credit application process, a case study of organisational control principles. In *ACM Symposium of Applied Computing*, Cyprus.

Schulz and Orlowska, 2004. Schulz, K. and Orlowska, M. (2004). Facilitating cross-organisational workflows with a workflow view approach. *Data & Knowledge Engineering*, 51(1):109–147.

Role Slices: A Notation for RBAC Permission Assignment and Enforcement

J.A. Pavlich-Mariscal, T. Doan, L. Michel, S.A. Demurjian, and T.C. Ting

Department of Computer Science & Engineering, The University of Connecticut,
Unit-2155, 371 Fairfield Road, Storrs, CT 06269- 2155
jaime.pavlich@uconn.edu
{thuong, ldm, steve, ting}@engr.uconn.edu

Abstract. During the past decade, there has been an explosion in the complexity of software applications, with an increasing emphasis on software design via model-driven architectures, patterns, and models such as the unified modeling language (UML). Despite this, the integration of security concerns throughout the product life cycle has lagged, resulting in software infrastructures that are untrustworthy in terms of their ability to authenticate users and to limit them to their authorized application privileges. To address this issue, we present an approach to integrate role-based access control (RBAC) into UML at design-time for permission assignment and enforcement. Specifically, we introduce a new UML artifact, the *role slice*, supported via a new UML role-slice diagram, to capture RBAC privileges at design time within UML. Once captured, we demonstrate the utilization of aspect-oriented programming (AOP) techniques for the automatic generation of security enforcement code. Overall, we believe that our approach is an important step to upgrading security to be an indispensable part of the software process.

1 Introduction

In recent years, the importance of security in software systems has risen to a high level. The typical approach of integrating security into software applications at latter stages of the process can lead to serious security flaws. In order to minimize this problem, security must be considered as a first-class citizen throughout the software process. The issues that must be considered when adding security to a software application include: *security policy definition* to capture the security requirements using tools and artifacts to define and check for consistency in the security rules in order to minimize errors; and, *secure application implementation* to automatically generate security enforcement code that realizes and integrates the security policy with the application code.

In support of security policy definition, we have employed the unified modeling language, UML [17], which is the de facto standard for software modeling. In UML, while there are parallels between security and UML elements, direct support for security specification is not provided. Our ongoing work [9,8,7] has focused on the inclusion of RBAC[12] and MAC[4] by aligning the concept of role

S. Jajodia and D. Wijesekera (Eds.): Data and Applications Security 2005, LNCS 3654, pp. 40–53, 2005.

with actor, and by adding security properties to use-case, class, and sequence diagrams to capture MAC and RBAC characteristics as well as lifetimes (i.e., the legal time intervals of access to UML elements), and translate them into constraints. In support of RBAC, an actor represents one organizational role as defined by the security officer. This organizational role differs from actor-use-case roles in UML, which are used by actors to communicate with each specific use-case. Each security requirement constraint is characterized mainly by the UML elements involved, and the type of the constraints (e.g., Static Mutual Exclusion between actors and other non-actor elements). Intuitively, when the designer creates, modifies, or deletes a design element, s/he has changed the design to a new state with respect to the set of design elements that previously existed. Over time, a UML design can be characterized as the set of all states representing a specific design snapshot. Given a point of design time, a state function returns the information of the design space (UML elements, connections and security requirements) and whether an element is validly applicable at that design time. With the state information, we can perform security analysis to check the validity of the design, thereby providing a degree of security assurance.

Our work to date distributes security definition across use cases, class and sequence diagrams. While this has the advantage of closely associating security with the involved UML elements, it has the disadvantage of having the combination of the security permissions (security policy) not easily understood by designers and programmers. To complement this effort, and to provide a more seamless transition from design to code, we introduce a new artifact, the *role slice*, to visually represent permissions among roles in RBAC. In addition, our role-slice approach can separate the security aspect from the non-security aspects of code, by defining mappings to aspect-oriented programming (AOP) [15] for enforcing the access control policies that have been defined. The role-slice notation uses specialized class diagrams that define permissions and roles, in the form of UML classes and stereotyped packages, respectively, and employs UML stereotyped dependency relationships for representing role hierarchies, relying on model composition [5] for defining the permissions for each role, according to its position in the hierarchy. Since the role-slice diagram utilizes a structure akin to a class diagram, in concept, this security extension to UML occurs at the design level rather than analysis; however, MAC and RBAC defined for actors, use-cases, etc., can all be leveraged as part of the process of defining role slices.

In support of secure application implementation, once the policy has been defined and checked for consistency, the integration of security into an application's code can be greatly improved by an adequate modularization of the security-enforcement code. Using AOP, our intent is to separate application's security and non-security code, providing the means to more easily identify and locate security definitions when changes are required, thereby lessening the impact of these changes on the application. Object-oriented design/programming is centered around the ability to decompose a problem into a solution that captures only one concern (perspective) of an application. AOP addresses this limit by providing the ability to independently specify multiple orthogonal concerns.

To support this, AOP provides abstractions to define concerns with *aspects*, and a compilation technique, *aspect weaving*, that integrates aspects with the main application code via an AOP compiler. In this paper, we present the role-slice artifact and its mapping to access-control enforcement code via aspects.

The remainder of this paper is organized into four sections. Section 2 explains background concepts on RBAC, model composition, and AOP. Using this as a basis, our presentation on a model for secure design is divided into two parts: Section 3 details the definition of role slices; and, Section 4 describes techniques for mapping these definitions to AOP enforcement code. Section 5 reviews other related research efforts efforts, highlighting the influence to our work, and detailing the commonalities and differences. Section 6 contains the conclusions and reviews ongoing research.

2   Background Concepts

In this section, we review background concepts on role-based access control, model composition, and aspect-oriented programming. Our objective is to provide the necessary material to set the context of our work for subsequent sections.

2.1   Role-Based Access Control (RBAC)

Role-based access control, RBAC [12], is a security policy schema that assumes that the owner of the information in a software system is not the users, but the organization to which they belong. Moreover, RBAC states that the access to that information must be constrained according to the *role* that each user has been authorized and activated to interact with the system. User-role authorization is based on a set of tasks that the user performs inside the organization [11]. Users are authorized to access the system via a specific role, which holds the set of *privileges* that the user will have when interacting with the system.

There are several different interpretations for privileges or *permissions*, (we use both terms interchangeably). Depending on the specific application in which privileges/permissions are used, they can represent different concepts, such as: file access permissions in filesystems; query executions, table access, column or tuple access in database systems; or, instance access, class access, method access or attribute access in object-oriented systems. When using the object-oriented paradigm, there is a class model that represents the main structure and functionality of an application. Our assumption for incorporating RBAC into these kinds of applications, is that permissions are defined over the set of public methods present in the class model. For the purposes of the work on role slices presented herein, we define a permission as the *ability to invoke the method of a class*. We also consider negative permissions, which explicitly deny the right to invoke a method.

2.2   Aspect-Oriented Programming (AOP)

Software systems are inherently complex, and as information technologies evolve (e.g., faster CPUs, more memory, etc.), their complexity continues to increase.

Software developers faced challenges in the past when trying to manage that complexity, which they solved via abstraction and modularization mechanisms in programming languages, which has evolved into object-oriented design (UML) and programming (Java, C++, etc). As complexity of software applications continues to increase, there has been an emphasis on providing techniques that reduce complexity while still promoting the ability to construct large-scale applications. One classic technique is *separation of concerns* that focuses on distinguishing all of the important concerns of an application in modular units, allowing them to be managed independently. According to Tarr et al. [19], in order to achieve this goal, software formalisms may be required to provide: decomposition mechanisms that can partition the software into simpler pieces that are easier to manage; and, composition mechanisms to join all of the component elements into a complete system.

In the object-oriented paradigm, the main composition and decomposition mechanism is the *class*, which while offering a degree of separation of concerns, is limited in its ability to support *crosscutting concerns*, which are requirements of an application that have two common problems:

Scattering: Many concerns, which are specified in the requirements, tend to be implemented by using different classes both in the design specification and in the source code. For instance, the code for implementing persistence (e.g., connecting to a database via ODBC/JDBC and issuing queries) in a banking application can be scattered among multiple classes.

Tangling: One class can implement several different requirements simultaneously. Using the example above, each class that has code to access the database may also have code which is related to business requirements, such as cash flow calculations, mortage rates, etc.

There are several approaches that address crosscutting concerns [15,19,13]. The key idea for most of them consists of a new form of modularization that decomposes a model into pieces that, if defined and chosen carefully, can be mapped easily from requirements specification into design artifacts and code. Each piece may represent a particular view of the system (the crosscutting concern) consisting of sets of code that (ideally) are designable and implementable separately by independent developers.

One such alternative is *aspect-oriented programming* (AOP). AOP defines a unit of decomposition, called an *aspect*, in order to isolate each crosscutting concern code into one location, and a *weaving mechanism*, to compose the aspect code with the rest of the application as part of the compilation process. Each aspect specifies the way to integrate its code with the rest of the application by using:

Join Points, which are points in the execution of the program where the occurence of events of interest to the crosscutting concerns can be observed, and where an aspect *advice* that reacts to such events is inserted.

Pointcuts, which are sets of join points that are defined through static syntactic and semantic conditions on the context surrounding the joint point. For example, in AspectJ, pointcuts can be defined as all of the call sites to a polymorphic method within a class hierarchy.

Advices, which contain the code that is intended to be woven at specific join points specified within a pointcut.

Another approach to separation of concerns that complements AOP is *model composition* [5], which has its roots in *subject-oriented programming, SOP,* [13] and *multidimensional separation of concerns* [19]. Model composition is an extension to UML that decomposes a class model into pieces, called *subjects*, that represent a particular view of the system. Subjects are essentially class models that can be used to represent crosscutting concerns. Later, they are composed into larger class models until the system is finished and has all of the required functionality.

3   Role Slices and Secure Design

Role slices are intended to allow a software designer to capture security information in parallel with class design. The role slice provides an abstraction to collect information on the security of a role that cuts across all of the classes in an application, and to organize this information into a role-slice diagram, similar in concept to a UML class diagram. In this section, we introduce role slices, and their placement within the security design process. Specifically, Section 3.1, presents an example used throughout this paper. Next, Section 3.2 explores the role-slice artifact, including both positive and negative permissions. Lastly, Section 3.3 considers other issues related to the usage of role slices for real-world applications.

3.1   A Survey Institution Example

To serve as a basis for illustrating the concepts related to role slices and the generation of aspect-oriented enforcement code, we define an example application based on the following scenario:

> *A Survey Institution performs and manages public surveys. After the raw data of the survey is collected, the senior staff person adds a survey header into the database. Then, a senior or junior staff adds questions into that survey, may categorize questions, or add a new question category. Special questions with sensitive content are restricted to senior staff, who are the only ones who can modify them. Every staff person can search for surveys in the system, and, according to their privileges, access them for modification. Some survey results are public, so they can be accessed by anybody who is intersted in viewing the results.*

For simplicity and space limits, we utilize a simple design model that is better suited to explaining the concepts rather than a real-world design.

Given this scenario, Fig. 1 shows the class diagram where: *Public_Survey_Results* holds public data about statistics and questions; *Survey_List* and *Survey_Header* provide an interface to access and modify the information about surveys. Since the class *Public_Survey_Results* holds only public data, we decide to control access only to the subsystem defined by the classes *Survey_List* and *Survey_Header*. We call this set of classes a *secure subsystem*.

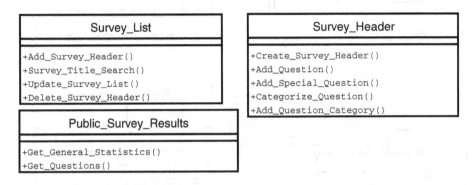

Fig. 1. Class Model of a Survey Management Application

3.2 Role Slices

A *role slice* is a structure that denotes the set of class methods that a given role can access in an application. Since we may not want to apply security to every class in the class model of the application, we define role-slice permission assignment with respect to a *secure subsystem*; the classes *Survey_List* and *Survey_Header* in Fig. 1. Visually, we represent a role slice as a UML stereotyped package containing a specialized class diagram, which is a subset of the class model of the application. Fig. 2 contains a diagram with roles slices for: *Staff* that contains common privileges; *Senior Staff* for users that have the ability to add a survey header and survey questions; and, *Junior Staff* with more limited access. Each class present in the role slice will have only methods that are assigned to the corresponding role as positive or negative permissions. An *abstract role slice*, *Staff* in Fig. 2, is tagged with the value *abstract*, cannot be assigned to a user, and is intended to be used as a mean to classify roles that have common permissions.

To represent role hierarchies, we define the *role-slice composition relationship*, which represents a hierarchical relationship between a *child* role slice and a *parent* role slice. The child role slice inherits the permissions from the parent role slice. Visually, we represent this relationship as a stereotyped dependency arrow that starts in the child and points to the parent. This relationship is shown in Fig. 2 with *Senior Staff* and *Junior Staff* as children of *Staff*. To obtain the complete set of permissions for a role in a hierarchy, we utilize the *composition with override integration* defined in [5], which composes two class diagrams by unifying their classes and methods into one diagram. For role slices, we match

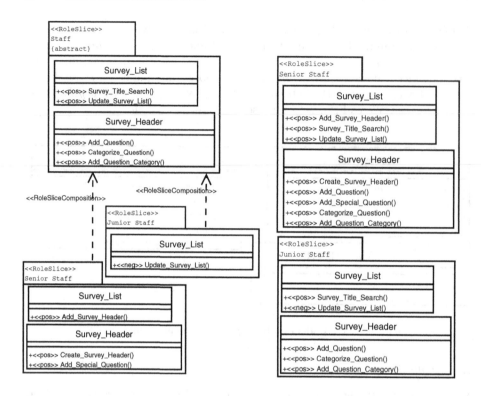

Fig. 2. Role-Slice Diagram   **Fig. 3.** Composed Role-Slice Diagram

the names of the classes (i.e., classes with the same name in both role slices compose into one class in the final diagram), and make the child override any permission definition in the parent.

We define permissions for the roles in Fig. 2 as follows: *Staff* is abstract and cannot be assigned to a user; and, *Senior Staff* and *Junior Staff*, which are non-abstract roles and assignable to users. The *Staff* role defines a set of common permissions: *Survey_Title_Search*, *Update_Survey_List*, *Add_Question*, *Categorize_Question* and *Add_Question_Category*. For Senior Staff, the assigned methods are: *Add_Survey_Header*, *Create_Survey_Header*, and *Add_Special_Question*. For Junior Staff, no permissions are directly assigned, but the permission to call *Update_Survey_List* is explicitly denied. Note that the method stereotypes ≪ *pos* ≫ and ≪ *neg* ≫ are used in the UML role-slice diagram for representing positive and negative permissions, respectively. The final set of permissions for each non-abstract role is defined through the composition of every non-abstract role slice with their ancestors, as shown in Fig. 3. Each final role slice has the union of all of the permissions from the ancestors (in this case, the parent Staff) and the respective child (Senior Staff or Junior Staff), with the exception of *Update_Survey_List*, which was overriden and restricted (negative) by Junior Staff.

3.3   Considerations for Real-World Scenarios

The main objective of the role-slice model is to represent a complex access control policy in a diagram that is easy to modify by security officers, and easy to understand by software designers and developers. From a practical standpoint, some issues must be taken into account:

- Any reasonably-sized application contains hundreds of classes, and the first critical decision in the security-policy definition process is to determine the subset of these classes to be included in the secure subsystem. A good approach is to only include the classes in the domain model that require access control and to exclude classes related to other concerns (e.g., I/O libraries, GUI components, etc.), since their presence would clutter the definition of role slices.
- The conceptualization of permissions during software development must be both be comprehensive and easy to understand by security officers and designers. To facilitate this, the composition relationship can be used to not only generate the final set of permissions for a security policy, but also to represent the permissions of each role at any point during the software process. This is especially useful when designing large role hierarchies, since the permissions of a concrete role can be difficult to visualize when spread across a significant portion of the role hierarchy.

Overall, issues related to the definition of security policies, their realization via role-slice diagrams, and the interplay of role-slice diagrams and application classes, are all critical to fully integrate the approach into the software process.

4   Mapping Role Slices to an Aspect-Oriented Application

This section details the transformation of role-slice definitions (as given in Section 3) into the application's code using aspect-oriented programming (AOP). Recall that the main purpose of a role slice is to define the access-control policy of an application regarding the authorized or prohibited methods (permissions) for each user (playing that role) interacting with the application. To map this information to aspect-oriented code and control the access to a method, it is necessary to check whether that method is denied for the active role (the role that the current user has when logged in) and raise an exception if that occurs; otherwise, the method is allowed to execute. This process is achievable with a set of AOP advices. All of the information for security permissions (role slices) are stored in a database. When a user logs into the system, an access-control aspect obtains its role-slice permissions by intercepting the login method in the class model and retrieves from the database the pertinent role slice for the user based on his/her credentials. For method permissions, an advice intercepts every call to methods in the secure subsystem (the classes *Survey_List* and *Survey_Header* in Fig. 1), made from methods external to the subsystem (every call that originates from *Public_Survey_Results* in Fig. 1), and allow their execution if and only if they are defined as a positive permission in the corresponding role slice.

The process of mapping from a role-slice diagram to aspect-oriented enforcement code will ultimately be automated with a code generator as shown in Fig. 4. This tool, currently under development at UConn, takes a role-slice specification (diagram and composed slices) as input, and outputs:

– A *policy database* that contains all of the information on roles and permissions (as defined in the composed role slices), and an authorization schema to store user instances and their assigned roles. We assume that a user is only permitted to play a single role at any given time (but can switch roles).
– An *access-control aspect* with the following characteristics:
  • The role-slice specification, particularly the secure subsystem definition, identifies the method invocations subject to access control. From this information, pointcut definitions for the access-control aspect are obtained.
  • The advice code that is woven at the pointcuts defined previously, must have access to the policy database, and be able to grant or deny access to a user invoking access controlled methods, based on his/her active role, and the call site.

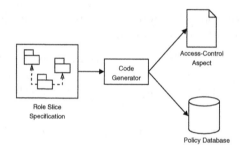

Fig. 4. Code Generator Scheme

We now explore an example aspect code, generated by our prototype, that enforces access control for the survey management application. Different portions of this aspect, implemented in AspectJ, are shown in Figs. 5, and 6.

Fig. 5 illustrates the portion of the access-control aspect that obtains the current active user. The `login` pointcut references a call to a method in the class `SecurityAdmin`, which returns the authenticated user. In this example, assume a multi-threading environment where each thread serves only one user. The advice using the pointcut stores the active user identification in a thread's local storage area.

Fig. 6 illustrates the code of the aspect that controls the access to methods from call sites outside the secure subsystem. The `externalCall` pointcut identifies all of the calls made to classes in the secure subsystem (i.e., `Survey_List` and `Survey_Header`), that originate from exogenous call sites. The advice code associated to this pointcut definition obtains the user's active role, and checks if s/he has a positive permission for to the intercepted method call. If not, an

```
public aspect AccessControl {
    ...
    pointcut login() : call(User SecurityAdmin.logIn(..));

    User around():login() {
        User u = proceed();
        activeUser.set(u);
        return u;
    }

    private ThreadLocal activeUser = new ThreadLocal() {
        protected Object initialValue() {
            return null;
        }
    };

    private User getActiveUser() {
        return (User)activeUser.get();
    }
    ...
}
```

Fig. 5. Obtaining Active User

exception is raised. Due to Java's semantics for exception handling, only runtime exceptions can be raised from this aspect. In summary, this example as given in Figs. 5 and 6, clearly illustrates the basic elements of the mapping from role slices to AOP enforcement code. Note that we are currently in the process of formalizing and implementing the role-slice code generator, as part of our overall prototyping work using Borland's UML tool Together Control Center [9,8,7].

```
public aspect AccessControl {
    ...
    pointcut externalCall() : (call(* Survey_List.*(..)) || call(* Survey_Header.*(..)))
                            && !within(Survey_List) && !within(Survey_Header);
    before() : externalCall() {
        Role r = getActiveUser().getActiveRole();
        if (!r.hasPosPermission(thisJoinPointStaticPart)) {
            throw new org.aspectj.lang.SoftException(new PermissionDeniedException());
        }
    }
    ...
}
```

Fig. 6. Checking of Permissions from Outside Calls

5   Related Work

In terms of related research, role slices are based on [10], which proposes a Network Enterprise Framework using UML to represent RBAC requirements for a specific framework given in [20]. Permissions are represented as methods of an interface-like artifact called *object handle*. Object handles are grouped in *keys*, which are stereotyped UML packages; role hierarchies are achieved by interface inheritance. In our approach, permissions are also represented as methods but, in contrast, they are grouped in role slices, which define specific rules of composition for them. Role slices also add negative permissions and permission overriding by descendent role slices. Our approach aims to be implementation-independent for object-oriented systems.

Another effort that relates to role slices is [3], which defines a metamodel to generate security definition languages. SecureUML [3,16] is an instance defined by this approach; a platform-independent security definition language for RBAC. The syntax of SecureUML has two parts: an *abstract syntax* independent from the modeling notation; and, a *concrete syntax* which can be used as an extension to a modeling language, such as UML. The abstract syntax defines basic elements to represent RBAC: *roles*, which can be assigned to *users* or *groups* of users; *permissions*, which are assigned to roles based on specific associated *constraints*; and, *actions*, which are associated with *permissions*, where a role can have a permission to execute one or more actions. Actions can be *atomic*, which means that they can be mapped directly to an action in the target platform, or *composite* actions, which are higher-level actions that may not be mapped directly to the target platform, and may contain lower-level actions within them. SecureUML's concrete syntax is defined by mapping elements in the abstract syntax to concrete UML elements [3]. We note that our role-slice diagram and associated concepts can be an instance of the concrete-syntax of the SecureUML notation, and that our syntax and associated mappings to UML elements differ from their approach. We also note that the role-slice diagram is only one component of our overall research. Specifically, our usage of composition in the role-slice diagram and the subsequent transition of the composed diagram into AOP enforcement code, is significantly different than the approach in SecureUML.

Another related approach, AuthUML [1,2] focuses on a process and a modeling language to express RBAC policies using *only* use cases. Permissions are defined by allowing or denying to actors the execution of use cases, and at a lower level, the execution of finer-grained conceptual operations that describe use-case behavior. Prolog-like predicates are used to represent the information and to check its consistency. In contrast, our approach uses classes to group permissions (methods), and role slices to group the entire set of permissions for a role. We do not define a specific process to develop software, so the decision of the way to utilize role slices to represent security information depends on the designers and developers. If the design of a particular application mapped each use case to a class, and each conceptual operation of a use case to a method, then both approaches would represent the same information about permissions.

The UMLsec approach [14] is another effort in security modeling related to our research. UMLsec is an extension to UML that defines several new stereotypes towards formal security verification of elements such as: fair exchange to avoid cheating for any party in a 2-party transaction; secrecy/confidentiality of information (accessible only to the intended people); secure information flow to avoid partial leaking of sensitive information; and, secure communication links like encryption. As currently structured, the UMLSec model is not tightly tied to RBAC, but the information it represents can be used to outline access control policies.

Regarding the aspect-oriented paradigm, [18] contains an example of composition of access-control behavior into an application by using aspect-oriented modeling techniques, with the aim of integrating security into a class model that allows designers to verify its access-control properties. Their approach takes a generic security design and instantiates it in a model tied to the domain of the application. In contrast, our code generation also requires the instantiation of the design, but only the access control aspect has dependencies with the domain class model. In addition, the role-slice notation provides a language to represent the policy that can be implemented using the aspect-oriented paradigm.

Another similar effort [6], provides a general framework to incorporate security into software using AOP. Similarities to our work include: the management of authentication; and, the interception of method invocations to constrain them based on permissions. The main difference is related to permissions. In their work, each permission is represented as a specific method tied to a framework of server objects that define them, and a set of client objects that invoke them. In contrast, in our role-slice approach, permissions are definable over any method in the class diagram, regardless of its structure.

6   Conclusions and Future Work

This paper has presented our efforts to define a new UML artifact to capture RBAC, the role slice and an associated diagram, and has detailed the transition from a role-slice diagram to security enforcement code, based on aspect-oriented programming (AOP). We believe that the role-slice notation, as presented in this paper, can assist designers and developers in the conceptualization of security policy, and facilitate its evolution throughout the design process. In addition, the automated mapping from a role-slice diagram (composed) to AOP enforcement code can provide a seamless transition from a security specification to code, and greatly facilitate the separation of concerns at the implementation level.

Ongoing and future research is focusing on achieving security policy composition via AOP, with the potential to also consider other, similar paradigms. We are interested in enhancing our model with additional security concerns, including: *mandatory access control* for security of methods based on classification and clearance; and, *delegation* for the ability to pass on authority (role) from one user to another. With three separate concerns (RBAC, MAC, and delegation), we must have the ability to compose any combination, which may require dynamic weaving of more than one set of constraints for access control, and the definition of different policies for separated secure subsystems. To facilitate this work on analysis and security extensions, we are formalizing role slices and their mapping to access-control aspects.

Another planned topic of research is to refine the definition of permissions, so they can support a wider-range of requirements. Specifically, we are interested in defining instance-based permissions, where roles would be authorized to invoke a method based on the instance of its class, and the value of their parameters. For example, different Senior Staff members in our example might be in charge of different surveys; even if their roles are the same, we would want the role parameterizable by instance so that they are restricted to particular survey instances. This research is related to aspect compilers, since it needs an aspect language that could support dynamic (runtime) join points that can be selected according to instance data (class instances, parameters), so that access control can be implemented seamlessly.

Lastly, we continue our joint implementation effort, focusing on integrating the work described herein with our other UML research [9,8,7]. Our objective is to provide a complete modeling framework from analysis and design through coding, which will also include the implementation of a role-slice diagramming tool, and the mapping from role slices to AOP security enforcement code. We are utilizing Borland's UML tool Together Control Center in support of this effort.

References

1. K. Alghathbar and D. Wijesekera. authUML: a three-phased framework to analyze access control specifications in use cases. In *FMSE '03: Proceedings of the 2003 ACM workshop on Formal methods in security engineering*, pages 77–86. ACM Press, 2003.
2. K. Alghathbar and D. Wijeskera. Consistent and complete access control policies in use cases. In Perdita Stevens, Jon Whittle, and Grady Booch, editors, *UML 2003 - The Unified Modeling Language. Model Languages and Applications. 6th International Conference, San Francisco, CA, USA, October 2003, Proceedings*, volume 2863 of *LNCS*, pages 373–387. Springer, 2003.
3. D. Basin, J. Doser, and T. Lodderstedt. *Model driven security, Engineering Theories of Software Intensive Systems*. 2004.
4. D. Bell and L. LaPadula. Secure computer systems: Mathematical foundations model. Technical report, Mitre Corporation, 1975.
5. S. Clarke. *Composition of object-oriented software design models*. PhD thesis, Dublin City University, January 2001.
6. B. De Win, B. Vanhaute, and B. De Decker. Security through aspect-oriented programming. In *Proceedings of the IFIP TC11 WG11.4 First Annual Working Conference on Network Security*, pages 125–138. Kluwer, B.V., 2001.
7. T. Doan, S. Demurjian, R. Ammar, and T.C. Ting. UML design with security integration as a first class citizen. In *Proc. of 3rd Intl. Conf. on Computer Science, Software Engineering, Information Technology, e-Business, and Applications (CSITeA'04)*, Cairo, December 2004.
8. T. Doan, S. Demurjian, T.C. Ting, and A. Ketterl. MAC and UML for secure software design. In *Proc. of 2nd ACM Wksp. on Formal Methods in Security Engineering*, Washington D.C., October 2004.
9. T. Doan, S. Demurjian, T.C. Ting, and C. Phillips. RBAC/MAC security for UML. In C. Farkas and P. Samarati, editors, *Research Directions in Data and Applications Security XVIII*, July 2004.
10. P. Epstein and R. Sandhu. Towards a UML based approach to role engineering. In *Proceedings of the fourth ACM workshop on Role-based access control*, pages 135–143, 1999.
11. D. Ferraiolo and R. Kuhn. Role-based access controls. In *15th NIST-NCSC National Computer Security Conference*, pages 554–563, 1992.

12. D. Ferraiolo, R. Sandhu, S. Gavrila, R. Kuhn, and R. Chandramouli. Proposed NIST standard for role-based access control. *ACM Trans. Inf. Syst. Secur.*, 4(3):224–274, 2001.
13. W. Harrison and H. Ossher. Subject-oriented programming: a critique of pure objects. In *Proceedings of the eighth annual conference on Object-oriented programming systems, languages, and applications*, pages 411–428, 1993.
14. J. Jürjens. UMLsec: Extending UML for secure systems development. In *Proceedings of the 5th International Conference on The Unified Modeling Language*, pages 412–425. Springer-Verlag, 2002.
15. G. Kiczales. Aspect-oriented programming. *ACM Comput. Surv.*, 28(4es):154, 1996.
16. T. Lodderstedt, D.A. Basin, and J. Doser. SecureUML: A UML-based modeling language for model-driven security. In *Proceedings of the 5th International Conference on The Unified Modeling Language*, pages 426–441. Springer-Verlag, 2002.
17. OMG. OMG-unified modeling language, v.1.5. UML Resource Page http://www.omg.org/uml, March 2003.
18. E. Song, R. Reddy, R. France, I. Ray, G. Georg, and R. Alexander. Verifiable composition of access control features and applications. In *Proceedings of 10th ACM Symposium on Access Control Models and Technologies (SACMAT 2005)*, 2005.
19. P. Tarr, H. Ossher, W. Harrison, and M. Sutton, Jr. Stanley. N degrees of separation: multi-dimensional separation of concerns. In *Proceedings of the 21st international conference on Software engineering*, pages 107–119. IEEE Computer Society Press, 1999.
20. D. Thomsen, D. O'Brien, and J. Bogle. Role based access control framework for network enterprises. In *Proceedings of 14th Annual Computer Security Application Conference*, pages 50–58, Phoenix, AZ, December 7-11 1998.

Designing Secure Indexes for
Encrypted Databases

Erez Shmueli[1], Ronen Waisenberg[1], Yuval Elovici[1], and Ehud Gudes[2]

[1] Ben-Gurion University of the Negev, Faculty of Engineering,
Department of Information Systems Engineering,
Postfach 653, 84105 Beer-Sheva, Israel
{erezshmu, ronenwai, elovici}@bgu.ac.il
[2] Ben-Gurion University of the Negev, Department of Computer Science,
Postfach 653, 84105 Beer-Sheva, Israel
ehud@cs.bgu.ac.il

Abstract. The conventional way to speedup queries execution is by using indexes. Designing secure indexes for an encrypted database environment raises the question of how to construct the index so that no information about the database content is exposed. In this paper, the challenges raised when designing a secure index for an encrypted database are outlined; the attacker model is described; possible attacks against secure indexes are discussed; the difficulty posed by multiple users sharing the same index are presented; and the design considerations regarding keys storage and encryption granularity are illustrated. Finally, a secure database-indexing scheme is suggested. In this scheme, protection against information leakage and unauthorized modifications is provided by using encryption, dummy values and pooling. Furthermore, the new scheme supports discretionary access control in a multi-user environment.

1   Introduction

Increasingly, organizations prefer to outsource their data center operations to external application providers. As a consequence of this trend toward outsourcing, highly sensitive data is now stored on systems that are not under the data owners' control. While data owners may not entirely trust providers' discretion, preventing a provider from inspecting data stored on their own machines is difficult. For this kind of service to work successfully, it is of primary importance to provide means of protecting the secrecy of the information remotely stored, while guaranteeing its availability to legitimate clients [1].

Communication between the client and the database service provider can be secured through standard means of encryption protocols, such as SSL (Secure Socket Layer), and is therefore ignored in the remainder of this paper. With regard to the security of stored data, access control has proved to be useful, on condition that data is accessed using the intended system interfaces. However, access control is useless if the attacker simply gains access to the raw database data, thus bypassing the traditional mechanisms [2]. This kind of access can

S. Jajodia and D. Wijesekera (Eds.): Data and Applications Security 2005, LNCS 3654, pp. 54–68, 2005.
© IFIP International Federation for Information Processing 2005

easily be gained by insiders, such as the system administrator and the database administrator (DBA).

Database encryption introduces an additional layer to conventional network and application security solutions and prevents exposure of sensitive information even if the raw data is compromised [3]. Database encryption prevents unauthorized users from viewing sensitive data in the database and, it allows database administrators to perform their tasks without having access to sensitive information. Furthermore, it protects data integrity, as unauthorized modifications can easily be detected [4].

A common technique to speed up the execution of queries in databases is to use a pre-computed index [5]. However, once the data is encrypted, the use of standard indexes is not trivial and depends on the encryption function used. Most encryption functions preserve equality, thus, "Hash" indexes can be used, however information such as the frequencies of indexed values is revealed. Most encryption functions do not preserve order, so "B-Tree" indexes, can no longer be used once the data is encrypted.

Moreover, if several users with different access rights use the same index, each one of them needs access to the entire index, possibly including indexed elements that are beyond his access rights. For example, Google Desktop, allows the indexing and searching of personal computers data. Using this tool, a legitimate user is able to bypass user names and passwords and view personal data belonging to others who use the same computer, since it is stored in the same index [6].

The contribution of this paper is threefold. First, we describe the challenges arising when designing a secure index for an encrypted database. Second, we outline design considerations regarding keys storage and encryption granularity. Third, we present a new indexing scheme that answers most of these challenges.

The remainder of the paper is structured as follows: in section 2, related works are outlined; in section 3, the problem statement is defined; in section 4, design considerations regarding database encryption are described; in section 5, we present a new secure database index; and section 6 presents our conclusions.

2   Related Work

The indexing scheme proposed in [7] suggests encrypting the whole database row and assigning a set identifier to each value in this row. When searching a specific value, its set identifier is calculated and then passed to the server, who, in turn, returns to the client a collection of all rows with values assigned to the same set. Finally, the client searches the specific value in the returned collection and retrieves the desired rows. In this scheme, equal values are always assigned to the same set, so some information is revealed when statistical attacks are applied, as stated in [1].

The indexing scheme in [1] suggests building a B-Tree index over the table plaintext values and then encrypting the table at the row level and the B-Tree at the node level. The main advantage of this approach is that the B-Tree content is not visible to the untrusted database server. However, only the client can now perform the B-Tree traversal, by executing a sequence of queries. Each query retrieves a node located at a deeper level of the B-Tree.

The indexing scheme provided in [2] is based on constructing the index on the plaintext values and encrypting each page of the index separately. Whenever a specific page of the index is needed for processing a query, it is loaded into memory and decrypted. Since the uniform encryption of all pages is likely to provide many cipher breaking clues, the indexing scheme provided in [8] proposes encrypting each index page using a different key depending on the page number. However, these schemes, which are implemented at the level of the operating system, are not satisfactory, since in most cases it is not possible to modify the operating system implementation. Moreover, in these schemes, it is not possible to encrypt different portions of the database using different keys. The disadvantage of using only one key is discussed in subsection 3.6.

The database encryption scheme in [4] suggests encrypting each database cell with its unique cell coordinates $\mu(T, R, C)$ and each index value concatenated with its unique row identifier, as illustrated in Fig. 1.

Figure 1 illustrates the database and index encryption as described in [4]. The use of cell coordinates for the encryption of the database table and of row identifiers for the index entries, ensures that there is no correlation between

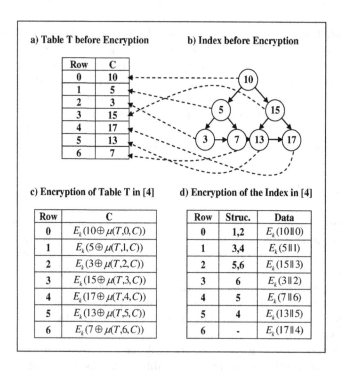

Fig. 1. Database and index encryption as described in [4]

the indexed values and the database ciphertext values. However, this indexing scheme is not resistant to tampering attacks.

The encryption function suggested in [9] preserves order, and thus allows range queries to be directly applied to the encrypted data without decrypting it. In addition it enables the construction of standard indexes on the ciphertext values. However, the order of values is sensitive information in most cases and should not be revealed.

In [10], a smart card with encryption and query processing capabilities is used to ensure the authorized and secure retrieval of encrypted data stored on untrusted servers. Encryption keys are maintained on the smart card. The smart card can translate exact match queries into equivalent queries over encrypted data.

In [11], the security of databases stored on smart cards is explored. However, retrieval performance is not the focus of their work and it is not clear how much of their techniques applies to general-purpose databases not stored on smart cards, as stated in [9].

3   The Problem Statement

3.1   The Attacker Model

The attacker can be categorized into three classes: *Intruder* - A person who gains access to a computer system and tries to extract valuable information. *Insider* - A person who belongs to the group of trusted users and tries to get information beyond his own access rights. *Administrator* - A person who has privileges to administer a computer system, but uses his administration rights in order to extract valuable information [10].

All of the above attackers can use different attack strategies: *Direct storage attacks* - Attacks against storage may be performed by accessing database files following a path other than through the database software, by physical removal of the storage media or by access to the database backup disks. *Indirect Storage attacks* - An adversary can access schema information, such as table and column names, metadata, such as column statistics, and values written to recovery logs in order to guess data distributions. *Memory attacks* - An adversary can access the memory of the database software directly [9] (The last one is usually protected by the Hardware/OS level).

3.2   Information Leakage

According to [4], a secure index in an encrypted database should not reveal any information on the database plaintext values. We extend this requirement, by categorizing the possible information leaks:

Static leakage - Gaining information on the database plaintext values by observing a snapshot of the database at a certain time. For example, if the index is encrypted in a way that equal plaintext values are encrypted to equal ciphertext values, statistics about the plaintext values, such as their frequencies can easily be learned.

Linkage leakage - Gaining information on the database plaintext values by linking a database value to its position in the index. For example, if the database value and the index value are encrypted in the same way (both ciphertext values are equal), an observer can search the database ciphertext value in the index, determine its position and estimate its plaintext value.

Dynamic leakage - Gaining information about the database plaintext values by observing and analyzing the changes performed in the database over a period of time. For example, if a user monitors the index for a period of time, and if in this period of time only one value is inserted (no values are updated or deleted), the observer can estimate its plaintext value based on its position in the index.

3.3   Unauthorized Modification

In addition to the passive attacks that *monitor* the index, active attacks that *modify* the index should also be considered. Active attacks are more problematic, in the sense that they may mislead the user. For example, modifying index references to the database rows may result in queries returning erroneous set of rows, possibly benefiting the adversary.

Unauthorized modifications can be made in several ways: *Spoofing* - Replacing a ciphertext value with a generated value. *Splicing* - Replacing a ciphertext value with a different ciphertext value. *Replay* - Replacing a ciphertext value with an old version previously updated or deleted [11].

3.4   Structure Perseverance

When applying encryption to an existing database, it would be desirable that the structure of the database tables and indexes is not modified during the encryption. This ensures that the database tables and indexes can be managed in their encrypted form by a database administrator as usual, while keeping the database contents hidden. For example, if a hash index is used and the values therein do not distribute equally, performance might be undermined, and the DBA might wish to replace the hash function. In such a case, the DBA needs to know structure information, such as the number of values in each list, but does not need to know the values themselves.

3.5   Performance

Indexes are used in order to speed up queries execution. However, in most cases, using encrypted indexes causes performance degradation due to the overhead of decryption. Indexes in an encrypted database raise the question of how to construct the index so that no information about the database content is revealed, while performance in terms of time and storage is not significantly affected.

3.6   Discretionary Access Control (DAC)

In a multi-user (discretionary) database environment each user only needs access to the database objects (e.g., group of cells, rows and columns) needed to perform his job.

Encrypting the whole database using the same key, even if access control mechanisms are used, is not enough. For example, an insider who has the encryption key and bypasses the access control mechanism can access data that are beyond his security group. Encrypting objects from different security groups using different keys ensures that a user who owns a specific key can decrypt only those objects within his security group [15]. Following this approach, different portions of the same database column might be encrypted using different keys. However, a fundamental problem arises when an index is used for that column as illustrated in Fig. 2.

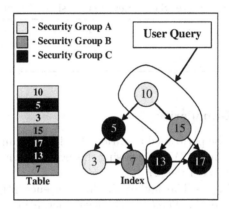

Fig. 2. An Indexed Column Encrypted using Different Keys

Figure 2 illustrates an index that is queried by users who belong to different security groups. Each one of them needs access to the entire index, possibly to indexed elements, which are beyond their access rights. The same problem arises when the index is updated.

4   Design Considerations

4.1   Key Storage

One important issue in any encrypted database is that of keys storage [1,2,12]. Several alternatives were proposed in the literature:

Storing the encryption keys at the server side - The server has full access to the encryption keys. All computations are performed at the server side.

Storing encryption keys at the client side - The client never transfers the keys to the server and is solely responsible for performing all encryption and decryption operations. When the database server has no access to the encryption keys, most computations cannot be performed at the server side, since they require decryption.

Keys per session - The database server has full access to the encryption keys during the session but does not store them on disk. This ensures that during the session, the user transaction can be performed entirely at the server side.

Table 1 summarizes the dependency between the trust in the server and the keys storage. If we have no trust in the database server, we would prefer to keep the encryption keys at the client side only. In cases where the database server itself is fully trusted, but its physical storage is not, we can store the keys at the server side in some protected region.

Table 1. Keys Storage vs. Trust in Server

	Server Side	Keys per Session	Client Side
Absolute	+	+	+
Partial	-	+	+
None	-	-	+

4.2   Encryption Granularity

Index encryption can be performed at various levels of granularity: single values, nodes, pages or whole index. When choosing the level of granularity, the following should be considered (see Table 2):

Information Leakage - The higher the level of encryption granularity, the less information is revealed. *Single values* level encryption of the index reveals sensitive information, such as frequencies of the index values. *Whole Index* level encryption ensures that information about the indexed data cannot be leaked, since the index is encrypted as one unit.

Unauthorized Modifications - Encryption at higher levels of granularity makes it harder for the attacker to tamper with the data. *Single values* level encryption of the index allows an attacker to switch two ciphertext values without being noticed. *Whole Index* level encryption implies that a minor modification to the encrypted index has a major effect on the plaintext index and can easily be detected.

Structure Perseverance - Higher levels of encryption granularity conceal the index structure. *Whole Index* level encryption changes the structure of the index since the basic element of reference is changed from a single value to the entire index. *Single values* level encryption of the index preserves its structure.

Performance - Finer encryption granularity affords more flexibility in allowing the server to choose what data to encrypt or decrypt. *Whole Index* level encryption requires the whole index to be decrypted, even if a small number of index nodes are involved in the query. *Single values* level encryption of the index enables decryption of values of interest only.

Table 2. Comparing Different Levels of Encryption Granularity

	Information Leakage	Unauthorized Modifications	Structures Perseverance	Performance
Single values	Worst	Worst	Best	Best
Nodes	Low	Low	Medium	Medium
Pages	Medium	Medium	Low	Low
Whole Index	Best	Best	Worst	Worst

Better performance and preserving the structure of the database cannot be achieved using pages or whole index encryption granularity. However, special techniques can be used in order to cope with unauthorized modifications and information leakage, when single values or nodes granularity encryption are used.

In our scheme, which is presented in the remainder of this paper, we assume that the encryption keys are kept per session and that the index is encrypted at the single values level of granularity.

5   A New Secure Database Index

In this section, a secure database index, encrypted at the single values level of granularity is suggested. Best performance and structure perseverance are simply obtained since single values granularity encryption is used. Information leakage and unauthorized modifications are protected against using encryption, dummy values and pooling. Finally, a technique that supports discretionary access control in a multi-user environment is presented.

5.1   Encryption

Let us assume that a standard index entry is of the form:

$$(V_{trc}, IRs, ER) \tag{1}$$

Where:

V_{trc} - An indexed value in table t, row r and column c.
IRs - The internal reference (references between index entries)
ER - The external reference (reference to the database row).

An entry in the proposed secure index is defined as follows:

$$(E_k(V_{trc}), IRs, E'_k(ER), MAC_k(V_{trc} \parallel IRs \parallel ER \parallel SR)) \tag{2}$$

Where:

k - An encryption key.
E_k - A nondeterministic encryption function.
E'_k - An ordinary encryption function.
SR - The entry self reference.
MAC_k - A message authentication code function.

The E_k Function. The implementation of E_k introduces a tradeoff between *static leakage* and *performance* (see Table 3). If E_k is a non-deterministic encryption function (that is, equal plaintext values are encrypted to different ciphertext values), statistics such as the frequencies and distribution of values are concealed, but comparing index values requires their decryption. On the other hand, if E_k is an order preserving encryption function, some information about the index values is revealed (e.g., their order) but it is possible to compare values without the need to decrypt them.

Table 3. The Tradeoff between Security and Performance for E_k implementation

	Security	Performance
Nondeterministic	High	Worst
Equality Preserving	Medium	Low
Order Preserving	Low	Medium
No Encryption	Worst	High

We suggest using a non-deterministic E_k. A possible implementation of E_k follows:

$$E_k(x) = E_k''(x||r) \tag{3}$$

Where:
k - An encryption key.
E_k'' - An ordinary encryption function.
r - A random number with a fixed number of bits.

Using the above implementation of E_k there is no correlation between $E_k(V_{trc})$ and the corresponding column ciphertext value (random numbers are used before encryption) and thus *linkage leakage* attacks are eliminated.

The MAC_k Function. Most commercial databases implement indexes like tables (as heap files). In this implementation, index entries are uniquely identified using the pair: *page id* and *slot number* [5] (in our notations SR and IR).

Message authentication codes (MAC) are used to protect against unauthorized modifications of messages. They mix the message cryptographically under a secret key, and the result is appended to the message. The receiver can then recompute the MAC and verify its correctness. It should be impossible for an attacker to forge a message and still be able to compute the correct MAC without knowing the secret key.

In our scheme, we use a MAC_k function to protect the index entries against unauthorized modifications. *Spoofing* attacks are eliminated, since the MAC value depends on V_{trc}, and once $E_k(V_{trc})$ is tampered with, V_{trc} will not match the V_{trc} used in the MAC. *Splicing* attacks are eliminated since the MAC value depends on SR and trying to substitute two encrypted index entries will be detected, since SR would not match the SR used in the MAC. *Replay* attacks can be eliminated by adding a new dimension, that of time, to each index node. This enables the validity of the node version to be verified, just as SR was used in order to verify its logical location.

The MAC value added to each index entry causes data expansion and thus, its size introduces a tradeoff between security and data expansion.

Evaluating a Query. The following pseudo code illustrates a query evaluation using the encrypted index [1]:

```
INPUT:
     A table: T
     A column: C
     A value: V
     A query: SELECT * FROM T WHERE T.C>=V

OUTPUT:
     A collection of row-ids.

X := getIndex(T, C).getRootNode();
While (not X.isLeaf()) Do
    If (not x.isValid())
        Throw IllegalStateException();
    Else
        If X.getValue()<V Then
             X := X.getRightSonNode();
        Else
             X := X.getLeftSonNode();
        End If;
    End If;
End While;

RESULT := {};

While X.getValue()<V Do
    X := X.getRightSiblingNode();
End While;

While X is not null Do
    RESULT := RESULT union {X.getRowId()};
    X := X.getRightSiblingNode();
End While;

Return RESULT;
```

While *isLeaf*, *getRightSonNode*, *getLeftSonNode* and *getRightSiblingNode* methods relate to the index structure and their implementation does not change,

---

[1] The encrypted index is assumed to be implemented as a binary tree. However, the pseudo code can be easily be generalized to handle a B-Tree implementation.

getValue and *getRowId* are implemented differently so that encryption and decryption support is added. The new method, *isValid*, verifies the index entry integrity using the MAC value.

Performance can be furthermore improved, if entries' verification is performed periodically on the entire index and not as part of each index operation.

5.2   Using Dummy Values and Pooling

In order to cope with *dynamic leakage* attacks, we need to reduce the *level of confidence* an adversary has about the effect of new inserted data on the database indexes. There is a trade-off between how much of the index is updated and how much information an adversary is able to learn [13]. In this subsection, we propose two techniques for reducing the adversary level of confidence:

Dummy values - We can insert dummy values to the index with each insertion made by the user, and thus reduce the level of confidence. However, inserting dummy values with each insertion results in data expansion. The number of dummy values added in each insertion determines the level of confidence an adversary has about the position of a value within the index.

Pooling - The use of pooling in order to improve performance of insertions to database indexes was suggested by [14]. We suggest the use of pooling for security reasons. We define a fixed size pool for each index holding the new inserted values. Only when the pool is full, will the indexes be updated with these values. Furthermore, the extraction of values from the pool should be done in a random order, since it makes it difficult to link the extracted values and their corresponding inserted values. When a query is to be executed, we first need to search the pool, and then to search the rest of the index. The pool size determines the level of confidence an adversary has about the position of a value within the index. Note that a full scan has to be performed on the pool whenever the index is used. Thus, the size of the pool is a privacy-performance trade-off. Using a pool size that has space complexity of $O(\log |table\ size|)$ will not affect the time complexity of the queries.

Figure 3 illustrates a database index using pooling. Figure 3a illustrates the database table, index and pool after the insertion of three values: 17,5,24 where the pool size is four values. Figure 3b illustrates the database table, index and pool after the insertion of a fourth value: 36, that fills the pool. The values in the pool are then extracted in random order and inserted into the database table and index.

5.3   Supporting DAC

If indexes are used only by one user or if they are never updated, it is possible to maintain a local index for each user. Securing indexes stored locally is relatively easy. However, such local indexes do not work well in a multi-user environment, since synchronizing them is difficult. Thus, it is necessary to store the indexes in one site, such as the database server, and share them between users.

As mentioned in subsection 3.6, a fundamental problem arises when multiple users share the same encrypted index and each user has different access rights.

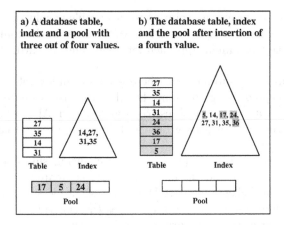

Fig. 3. A Database Index Using Pooling

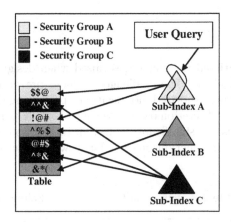

Fig. 4. An Encrypted Database Column and its Corresponding Sub-Indexes

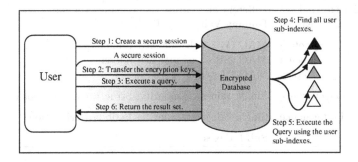

Fig. 5. Query Execution Using Sub-Indexes

We suggest a simple but elegant solution to this problem: split the index into several sub-indexes where each sub-index relates to values in the column encrypted using the same key. A similar approach for disseminating XML documents was proposed in [15].

Figure 4 illustrates sub-indexes where each sub-index relates to values in the column encrypted using the same key. In order to evaluate a query, only ciphertext values with the same access right are queried. All the values in a sub-index belong to the same security group, and thus the problem that is illustrated in Fig. 2 is eliminated.

Figure 5 illustrates how a query is executed using sub-indexes. A secure session between the user and the database server is created (step 1). The user supplies his encryption keys[2] (step 2). During the secure session, the user submits queries to the server (step 3). The server uses the encryption keys in order to find the set of indexes that the current user is entitled to access[3] (step 4). The query is executed on the set of indexes found (step 5). The result set is returned to the user (step 6).

6   Conclusions

In this paper, we outlined the challenges raised when designing a secure index for an encrypted database. The challenges include: prevention of information leakage; detection of unauthorized modifications; preserving the structure of the index; and supporting discretionary access control; while performance in terms of time and storage is not significantly affected. In addition, two design considerations, keys storage and encryption granularity, were discussed. For each design

Table 4. Summary of Challenges and Solutions

Challenge	Solution
Static Leakage	E_k is nondeterministic
Linkage Leakage	Different encryption functions for the index and the table
Dynamic Leakage	Dummy Values and Pooling
Spoofing	MAC (V_{trc} - the indexed value)
Splicing	MAC (SR - the node self reference)
Replay	MAC (Version)
Structure Perseverance	Single values granularity; Structure data is not encrypted
Performance	Single values granularity; Periodic verification
DAC	Sub-Indexes

---

[2] The encryption keys can be supplied using smart card architecture.

[3] The database server can maintain a directory that maps the hash of a given encryption key to the corresponding sub-index.

consideration, we proposed several alternatives and elaborated on the tradeoffs between them.

A secure database index encrypted at the single values level of granularity was suggested. Performance and structure perseverance are simply obtained since single values granularity encryption is used. We used encryption, dummy values and pooling in order to prevent information leakage and unauthorized modifications. Finally, in order to support discretionary access control in a multi-user environment, we suggested splitting the index into several sub-indexes, where each sub-index relates to values in the column encrypted using the same key.

Table 4 summarizes the challenges and solutions that were suggested throughout this paper.

References

1. Damiani, E., De Capitani diVimercati, S., Jajodia, S., Paraboschi, S. and Samarati, P.: Balancing Confidentiality and Efficiency in Untrusted Relational DBMSs. CCS'03, Washington (2003) 27-31.
2. Iyer, B., Mehrotra, S., Mykletun, E., Tsudik, G. and Wu, Y.: A Framework for Efficient Storage Security in RDBMS. E. Bertino et al. (Eds.): EDBT 2004, LNCS 2992 (2004) 147-164.
3. Davida, G.I., Wells, D.L., and Kam, J.B.: A Database Encryption System with subkeys. ACM Trans. Database Syst. 6 (1981) 312-328.
4. Elovici, Y., Waisenberg, R., Shmueli, E., Gudes, E.: A Structure Preserving Database Encryption Scheme. SDM 2004, Workshop on Secure Data Management, Toronto, Canada, August, (2004).
5. Ramakrishnan, R and Gehrke, J.:Database Management Systems. McGraw-Hill (2000).
6. Spring, T.: Google Desktop Search: Security Threat? http://blogs.pcworld.com/staffblog/archives/000264.html, October, (2004);
7. Hacigümüs, H., Iyer, B., Li, C., and Mehrotra, S.: Executing SQL over encrypted data in the database-service-provider model. In Proc. of the ACM SIGMOD'2002, Madison, USA (2002).
8. Bayer, R. and Metzger, J.K.: On the Encipherment of Search Trees and Random Access Files. ACM Trans Database Systems, Vol. 1 (1976) 37-52.
9. Agrawal, R., Kiernan, J., Srikant, R. and Xu, Y.: Order Preserving Encryption for Numeric Data. In Proc. of the ACM SIGMOD'2004, Paris, France (2004).
10. Bouganim, L. and Pucheral, P.: Chip-secured data access: confidential data on untrusted servers. In Proc. of the 28th Int. Conference on Very Large Data Bases, Hong Kong, China (2002) 131-142.
11. Vingralek, R.: Gnatdb: A small-footprint, secure database system. In Proc. of the 28th Int'l Conference on Very Large Databases, Hong Kong, China, August (2002) 884-893.
12. Hore, B., Mehrotra, S. and Tsudik, G.: A Privacy Preserving Index for Range Queries. In Proc. of the 30th International Conference on Very Large Data Bases, Toronto, Canada(2004) 720-731.
13. Song, D.X., Wagner, D. and Perrig, A.: Practical Techniques for Searches on Encrypted Data. In Proc. of the 2000 IEEE Security and Privacy Symposium, May (2000).

14. Jermine, C. Datta, A. and Omiecinski, E.: A Novel Index Supporting High Volume Data Warehouse Insertions. In Proc. of the 25th Int. Conference on Very Large Data Bases, Edinburgh, Scotland (1999) 235-245.
15. Bertino, E. and Ferrari, E.: Secure and Selective Dissemination of XML Documents. ACM Transactions on Information and System Security Vol. 5 No. 3 (2002) 290-331.
16. Denning, D.E.: Cryptography and Data Security. Addison-Wesley, Massachusetts (1982).
17. Menezes, A., Van Oorschot, P. and Vanstone, S.: Handbook of Applied Cryptography. CRC Press (1996).
18. National Bureau of Standards. Data Encryption Standard. FIPS, NBS (1977).
19. Database Encryption in Oracle9i^{TM}. An Oracle Technical White Paper (2001).

Efficiency and Security Trade-Off in Supporting Range Queries on Encrypted Databases*

Jun Li and Edward R. Omiecinski

College of Computing,
Georgia Insitute of Technology,
801 Atlantic Drive, Atlanta, GA 30332
{junli, edwardo}@cc.gatech.edu

Abstract. The database-as-a-service (DAS) model is a newly emerging computing paradigm, where the DBMS functions are outsourced. It is desirable to store data on database servers in encrypted form to reduce security and privacy risks since the server may not be fully trusted. But this usually implies that one has to sacrifice functionality and efficiency for security. Several approaches have been proposed in recent literature for efficiently supporting queries on encrypted databases. These approaches differ from each other in how the index of attribute values is created. Random one-to-one mapping and order-preserving are two examples. In this paper we will adapt a prefix-preserving encryption scheme to create the index. Certainly, all these approaches look for a convenient trade-off between efficiency and security. In this paper we will discuss the security issues and efficiency of these approaches for supporting range queries on encrypted numeric data.

1 Introduction

The database-as-a-service (DAS) model [1] is a new computing paradigm that has emerged recently. To save cost, data storage and management are outsourced to database service providers. In other words, highly sensitive data are now stored in locations that are not under the data owner's control, such as leased space and partners' sites. This can put data confidentiality at risk. Therefore, it is desirable to store data in encrypted form to protect sensitive information. Also queries may reveal private information about the user [2]. In this paper, we discuss how to efficiently support searching functionality, in particular, range queries, while preserving data confidentiality and user privacy. The motivation within this model of processing is to provide security and privacy but also have the database service provider do most of the query processing. Several approaches have been proposed to generate the index that enables queries to be processed against encrypted data with different levels of efficiency and security [3,4,5,6]. In this paper, we will adapt a prefix-preserving encryption scheme to create the

---

* This work has been supported in part by National Science Fundation Grant CCR-0121643.

index. We will also discuss the security issues and efficiency of these approaches for supporting range queries on encrypted data.

One simple way to preserve the confidentiality is to decrypt the data when performing search. There are several drawbacks with this approach. First, all the data stored in the database needs to be decrypted for every query. Second, this approach assumes the server is secure and fully trusted. This assumption is less justified in the DAS paradigm.

A major type of database queries is *range-based*, composed of *intervals* in the underlying domain of the attributes. Attributes such as name, not typically thought of as numerical, can be indexed and therefore linearized in some fashion. In this paper we will mainly be concerned with *interval-matching* or *exact-matching* as query conditions. Interval-matching is defined as a boolean function $f_{[a,b]}(x)$, which returns true if and only if $x \in [a, b]$. Because computers can handle only inherently finite and discrete attribute values, one can assume without loss of generality x, a and b are all nonnegative integers. Exact-matching is a special case of interval-matching in which a is equal to b.

The paper is organized as the follows, in Sect. 2, we survey the related work and discuss possible solutions based on well-known mechanisms. Section 3 shows how a relation is encrypted and stored on the server. In Sect. 4, we present a scheme that efficiently supports interval-matching as query conditions. First we show how an interval-matching problem can be transformed into a set of prefix-matching problems. Then the prefix-preserving encryption algorithm is presented. At the end of the section, we describe that with prefix-preserving encryption how a condition in a range query is translated to a condition over server-side representation and how select operations are implemented. Section 5 analyzes one possible attack against the random one-to-one mapping scheme and the prefix-preserving scheme, while in Sect. 6 we have some additional discussion on the security of the prefix-preserving scheme. Section 7 compares the prefix-preserving scheme with the random one-to-one mapping scheme in the aspects of client side cost, server side cost and communication cost for supporting range queries. We then conclude the paper in Sect. 8.

2   Related Work

Recently providing security and privacy in DAS has drawn considerable attention [3,4,5,6]. The bucket index technique proposed in [3,6] relies on partitioning attribute domains of a client's table into sets of buckets. The index value of each remote table attribute value is the bucket number to which the corresponding plain value belongs. This representation supports efficient evaluation of both exact-matching and interval-matching predicates on the database service provider; however, it makes it awkward to manage the correspondence between bucket numbers and the actual attribute values present in the database. For the convenience of comparison, in the rest of this paper, when we discuss about this approach, we will assume that the size of each bucket is 1 and the bucket number is generated by a random one-to-one mapping of the plaintext value. In this case, the server will not return any redundant data to the client. Therefore, the client does not need any database functionality to filter out unsolicited data. This fulfills the goal of the DAS model, i.e., outsourcing database management and having the database server do most of the work.

In [4], the authors quantitatively evaluate the level of inference exposure associated with the publication of attribute indexes generated by a random one-to-one mapping. In the solution they propose for supporting interval-based queries, the task of determining B^+-tree information is left to the customer. The advantage of their solution is that the content of B^+-tree is not visible to an untrusted database service provider. The disadvantage is that a lot of data processing has to occur on client machines. This mitigates the advantage of the DAS model.

In [7], a sequence of strictly increasing polynomial functions is used for encrypting integer values while preserving their order. In [5], another form of order-preserving encryption is provided for computing the index. It takes a user-provided target distribution as input and transform the plaintext values in such a way that the transformation preserves the order while the transformed values follow the target distribution. The authors assume an application environment where the goal is safety from an adversary who has access to all (but only) encrypted values (the so called ciphertext only attack [8]). In this paper, we will not only examine the prefix-preserving scheme under ciphertext only attack, but also examine it under known plaintext attack [8] (i.e., an adversary is assumed to gain full knowledge to certain number of ⟨plaintext, ciphertext⟩ pairs through means other than compromising the key).

All of the aforementioned schemes including the scheme proposed in this paper suffer from a same problem, i.e., they preserve statistics. That is, an adversary may know exactly how many entries each value has, even though the plaintexts of the indexes themselves are unknown. This can lead the adversary into an easier inference. Elovici *et al.* proposed an index scheme that does not reveal database statistics [9]. However, it assumes that the cell coordinates (including Table ID, Row ID, and Column ID) are stable. That is, insert, update and delete operations do not change the coordinates of existing cells. This puts additional restrictions to the implementation of the DBMS.

A potential technique that can support searching on encrypted data is computing with encrypted data [10]. However, an expensive protocol between clients and database service providers is needed. A closely related topic is Private Information Retrieval (PIR) [2]. PIR mechanisms allow clients to query databases without revealing which entries are of interest. PIR schemes often require multiple non-colluding servers, consume large amounts of bandwidth, and do not guarantee the confidentiality of the data.

3   Data Organization

In a relational DBMS, data are organized in tables (e.g., the Employee data in Table 1, where the underlined attribute represents the key of the table). The database can be encrypted with regard to different units, which can be individual

Table 1. Employee

FNAME	LNAME	SSN	ADDRESS	SALARY	DNO
John	Smith	123456789	731 Fondren, Storrs, CT	30000	5
Franklin	Wong	333445555	638 Voss, Storrs, CT	40000	5
Alicia	Zelaya	999887777	3321 Castle, Storrs, CT	25000	4
Ahmad	Jabbar	987987987	980 Dallas, Storrs, CT	25000	5
James	Borg	888665555	450 Stone, Storrs, CT	55000	1

Table 2. Encrypted_Employee

Enc_tuple	I_{SSN}	I_{SALARY}	I_{DNO}
fjftejcCcWsGqfChXcHuRzoriODCRxvD	068764019	6488	250
tprJMmfjXJNs74fZZfL1TridemjZnWvY	277737042	45639	250
edVI8JvVSjmzXsrmDIiosZabdFnnorwy	080581877	53798	224
z4tzGJUdsyy7Eb0puESatLCXOXckVTWA	203690710	53798	250
zzdqGlqngQgwJurSqsyFrejiia6KCNMk	929644962	20577	59

table, a column of a table, a row (tuple) of a table or a given column within each row (i.e., the data item value). Encrypting at a coarser level of granularity such as a table implies that the entire table must be returned as the result of a query, although encryption/decryption will be more efficient. Encrypting at a finer level such as a data item allows for more efficient query processing but requires increased overhead for encryption/decryption [1]. As in [3,4,5,6], we assume encryption to be performed at the tuple level. To provide the server with the ability to select a set of tuples to be returned in response to a query, we associate each encrypted tuple with a number of indexing attributes. An index can be associated with each attribute in the original relation on which conditions need to be evaluated for query processing.

Each plaintext relation will be stored as a relation with one attribute representing the encrypted tuple and additional attributes representing the indexes. Each plaintext tuple $t(A_1, ..., A_n)$ is mapped onto a tuple $t'(E(t), I_1, ..., I_m)$ where $m \leq n$. The attribute $E(t)$ stores an encrypted string that corresponds to the entire plaintext tuple, and each I_i corresponds to the index over some A_j. The encryption function E is treated as a black box in our discussion. Any block cipher such as AES [11], DES [12] etc., can be used to encrypt the tuples. Table 2 illustrates an example of the corresponding encrypted/indexed relation Encrypted_Employee where Enc_tuple contains the encrypted tuples, while I_{SSN}, I_{SALARY}, and I_{DNO} are indexes over attributes SSN, SALARY, and DNO respectively.

4   A Prefix-Preserving Encryption Based Scheme

4.1   Transforming Interval-Matching into Prefix-Matching

In this section, we will transform interval-matching into prefix-matching. Prefix-matching has been used widely in databases and networks. The transformation is based on the fact that an arbitrary interval can be converted into a union of *prefix ranges*, where a prefix range is one that can be expressed by a prefix [13]. For example, the interval [32, 111], the 8-bit binary representation of which is [00100000, 01101111], can be represented by a set of prefixes $\{001*, 010*, 0110*\}$. Throughout this paper, the notation $*$ is used to denote an arbitrary suffix. To verify that a number is in the interval is equivalent to check that the number matches any of those prefixes in the set. For example, 37 (00100101 in binary) is in the interval as it matches prefix $001*$, while 128 (10000000 in binary) is not in the interval since it matches none of those three prefixes.

Let n denote the length of the binary representation of the data, and let p_n denote the number of prefixes needed to represent an interval. We have the following theorem on the upper bound of p_n.

Theorem 1. *For any interval* $[a_1a_2\cdots a_n, b_1b_2\cdots b_n]$ $(n \geq 2)$, $p_n \leq 2(n-1)$.

The proof of this theorem is omitted here due to the lack of space and can be found in our technical report [14]. Note that for interval $[1, 2^n - 2]$, it can be easily verified that p_n is equal to $2(n-1)$. Therefore, the upper bound is tight.

Theorem 2. *For a given* n, *considering all possible intervals* $[a_1a_2\cdots a_n,$ $b_1b_2\cdots b_n]$, *if we assume all the intervals appear with the same probability, i.e., all queries are equi-probable, the average number of* p_n *is equal to* $\frac{(n-2)2^{2n-1}+(n+1)2^n+1}{2^{2n-1}+2^n-1}$, *which is approximately equal to* $n-2$, *when* n *is large.*

The proof of this theorem is omitted here due to the lack of space and can be found in our technical report [14]. From these two theorems we see that the upper bound of p_n is a linear function of n and the average number of p_n is approximately a linear function of n. This is a very nice feature.

In Fig. 1 we present a recursive algorithm to generate the set of prefixes for a given interval $[a_1a_2\cdots a_n, b_1b_2\cdots b_n]$.

---

1. Starting from $k = 1$, find the most significant bit, numbered k, for which $a_k < b_k$.

2. If k is not found, i.e., for all $1 \leq i \leq n$, $a_i = b_i$, then the interval can be denoted by prefix $a_1a_2\cdots a_n$. Return $a_1a_2\cdots a_n$.

3. If for all $k \leq i \leq n$, $a_i = 0$ and $b_i = 1$, then return $a_1a_2a_{k-1}*$ (return $*$ if $k = 1$).

4. Transform interval $[a_1a_2\cdots a_n, b_1b_2\cdots b_n]$ into $[a_1\cdots a_{k-1}0a_{k+1}\cdots a_n, a_1\cdots a_{k-1}011\cdots 1]$ $\cup$ $[a_1\cdots a_{k-1}100\cdots 0, a_1\cdots a_{k-1}1b_{k+1}\cdots b_n]$.

5. Run this algorithm with interval $[a_{k+1}\cdots a_n, 11\cdots 1]$ as input, concatenate $a_1\cdots a_{k-1}0$ before all the returned prefixes. Then run this algorithm with interval $[00\cdots 0, b_{k+1}\cdots b_n]$ as input, concatenate $a_1\cdots a_{k-1}1$ before all the returned prefixes. Return all the prefixes.

Fig. 1. The algorithm for transforming interval $[a_1a_2\cdots a_n, b_1b_2\cdots b_n]$ into prefixes

We have seen that matching an interval based on a set of prefix-matchings is both simple and efficient. Therefore prefix-preserving encryption algorithm can be used to efficiently support interval-matching as a query condition while preserving the confidentiality of data and queries.

4.2   Prefix-Preserving Encryption

After transforming interval-matching into prefix-matching, we need a prefix-preserving encryption scheme to generate the index, so that the database system will be able to answer the queries based on encrypted data and queries. We apply an encryption scheme proposed by Xu et $al.$ [15] for prefix-preserving IP address anonymization.

Definition 1. (Prefix-preserving encryption) *([15]) We say that two n-bit numbers $a = a_1 a_2 \cdots a_n$ and $b = b_1 b_2 \cdots b_n$ share a k-bit prefix $(0 \le k \le n)$, if $a_1 a_2 \cdots a_k = b_1 b_2 \cdots b_k$, and $a_{k+1} \ne b_{k+1}$ when $k < n$. An encryption function E_p is defined as a one-to-one function from $\{0,1\}^n$ to $\{0,1\}^n$. An encryption function E_p is said to be prefix-preserving, if, given two numbers a and b that share a k-bit prefix, $E_p(a)$ and $E_p(b)$ also share a k-bit prefix.*

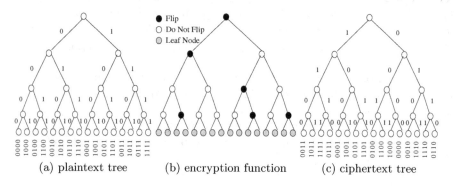

(a) plaintext tree   (b) encryption function   (c) ciphertext tree

Fig. 2. An example of prefix-preserving encryption

It is helpful to consider a geometric interpretation of prefix-preserving encryption [15]. If a plaintext can take any value of a n-bit number, the entire set of plaintexts can be represented by a complete binary tree of height n. This is called the *plaintext tree*. Each node in the plaintext tree (excluding the root node) corresponds to a bit position, indicated by the height of the node, and a bit value, indicated by the direction of the branch from its parent node. Figure 2(a) shows a plaintext tree (using 4-bit plaintexts for simplicity).

A prefix-preserving encryption function can be viewed as specifying a binary variable for each non-leaf node (including the root node) of the plaintext tree. This variable specifies whether the encryption function "flips" this bit or not. Applying the encryption function results in the rearrangement of the plaintext tree into a *ciphertext tree*. Figure 2(c) shows the ciphertext tree resulting from the encryption function shown in Fig. 2(b). Note that an encryption function will, therefore, consist of $2^n - 1$ binary variables, where n is the length of a plaintext.

A general form of prefix-preserving encryption function is presented in [15]. Let f_i be a function from $\{0,1\}^i$ to $\{0,1\}$, for $i = 1, 2, \cdots, n-1$ and f_0 is a constant function. Given a plaintext $a = a_1 a_2 \cdots a_n$, the ciphertext $a'_1 a'_2 \cdots a'_n$ will be computed by the algorithm given in Fig. 3. According to Theorem 1 (canonical form theorem) in [15], the algorithm given in Fig. 3 is a prefix-preserving encryption algorithm.

---

1. Compute a'_i as $a_i \oplus f_{i-1}(a_1 a_2 \cdots a_{i-1})$, where $\oplus$ stands for the exclusive-or operation, for $i = 1, 2, \cdots, n$.
2. Return $a'_1 a'_2 \cdots a'_n$.

Fig. 3. Prefix-preserving encryption algorithm

In [15], the prefix-preserving encryption scheme is defined as instantiating functions f_i with cryptographically strong stream ciphers or block ciphers as follows:

$$f_i(a_1 a_2 \cdots a_i) := \mathcal{L}(\mathcal{R}(a_1 a_2 \cdots a_i, \kappa)) \tag{1}$$

where $i = 1, \cdots, n-1$ and $\mathcal{L}$ returns the "least significant bit". Here $\mathcal{R}$ is a pseudorandom function or a pseudorandom permutation (i.e., a block cipher). κ is the cryptographic key used in the pseudorandom function $\mathcal{R}$. Its length should follow the guideline specified for the pseudorandom function that is actually adopted.

The encryption function can be performed quickly as it only involves $n-1$ symmetric key cryptographic operations, and these $n-1$ operations can be done in parallel. A prefix expresses a prefix range, thus a prefix-matching query can be efficiently processed as a range query with a B$^+$-tree index structure. We will compare the performance of the prefix-preserving scheme with the random one-to-one mapping scheme in Sect. 7.

4.3 Implementing Range Queries over Encrypted Relations

With the prefix-preserving encryption algorithm, denoted by E_p, we can translate specific query conditions in operations (such as selects and joins) to corresponding conditions over server-side representation. This translation function is called Map_{cond}. Since this paper is mainly focused on supporting range queries, we will only consider select operations in this paper. This scheme can handle other relational operations as well. The discussion is omitted here due to the lack of space and can be found in our technical report [14].

A select query condition is a boolean expression specified on relation attributes. It can be made up of a number of *clauses* of the form
<attribute> <comparison op> <value>,

where <attribute> is the name of an attribute, <comparison op> is one of the operations $\{=, \leq, \geq\}$, and <value> is a constant value from the attribute domain. Clauses can be arbitrarily connected by the boolean operators AND, OR, and NOT to form a general query condition. It has been discussed in [3] how to translate a composite condition to the corresponding condition over server-side representation after each clause is translated. Hereafter we discuss how to translate a single clause.

attribute = value: Since the prefix-preserving encryption is a one-to-one mapping, the mapping is simply defined as follows:
$Map_{cond}(A_i = v) \Rightarrow E_p(A_i) = E_p(v)$.

attribute $\leq$ value (attribute $\geq$ value): A query condition $A_i \leq v$ ($A_i \geq v$) is equivalent to an interval-matching of $f_{[v_{min}, v]}(A_i)$ ($f_{[v, v_{max}]}(A_i)$), where v_{min} (v_{max}) is the lower (upper) bound of the attribute domain. The interval $[v_{min}, v]$ ($[v, v_{max}]$) can be converted into a union of prefix ranges, $\{P_1, P_2, \cdots, P_l\}$, with Algorithm 1. Therefore, interval-matching $f_{[v_{min}, v]}(A_i)$ can be transformed to a set of prefix-matchings $\{M_{P_1}(A_i), M_{P_2}(A_i), \cdots, M_{P_l}(A_i)\}$ ($M_{P_k}(A_i)$ denotes the boolean function, which returns true if and only if the value of A_i matches prefix P_k). Then the prefix-preserving encryption can be applied on the prefixes. Therefore, the mapping is defined as follows:
$Map_{cond}(A_i \leq v) \Rightarrow$
$\{M_{E_p(P_1)}(E_p(A_i))$ OR $M_{E_p(P_2)}(E_p(A_i))$ OR $\cdots$ OR $M_{E_p(P_l)}(E_p(A_i))\}$.

Consider a select operation $\sigma_C(R)$ on a relation R, where C is a condition specified on one or more of the attributes $A_1, A_2, \cdots, A_n$ of R. The operation can be rewritten as follows:
$\sigma_C(R) = D(\sigma_{Map_{cond}(C)}(E(R))$,
where $E(R)$ is the encrypted relational table (e.g., the Encrypted_Employee table presented in Table 2), and D is the corresponding decryption function of E. The operation $\sigma_{Map_{cond}(C)}(E(R))$ will be executed at the server. The results will be transmitted to the client. The client then can get the query results by applying decryption function D.

5   Attack with a Set of Queries

In this section, we will discuss the security issues of the prefix-preserving scheme proposed in this paper and the schemes proposed in the literature, i.e., random one-to-one mapping and order-preserving. There are many possible attacks against these schemes [4,5]. We are not going to examine all the possible attacks, instead we will discuss a particular one, which can be applied to both the random one-to-one mapping scheme and the prefix-preserving scheme.

An adversary may compromise the confidential information by gathering query predicate conditions. Sometimes it is reasonable for an adversary to assume that the index set against one attribute from each query may be derived from a single interval. In other words, each index set, though contains multiple indexes, represents only a single interval. Based on this assumption, the encryption mapping may be revealed partially, i.e., the adversary can figure out a coarse order of a set of indexes. This will be further explained in the rest of this section.

The feasibility of this attack is constrained by the ability of adversaries to collect enough queries. Furthermore, clients may not obey the assumption, i.e., they may not always submit a single interval-matching for each predicate against one index attribute in a query. This will complicate the attack as well.

To alleviate this problem, clients may specify different keys to generate indexes for different attributes, thus preventing an adversary from aggregating information from different attributes. Also, clients can inject some noise into their queries to undermine the adversary's assumption. But the price paid is that the clients will receive some data that are not of interest. This compromises the purpose of the DAS model, since the clients still need certain database functionality to be able to filter out redundant results.

The order-preserving encryption preserves the order of plaintexts, so it is trivial for the adversary to figure out the order of any set of indexes generated from the order-preserving scheme. In the remainder of this section we will analyze possible attacks against the random one-to-one mapping scheme and the prefix-preserving scheme.

5.1   Against the Random One-to-one Mapping Scheme

An adversary is assumed to be able to collect a set of queries. In each query there is a tuple of index sets. Based on our assumption, the indexes in a set should represent a single interval. Assume the size of the index domain is 2^n. If the adversary is able to collect all the $2^n - 1$ *two-index sets* which contain two consecutive indexes, then he/she will be able to figure out an order of all the indexes, but without knowing whether it is an ascending or descending order. If the adversary knows at least one plaintext/ciphertext pair, then he/she will be able to decrypt any index. For example, when $n = 2$, if the adversary is able to collect 3 index sets, $\{a, b\}, \{b, c\}, \{c, d\}$, the he/she will be able to figure out an order of the indexes, a, b, c, d, without knowing if it is an ascending or descending order.

An algorithm to collect two-index sets from a list of index sets is given in Fig. 4.

---

1. Discard one-index sets.
2. For any two sets A, B in the list of index sets, if none of $A \cap B$, $A \cap \overline{B}$, $\overline{A} \cap B$ is an empty set, then add these sets into the new list of index sets (Note that any of these resulted sets still represents a single interval).
3. If any new set is added, go to step 1. Otherwise, collect all two-index sets.

Fig. 4. The algorithm for attacking queries against the random one-to-one mapping

5.2   Against the Prefix-Preserving Scheme

To better illustrate the attack against the prefix-preserving scheme, we introduce a definition as follows.

Definition 2. *Given two k-bit (k ≥ 2) encrypted prefixes $a = a_1 a_2 \cdots a_k *$ and $b = b_1 b_2 \cdots b_k *$, if there exists an i, $1 \le i \le k-1$ such that $a_i \ne b_i$ and the range of a and b can be merged into a single interval, then we call the set of prefixes $\{a, b\}$ a* **non-trivial two-prefix set with length** *k. We call an encrypted two-prefix set $\{a_1 a_2 \cdots a_{k-1} a_k *, a_1 a_2 \cdots a_{k-1} \overline{a_k} *\}$ a* **trivial two-prefix set.**

It is easy to see that if an adversary has all $(2^{k-1} - 1)$ non-trivial two-prefix sets of length k, then he/she will be able to create an order for all encrypted k-bit prefixes without knowing if it is an ascending or descending order. If the adversary knows at least one plaintext/ciphertext pair, then he/she will be able to decrypt any encrypted k-bit prefix. For example, if an adversary has the following three non-trivial two-prefix sets of length 3, $\{a_1 a_2 a_3 *, a_1 \overline{a_2} b_3 *\}$, $\{a_1 \overline{a_2} \overline{b_3} *, \overline{a_1} b_2 c_3 *\}$, $\{\overline{a_1} b_2 \overline{c_3} *, \overline{a_1} \overline{b_2} d_3 *\}$, then he/she will be able to figure out the following order for all 3-bit prefixes: $a_1 a_2 \overline{a_3}$, $a_1 a_2 a_3 *$, $a_1 \overline{a_2} b_3 *$, $a_1 \overline{a_2} \overline{b_3} *$, $\overline{a_1} b_2 c_3 *$, $\overline{a_1} b_2 \overline{c_3} *$, $\overline{a_1} \overline{b_2} d_3 *$, $\overline{a_1} \overline{b_2} \overline{d_3} *$ without knowing whether it is an ascending or descending order. If the plaintext of $a_1 a_2 a_3 *$ is known to be $001*$, the adversary will be able to decrypt any encrypted 3-bit prefix.

An adversary is assumed to be able to collect a set of queries. In each query there is a tuple of encrypted prefix sets. Based on our assumption, the encrypted prefixes in a set should represent a single interval. An algorithm to collect non-trivial two-prefix sets of length k from a list of encrypted prefix sets is given in Fig. 5.

---

1. Preprocess the encrypted prefix sets.

 – For any prefix longer than k-bit, $a_1 a_2 \cdots a_k a_{k+1} \cdots a_l *$ $(l > k)$, replace it by $a_1 a_2 \cdots a_k *$.
 – For any prefix shorter than k-bit, $a_1 a_2 \cdots a_l *$ $(l < k)$, replace it by all the k-bit prefixes which share the l-bit prefix.
   (Note that after the preprocessing, the encrypted prefixes in a set still represent a single interval)

2. Discard trivial two-prefix sets and one-prefix sets.
3. For any two sets A, B in the list of prefix sets, if none of $A \cap B$, $A \cap \overline{B}$, $\overline{A} \cap B$ is an empty set, then add these sets into the new list of prefix sets (Note that any of these resulted sets still represents a single interval).
4. If any new set is added, go to step 2. Otherwise, collect all non-trivial two-prefix sets.

Fig. 5. The algorithm for attacking queries against the prefix-preserving scheme

Hereafter we give a simple example of this attack. Suppose an adversary wants to attack the 3-bit prefixes, and he/she has the following encrypted prefix sets from the queries. $A = \{a_1 a_2 a_3 *, a_1 \overline{a_2} *, \overline{a_1} b_2 *, \overline{a_1} \overline{b_2} b_3 *\}$, $B = \{a_1 \overline{a_2} c_3 *, \overline{a_1} b_2 *, \overline{a_1} \overline{b_2} b_3 *\}$, $C = \{\overline{a_1} b_2 d_3 a_4 *, \overline{a_1} \overline{b_2} *\}$. The adversary can get the following 3-bit prefix sets. $A' = \{a_1 a_2 a_3 *, a_1 \overline{a_2} c_3 *, a_1 \overline{a_2} \overline{c_3} *, \overline{a_1} b_2 d_3 *, \overline{a_1} b_2 \overline{d_3} *, \overline{a_1} \overline{b_2} b_3 *\}$, $B' =$

$\{a_1\overline{a_2}c_3*, \overline{a_1}b_2d_3*, \overline{a_1}b_2\overline{d_3}*, \overline{a_1}\overline{b_2}b_3*\}$, $C' = \{\overline{a_1}b_2d_3*, \overline{a_1}\overline{b_2}b_3*, \overline{a_1}\overline{b_2}b_3*\}$. Then he/she will get the following non-trivial two-prefix sets: $A' \cap \overline{B'} = \{a_1a_2a_3*, a_1\overline{a_2c_3}*\}$, $A' \cap C' = \{\overline{a_1}b_2d_3*, \overline{a_1}\overline{b_2}b_3*\}$, $B' \cap \overline{C'} = \{a_1\overline{a_2}c_3*, \overline{a_1}b_2\overline{d_3}*\}$. Finally the adversary will be able to figure out the following order of the 3-bit prefixes: $a_1a_2\overline{a_3}*$, $a_1a_2a_3*$, $a_1\overline{a_2c_3}*$, $a_1\overline{a_2}c_3*$, $\overline{a_1}b_2\overline{d_3}$, $\overline{a_1}b_2d_3*$, $\overline{a_1}\overline{b_2}b_3*$, $\overline{a_1}\overline{b_2}b_3*$, without knowing whether it is an ascending or descending order.

6 Additional Security Analysis for Prefix-Preserving Encryption

In this section we will have more discussion about the security of the prefix-preserving encryption scheme. It has been proved that with the instantiating functions as (1) the prefix-preserving encryption scheme is indistinguishable from a *random prefix-preserving function*, a function uniformly chosen from the set of all prefix-preserving functions when the adversaries are assumed to be computationally bounded. This is elaborated in [15]. Moreover, as mentioned in Sect. 4.2, when plaintexts can take any value of a n-bit number, the prefix-preserving encryption function consists of $2^n - 1$ binary variables. Therefore, we have a key of $2^{2^n - 1}$ possibilities. For example, when n is only 16, the number of possible keys is 2^{65535}. Therefore, the key κ in (1) can be sufficiently long such that it is impractical for adversaries to try each possible key to compromise the prefix-preserving scheme.

In the remainder of this section, we discuss another possible way in which the prefix-preserving scheme may be attacked. An adversary is assumed to have compromised (gain full knowledge to) certain number of $\langle$plaintext, ciphertext$\rangle$ pairs through means other than compromising the key, i.e., the known plaintext attack model [8]. Then he/she will be able to infer information from other ciphertexts by prefix-matching, because the encryption is prefix-preserving. For example, if an adversary knows $\langle$plaintext, ciphertext$\rangle$ pair $\langle a_1a_2\cdots a_n, a_1'a_2'\cdots a_n'\rangle$, then given another ciphertext $a_1'a_2'\cdots a_{k-1}'\overline{a_k'}b_{k+1}'\cdots b_n'$, he/she knows the k-bit prefix of the plaintext should be $a_1a_2\cdots a_{k-1}\overline{a_k}$. Note that if an adversary knows one $\langle$plaintext, ciphertext$\rangle$ pair $\langle a_1a_2\cdots a_n, a_1'a_2'\cdots a_n'\rangle$, then he/she should also know the $\langle$plaintext, ciphtertext$\rangle$ pair $\langle a_1a_2\cdots \overline{a_n}, a_1'a_2'\cdots \overline{a_n'}\rangle$. Therefore, an adversary always knows an even number of $\langle$plaintext, ciphertext$\rangle$ pairs.

Suppose an adversary knows 2 pairs of $\langle$plaintext, ciphertext$\rangle$. Given a random ciphertext, let $A(n)$ denote the average length of the prefix that can be inferred by prefix-matching, where n is the length of the binary representation of the data. The probability that the k-bit prefix of the plaintext can be inferred is $\frac{1}{2^k}$, for $1 \leq k \leq n - 1$, while for $k = n$, the probability is $\frac{2}{2^n}$. Therefore, $A(n) = \sum_{i=1}^{n-1} \frac{i}{2^i} + \frac{2n}{2^n} = \sum_{i=0}^{n-1} \frac{1}{2^i} = 2 - \frac{1}{2^{n-1}} < 2$. In other words, on the average an adversary can infer no more than 2 bits from a random ciphertext, if he/she knowns 2 pairs of $\langle$plaintext, ciphertext$\rangle$ [1].

---

[1] We are assuming the plaintext is uniformly distributed. The information leaked by the known-plaintext attack can be significantly higher, if we consider that the possible values are not uniformly distributed.

We also analyze the situation that an adversary knows $2k$ ($k > 1$) pairs of ⟨plaintext, ciphertext⟩ in our technical report [14]. In summary, when $n \rightarrow \infty$, given a ciphertext, the average length of the prefix that can be inferred is bounded by $\log_2 k + 2$ based on numerical results. So the prefix information an adversary can obtain by comparing a ciphtertext against a few pairs of ⟨plaintext, ciphertext⟩ is limited. Therefore, we claim that the prefix-preserving scheme is secure even if a few pairs of ⟨plaintext, ciphertext⟩ are known by an adversary. To make the system even more secure, the data owner may specify different keys to generate indexes for different attributes, thus preventing an adversary from aggregating information from different attributes.

7   Performance Comparison

7.1   Communication Cost

With the prefix-preserving scheme, the total length of the indexes for an interval-matching query condition is less than $2n(n-1)$ bits. With random one-to-one mapping, the total length is $l \cdot n$, where l is the length of the interval. So when l is larger than $2(n-1)$, the prefix-preserving scheme is more efficient. If we assume all the intervals appear with the same probability, the average length of the interval is $\frac{\sum_{i=1}^{2^n} \frac{i(i+1)}{2}}{\sum_{i=1}^{2^n} i} = \frac{2^{3n-1}+3\cdot 2^{2n-1}+2^n}{3(2^{2n-1}+2n-1)}$, which is approximately equal to $2^n/3$, when n is large. Therefore, the average number of bits of the indexes is about $n \cdot 2^n/3$, which is much greater than $2n(n-1)$, when n is large.

7.2   Client Side Cost

During the encryption of the database, it costs more to use the prefix-preserving scheme to compute the indexes for the records. Since normally the length of the index attribute is smaller than the block size of a typical block cipher, to compute one index, the prefix-preserving encryption will require $n-1$ block cipher encryptions. In contrast, the random one-to-one mapping will require only 1 encryption. Similarly, to encrypt an exact matching query condition, it costs more with prefix-preserving encryption. However, to encrypt an interval-matching query condition, with prefix-preserving, at most $2(n-1)^2$ encryptions are needed. With random one-to-one mapping, the number of encryptions needed is equal to the length of the interval l. So when l is larger than $2(n-1)^2$, the prefix-preserving scheme is more efficient. If we assume all intervals appear with same probability, then the average length of the interval is about $2^n/3$, which is larger than $2(n-1)^2$, when n is larger than 8.

7.3   Server Side Cost

As for the server side cost, we will be mainly concerned about the cost of disk accesses for executing an interval-matching query, since in most cases it is the bottleneck. To estimate the cost of disk accesses, we must know the number of the records (r), and the number of blocks (b) (or close estimates of them). Also, we

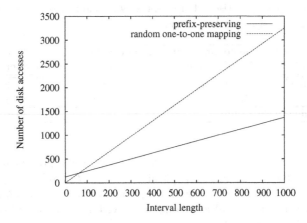

Fig. 6. Number of disk accesses by varying the length of the interval

need to know the number of levels (h) of B$^+$-tree, which is the typical database storage structure for indexes. Another important parameter is the selectivity (sl) of an attribute, which is the fraction of records satisfying an exact-matching condition on the attribute.

Without any index structure, to do a sequential scan of the whole database table, the cost of disk accesses is $b \cdot t_s$, where t_s is the time needed for a sequential disk block access. In the random one-to-one mapping scheme, with a B$^+$-tree index structure the number of disk accesses needed for retrieving the indexes is $l \cdot h$, where l is the length of the interval, and the number of disk accesses needed for retrieving the actual records is $l \cdot f \cdot sl \cdot b$, where f is the percentage of the values in the interval that actually exist in the table. Therefore, the total timing cost of disk accesses is $l(h + f \cdot sl \cdot b) \cdot t_r$, where t_r is the time needed for a random disk block access. As mentioned in Sect. 4.2, a prefix-matching query can be processed as a range query. In the prefix-preserving scheme, with a B$^+$-tree index structure the number of disk accesses needed for retrieving the indexes is less than $2(n-1)(h-1) + l$, and the number of disk accesses for accessing the actual records is $l \cdot f \cdot sl \cdot b$. So the timing cost of disk accesses is less than $(2(n-1)(h-1) + l + l \cdot f \cdot sl \cdot b)t_r$. Therefore, when $l > 2(n-1)$, the prefix-preserving scheme is more efficient then the random one-to-one mapping scheme, if sequential scan is not needed. A typical value of n could be 32. Then when $l > 62$, the prefix-preserving scheme is more efficient. A typical disk block size is 32 K bits. A typical size of a pointer to a disk block is 32 bits. Assume the number of records r in the database is 1 M, i.e., 2^{20}. Then the order of the B$^+$-tree should be $32\,\text{K}/(32+32) = 2^9$, and the height h should be $\log_{2^9} 2^{20} = 3$. Figure 6 shows the number of disk accesses with random one-to-one mapping/prefix-preserving, assuming f to be 100%, $sl = 1/r = 2^{-20}$, and the total number of disk blocks in the database b is 256 K. Note that, assuming $t_r = 64 \cdot t_s$, for the random one-to-one mapping scheme, it will be more efficient to do a sequential scan of

Table 3. Performance comparison of prefix-preserving and random one-to-one mapping for supporting an interval-matching query

	Average communication cost (length of indexes)	Average client side cost (number of encryptions)	Server side cost (number of disk accesses)
Prefix-preserving	$\leq 2n(n-1)$ bits	$\leq 2(n-1)^2$	$\leq 2(n-1)(h-1)+l+$ $l \cdot f \cdot sl \cdot b$
Random mapping	$n \cdot 2^n/3$ bits	$2^n/3$	$l(h + f \cdot sl \cdot b)$

the whole database table when $l > 1260$. With the prefix preserving scheme, it might be more efficient to do a sequential scan when $l > 3177$.

In summary, we present the communication cost, client side and server side cost for supporting an interval-matching query with random one-to-one mapping /prefix-preserving in Table 3.

8 Conclusions

This paper discusses concerns about protecting sensitive information of data and queries from adversaries in the DAS model. Data and queries need to be encrypted, while the database service provider should be able to efficiently answer queries based on encrypted data and queries. Several approaches are studied in this paper, random one-to-one mapping and prefix-preserving. Possible attacks against these approaches and the performance of these approaches are investigated. The prefix-preserving scheme is more efficient than the random one-to-one mapping scheme for supporting interval-matching queries. In terms of communication cost, with prefix-preserving the length of indexes for an interval is less than $2n(n-1)$ bits, while with random one-to-one mapping the average is about $n \cdot 2^n/3$ bits. In terms of client side cost, with prefix-preserving the number of encryptions needed is less than $2(n-1)^2$, while with random one-to-one mapping the average is about $2^n/3$. In terms of server side cost, the number of disk accesses with the prefix-preserving scheme is smaller than the random one-to-one mapping scheme, when the length of the interval is larger than $2(n-1)$. However, the prefix-preserving scheme is less secure than the random one-to-one mapping scheme, because of the constraint of prefix-preserving. For example, with the prefix-preserving encryption a coarse ordering of the encrypted data can be determined by a grouping based on a k-bit prefix, but not with a random one-to-one mapping.

Acknowledgement. The authors would like to thank the anonymous referees for their insightful and constructive comments, and Professor Alexandra Boldyreva for her technical comments.

References

1. Hacigumus, H., Iyer, B., Mehrotra, S.: Providing database as a service. In: Proceedings of ICDE'02. (2002) 29–38
2. Chor, B., Goldreich, O., Kushilevitz, E., Sudan, M.: Private information retrieval. In: Proceedings of the 36th IEEE Symposium on Foundations of Computer Science. (1995) 41–50
3. Hacigumus, H., Iyer, B., Li, C., Mehrotra, S.: Executing SQL over encrypted data in the database-service-provider model. In: Proceedings of the 2002 ACM SIGMOD International Conference on Management of Data. (2002) 216–227
4. Damiani, E., Vimercati, S.D.C., Jajodia, S., Paraboschi, S., Samarati, P.: Balancing confidentiality and efficiency in untrusted relational dbmss. In: Proceedings of CCS'03. (2003) 93–102
5. Agrawal, R., Kiernan, J., Srikant, R., Xu, Y.: Order preserving encryption for numeric data. In: Proceedings of the 2004 ACM SIGMOD International Conference on Management of Data. (2004) 563–574
6. Hore, B., Mehrotra, S., Tsudik, G.: A privacy-preserving index for range queries. In: Proceedings of VLDB'04. (2004) 720–731
7. Ozsoyoglu, S.C.G., Singer, D., Chung, S.S.: Anti-tamper databases: Querying encrypted databases. In: Proceedings of the 17th Annunal IFIP WG11.3 Working Conference on Database and Application Security. (2003)
8. Stinson, D.R.: Cryptography: Theory and Practice. CRC Press (2002)
9. Elovici, Y., Waisenberg, R., Shmueli, E., Gudes, E.: A structure preserving database encryption scheme. In: Secure Data Management. (2004) 28–40
10. Feigenbaum, J.: Encrypting problem instances, or ..., can you take advantage of someone without having to trust him? In: Proceedings of CRYPTO'85. (1986) 477–488
11. AES: Advanced encryption standard. FIPS 197, Computer Security Resource Center, National Institute of Standards and Technology (2001)
12. DES: Data encryption standard. FIPS PUB 46, Federal Information Processing Standards Publication (1977)
13. Srinivasan, V., Varghese, G., Suri, S., Waldvogel, M.: Fast and scalable layer four switching. In: Proceedings of ACM SIGCOMM'98. (1998) 191–202
14. Li, J., Omiecinski, E.R.: Efficiency and security trade-off in supporting range queries on encrypted databases. Technical Report GIT-CC-05-01, College of Computing, Georgia Institute of Technology (2005) Available at ftp://ftp.cc.gatech.edu/pub/coc/tech_reports/2005/GIT-CC-05-01.pdf.
15. Xu, J., Fan, J., Ammar, M.H., Moon, S.B.: Prefix-preserving IP address anonymization: measurement-based security evaluation and a new cryptography-based scheme. In: Proceedings of the 10th IEEE International Conference on Network Protocols. (2002) 280–289

Verified Query Results from Hybrid Authentication Trees

Glen Nuckolls

Department of Computer Sciences, University of Texas at Austin,
Austin, TX 78712-0233 USA
nuckolls@cs.utexas.edu
http://www.cs.utexas.edu/ nuckolls/

Abstract. We address the problem of verifying the accuracy of query results provided by an untrusted third party Publisher on behalf of a trusted data Owner. We propose a flexible database verification structure, the Hybrid Authentication Tree (HAT), based on fast cryptographic hashing and careful use of a more expensive *one-way accumulator*. This eliminates the dependence on tree height of earlier Merkle tree based proposals and improves on the VB tree, a recent proposal to reduce proof sizes, by eliminating a trust assumption and reliance on signatures. An evaluation of the Hybrid Authentication Tree against the VB tree and Authentic Publication showing that a HAT provides the smallest proofs and faster verification than the VB tree. With moderate bandwidth limitations, the HATs low proof overhead reduces transfer time to significantly outweigh the faster verification time of Authentic Publication. A HAT supports two verification modes that can vary *per query* and *per Client* to match Client resources and applications. This flexibility allows the HAT to match the best performance of both hash based and accumulator based methods.

1 Introduction

An increasing number and variety of applications and systems require access to data over a network. Third party architectures offer one way to address availability when the data source may have limited resources, by relying on a dedicated third party *Publisher* to provide responses. The related Edge Server model increases the availability of data services defined by a central server by replicating them at edge servers closer to clients. Maintaining data integrity along with high availability is a significant challenge. Providing database access introduces more complications. Typically, the number of different responses that can be generated from queries on a single data set is much larger than the data set itself. The integrity of query response involves showing that the response was correct, meaning the returned data was from the correct data set, and that the response is complete, meaning all matching data was returned.

We address the problem of verifying the accuracy of query results provided by an untrusted third party in the third party Publisher model. The *Owner* relies

S. Jajodia and D. Wijesekera (Eds.): Data and Applications Security 2005, LNCS 3654, pp. 84–98, 2005.
© IFIP International Federation for Information Processing 2005

on the untrusted Publisher to process *Client* database queries. In the related *Authentic Publication* model [6], the Publisher is assumed to be untrusted, but the Owner is trusted, so Clients use a small digest value computed over the database by the Owner, to verify the query results. The same digest verifies many different queries on the same database. This allows the Owner to rely on, presumably cheaper, untrusted resources to handle Client requests. Authentic Publication [6] uses the organization of a tree digest, based on Merkle trees, to provide efficient verification for Clients.

Proof overhead can be significant when bandwidth is limited relative to processing power. In the original Authentic Publication method, proof size depends on the number of data points in the answer and the tree height, $O(\log N)$ additional hash values for a tree over N data points. Pang and Tan [17] proposed to eliminate this dependence on tree height with the verifiable B-tree (VB tree). This requires some degree of trust in the Publisher, relies heavily on Owner signatures and a proposed one-way digest function based on modular exponentiation. The trust assumption is problematic and the use of expensive primitives adds excessive overhead to both proof size and verification time.

In this paper we propose a flexible verification method, the Hybrid Authentication Tree (HAT), that eliminates the dependence on the tree height. Our novel method carefully incorporates fast hash functions with a more expensive cryptographic primitive, a *one-way accumulator*. The accumulator helps break the dependence on tree height without relying on Owner signatures and the lighter weight hash function speeds up the Client verification process. The design finds an efficient balance between the two primitives, using the heavier accumulators sparingly. Using the same one-time digest value, the HAT design allows the verification method to vary *per query* and *per Client* according to Client bandwidth and application requirements. One verification mode relies on both fast hash operations and the accumulator. The other mode bypasses the expensive accumulator operations, relying only on fast hash operations in a Merkle tree like method similar to Authentic Publication. In effect, we design a digest that gives us two verification schemes in one. Our analysis shows that, even for reasonable bandwidths of 1 mbps or more, the low proof overhead of the HAT improves significantly over the VB-tree and the original Authentic Publication method.

1.1   Outline of the Paper

Section 2 gives some useful background. Section 3 presents the details of the HAT construction and digest, explaining the motivation for using accumulator functions to break the dependence on tree height in Section 3.1, describing how completeness is verified in Section 3.2, and then defining the digest and verification in 3.3 and 3.4. We establish parameters for evaluation in Section 4 and give a detailed evaluation and comparison of the HAT with Authentic Publication and the VB-tree in Section 5, looking at proof overhead in 5.1, verification cost in 5.2, and bandwidth considerations in 5.3.

Section 6 describes how a HAT can bypass the use of the accumulator when advantageous. We discuss related research in 7, discuss future directions in 8 and conclude in 9.

2   Preliminary Building Blocks

We briefly describe the hash functions, one-way accumulators, Merkle trees and Authentic Publication.

2.1   Collision Intractable Hash Function

Hash functions such as MD5 or SHA-1 can be used to detect modifications in files by recomputing the MD5 or SHA-1 checksum on the file in question and comparing to the original checksum value. It is assumed to be difficult to produce another file with the same MD5 checksum or the original. This property is known as collision resistance or collision intractability. Though not formal in the cryptographic sense, we can reasonably rely on the following notion of collision resistance.

Definition 1. *A function f mapping the set of all binary strings to the set of strings of some fixed length is collision resistant if, given a "random" input value x, and the image $f(x)$, it is computationally infeasible for an adversary to compute $x' \neq x$ such that $f(x') = f(x)$.*

One informality evident is the reference to a random input. Since the size of the input is not specified, the domain cannot be uniformly sampled. The formal cryptographic definition of collision resistance handles this, and the function we rely on, SHA-1, is widely relied on for collision resistance.

When f is a hash function, we write $f(x_1, x_2)$ to denote the application of f to a single string constructed by concatenating x_1 and x_2 and some unique delimiter between them. The hash can apply to any number of strings with no ambiguity about the value and number of inputs.

2.2   Merkle Trees and Authentic Publication

We review the basic Merkle tree construction [13] since it is a common thread to many recent efforts in efficient query answer verification. The structure is a binary search tree, over a data set D of size N, with the key key(d) and data for each item $d \in D$ stored at the leaves. The key is simply a unique identifier for d e.g. the primary key for a relational tuple. Our example, shown on the left in Figure 2.2, uses a set of integer keys and ignores any associated data attributes. The tree is digested using a collision-resistant hash function h to produce a value $f(v)$ at each node v as follows: Starting at the leaves, the value of a leaf is its key value and the value of an internal node is the hash of the child values. Alternately we can hash the associated attributes with the key to produce the leaf value. The overall digest value of the tree, denoted Σ, is just the digest value at the root. With this digest value, an efficient proof, of size $O(\log N)$ can be given that a data item is or is not in the set. The proof consists of the intermediate hash value for each sibling of a node along the search path.

We follow the general Authentic Publication model [6]: a trusted data Owner relies on an untrusted third party Publisher to respond to Client queries on

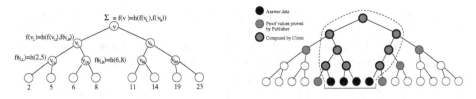

Fig. 1. Merkle hashing, left, and range query verification, right

a data set. First, a trusted Owner computes a digest of the data set (e.g. as in the binary search tree example). Next, the data is given to one or more untrusted Publishers and the digest is distributed to Clients. Publishers send additional proof values with each Client query response. Clients verify the answer by partially recomputing the root digest. Clients can send any number of queries on the data set to an untrusted Publisher and verify that the answers are the same as the Owner used to compute Σ. This approach scales well, with no security assumptions on Publishers.

2.3 An Efficient RSA Based One-Way Accumulator

Benaloh and de Mare [2] define an accumulator as a family of one-way, quasi-commutative hash functions. A hash function f is *one-way* if, given $x \in X$ and $y, y' \in Y$ it is hard to find $x' \in X$ such that $f(x, y) = f(x', y')$. The function f is *quasi-commutative* if

$$f(f(x, y_1), y_2) = f(f(x, y_2), y_1) \ \forall x \in X_k, y_i \in Y$$

We define $f(x, y_1, y_2, \ldots, y_N)$ to be $f(\ldots f(f(x, y_1), y_2) \ldots, y_N)$ for convenience. Given an initial value x, if $z = f(x, y_1, y_2, \ldots, y_N)$, the y_i values can be input into the accumulator in any order and still produce z. Now, given a value $y_i \in Y$, let z_i be the result of applying f to all the values in $Y - \{y_i\}$ with initial value x. Then $f(z_i, y_i) = z$ and, z_i serves as a proof that y_i was used to compute z.

The one-way property is weaker than strict collision resistance since the adversary can not choose y'. However, quasi-commutativity directly provides the means to break collision-resistance, and one-way is often sufficient since the values $y_i \in Y_k$ used as input to the accumulator are themselves often the result of a cryptographic collision resistant hash function. In fact, the domain set Y_k can be restricted to the result of a hash on some input. In order to forge a proof for a value that hashes to $\tilde{y}$ with respect to a collection $\{y_i\}_1^N$, an adversary would need to find an alternate proof $\tilde{z}_j$ for a value $\tilde{y}$ that can be changed, by choosing a different value to hash, but not chosen, since the hash output is unpredictable. We restrict input to accumulators to be the output of a collision resistant hash function.

Benaloh and de Mare propose a one-way quasi-commutative accumulator based on an RSA modulus and prove it's security in [2]. Given n we define H_n by $H_n(x, y) = x^y \mod n$. H_n is quasi-commutative by the laws of exponents: $(x^{y_1})^{y_2} = (x^{y_2})^{y_1}$. To ensure H_n is one-way, the modulus n is chosen to be a *rigid* integer, meaning $n = p \cdot q$ where p and q are safe primes of the same bit size. A prime p is *safe* if $p = 2p' + 1$ and p' is an odd prime. The factorization of n is considered trapdoor knowledge and in our model is known only by the Owner. Efficient methods for choosing rigid moduli are discussed in [2] and [12].

For a set $Y = \{y_1, \ldots y_N\}$ and $z = H_n(x, y_1, \ldots, y_N)$, $z_i = x^{y_1 y_2 \cdots y_{i-1} y_{i+1} \cdots y_N}$ serves as a proof for $y_i \in Y$. The value of x is also chosen by the Owner, but is not trapdoor knowledge. The Owner, knowing p, q, and thus $\phi(n) = (p-1)(q-1)$, can exponentiate by first reducing the exponent mod $\phi(n)$. This is an advantage we cannot give the Publisher and Client since $\phi(n)$ easily reveals p and q. However, the Publisher can still compute a proof by exponentiating.

3   The Hybrid Authentication Tree

We combine an accumulator function with Merkle hashing to providing proofs for answer correctness and completeness that are independent of tree height is fairly straightforward. However, since accumulator operations are so much more expensive than hashing, minimizing their use requires special consideration. We then describe how completeness is verified and then present the complete digest and verification processes.

3.1   Breaking the Dependence on Tree Height

A HAT is just a binary search tree with data stored at the leaves, along with a digest procedure that incorporates a fast collision intractable hash function h and an accumulator H. We want to take advantage of the input reordering allowed by an accumulator to avoid checking the entire hash path to the root as done when using Merkle trees as in Authentic Publication [6] and related schemes. However, accumulators have larger output, typically near the 1024 bits of an RSA modulus compared to the 160 bit output of SHA-1, and take longer to verify a value y_i against a proof z_i for a set value z. For example, suppose our range returned exactly one leaf w. Instead of the client verifying that w is the correct answer by hashing from w up to the root of the tree, the client could simply verify that w was included in a final accumulation value, requiring only a constant size proof. Answer completeness would need to be addressed, but could still be done with a constant size proof. This method breaks the dependence on the height of a Merkle tree but does not scale well to larger answer sizes.

Our approach uses Merkle hashing to certain nodes of the tree and then use the accumulator to verify the values of those nodes, eliminating the hashing along remaining path to the root. One natural set of nodes to consider for a range query is the set of *canonical covering roots* (CCRs) for the range in the tree as shown in Figure 2. The set of CCRs in a search tree for a range query is the set of nodes with disjoint subtrees whose leaves are the exact answer to the range query. For a range returning T leaves, is not hard to show that there are $O(\log T)$ CCRs and they have height $O(\log T)$.

The CCRs seem like good nodes to switch from Merkle hashing to accumulation. Their size and number depend only on the answer size so they break the

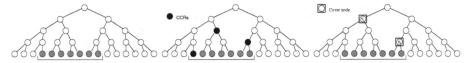

Fig. 2. The range, left, associated CCRs, center, and Covering Nodes v_L, v_R

dependence on the tree height. In fact, using CCRs provides smaller proofs than the scheme we present, but the number of accumulator computations required is still high. In order to further reduce the number of accumulator computations, we rely on the following.

Given a full binary search tree and range with T satisfying leaves, there are at most two nodes of height $O(\log T)$ whose leaves contain all the leaves in the range.

The pair with the smallest subtree is the *covering pair* for the range, or *covering node* in case there is only one. The verification switches from Merkle hashing to accumulator computations at the covering nodes (see Figure 2). This reduces the accumulator verification to one or two values.

3.2   Completeness and Covering Node Adjacency

The previous section only addressed verification that data is from the correct data set. We have not addressed how we can provide a proof that the answer is complete, containing all values within the range. The client will be able to verify that data matches the range, but not that all data matching the range has been returned.

First, note that Merkle hashing does much of this implicitly. Nodes in the middle of the range can't be left out without changing the root hash value without breaking the hash function. Verifying that no leaves were left off either end is the only requirement. Authentic publication includes the next highest and next lowest leaves in order to prove range completeness. It is easy to avoid revealing the data not in the range by providing only the data key and a hash of the data itself. However, they key, or at least some part of it, must be revealed. One alternate approach includes the split values in the hash at each node. These are checked in the verification and ensure range completeness. This approach is described in [11]. The additional split values would introduce a significant amount of additional proof overhead and it is not clear that much privacy can be gained over the inclusion of boundary key values. Privacy with completeness is an important concern, but is left to future research.

Given that we stop hashing at two covering nodes, and that the quasi-commutative property of accumulators makes completeness harder, we have two tasks. Prove that the ends are complete, and prove that the leaves of the two covering nodes form a continuous range in the tree. Two nodes are adjacent if their subtrees are disjoint and have adjacent leaves (see Figure 3). If we can show

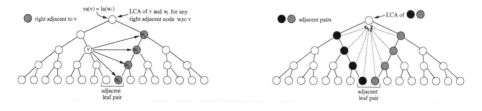

Fig. 3. Node v's right adjacent nodes and all adjacent pairs with same LCA

that our two covering nodes are adjacent, the Merkle hashing scheme used in each subtree will ensure that the range is complete. A fact about trees provides a simple and efficient way to show that any two adjacent nodes are, in fact, adjacent.

Looking at any tree, it is clear that all adjacent node pairs defined by the same adjacent leaf pair have the same least common ancestor, and that for any single node v all of the left adjacent nodes to v produce the same lca. The same holds for the right. We use $\mathsf{la}(v)$ and $\mathsf{ra}(v)$ to denote this single lca of v with all left and right adjacent nodes respectively (see Figure 3). The fact that $\mathsf{ra}(v) = \mathsf{la}(w_i)$ serves as a compact proof that v and w_i are adjacent in the tree. These left and right adjacency values are hashed in with the f_1 value at each node after the standard Merkle hash and are given to Clients to use in verification. After this, the resulting f_2 values at each node (see Section 3.3) will then be used to compute a single value using the accumulator. The final digest value is the hash of the root value of the Merkle hash and the accumulated value.

The Owner could achieve more or less the same effect as using the lca adjacency hash value by assigning some random value instead to serve as this proof, but this has a number of potential disadvantages. In particular, it prevents the Publishers from computing the digest on their own from the data and knowledge of the general digesting scheme. The hash of this lca node is computed directly from the structure and data set just as the root digest. Requiring that these random number be sent for each adjacent leaf pair adds unnecessary complication.

3.3   Digest

For each data item $d \in D$, $\mathsf{key}(d)$ and the hash output $h(d)$ are both computed in a way known to all parties from the attributes of d. Each leaf node of the binary search tree corresponds to some $d \in D$ and they appear in the tree sorted by $\mathsf{key}()$ value. Internal nodes v have left $\mathsf{lc}(v)$ and right $\mathsf{lc}(v)$ child fields, and every node has a left $\mathsf{la}(v)$ and right $\mathsf{ra}(v)$ adjacent lca node field as defined in section 3.2. If no such node exists, the field is assigned some fixed value indicating the left or right end. The digest uses a publicly known collision resistant hash function h and accumulator H to compute the final digest value Σ that the Owner provides to Clients.

1. f_1 is a standard Merkle hash using h.

$$
f_1(v) = \begin{cases} h(f_1(\mathsf{lc}(v))), f_1(\mathsf{rc}(v))) & v \; \textit{internal} \\ h(\mathsf{key}(d), h(d)) & v \; \textit{is a } \textit{leaf} \textit{ with associated data } d \end{cases}
$$

2. f_2 incorporates the hash values from adjacency lca nodes.

$$f_2(v) = h(f_1(v), f_1(\mathsf{la}(v)), f_1(\mathsf{ra}(v)))$$

3. A value A is computed using the accumulator H with some initial value x. If $v_1, v_2, \ldots v_m$ are thee nodes of the tree,

$$A = H(x, f_2(v_1), f_2(v_2), \ldots, f_2(y_m))$$

H is quasi-commutative so the node order will not affect the result.

4. Let *root* denote the root of the tree. The final digest value Σ is computed as

$$\Sigma = h(A, f_2(root))$$

3.4 Proof and Client Verification

The Client submits a range query $[a, b]$ that returns T satisfying leaf nodes. We assume that the Client has $\mathsf{key}(d)$ and $h(d)$ for data item d associated with each returned leaf v and the two boundary leaves. The Client can compute $\mathsf{key}(d)$ and $h(d)$ from the answer data except for the boundary leaves. We assume there are exactly two covering nodes denoted v_L and v_R. For a node v, z_v denotes the proof that $f_2(v)$ was used to compute the value A using accumulator H as described in Section 2.3. Verification proceeds as follows:

1. Compute $f_1(v_L)$ and $f_1(v_R)$
   In addition to the $\mathsf{key}(d)$ and $h(d)$ values the Client already has, the boundary values are required and the $2 \log T$ supporting hash values for each of the covering nodes as in the Authentic Publication method.
2. Compute $f_2(v_L)$ and $f_2(v_R)$ values and check that v_L and v_R are adjacent. Check that $f_1(\mathsf{ra}(v_L)) = f_1(\mathsf{la}(v_R))$, and thus v_L and v_R are adjacent. Requires $f_1(\mathsf{ra}(v_L)) = f_1(\mathsf{la}(v_R))$, $f_1(\mathsf{la}(v_L))$ and $f_1(\mathsf{ra}(v_R))$
3. Check that $H(z_{v_L}, f_2(v_L)), H(z_{v_R}, f_2(v_R))$ both equal A. Requires accumulator proofs z_{v_L} and z_{v_R} and value A.
4. Check that $h(f_2(root), A) = \Sigma$. Requires $f_2(root)$.

4 Proof Size and Verification Cost

We derive expressions for the proof overhead and verification in this section. In Section 5 we instantiate the hash and accumulator functions and give a detailed analysis of realistic overhead and cost values in order to compare our protocol with related proposals.

We assume that any node of the tree with M leaves has height at most $2 \log M$. We also assume that the key size is negligible. The expression $\mathsf{proof}_{\mathsf{HAT}}$ is in bits and and $\mathsf{verify}_{\mathsf{HAT}}$ is in bit operation per second. They are derived from Section 3 and the balance assumption.

$$\mathsf{proof}_{\mathsf{HAT}} = (4 \log T) S_{hash} + 2 S_{acc}$$
$$\mathsf{verify}_{\mathsf{HAT}} = (T + 2 \log T) T_{hash} + 2 T_{acc}(160)$$

Hashing to the cover nodes takes at most $2T$ hashes. We assume here that the few value comparisons involved are not significant.

We take our VB tree analysis from [17] and use a branching factor of 2 since larger factors add significantly to proof size. We conservatively ignore overhead from projections. Projections with VB trees do not handle duplicate elimination and the other schemes produce smaller proofs in this case.

Figure 4 shows results for returned answer set sizes up to 10^8 and data set sizes up to 10^9 for Authentic Publication. We assumed a tree balanced within a factor of two at each subtree. The HAT has smallest overhead of any of the schemes and is close to AP only when T is near N. HATs have roughly 3 to 4 times smaller proofs for small answer sizes.

5.2   Verification Cost

We use values derived from a detailed analysis, omitted here, and round conservatively. As before, these expressions were derived from a detailed analysis omitted due to space considerations.

$$\begin{aligned}
\text{verify}_{\text{HAT}} &= 28,500 \cdot T + 6.5 \times 10^8 \\
\text{verify}_{\text{AP}} &= 57,000 \cdot \log N + 28,500 \cdot T \\
\text{verify}_{\text{VBtree}} &= 4 \times 10^9 \cdot T + 10^{10} \cdot \log T - 4 \times 10^9
\end{aligned}$$

We assume a 1024 bit modulus for the one-way hash used in the VB tree and the same modulus for the Owner RSA signatures. We also choose a low 16 bit public exponent for efficiency. As before, a binary branching factor is the most efficient instantiation of a VB tree, and projection does not improve the comparison. For Authentic Publication, Clients simply hash to the root using, for our comparison, SHA-1. Verification depends on N in this case.

The Authentic Publication verification is only has faster than a HAT for answer sizes up to 10^5. The VB tree is the slowest and is nearly infeasible for answer sizes more than 100,000. For answers of size less than 10,000, a HAT remains roughly constant, dominated by the modular exponentiation on the two 160 bit hash values to check against the accumulator proof value. Only one exponentiation may be required. Clearly our method is more practical than the VB tree. For answer sizes above 10^5, a HAT is as efficient as the Authentic Publication, yet has smaller proof size.

5.3   Bandwidth Versus CPU

When bandwidth is limited in comparison to processing resources, proof overhead is a larger factor. We compare the total time to transfer and verify proofs with and without full data transfer for HATs and Authentic Publication. Both comparisons are of interest since the Client may obtain data and proof from different sources or channels. The Client may also want a proof without needing all data sent. For an expired result similar to the current version, transmitting changes may be much smaller than the data set.

However, we still compare transmission including data as well. We assume that the data size per item is small, only 1024 bits, or 128 bytes. Clearly for much larger data sizes, this transmission cost will dominate, but it is useful to consider smaller, but reasonable sizes.

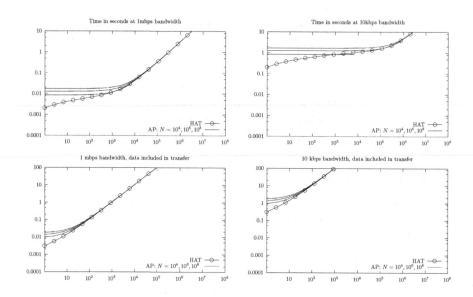

Fig. 5. Transmission time in seconds vs number T of items in answer, assuming a 1 gigahertz 64 bit processor at 64×10^9 bit ops per second

$$T_{total} = \frac{1024 \cdot T}{t} + \frac{\text{proof}}{t} + \frac{\text{verify}}{p}$$

T_{proof} excludes the first term of T_{total}. We keep the 1 GHz 64 bit processor assumption since varying bandwidth will have largest affect and varying both parameters adds too much complexity. Figure 5 shows total transfer and verification time for proof only and data included for average bandwidths to the Publisher of 1 mbps and 10 kbps. For small answer sets, the HAT takes between 3 and 10 times less time depending on the size N and if the data is included. The improvement is similar for both bandwidth values, but a little better as expected for the lower value. The improvement is sustained up to answer sizes of 10^4 for 1 mbps and over 10^5 for 10 kbps, for proof transmission only, and for answer sizes of less than 100 when answer data is included. Clearly, when bandwidth is very high, much higher than 1 mbps, Authentic Publication's verification time will win for smaller answers, but for reasonable bandwidth assumptions, low proof overhead shows significant improvement for smaller answer sizes.

6   Flexible per Query Tradeoffs: A Hybrid Tree

The HAT digest structure supports a per query, per client choice of two verification modes, both equally compatible with a single computation of the digest value. We described the accumulator mode in Section 3.4 and evaluated it in later sections. The hash only mode bypasses the accumulator checks and simply hashes to the root as in the Authentic Publication scheme, treating the covering nodes the same as any other node. The only difference is that the Client hashes in the accumulated value A with the root f_2 value at the end. This option is available *per query* and effectively produces a hybrid scheme able to bypass the accumulator step if advantageous.

The analysis and comparisons of Section 5 demonstrate one advantage of this flexibility. It also allows Publishers responding to a heterogeneous Client set to choose and adapt a verification strategy tailored to the Client's (possibly changing) resources, bandwidth, and application requirements.

7   Related Work

As discussed in Section 2.2 the proposed techniques are based on the original work by Merkle [13]. Naor and Nissim [15] made refinements in the context of certificate revocation. Goodrich and Tamassia [7] and Anagnostopoulos et al. [1] developed authenticated dictionaries. Authentic Publication was introduced in [6] where they showed how to securely answer some types of relational database queries. Devanbu, et al. described authentication for queries on XML document collections in [5]. Bertino, et al. focus in detail on XML documents in [3] and leverage access control mechanisms as a means of providing client proofs of completeness. They also expand supported query types and provide a detailed investigation of XML authentication issues including updates, and address important implementation issues.

Martel, et al. [11] establish a general model, Search DAGs, and provide security proofs for authenticating a broad class of data structures. Goodrich et al. [8] show that a broad class of geometric data structures fit the general model in [11] and thus have efficient authenticated versions. Similar Merkle hash tree based techniques have been used by Maniatis and Baker [10] and most recently Li, et al. [9] for secure storage. Buldas, et al. [4] describe methods that support certificate attestation when there is no trusted Owner. Nuckolls, et al. show how to extend the techniques in [6] to a distributed setting, allowing a collection of Owners to rely on an untrusted Publisher or other untrusted resources to achieve the same effect as a single trusted Owner while distributing the costs among the trusted parties.

Pang and Tang [17] proposed the VB tree as a way of eliminating dependence of proof size on the tree height, but require some trust of the Publisher since they only ensure that answer data is a subset of the original set. They also incorporate more expensive signatures and a proposed one-way function based on modular exponentiation. We discuss the VB tree in our performance analysis section and compare it to our proposed method.

Proving that values are not excluded in set membership queries, Micali, et al. [14] have shown how to construct zero-knowledge databases that preserve privacy, in addition to authentication. Ostrovsky, et al. [18] tackle the same problem for multi-attribute queries using a multidimensional range tree (MDRT).

Accumulators were proposed by Benaloh and de Mare [2] more constructions followed in [16]. Many of the RSA based accumulators contain a trap door and a proposal for accumulators without trapdoors has been given by Sander in [19].

8 Future Directions

We'd like to extend the methods here to a wider range of structures. So far, no systematic approach has been suggested for extending query verification techniques to the relational model. Devanbu et al. [6] discuss projection and joins, Martel et al. [11] present a solution for multidimensional range trees that support multi-attribute queries, and [17] suggest an approach to projections, but do not address the issue of duplicate values. There are many remaining issues with integrity on all types of relational queries.

The HAT relies on an accumulator with trapdoor information that must be kept secret by the Owner. Accumulators without trapdoors exist [19] but are not efficient enough for our purposes. An efficient quasi-commutative accumulator without a trapdoor would speed up our verification time.

Efficiently eliminating the dependence on the tree size lends increased flexibility to the verification process. This improves support for different types of Client applications and is worth exploring in the short term. One example is supporting Client verification of data in an order appropriate to the end application. The proposal in this paper easily adapts to provide priority verification for subranges of a query and then subsequently, if required, full query verification, and should also support incremental verification for small changes to previous requests.

We are also hopeful about the prospect of incorporating privacy in efficient database query authentication. Another promising goal is to bridge the differences between the work started in [14,18] and the current state of the more efficient authentication only methods, including the proposals of this paper. In addition to privacy, we hope to see progress on the longer term goal of ensuring that databases operated entirely by an untrusted and possibly distributed third party, satisfy arbitrary and general security requirements.

9 Conclusion

We carefully evaluated three methods: 1) fast hashing, specifically Authentic Publication over a binary search tree, 2) our hybrid authentication tree in accumulator mode, and 3) the VB tree. We show that both Authentic Publication and our accumulator based method significantly out perform the VB tree. We also show that the HAT always produces a smaller proof size than Authentic Publication and improves by a factor of 3 or 4 for smaller answer sizes.

HT Proof size is also smaller for answers significantly smaller than the database size. Authentic publication, as expected, has more efficient verification, but when bandwidth and transmission time is considered, the smaller HAT proofs provide up to 10 times faster overall verification time than the Authentic Publication method for smaller answer sizes. Even assuming infinite bandwidth, for answer sizes around 10^5 or higher, the HAT matches the performance of fast hashing in the Authentic Publication method. Our scheme is also competitive when considering storage overhead, digest computation, proof retrieval/generation, and updates.

For high bandwidths, Authentic Publication will provide faster verification, but our analysis shows there are significant benefits from a hybrid scheme that takes the best of the fast hashing and accumulator methods. Good tradeoff values can be analytically determined, changed on the fly *per query* with changing network conditions and client preferences.

Our analysis assumes a nearly balanced tree. Skewed trees could make our method even more attractive since hash trees performance depends on the length of paths to the root. Many applications and specialized data structures, such as XML document structures, are often not balanced. A HAT may provide flexibility in the data structure choice, reducing or eliminating the effect of unbalanced trees on Client costs.

Acknowledgments

The author thanks Mike Dahlin and Felipe Voloch for helpful discussions and the valuable comments of the anonymous reviewers.

References

1. A. Anagnostopoulos, M. T. Goodrich, and R. Tamassia. Persistent authenticated dictionaries and their applications. *Lecture Notes in Computer Science*, 2200:379, 2001.
2. J. Benaloh and M. de Mare. One-way accumulators: A decentralized alternative to digital signatures. In *Advances in Cryptology - EUROCRYPT '93*, number 765 in LNCS, pages 274–285, 1994.
3. E. Bertino, B. Carminati, E. Ferrari, B. Thuraisingham, and A. Gupta. Selective and authentic third-party distribution of xml documents. *IEEE Transactions on Knowledge and Data Engineering*, 16(10):1263–1278, 2004.
4. A. Buldas, P. Laud, and H. Lipmaa. Eliminating counterevidence with applications to accountable certificate management. *Journal of Computer Security*, 10:273–296, 2002.
5. P. Devanbu, M. Gertz, A. Kwong, C. Martel, G. Nuckolls, and S. G. Stubblebine. Flexible authentication of xml documents. In *Proceedings of the 8th ACM Conference on Computer and Communications Security (CCS-8)*, pages 136–145, 2001.
6. P. T. Devanbu, M. Gertz, C. U. Martel, and S. G. Stubblebine. Authentic publication over the internet. *Journal of Computer Security*, 3(11):291–314, 2003.
7. M. Goodrich, R. Tamassia, and A. Schwerin. Implementation of an authenticated dictionary with skip lists and commutative hashing. *DISCEX II*, 2001.
8. M. T. Goodrich, R. Tamassia, N. Triandopoulos, and R. Cohen. Authenticated data structures for graph and geometric searching. In *Topics in Cryptology - CT-RSA 2003, Proceedings of the Cryptographers' Track at the RSA Conference*, volume 2612 of *LNCS*, pages 295–313, 2003.
9. J. Li, M. N. Krohn, D. Mazires, and D. Shasha. Secure untrusted data repository (sundr). In *Proceedings of the 6th Symposium on Operating Systems Design and Implementation*, pages 91–106, 2004.
10. P. Maniatis and M. Baker. Enabling the archival storage of signed documents. In *Proceedings of the USENIX Conference on File and Storage Technologies (FAST 2002)*, pages 31–45, Monterey, CA, USA, Jan. 2002. USENIX Association.

11. C. U. Martel, G. Nuckolls, P. T. Devanbu, M. Gertz, A. Kwong, and S. G. Stubblebine. A general model for authenticated data structures. *Algorithmica*, 39(1):21–41, 2004.

12. A. J. Menenzes, P. C. van Oorschot, and S. A. Vanstone. *Handbook of Applied Cryptography*. CRC Press, 1996.

13. R. Merkle. Protocols for public key cryptosystems. In *Proceedings of the IEEE Symposium on Security and Privacy*, pages 122–134. IEEE Computer Society Press, 1980.

14. S. Micali, M. O. Rabin, and J. Kilian. Zero-knowledge sets. In *Proceedings of the 44th Symposium on Foundations of Computer Science (FOCS 2003)*, pages 80–91, 2003.

15. M. Naor and K. Nissim. Certificate revocation and certificate update. *IEEE Journal on Selected Areas in Communications*, 18(4):561–570, 2000.

16. K. Nyberg. Fast accumulated hashing. In *Proceedings of the Third Fast Software Encryption Workshop*, number 1039 in LNCS, pages 83–87, 1996.

17. H. Pang and K.-L. Tan. Authenticating query results in edge computing. In *Proceedings of the 20th International Conference on Data Engineering (ICDE'04)*, 2004.

18. A. S. Rafail Ostrovsky, Charles Rackoff. Efficient consistency proofs for generalized queries on a committed database. In *Proceedings of the 31st International Colloquium on Automata, Languages and Programming (ICALP 2004)*, volume 3142 of *LNCS*, pages 1041–1053, 2004.

19. T. Sander. Efficient accumulators without trapdoor. In *Proceedings of the Second International Conference on Information and Communication Security - ICICS'99*, number 1726 in LNCS, pages 252–262, 1999.

Multilevel Secure Teleconferencing over Public Switched Telephone Network

Inja Youn[1], Csilla Farkas[2], and Bhavani Thuraisingham[3]

[1] Department of Information and Software Engineering,
George Mason University, Fairfax, VA 22030
iyoun@gmu.edu
[2] Dept. of Computer Science and Engineering,
University of South Carolina, Columbia, SC 29208
farkas@cse.sc.edu
[3] Erik Jonsson School of Engineering and Computer Science,
University of Texas at Dallas, Richardson, TX 75080
bhavani.thuraisingham@utdallas.edu

Abstract. Two-way group voice communications, otherwise known as teleconferencing are common in commercial and defense networks. One of the main features of military teleconferences is the need to provide means to enforce the Multilevel Security (MLS) model. In this paper we propose an architecture and protocols facilitating MLS conferences over Public Switched Telephone Network (PSTN). We develop protocols to establish secure telephone conferencing at a specific security level, add and drop conference participants, change the security level of an ongoing conference, and tear down a conference. These protocols enforce MLS requirements and prevent against eavesdropping. Our solution is based on encryption methods used for user and telephone authentication and message encryption, and trusted authentication centers and certificate authorities. We provide an initial estimate of signaling delays of our protocols incurred due to the enforcement of the MLS requirements.

1   Introduction

The need to provide secure communication via public telephone systems has resulted in custom designed and dedicated devices, like the secure telephone unit third generation (STU-III) [3] and TeleVPN [2]. While these methods provide some level of confidentiality, they require extensive setup procedures and dedicated hardware or do not require telephone device authentication. Our aim is to enable current telephone technologies to provide voice privacy without the extensive setup and maintenance requirements of the current systems.

Public Switched Telephone Networks (PSTN [13] - a circuit switched network with almost zero down time and acceptable quality audio signals - use Signaling System 7 (SS7) [4,5,9,7,8,6,11] as its signaling network to set up, configure, maintain, and tear down voice circuits that are used to transmit continuous voice

S. Jajodia and D. Wijesekera (Eds.): Data and Applications Security 2005, LNCS 3654, pp. 99–113, 2005.

streams. Moreover, increasingly popular mobile telephones can also depend on SS7. However, SS7 provides limited security to its signaling and voice networks, as shown by Lorencz et al. [10]. Recognizing these limitations, Sharif et al. [12] present protocols to ensure voice confidentiality over PSTN using the Discretionary Access Control (DAC) model. Their solution uses public and secret key encryption methods to authenticate the users and telephone devices, and to provide encrypted end-to-end communication. They show that authentication delays are within acceptable range for PSTN. Youn et al. [14] extend the protocols of Sharif et al. to DAC based secure teleconferences over PSTN. That is, participation in a conference is decided on the identity of the user (telephone device). However, their methods do not satisfy the security needs of military conferences. In this paper, we extend both these works to MLS based teleconferencing. We adopt the Bell-LaPadula (BLP) [1] access control model.

BLP policies are expressed via security classification labels, assigned to subjects (i.e., active computer system entities) and to objects (i.e., passive resources). Classification labels form a lattice with a dominance relation among the labels. BLP controls read and write operations on the objects based on the classification labels of the requested data objects and the clearance of the subject requesting the operation. For example, BLP ensures that a subject can read an object only if the subject's clearance dominates the object's classification (simple-security property) and that a subject can write an object only if the object's classification dominates the subject's clearance (*-property). Trusted subjects are permitted to bypass the *-property of the BLP. The two axioms of BLP ensure confidentiality by permitting information flow from a dominated security class to a dominating security class but not in the other direction. While MLS is considered too restrictive for general purpose applications, it is required in the military domain.

In this paper we propose an MLS teleconference security model and provide a set of protocols to establish and maintain an MLS teleconference at a specified security level. In our model, a user (conference participant) and his/her telephone device together are considered as the subject; the conference (i.e., its content) is considered as the object. The user who initiates the conference, called call controller, requests the join (add) of a user/telephone to an active conference. However, the actual "adding" of a user/telephone must be permitted by a referential monitor that enforces the simple security property of BLP. That is, a user/telephone is permitted to join a conference only if the security classification of the conference is dominated by the greatest lower bound of the security clearances of the user and the telephone device. The human users are trusted not to violate the *-property, i.e., a user is trusted not to reveal any information that is classified higher than the level of the conference. Call controllers are also trusted (trusted subject) to lower the security clearance of an ongoing conference. To ensure that telephone devices cannot leak confidential information, they are cleared based on their encryption capabilities and verified hardware. We develop a set of protocols to ensure that the conference content is protected from unauthorized disclosure at any time. We also perform analysis of the conference dynamics and the necessary security evaluations to guarantee message confidentiality. Our aim is to limit the necessary delays incurred by the authentication, security checking, and the conference key refreshment. We give an analysis of the incurred delays for our secure teleconference.

The organization of the paper is as follows. Section 2 introduces our security architecture and the MLS teleconferencing model. In Section 3 we present descriptions of our protocols and the corresponding security requirements. Section 4 contains the delay calculation. Finally, we conclude and recommend future research directions in Section 5. We included sample protocols in Appendix A and the break down of the delay calculation in Appendix B.

2   Security Model

The main aim of our research is to build on top of the existing communication infra-structure. Our protocols to set up, maintain, and tear down secure teleconferences use libraries on the Signaling System 7 (SS7) protocol stack. MLS teleconferencing uses secure bridges [12,14].

2.1   Secure Teleconferencing Architecture

We distinguish between a single master-secure bridge (MSB) and slave-secure bridges (SB). MSB has all the capabilities needed for teleconferencing and to enforce MLS requirements. MSB connects to the call-master, i.e., the participant who is initiating the conference. Slave-secure bridges (SB), connecting the conference participants, performs participant and telephone authentication. Each secure bridge is associated with an 1) Authentication Center (AC) to authenticate users and telephones, and to manage secret keys, and a 2) Certificate Authority (CA) to manage digital certificates and generate public/private key pairs. Our model requires that each telephone has cryptographic capabilities using symmetric and public keys. Telephones (and their corresponding secure bridges) are trusted based on these cryptographic capabilities as well as hardware verification of the physical device.

Additional PSTN components, like the Service Switching Points (SSP), Service Control Points (SCP), and Signal Control Point, together with the secure bridges form the secure teleconferencing architecture [14]. Our protocols use the Digital Subscriber Signaling System no 1 (DSS1) to communicate between the telephones and the local SSPs. ISDN user part (ISUP) is used for communication between SSPs and Transaction capabilities Library (TCAP) as well as for transactions between SSPs, ACs, CAs, and Line Information Translation Database (LIDBs).

2.2   Security Model

Our goal is to protect the confidentiality of the telephone conversation from unauthorized disclosure. Note, that the problem of hiding the existence of an unauthorized conference is outside of the scope of this paper. We propose methods to apply the BLP security model to teleconferencing. The subject of our model is the telephone device and the human user (conference initiator and participants) using the telephone. Telephones are authenticated based on the telephone line numbers (TLN), telephone device numbers (TDN), and the private keys assigned to them. A security clearance label is assigned for each telephone, based on its encryption capabilities, verification of hardware components (e.g., trusted hardware and reliability), and physical security. Telephone clearances are considered relatively static. Increasing or decreasing a telephone's clearance level requires technical modifications, like encryption updates. We assume that users are aware of the clearance of the telephone devices.

User authentication is performed by a claimed user identity and the corresponding password. Each user with maximum security clearance λ is associated with a set of passwords, where each password λ' in the set corresponds to a specific security level and $\lambda \geq \lambda'$. To prevent the exposure of a higher security password on a lower security telephone device, we require that each user is authenticated with the password that is assigned to him/her for the level of the telephone device. For example, a user U with Top-Secret (TS) security clearance has different passwords for Unclassified, Secret, and Top-Secret levels. When U uses a telephone with Secret clearance, the user is authenticated based on his/her Secret level password. Note, that different approaches could be used to limit exposure of user passwords on telephones. For example, users may be restricted to use telephone devices only if the clearance level of the device dominates the clearance level of the user. Finding the optimal approach is outside of our current research and is dependent on the application area, the number of levels, and the available hardware resources.

A secure bridge, serving a telephone with clearance λ, stores the appropriate (user-id, password) pairs for all levels λ', where $\lambda \geq \lambda'$. For each call activation by a user U_i, using the telephone T_i, the permitted security clearance is calculated as the greatest lower bound of $[\ \lambda(U_i),\ \lambda(T_i)]$, where $\lambda(U_i)$ and $\lambda(T_i)$ are the clearances of user U_i and device T_i, respectively.

The protection object is the content of the telephone conference. Each conference is initiated at a specified security level. Conference classification levels may increase and decrease along the dominance relation of the security lattice. We require that a user/telephone pair is permitted to initiate or join a conference only if the greatest lower bound of their joint security clearance dominates the security classification of the conference.

This paper studies the conference dynamics, including initiating the conference, adding and dropping participants, changing security classification of an ongoing conference, and changing the call controller of an ongoing conference. Our security requirement is that an unauthorized user should not be able to disclose the conference content. That is, unauthorized users should not be permitted to become participants of a conference or gain access to the secret key used to encrypt the content of the conference. The later requirement protects against passive eavesdropping. Our security requirements are supported by the properties of existing secret and public key encryption methods and by safeguarding the encryption/decryption keys. In addition to the security requirement we want to limit the number of authentication procedures and key updates that cause delays in the teleconferencing.

3   Protocols

We developed eight protocols to support secure telephone conferencing: 1) Establish a conference, 2) Add a new conferee by the call controller, 3) Add a new conferee by his/her own request, 4) Drop a conferee by the call controller, 5) Drop a conferee by his/her own choosing (hang up), 6) Change the classification of an ongoing conference 7) Call teardown by the call controller hanging up, and 8) Call teardown when the last slave conferee hangs up. Due to the space restrictions of the paper we only present some of our protocols.

3.1   Protocol 1 - Teleconference Call Setup Process

The teleconference call setup process has five phases: 1) Telephone authentication, 2) User authentication, 3) Cross certification of the MSB, 4) Remote telephone authentication, 5) Remote user authentication, 6) Cross certification of the SSBs, and 7) Key distribution. Figure 1 shows the control messages for

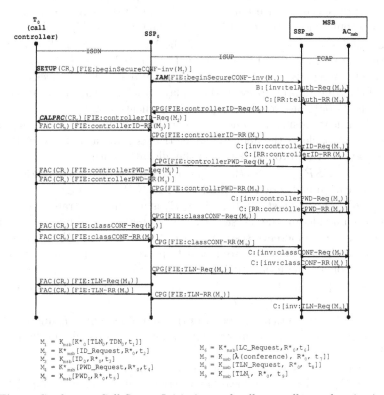

Fig. 1. Conference Call Setup: Initiation and call controller authentication

conference set up steps and the authentication of the call controller. The protocol is given below. The call controller's (user U_0) security clearance is determined by the security clearance of the telephone device (T_0) used to initiate the conference and the security clearance of the ($U_0, password_0$) pair. The permitted classification level of the conference to be initiated by U_0 is $\lambda(U_{0-permitted}) = GLB[\lambda(T_0), (\lambda(U_0, password_0))]$. The call controller is permitted to initiate a conference with security classification λ', where $\lambda(U_{0-permitted}) \geq \lambda'$. The actual protocol steps are given in Appendix A.

1. [T_0] The call controller (U_0) dials the teleconference access code. Once the telephone enters the teleconference mode, the call controller enters the telephone line number (TLN) of the master secure bridge (MSB).

2. [$T_0 \rightarrow SSP_0 \rightarrow SSP_{msb} \rightarrow AC_{msb}$] T_0 invokes the facility that initiates the conference sending $M_1 = K_{msb}[K_0^*[TLN_0, TDN_0, t_0]]$ to MSB, where K_{msb} is the public key of the MSB, and K_0^* is the private key of T_0.
   This message is used for the authentication of the telephone device and travels in the SETUP message (ISDN) between T_0 and SSP_0, and in the IAM primitive (ISDN) between SSP_0 and SSP_{msb}. While the IAM message travels through the SS7 network, the intermediate exchanges allocate the voice trunks. The destination exchange (SSP_{msb}) allocates the resources for the secure teleconference (the Master Secure Bridge - MSB) and initiates the teleconference transaction by sending the message M_1 to AC_{msb}.

3. [AC_{msb}] The authentication center of the Master Secure Bridge verifies the authenticity of the telephone set by extracting TLN_0 and TDN_0 and comparing them against the ones stored in the database. It also checks the validity of the timestamp to prevent the replay attack. The authentication center looks in its database for the telephone classification $\lambda(T_0)$.
   If authentication succeeds and the algorithm continues with the step 4.
   Else SSP_{msb} clears the allocated voice trunks using a RELEASE/RLCOM message pair that propagates along the allocated path.

4. [$AC_{msb} \rightarrow SSP_{msb} \rightarrow SSP_0 \rightarrow T_0$] MSB replies with a request for user authentication embedded in a Call Progress (CPG) message:
   $M_2 = K_{br}^*[ID\_Request, R_0^*, t_1]$, where R_0^* is a nonce generated by AC that will be embedded in the message exchanged between call master and MSB during the teleconference session, and t_1 is a timestamp. Both the random number and the timestamp are meant to prevent the replay attack. An IVR message solicits the user to dial her user ID.

5. [$T_0 \rightarrow SSP_0 \rightarrow SSP_{msb} \rightarrow AC_{msb}$] The call controller enters her/his ID (ID_0): $M_3 = K_{msb}[ID_0, R_0^*, t_3]$

6. [AC_{msb}] The authentication center of the MSB decrypts M_3 and checks the validity of the random number, timestamp, and looks in the database for ID_0.
   If authentication succeeds the protocol continues with the step 7.
   Else, SSP_{msb} clears the allocated voice trunks using a RELEASE/RLCOM message pair and ends the transaction with AC_{msb}

7. $[AC_{msb} \rightarrow SSP_{msb} \rightarrow SSP_0 \rightarrow T_0]$ The authentication center sends a signed acknowledgement in a CPG message, which contain a request for password: $M_4 = K^*_{msb}[PWD\_Request, R^*_0, t_4]$

8. $[T_0 \rightarrow SSP_0 \rightarrow SSP_{msb} \rightarrow AC_{msb}]$ The call controller dials her password (PWD_0), which will be again send to AC_{msb} in a CPG message encrypted by the public key of MSB. $M_5 = K_{msb}[PWD_0, R^*_0, t_5]$

9. $[AC_{msb}]$ The MSB decrypts the message and checks the timestamp and the (ID_0, PWD_0) pair.

   If authentication succeeds, i.e., there is an (ID_0, PWD_0) pair, the AC_{msb} maps the user clearance $\lambda(U_0, password_{U_0})$. AC_{msb} computes $\lambda(permitted)$ $= GLB[\lambda(T_i), \lambda(U_0, password_{U_0})]$. The protocol continues to assign security classification for the conference.

   Else, SSP_{msb} clears the allocated voice trunks using a RELEASE/RLCOM message pair and ends the transaction with AC_{msb}

3.2 Protocol 2 - Add a Participant to an Ongoing Conference

After the conference is set up, new participants U_x may join the ongoing conference. U_0 (call controller) places the teleconference on hold by pressing the HOLD button. The other conferees are still able to talk while the conference is on hold. U_0 initiates the new participant by dialing the U_x's telephone number. The minimal requirement after successful authentication of T_x and U_x is that $GLB[\lambda(T_x), \lambda(U_x, password_x)] \geq \lambda(conf)$. Based on the conference dynamics, the encryption key used for the conference may or may not need to be updated (see Section 3.4).

3.3 Protocol 3 - Drop a Participant from an Ongoing Conference

Conference participants may be dropped from an active conference voluntarily (conferee hangs up) or non-voluntarily (call controller drops the user to maintain the MLS requirements). For example, a user with Secret clearance may decide to discontinue participation in a Secret conference. The same user may rejoin the conference at a later time. On the other hand, a user with Secret clearance is "forced" to be dropped from a conference when the conference classification is increased from Secret to Top-Secret. The MSB is responsible for enforcing the drop of the participants, reallocating the system resources, and initiating a new encryption key if a forced drop occurred.

3.4 Protocol 4 - Change the Security Classification of an Ongoing Conference

The security classification of an ongoing conference may be changed during the conference. For example, after discussing a Top-Secret topic, the security classification of the conference may be decreased to Secret to allow participation of Secret users. Any change in the conference classification may have an effect on the 1) minimum clearance requirement of the call controller, 2) new clearance requirements of the participants of the ongoing conference, 3) dropping conference participants, and 4) need of new encryption key. Figure 2 shows the message transfer to change the conference classification.

To change the security classification of an ongoing conference to a new classification, the call controller U_0 must be cleared to the new classification. That is, if $\lambda(conf_0)$ denotes the security classification of the ongoing conference, and $\lambda(conf_{new})$ denotes the requested security classification, then the new level is permitted only if $\lambda(U_0) \geq \lambda(conf_{new})$. Moreover, to decrease the classification of a conference, the call controller must be trusted. If $\lambda(U_i) \geq \lambda(conf_{new})$ is not true for all participants U_i then U_i must be dropped and a new message encryption key must be distributed among the remaining participants. Also, if the conference classification is decreased and a new user U_i is added such that $\lambda(conf_0) > \lambda(U_i) \geq \lambda(conf_{new})$ then a new message encryption key must be distributed among the participants.

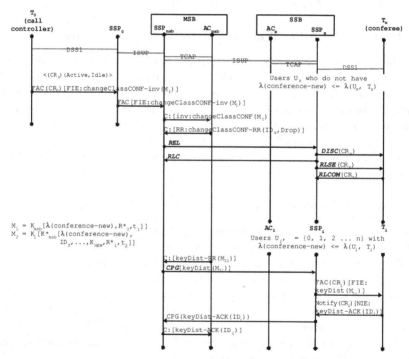

Fig. 2. Changing an ongoing conference classification

We consider the following three scenarios: decrease conference classification, increase conference classification, and change the classification to an incomparable level. Table 1 show our security analysis for these scenarios from the perspectives of security requirements for the call controller, active participants, new participants, and the need of new key generation.

Note, that any change in the conference classification can be modeled as a series of single steps in the security lattice. That is, a change from label λ_1 to λ_k is

Table 1. Conference dynamics and security requirements

	Decrease conference level $\lambda(conf_0) > \lambda(conf_{new})$	Increase conference level $\lambda(conf_{new}) > \lambda(conf_0)$	Change to non-compatible level $\lambda(conf_{new}) \not\geq \lambda(conf_0)$, $\lambda(conf_0) \not\geq \lambda(conf_{new})$
Security requirement for call controller (U_0)	Trusted Subject	$GLB[\lambda(T_0), \lambda(U_0, password_0)] \geq \lambda(conf_{new})$ must hold to authorize the change	Trusted Subject and $GLB[\lambda(T_0), \lambda(U_0, password_0)] \geq LUB[\lambda(conf_0), \lambda(conf_{new})]$ must hold to authorize the change
Security requirement for active user (U_i)	None, since $GLB[\lambda(T_i), \lambda(U_i, password_i)] \geq \lambda(conf_0) > \lambda(conf_{new})$	$GLB[\lambda(T_i), \lambda(U_i, password_i)] \geq \lambda(conf_{new})$ must hold not to be dropped	$GLB[\lambda(T_i), \lambda(U_i, word_i)] \geq \lambda(conf_0), \lambda(conf_{new})]$ must hold not to be dropped
Security requirement for new user (U_x)	$GLB[\lambda(T_x), \lambda(U_x, password_x)] \geq \lambda(conf_{new})$ must hold to join	$GLB[\lambda(T_x), \lambda(U_x, password_x)] \geq \lambda(conf_{new})$ must hold to join	$GLB[\lambda(T_x), \lambda(U_x, password_x)] \geq \lambda(conf_{new})$ must hold to join
Need of new message encryption key distribution	**YES** if a new participant with $\lambda(conf_{new}) \leq \lambda(U_x) < \lambda(conf_0)$ joins the conference **NO-if no new joins**	**YES** if any participants with $\lambda(U_i) < \lambda(conf_{new})$ has dropped out (voluntarily or forced) **NO-if no drops**	**YES** if a new join with $\lambda(conf_{new}) \leq \lambda(U_x)$ but NOT $\lambda(conf_0) \leq \lambda(U_x)$ or if any participants with NOT $\lambda(conf_{new}) \leq \lambda(U_i)$ has dropped out **NO-if no new joins and drops**

modelled as navigating the security lattice along the path $\lambda_1 \rightarrow \lambda_2 \rightarrow \ldots \rightarrow \lambda_k$, where for all $\lambda_i \rightarrow \lambda_j$ either $\lambda_i > \lambda_j$ or $\lambda_j > \lambda_i$. For a call master to initiate the change of a conference level from λ_1 to λ_k must be cleared to all intermediate levels, that is $GLB[\lambda(T_0), [\lambda(U_0, password_0)] \geq LUB[\lambda(conf_0), \lambda(conf_{new})]$ must hold. Similar restrictions hold for any active participant. Our analysis on the need of new encryption key incorporates the possibility that any non-active user may be eavesdropping on the conference before or after the change. The requirements for distributing a new key are based on this possibility of eavesdropping. Application requirements may require periodic refreshment of the message encryption key even if this is not necessary based on the conference dynamics.

4   Performance Analysis

We compute the delays of our protocol, using standard telecommunication connections delays [16,17,18], published encryption/decryption delays for text [3], and the switch response time delays. Table 2 in Appendix B summarizes our findings. The encryption and decryption time for RSA encryption and decryption is considered to be 12ms, (we do not consider the possibility of a small public key, therefore the encryption and decryption time is about the same). Table 3 in Appendix B shows the network delays corresponding to our protocols. The delays corresponding to the user interaction (like the time before an user answer the phone, the time necessary for a user to enter the password, or playing messages) are hard to measure and are user dependent, therefore are not considered here. The user interaction delay may take considerable time, but it is unavoidable and also part of traditional (un-secure) teleconferencing. The worst case calculation, given in Table 3, shows that teleconference setup delay is slightly less than 20 seconds under the assumption that all slave conferees are authenticated simultaneously (i.e., parallel authentication). Adding a user delay is about 11 seconds. Dropping a user and changing the conference classification create small (2-3 seconds) delays.

5   Conclusions

In this paper we present an architecture and protocols to facilitate multilevel secure teleconferences over Public Switched Telephone Network (PSTN). Our goal is to protect conversation confidentiality. Our protocols enable to establish secure telephone conferencing at a specific security level, add and drop conference participants, change the security level of an active conference, and tear down a conference. The protocols protect against eavesdropping and unauthorized participation in a MLS conference. MLS requirements are enforced by safeguarding the message encryption key of the conference. We also provide an initial estimates of delays incurred during setup (20 seconds) and adding a user (11 seconds).

The authors are not aware of any published acceptance delay range for automated teleconferencing. Based on our experiences using such services (e.g., observed delays of several minutes for conference set up) indicates that the delays, incurred by our protocols, are within the acceptable range. Nevertheless, for future references, we are planning to request evaluation of our protocols by vendors and developers. For future work we are planning to simulate our protocols to generate realistic measurements over the incurred delays. Furthermore, we are investigating methods to include a protocol for negotiating encryption algorithms, keys, and configurations specifications between the participants.

Acknowledgement

Farkas' work was partially supported by the National Science Foundation under Grant IIS-0237782.

References

1. D. Bell and L. Lapadula. Secure computer systems : Unified exposition and multics interpretation. Technical Report ESD-TR-75-306, MITRE Corporation, 1975.
2. SecureLogix Corporation. TeleVPN call shield 1.0. http://www.securelogix.com/applications/televpn.htm.
3. Department of Defense Security Institute, http://www.tscm.com/STUIIIhandbook.html. *STU-III Handbook for Industry*.
4. ITU-T Recommendation Q.706. *Specifications of Signaling System No. 7–Message Transfer Part Signaling Performance*, March 1993.
5. ITU-T Recommendation Q.706. *Specifications of Signaling System No. 7–Signaling performance in the Telephone Application*, March 1993.
6. ITU-T Recommendation Q.709. *Specifications of Signaling System No.7–Hypothetical Signaling Reference Connection*, 1993.

7. ITU-T Recommendation Q.734. *Stage 3 description for multiparty supplementary Specifications of signaling system no. 7.*, 1993.
8. ITU-T Recommendation Q.84. *Stage 2 description for multiparty supplementary services*, 1993.
9. ITU-T Recommendation Q.954. *Stage 3 description for multiparty supplementary services using DSS 1*, 1993.
10. G. Lorenz, T. Moore, J. Hale, and S. Shenoi. Securing SS7 telecommunications networks. In *Proceedings of the 2001 IEEE Workshop on Information Assurance and Security*, 2001.
11. T. Russell. *Signaling system 7.* McGraw-Hill, New York, 2002.
12. M. Sharif and D. Wijesekera. Providing voice privacy over public switched telephone networks. In *Proceeding of IFIP 11.5*, pages 25–36, 2003.
13. J. G. von Bosse. *Signaling in Telecommunication Networks.* John Wiley & Sons, New York, 1998.
14. I. Youn and D. Wijesekera. Secure bridges: A means to conduct secure teleconferences over public telephones. In *Proc. of the 18th Annual Conference on Data and Applications Security*, 2004.

Appendix A

Protocol 1 – Conference Set Up:

A. Call Controller Authentication:

1. $[T_0]$ The call controller (U_0) dials the teleconference access code. Once the telephone enters the teleconference mode, the call controller enters the telephone line number (TLN) of the master secure bridge (MSB).

2. $[T_0 \rightarrow SSP_0 \rightarrow SSP_{msb} \rightarrow AC_{msb}]$ T_0 invokes the facility that initiates the conference sending $M_1 = K_{msb}[K_0^*[TLN_0, TDN_0, t_0]]$ to MSB, where K_{msb} is the public key of the MSB, and K_0^* is the private key of T_0. This message is used for the authentication of the telephone device and travels in the SETUP message (ISDN) between T_0 and SSP_0, and in the IAM primitive (ISDN) between SSP_0 and SSP_{msb}. While the IAM message travels through the SS7 network, the intermediate exchanges allocate the voice trunks. The destination exchange (SSP_{msb}) allocates the resources for the se-cure teleconference (the Master Secure Bridge - MSB) and initiates the teleconference transaction by sending the message M_1 to AC_{msb}.

3. $[AC_{msb}]$ The authentication center of the Master Secure Bridge verifies the authenticity of the telephone set by extracting TLN_0 and TDN_0 and comparing them against the ones stored in the database, and by checking also the validity of the timestamp to prevent the replay attack. The authentication center looks in its database for the telephone classification $\lambda(T_i)$ and associates it with the initiated teleconference.

   If authentication succeeds and the algorithm continues with the step A.4.

   Else, SSP_m clears the allocated voice trunks using a RELEASE/RLCOM message pair that propagates along the allocated path.

4. $[AC_{msb} \rightarrow SSP_{msb} \rightarrow SSP_0 \rightarrow T_0]$ MSB replies with a request for user authentication embedded in a Call Progress (CPG) message:
   $M_2 = K_b^* r[ID\_Request, R_0^*, t_1]$, where R_0^* is a nonce generated by AC that will

be embedded in the message exchanged between call master and MSB during the teleconference session, and t_1 is a timestamp. Both the random number and the timestamp are meant to prevent the replay attack. An IVR message solicits the user to dial her user ID.

5. $[T0 \rightarrow SSP_0 \rightarrow SSP_{msb} \rightarrow AC_{msb}]$ The call controller enters her ID (ID_0): $M_3 = K_{msb}[ID_0, R_0^*, t_3]$

6. $[AC_{msb}]$ The authentication center of the MSB decrypts M_3 and checks the validity of the random number, timestamp, and looks in the database for ID_0.
   If authentication succeeds the protocol continues with the step A.7.
   Else, SSP_{msb} clears the allocated voice trunks using a RELEASE/RLCOM message pair and ends the transaction with AC_{msb}

7. $[AC_{msb} \rightarrow SSP_{msb} \rightarrow SSP_0 \rightarrow T_0]$ The authentication center sends a signed acknowledgement in a CPG message, which contain a request for password: $M_4 = K_{msb}^*[PWD\_Request, R_0^*, t_4]$.

8. $[T0 \rightarrow SSP_0 \rightarrow SSP_{msb} \rightarrow AC_{msb}]$ The call controller dials her password (PWD_0), which will be again send to AC_{msb} in a CPG message encrypted by the public key of MSB. $M_5 = K_{msb}[PWD_0, R_0^*, t_5]$

9. $[AC_{msb}]$ The MSB decrypts the message and checks the timestamp and the (ID_0, PWD_0) pair.
   If authentication succeeds, i.e., there is an (ID_0, PWD_0) pair, the AC_{msb} maps the user clearance $\lambda(U_0)$. AC_{msb} computes $\lambda(permitted) =$
   $GLB[\lambda(T_i), \lambda(U_0)]$. The protocol continues with step 10.
   Else, SSP_{msb} clears the allocated voice trunks using a RELEASE/RLCOM message pair and ends the transaction with AC_{msb}.

B. Conference Classification and the Telephone Line Numbers

1. The call master dials the number of the nc conferees, one by one (nc is a number between 1 and 30). We suppose that only n conferees ($n = nc$) succeed in connecting to the conference. The other $(nc - n)$ conferees do not connect or have authentication failure.

2. $[AC_{msb} \rightarrow SSP_{msb} \rightarrow SSP_0 \rightarrow T_0]$ The authentication center requests the call master to choose a classification for the conference (LC): $M_6 = K_{msb}^*[LC\_Request, R_0^*, t_6]$. This is requested as a list of options played using the IVR.

3. $[T_0 \rightarrow SSP_0 \rightarrow SSP_{msb} \rightarrow AC_{msb}]$ The call controller sends the classification for the conference: $M_7 = K_{msb}[\lambda(conference), R_0^*, t_7]$.
   If $\lambda(conference) \leq \lambda(permitted)$ then the protocol continues with step B.4.
   Else SSP_{msb} clears the allocated voice trunks using a RELEASE/RLCOM message pair and ends the transaction with AC_{msb}.

4. The following steps are repeated for all remote parties $(i = 1, 2 \ldots n)$
   (a) $[AC_{msb} \rightarrow SSP_{msb} \rightarrow SSP_0 \rightarrow T_0]$ MSB sends a request to the call controller to dial the telephone line number of the first conferee:
       $M_8 = K_{msb}[TLN\_request, R_0^*, t_{8i}]$
   (b) $[T_0 \rightarrow SSP_0 \rightarrow SSP_{msb} \rightarrow AC_{msb}]$ The call controller dials the telephone line number of $User_i$ (TLN_i): $M_9 = K_{msb}[TLN_i, R_0^*, t_{9i}]$

5. For $i = 1$ to nc repeat the following steps (1 through 9) (nc is the number of conferees called by U_0). If $\lambda(conference) \leq \lambda(permitted)$ for user U_i than associate $(U_i, \lambda(permitted))$ with the conference and continue the protocol. Else drop U_i and clear the connection.

C. Cross-Certification

1. $[AC_{msb} \rightarrow SSP_{msb} \rightarrow SSP_i]$ AC_{msb} signals to SSP_{msb} to send the initial address message (IAM) that seizes a trunk between the secure bridge for U_i and the local exchange of the remote user (SSP_i) to establish a bidirectional circuit between the secure bridge and the SSP_i, followed by a call progress (CPG) message that has as a parameter a ticket $M10 = K^*_{msb}[ID_0, ID_1 \ldots ID_{nc}, \lambda(conference), R_i, t_{10i}]$ signed by the bridge. M_{10} certifies the U_0, initiate the conference, and transmits the conference classification $\lambda(conference)$ to the $SSBs$.

2. $[SSP_i \rightarrow AC_i]$ SSP_i forwards M_10 to AC_i for authentication. If fails, the AC_i signals the SSP_i to drop the $User_i$. Otherwise, continues with step D.1.

D. Remote Parties Authentication

1. $[AC_i \rightarrow SSP_i \rightarrow T_i \rightarrow SSP_i]$ If authentication succeeds, AC_i sends authentication result to the SSP_i in TCAP message $M_{11} = K^*_{aci}[ID_0, ID_1 \ldots ID_{nc},$ $K_{msb}, R^*_i, t_{11i}]$. SSP_i sends the result to the T_i in an ISUP message. T_i sends back: $M_{12} = K_{aci}[K^*_i[TLN_i, TDN_i, R^*_i, t_{12i}]]$ encrypts and signs telephone device and line numbers.

2. $[SSP_i \rightarrow AC_i]$ The authentication center checks the telephone line and the device numbers in M_{12} sent through the TCAP message by decrypting the message with K^*_{aci}, and then checks the signature of T_i using K_i. After decryption and authentication, the AC_i also verifies whether the TLN_i and the TDN_i from the message M_{12} coincides with the one in the local database. Also, AC_i looks in its database for the telephone device classification $\lambda(T_i)$. If the authentication fails, or if the security condition $\lambda(conference) \leq \lambda(T_i)$ fails, AC_i sends an error message to the SSP_i, which initiates the disconnection procedure for the $User_i$ from the secure conference by sending a REL/RLCOM message pair to the MSB.

3. $[AC_i \rightarrow SSP_i \rightarrow T_i]$ AC_i sends $M_{13} = K^*_{aci}[ID\_Request, R^*_i, t_{13i}]$ in a TCAP message as the return result to the SSP_i where the random number R^*_i is included in the confirmation ticket sent by the AC_i to the MSB.

4. $[SSP_i \rightarrow T_i]$ SSP_i sends M_{13} to U_i in a FACILITY message with a FIE containing a user authentication request.

5. $[T_i \rightarrow SSP_i]$ T_i sends the ALERT (CR_i) message to SSP_i.

6. $[SSP_i \rightarrow SSP_0]$ SSP_i sends the ALERT

7. $[SSP_0 \rightarrow T_0]$ SSP_0 sends the ALERT (CR_0) message to T_0.

8. $[T_i \rightarrow SSP_i]$ When U_i picks up the handset, T_i sends the CONNECT message to SSP_i, and the SSP_i plays an IVR announcement informing U_i of the conference participants, after the SSP_i plays a new IVR announcement to the T_i: "Please enter your ID".

9. $[T_i \rightarrow SSP_i]$ U_i dials her ID that is encrypted with AC_i's public key. The U_i's telephone knows the AC_i's public key, and sends it to the AC_i over the network.

10. $[SSP_i \rightarrow AC_i]$ SSP_i forwards $M14 = Kaci[IDi, R * i, t14]$ to the AC_i in a TCAP message. The authentication center verifies the pair $(ID, password)$ sent over by the SSP_i. If the ID is not found in AC_i's database, or if the condition $\lambda(conference) = \lambda(T_i)$ is not fulfilled, the AC_i issues an error message to the SSP_i, and the local exchange starts clearing the connection. Thus we have: $\lambda(conference) = GLB[\lambda(T_i), \lambda(U_i)] = \lambda(T_i, U_i)$

11. $[AC_i \rightarrow SSP_i \rightarrow T_i]$ If the authentication succeeds, AC_i sends a PWD request to the $User_i$: $M_{15} = K^*aci[PWD\_Request, R^*_i, t_{15i}]$

12. $[T_i \rightarrow SSP_i \rightarrow AC_i]$ $User_i$ answers with $M_{16} = K^*_{aci}[PWD_i, R^*_i, t_{16i}]$

13. $[AC_i]$ AC_i checks the password, and if authentication fails, clears the connections with MSB and T_i. If authentication succeeds, it continues with step E.1.

E. Cross-Certification

1. $[AC_i \rightarrow SSP_i \rightarrow SSP_{msb} \rightarrow AC_{msb}]$ If authentication succeeds, SSP_i sends the following ticket to AC_{msb}, completing the cross-certification phase: $M_{17} = K^*_{aci}[ID_i, \lambda(U_{17i}]$. The MSB receives now U_i's public key and clearance, and also the telephone device classification. Thus, MSB and U_i are able to communicate without any further help from the slave secure bridge. MSB double-checks the condition $\lambda(conference) = GLB(\lambda(T_i), \lambda(U_i)) = \lambda(T_i, U_i)$

F. Key Distribution

1. The master secure bridge waits until either all users have connected or a connection timeout occurred, and adds the IDs of all connected users to a list.
2. For $i = 0, 1, \ldots n$ repeat following steps 1 and 2.
   (a) $[AC_{msb} \rightarrow SSP_{msb} \rightarrow SSP_i \rightarrow T_i]$. The secure bridge starts the group shared key distribution phase by sending $M_{18} = K_i[K^*_{br}[K_E, R^*_i, t_{18}]]$ in a TCAP message between the AC_{msb} and the SSP_{msb}, in a CPG message between the SSP_{msb} and the SSP_i and in a FACILITY message between SSP_i and T_i.
   (b) $[T_i \rightarrow SSP_i \rightarrow SSP_{msb} \rightarrow AC_{msb}]$ T_i decrypts M_{18}, checks the signature, the random number and the timestamp, and recovers the group shared key K_E. After this, the T_i sends the $Key - dist - ACK(ID_i)$ back to the AC_{msb}.
3. As soon as the users receive the symmetric key, they can start the secure group conversation. The voice is encrypted by the telephone device and is sent to the Master Secure Bridge. The MSB takes care of forwarding the encrypted signal to the destination telephone devices, where the signal is decrypted.

Appendix B

Table 2. Switch Response Delay Calculation

Type of Call Segment	Switch Response time (ms)	
	Mean	95% confidence interval
ISUP Message	$205 - 218$	$= 337 - 349$
Alerting	400	$= 532$
ISDN Access Message	$220 - 227$	$= 352 - 359$
TCAP Message	$210 - 222$	$= 342 - 354$
Announcement/Tone	300	$= 432$
Connection	300	$= 432$
End MF Address - Seize	150	$= 282$

Table 3. Network delay

Table Conference Call Phase	Delay	Delay under assumptions: n = 10, p = 10s, a$_i$ = b$_i$ = 50ms d = e = 12ms	Description of the parameters and assumptions
Call setup	$11007 + 667n$ $+(n+8)a_0$ $+8 \cdot \max\{a_1 \dots a_n\}$ $+2 \cdot \max\{b_1 \dots b_n\}$ $+21 \cdot (d+e)$ ms	$19,181ms$	The number of conferencing subscribers is n The transmission propagation delay between T_0 and AC_{msb} is a_0 and the transmission propagation
Add user by call controller	$9855 + 3a_0 + 6a_n$ $+2 \cdot \max a_1 \dots a_n$ $+2 \cdot \max b_1 \dots b_n$ $+11 \cdot (d+e)$ ms	$10,769ms$	delay between T_i and AC_i is a_i, where $i = 1,2 \dots n$. (see ITU-T Recommendation TABLE 1/Q.706). We will omit a maxi-
Drop user by call controller	$2001 + a_0$ $+2 \cdot \max\{a_1 \dots a_n\}$ $+2 \cdot \max\{b_1 \dots b_n\}$ $+3 \cdot (d+e)$ ms	$2,323ms$	mum 2.5ms delay between T_0 and SSP_0 (under the realistic assumption that the distance between T_0 and SSP0 is less then 500km),
Increase / change conference classification.	$2001 + a_0$ $+2 \cdot \max a_1 \dots a_n$ $+2 \cdot \max b_1 \dots b_n$ $+3 \cdot (d+e)$ ms	$2,323$ ms	since it is not significant compared with the total delay. The transmission propagation delay between AC_{msb} and AC_i is b_i, where $i = 1,2 \dots n$
Decrease conference classification	$2001 + a_0$ $+2 \cdot \max\{a_1 \dots a_n\}$ $+2 \cdot \max\{b_1 \dots b_n\}$ $+(d+e)$ ms	$2,275ms$	The delay to perform a RSA 1024 encryption/decryption is $e = d = 12ms$.

Secrecy of Two-Party Secure Computation*

Yi-Ting Chiang, Da-Wei Wang**, Churn-Jung Liau, and Tsan-sheng Hsu***

Institute of Information Science Academia Sinica, Taipei, 115, Taiwan
{ytc, wdw, liaucj, tshsu}@iis.sinica.edu.tw

Abstract. Privacy protection has become one of the most important issues in the information era. Thus, many protocols have been developed to achieve the goal of cooperatively accomplishing a computational task without revealing the participants' private data. Practical protocols, however, do not guarantee perfect privacy protection, as some degree of privacy leakage is allowed during the computation process for the sake of efficient resource consumption, e.g., the number of random bits required and the computation time. Although there are metrics for measuring the amount of resource consumption, as far as we know, there are no effective metrics that measure the degree of privacy leakage. Without such metrics, however, it is difficult to compare protocols fairly. In this paper, we propose a framework based on linear algebra and information theory to measure the amount of privacy leakage in protocols. This framework can be used to analyze protocols that satisfy certain algebraic properties. We use it to analyze three two-party scalar product protocols. The framework might also be extendable to the analysis of other protocols.

Keywords: Privacy Analysis, Private Computation, Scalar Product.

1 Introduction

Privacy protection is one of the most pressing issues in the information era. The massive databases spread over the Internet are gold mines for some and, at the same time, one of the greatest threats to privacy for others. How to cooperatively accomplish a computational task without revealing participants' private input has therefore gained a lot of attention and the development of efficient solutions is now an active research area. In theory [11,7], it is possible to securely compute almost any function without revealing anything, except the output. Unfortunately, the theoretical results are not readily applicable to real applications due to their high computational complexity.

Most theoretical approaches adopt a computationally indistinguishable view of secrecy and try to find provable secure solutions, but such a definition leaves

---

* Supported in part by Taiwan Information Security Center.

** Corresponding Author: Joint-appointment faculty member of National Yang Ming University, Taiwan. Supported in part by NSC (Taiwan) Grant 93-2213-E-001-031.

*** Supported in part by NSC (Taiwan) Grants 92-2213-E-001-005 and 93-2213-E-001-001.

S. Jajodia and D. Wijesekera (Eds.): Data and Applications Security 2005, LNCS 3654, pp. 114–123, 2005.

little room to quantify secrecy. Meanwhile, in application oriented studies, researchers usually take an intuitive approach to the definition of secrecy and try to prove the secrecy of protocols by refuting possible attacks. However, being intuitive, this approach cannot actually prove the security of protocols per se. It can only be argued that refuting possible attacks preserves some security. There is a gap between the theoretical and intuitive approaches in terms of provable secrecy. Although, privacy is a basic human right, it is not the only one. When multi-party private computation is applied to the public sector, sometimes privacy must be compromised to accommodate other important social values. It can also be applied to the private sector, such as in a business setting. For example, two (or more) companies might want to compute a function cooperatively; however, neither of them wants to share their private information. In both public sector and private sector applications, it would be beneficial to be able to quantify secrecy so that some tradeoff, for example, between secrecy and computational efficiency, could be made. In [5], similar arguments are presented about ideal secrecy and acceptable secrecy. In this paper, we propose an information theoretical framework toward a quantifiable definition of secrecy for multi-party private computation.

The remainder of this paper is organized as follows. We give a short review of related works in Section 2. In Section 3, we present our formal framework. In Section 4, we analyze several scalar product protocols to demonstrate our model and summarize the results. Finally, in Section 5, we present our conclusions and a short discussion about possible extensions of our model. We also indicate the direction of future work.

2   Related Work

Secure two-party computation was first studied by Yao [11] and extended to the multi-party case by Goldreich et al [7]. Through a sequence of effort, a satisfactory definitional treatment was developed and precise proofs for security were provided . A full description of these developments can be found in [6]. The general construction approach is as follow. To securely compute a function, it is first converted to a combinatorial circuit. For each gate in the circuit, all parties run a protocol to compute the result of that gate. Both the input and the output of the gate are shared randomly and the final output is also shared randomly among all parties, after which each party can exchange its share of the information to compute the final result. Although, this general construction approach is impressive, it implies that both the size of the circuit and the number of parties involved dominate the size, i.e., complexity, of the protocol. Note that the size of the circuit is related to the size of the input. Therefore, the approach is not a feasible solution for a real world problem with a large input and/or a large number of parties [9].

The high cost of the general approach for large problems has motivated researchers to look for efficient solutions for specific functions and many protocols have already been developed to solve specific problems. There are specific protocols for general computation primitives, such as, scalar products [1,10], set union and set intersection cardinality [8], and private permutation [2]. In addition, there are protocols for specific application domains, for example, data mining, computational geometry, statistical analysis, etc. An excellent survey of secure multi-party computation problems can be found in [3].

Almost all the approaches mentioned above are based on the notion of ideal secrecy, as indicated in [5]. In that paper the authors ask if it would be possible to lower the security requirement from an ideal level to an acceptable level so that an efficient protocol could be developed. We extend their work by quantifying the security level within an information theoretical framework.

3   Framework

In multi-party private computation, n players cooperate to compute a function, and each player holds some private input that is part of the parameters for computing the function. The goal is to compute the function and maintain the secrecy of each party's private input. Given a protocol, P, we use X_i^P to denote the private input of party i, and msg_i^P to denote the message received by party i. We use information theory to model the amount of information revealed after running P. Before running P, each party has no information about other parties' private input. However, after running P, each party may know something about some of the other parties' private inputs because of new information gathered during the execution of P. Let $H_i^P = H(X_i^P)$ denote the entropy of random variable X_i^P, and $H_{ij}^P = H(X_i^P | msg_j^P)$ denote the entropy of random variable X_i^P given msg_j^P. The conditional entropy corresponds to the intuitive idea of the amount of information (uncertainty) of X_i^P from party j's perspective after receiving msg_j^P.

We define the degree of secrecy of protocol P as $\min_{i,j}(H_{ij}^P / H_i^P)$, or $\min_{i,j}$ (H_{ij}^P); and call the former *relative secrecy* and the latter *absolute secrecy*. When comparing different protocols, we believe that relative secrecy is a better notion, since it is normalized to a number between zero and one, where one indicates perfect secrecy, and zero means no secrecy at all. However, for some specific applications, where the number of players and the types of private input are fixed, absolute secrecy gives the user a direct measurement of the degree of uncertainty that each private input contains after executing the protocol. Obviously we assume the existence of private communication channels between any two parties. To model the case of a broadcast channel, we simply replace msg_i^P with msg^P, where msg^P denotes the complete record of messages broadcast during the execution of the protocol. It is worth mentioning that our model can be extended to model situations such as parties forming a coalition, where there is asymmetry among data elements in the private inputs and among the parties. We do not try to describe such a general model here, as the extension might detract from our main points. In a later work, we hope to extend our model to a multi-party setting.

4   Analysis of the Protocols

4.1   Preliminaries

In this paper, we analyze the degree of secrecy of three two-party scalar product protocols, each of which has two players, Alice and Bob, who have private input X_A and X_B respectively. The private input of each player is an n dimensional vector. After running the protocol, Alice and Bob receive the numbers u and v respectively, such that $u + v$ is the inner product of X_A and X_B, i.e., $X_A \cdot X_B$. Let $*$ be the matrix product operator, and X_B^T be the transpose of X_B. Then, $u + v = X_A \cdot X_B = X_A * X_B^T$. Hereafter, we assume that $X_A, X_B \in GF(p)^n$, where $GF(p)$ is a Galois field of order p, and p is a prime number. We also assume that both parties are semi-honest, i.e., they both follow the protocol and do not deliberately deviate from it to get more information. Instead, they only deduce information from messages they receive.

We first list some facts from information theory.

Fact 1

1. $H(X|msg) = H(X, R|msg) - H(R|X, msg)$.
2. If R is a function of X and msg, then $H(R|X, msg) = 0$ and $H(X|msg) = H(X, R|msg)$.
3. If $H(R|X, msg) \neq 0$ and $H(X|R, msg) = 0$, then $H(X|msg) = H(R|msg) - H(R|X, msg)$.

Let V and C be two random sources. If it is known that some functional dependency exists between V and C, then knowing information about C reveals information about V. That is, the entropy of V is reduced. For the case where $V, C \in GF(p)^n$ and A is a matrix, we get the following:

Proposition 1. Let $V, C \in GF(p)^n$ be two vectors with all elements uniformly randomly selected from $GF(p)$, and let A be an $m \times n$ matrix with all its elements in $GF(p)$. If there exists a functional dependency $A * V = C$ and $rank(A) = k$, then $H(V|C) = (n - k) \log p$.

Proof: By $A * V = C$, let W_1 and W_2 be two vector spaces with ordered bases α and β such that there is a linear transformation $T: W_1 \to W_2$. $[T]_\beta^\alpha = A$. Since $rank(A) = k$, if C is known, we can find a vector space $U \subseteq W_1$ such that the dimension of U is $n - k$ and $V \in U$. Let $s = (s_1, \ldots, s_{n-k})$ be an ordered basis of U. Then V can be expressed in the form:

$$V = a_1 s_1 + a_2 s_2 + \cdots + a_{n-k} s_{n-k}.$$

Thus, $H(V|C) = H(a_1, \ldots, a_{n-k}) = (n - k) \log p$.   ∎

The following lemma can be derived directly from the above proposition.

Lemma 1. Let $A * V = C$ be a linear system of equations in $GF(p)$. If there are k linear independent equations in $A * V = C$, that is, $rank(A) = k$, and n unknowns in V, then $H(V|C) = (n - k) \log p$.

We now describe and analyze three scalar product protocols. In our analysis, let $\mathbf{I}_i$ be an $i \times i$ identity matrix, and $\mathbf{0}_{i \times j}$ be an $i \times j$ zero matrix.

4.2   Analysis of Protocol 1

The protocol is as follows. First Alice and Bob agree to an $n*n$ invertible matrix, M, and a positive integer, k, that is not larger than n.

Scalar Product Protocol 1 *[5]*

Alice	Bob
1. Compute $X'_A = X_A * M$.	Compute $X'_B = (M^{-1} * X^T_B)^T$.
Let $X'_A = [x_{A_1}, \ldots, x_{A_n}]$,	Let $X'_B = [x_{B_1}, \ldots, x_{B_n}]$,
$\bar{X}_A = [x_{A_1}, \ldots, x_{A_k}]$,	$\bar{X}_B = [x_{B_1}, \ldots, x_{B_k}]$,
$\underline{X}_A = [x_{A_{k+1}}, \ldots, x_{A_n}]$	$\underline{X}_B = [x_{B_{k+1}}, \ldots, x_{B_n}]$

2. $\qquad\qquad\qquad$ Alice $\xrightarrow{\bar{X}_A}$ Bob

$\qquad\qquad\qquad\qquad$ Alice $\xleftarrow{\underline{X}_B}$ Bob

3. $u = \underline{X}_A * X^T_B \qquad\qquad\qquad\qquad\qquad v = \bar{X}_A * \bar{X}^T_B$

Let U be a matrix whose column vectors are the leftmost k column vectors of matrix M, and let V be a matrix whose row vectors are the last $n-k$ row vectors of matrix M^{-1}. We organize messages received by Alice and Bob in a matrix form and use Lemma 1 to derive the conditional information of each private input after the other party receives the messages sent during the protocol.

- Alice receives the message $msg_A = \{\underline{X}_B\} = \{V * X^T_B\}$. Thus, $V * X^T_B = \underline{X}_B$ and $rank(V) = n - k$. By Lemma 1, $H(X_B|msg_A) = k \log p$.
- Similarly, Bob receives the message $msg_B = \{\bar{X}_A\} = \{U * X_A\}$. Hence, $U * X_A = \bar{X}_A$ and $rank(U) = k$. By lemma 1, $H(X_A|msg_B) = (n - k) \log p$.

Based on the above discussion, we have the following lemma.

Lemma 2. *In Protocol 1, the degree of secrecy for Alice is* $\frac{H(X_A|msg_B)}{H(X_A)} = \frac{(n-k)\log p}{n \log p} = (n - k)/n$, *and for Bob is* $\frac{H(X_B|msg_A)}{H(X_B)} = \frac{k \log p}{n \log p} = k/n$. *The degree of secrecy for Protocol 1 is* $\min(\frac{H(X_A|msg_B)}{H(X_A)}, \frac{H(X_B|msg_A)}{H(X_B)}) = \min(k, n - k)/n \le \frac{1}{2}$.

Remarks: In [5], it is mentioned, but not formally explained, that M should be invertible and k should be selected as $k = \lceil n/2 \rceil$. From our analysis, we know that selecting M to be invertible and $k = \lceil n/2 \rceil$ maximizes the degree of secrecy. It is also mentioned in [5] the selection of M should avoid the case where $\bar{X}_A = [x_{A_1}, \ldots, x_{A_k}]$; for example, that the selection of $M = \mathbf{I}_n$ is one of the bad cases. However, in our framework, picking $M = \mathbf{I}_n$ and picking M to be any invertible matrix are identical in terms of the degree of secrecy. Institutively, the advice mentioned above indicates that, the case where an individual value is fully revealed is definitely more serious than the cases where individual values are partially revealed, even though the total information remains are the same. The conflict will be resolved when our model is extended to consider asymmetry among the data elements of private inputs.

4.3 Analysis of Protocol 2

This protocol assumes the existence of a semi-honest party, C. In other words, C does not collude with Alice or Bob. First C generates two $1 \times n$ random matrices, R_a and R_b; and then randomly picks two integers, r_a and r_b, such that $r_a + r_b = R_a * R_b^T$. C sends R_a and r_a to Alice, and R_b and r_b to Bob.

Scalar Product Protocol 2 [4,5]

Alice	Bob
1. $X'_A = X_A + R_a$	$X'_B = X_B + R_b$
2.	$\text{Alice} \xrightarrow{X'_A} \text{Bob}$
	$\text{Alice} \xleftarrow{X'_B} \text{Bob}$
3.	Bob generates a random value v, and computes $s = X'_A * X_B^T + r_b - v$
4.	$\text{Alice} \xleftarrow{s} \text{Bob}$
5. $u = s - (R_a * X'^T_B) + r_a$	

Because, in this protocol, the commodity party C generates random variables without receiving any message, C gets no information about the private inputs of Alice and Bob.

Alice receives the message $msg_A = \{X'_B, r_a, s\}$ in Protocol 2, where

- $X'_B = \mathbf{I}_n * X_B^T + \mathbf{I}_n * R_b^T + 0 \cdot r_b + 0 \cdot v$,
- $r_a = \mathbf{0}_{1 \times n} * X_B^T + R_a * R_b^T - 1 \cdot r_b + 0 \cdot v$, and
- $s = X'_A * X_B^T + \mathbf{0}_{1 \times n} * R_b^T + 1 \cdot r_b - 1 \cdot v$.

Since $H(R_b|X_B, msg_A)$, $H(r_b|X_B, msg_A)$, and $H(v|X_B, msg_A)$ are all 0, we have $H(X_B|msg_A) = H(X_B, R_b, r_b, v|msg_A)$. Let $A_1 = \begin{bmatrix} \mathbf{I}_n & \mathbf{I}_n & 0 & 0 \\ \mathbf{0}_{1 \times n} & R_a & -1 & 0 \\ X'_A & \mathbf{0}_{1 \times n} & 1 & -1 \end{bmatrix}$,

$Z_1 = \begin{bmatrix} X_B^T \\ R_b^T \\ r_b \\ v \end{bmatrix}$, and $C_1 = \begin{bmatrix} X'^T_B \\ r_a \\ s \end{bmatrix}$.

Note that $rank(A_1) = n + 2$, $A_1 * Z_1 = C_1$, and C_1 is essentially msg_A. $H(X_B|msg_A) = n \log p$ by Lemma 1.

Bob gets the message $msg_B = \{r_b, X'_A\}$ in Protocol 2, where

- $\mathbf{I}_n * X_A^T + \mathbf{I}_n * R_a^T + 0 \cdot r_a = X'^T_A$, and
- $\mathbf{0}_{1 \times n} * X_A^T + R_b * R_a^T - 1 \cdot r_a = r_b$.

Let $A_2 = \begin{bmatrix} \mathbf{I}_n & \mathbf{I}_n & 0 \\ \mathbf{0}_{1 \times n} & R_b & -1 \end{bmatrix}$, $Z_2 = \begin{bmatrix} X_A^T \\ R_a^T \\ r_a \end{bmatrix}$, and $C_2 = \begin{bmatrix} X'^T_A \\ r_b \end{bmatrix}$.

It is easy to verify that $H(R_a|X_A, msg_B) = 0$, $H(r_a|X_A, msg_B) = 0$, and $rank(A) = n + 1$. Thus, $H(X_A|msg_B) = H(X_A, R_a, r_b|msg_B)$. We know $A_2 *$

$Z_2 = C_2$, and C_2 is essentially msg_B. By Lemma 1, $H(X_A|msg_B) = ((2n+1) - (n+1)) \log p = n \log p$.

Based on the above discussion, we have the following lemma.

Lemma 3. *The degree of secrecy for Protocol 2 is* $\min(\frac{H(X_A|msg_B)}{H(X_A)},$ $\frac{H(X_B|msg_A)}{H(X_B)})=1$.

4.4   Analysis of Protocol 3

This protocol assumes M is a public $n \times n$ matrix, m is a publicly known constant that is at most n, and $rank(M) = k$. Without loss of generality, we assume that n can be evenly divided by m, and $q = n/m$.

Scalar Product Protocol 3 *[10]*

Alice	Bob
1. *Generate a $1 \times n$ random matrix R. Let D be an $m \times n$ matrix whose elements are d_{ij}, where $d_{ij} =$* $\begin{cases} 1, \textit{if } j \in [(i-1) \cdot q + 1, i \cdot q] \\ 0, \textit{otherwise} \end{cases}$ *Define $X'_A = (X_A^T + M * R^T)^T$ and $Q = D * R^T$.*	
2.	Alice $\xrightarrow{Q, X'_A}$ Bob
3.	*Let $s = X'_A * X_B^T$, and generate a $1 \times m$ random matrix $R' = [r'_1, \ldots, r'_m]$. Let $W = [w_1, \ldots, w_n]$ be a $1 \times n$ matrix, where $w_{(i-1) \times q + j} = r'_i, \forall i \in [1, m]$ and $\forall j \in [1, q]$. Let $X'_B = X_B * M + W$.*
4.	Alice $\xleftarrow{X'_B, s}$ Bob
5. *Note that $s = X'_A * X_B^T$* $= X'_A * X_B^T + R * W^T - R * W^T$ $= X_A * X_B^T + R * X_B^{\prime T} - R * W^T$. *Since Alice knows X'_B, she can get $u = X_A * X_B - R * W^T$.*	*Bob can compute $v = R' * Q$. Notes that $R \cdot W^T = R' * Q$.*

Alice receives the message $msg_A = \{X_B^{\prime T}, s\}$, where

- $X_B^{\prime T} = M^T * X_B^T + \mathbf{I}_n * W^T$, and
- $s = X'_A * X_B^T + \mathbf{0}_{1 \times n} * W^T$.

Note that there are only m unknowns, $r'_1, \ldots, r'_m$, in W. Let $A = \begin{bmatrix} M^T & \mathbf{I}_n \\ X'_A & \mathbf{0}_{1 \times n} \end{bmatrix}$, $Z = \begin{bmatrix} X^T_B \\ W^T \end{bmatrix}$, and $C = \begin{bmatrix} X'^T_B \\ s \end{bmatrix}$.

We know that $H(W|X_B, msg_A) = 0$, $rank(A) = n + 1$, $A * Z = C$, and C is essentially msg_A. By Lemma 1, $H(X_B|msg_A) = (n + m - (n + 1))\log p = (m - 1)\log p$.

Bob receives the message $msg_B = \{X'_A, Q\}$ from Alice in Protocol 3, where

- $X'^T_A = \mathbf{I}_n * X^T_A + M * R^T$, and
- $Q = \mathbf{0}_{m \times n} * X^T_A + D * R^T$.

In Bob's case, $H(R|X_A, msg_B)$ may not be 0 if $rank(M) = k \neq n$. On the other hand, $H(X_A|R, msg_B) = 0$, even if k is not equal to n. So we have $H(X_A|msg_B) = H(R|msg_B) - H(R|X_A, msg_B)$.

We first compute $H(X_A, R|msg_B)$. Let $A_1 = \begin{bmatrix} \mathbf{I}_n & M \\ \mathbf{0}_{m \times n} & D \end{bmatrix}$, $Z_1 = \begin{bmatrix} X^T_A \\ R^T \end{bmatrix}$, and $C_1 = \begin{bmatrix} X'^T_A \\ Q \end{bmatrix}$.

It is clear that $rank(A) = n+m$, $A_1 * Z_1 = C_1$, and C_1 is essentially msg_B. By Lemma 1, $H(R|msg_B) = H(X_A, R|msg_B) = (2n - (n+m))\log p = (n-m)\log p$.

To compute $H(R|X_A, msg_B)$, X_A can be treated as a constant vector. Therefore, let $A_2 = \begin{bmatrix} M \\ D \end{bmatrix}$, $Z_2 = \begin{bmatrix} R^T \end{bmatrix}$, and $C_2 = \begin{bmatrix} X'^T_A - X^T_A \\ Q \end{bmatrix} = \begin{bmatrix} M * R \\ Q \end{bmatrix}$. From $A_1 * Z_1 = C_1$, we can derive $A_2 * Z_2 = C_2$.

Let $rank(A_2) = e$. From Lemma 1, $H(R|X_A, msg_B) = (n - e)\log p$. As a result, $H(X_A|msg_B) = H(R|msg_B) - H(R|X_A, msg_B) = ((n - m) - (n - e))\log p = (e - m)\log p$.

Note that $e \leq n$, m is an integer, and $\min(m - 1, e - m) \leq \min(m - 1, n - m) \leq (n - 2)/2$.

Based on the above discussion, we have the following lemma.

Lemma 4. *The degree of secrecy for Protocol 3 is:*

$$\min\left(\frac{H(X_A|msg_B)}{H(X_A)}, \frac{H(X_B|msg_A)}{H(X_B)}\right) = \min\left(\frac{e - m}{n}, \frac{m - 1}{n}\right) \leq \frac{1}{2} - \frac{1}{n} < \frac{1}{2}.$$

Remarks: In our analysis, Protocol 3 achieves its maximum level of secrecy when $m = \frac{n+1}{2}$ and $rank(A_2) = n$ However, we require that $m = n/q$ for some integer q, and m to be an integer. When n is even and $m = n/2$, the protocol achieves its maximum level of secrecy. This provides a guideline for choosing M and m.

5   Conclusion and Future Works

In this paper, we propose the measurement of secrecy in the information theoretical sense, and use our model to analyze three two-party scalar product protocols. The results are summarized in Table 1. We note that although Protocol 2 achieves the highest level of security with the least complexity, i.e., random bits, communication cost, and computational efforts, it requires a semi-honest third party, which may be costly to implement in real applications. Protocol 3 may be slightly more secure than Protocol 1.

Table 1. Summary of results

	Protocol 1	Protocol 2	Protocol 3
random bits	0	$(2n+1)\lceil \log p\rceil$	$(m+n)\lceil \log p\rceil$
communication cost	$O(n\log p)$	$O(n\log p)$	$O(n\log p)$
computational complexity	$O(n^2)$	$O(n)$	$O(n^2)$
degree of secrecy	$\le \frac{1}{2}$	1	$\le \min(\frac{n-m}{n}, \frac{m-1}{n})$ $\le \frac{1}{2} - \frac{1}{n}$
comments	requires a $n \times n$ inevitable matrix	requires a semi-honest third party	achieve max secrecy when $m = \lfloor n/2 \rfloor$

We consider that maintaining secrecy is an important factor in multi-party private computation, but it is not the sole goal. Thus, a tradeoff among computational complexity, communication complexity, and secrecy can be explored. The theoretical existential proof of solutions for multi-party private computation is elegant and impressive; however, it is not practical for real world, large-scale applications. For real applications, perfect secrecy is an ideal situation, but adequate secrecy is sometimes sufficient. Being able to quantify the secrecy preserved by protocols is important in deciding if an adequate secrecy level can be achieved. In this paper, we have proposed the use of an information theoretical framework to measure the secrecy of protocols. Furthermore, we have analyzed three two-party scalar protocols to demonstrate the efficacy of our approach.

Finally, there are two interesting research directions worthy of further study. First, it would interesting and challenging to develop general analysis methodologies. So far, we have only investigated the linearly dependent relationship between secret input and messages. More tools are needed to analyze more complex protocols. The second interesting direction would be to explore possible tradeoffs between secrecy and other performance related measurements.

References

1. M. J. Atallah and W. Du. Secure multi-party computational geometry. *Lecture Notes in Computer Science*, 2125:165–179, 2000.
2. W. Du and M. J. Atallah. Privacy-preserving cooperative statistical analysis. In *Proceedings of the 17th Annual Computer Security Applications Conference*, pages 102–110, New Orleans, Louisiana, USA, December 2001.

3. W. Du and M. J. Atallah. Secure multi-party computation problems and their applications: A review and open problems. In *New Security Paradigms Workshop*, pages 11–20, Cloudcroft, New Mexico, USA, September 2001.
4. W. Du and Z. Zhan. Building decision tree classifier on private data, 2002.
5. W. Du and Z. Zhan. A practical approach to solve secure multi-party computation problems. In *Proceedings of New Security Paradigms Workshop*, Virginia Beach, virginia, USA, September 2002.
6. O. Goldreich. *Foundations of Cryptography Volume II Basic Aplications*. Cambridge, 2004.
7. O. Goldreich, S. Micali, and A. Wigderson. How to play any mental game, or: A completeness theorem for protocols with honest majority. In *Proc. 19th ACM Symposium on Theory of Computing*, pages 218–229, 1987.
8. M. Kantarcoglu and C. Clifton. Privacy-preserving distributed mining of association rules on horizontally partitioned data. *IEEE Transactions on Knowledge and Data Engineering*, 16(9):1026–1037, 2004.
9. Dahlia Malkhi, Noam Nisan, Benny Pinkas, and Yaron Sella. Fairplay — a secure two-party computation system. In *Proceedings of the 13th Symposium on Security, Usenix*, pages 287–302, 2004.
10. J. Vaidya and C. Clifton. Privacy preserving association rule mining in vertically partitioned data. In *The Eighth ACM SIGKDD International Conference on Knowledge Discovery and Data Mining*, pages 639–644, July 2002.
11. A. C. Yao. How to generate and exchange secrets. In *Proceedings of the 27rd Annual IEEE Symposium on Foundations of Computer Science*, pages 162–167, November 1986.

Reliable Scheduling of Advanced Transactions

Tai Xin, Yajie Zhu, and Indrakshi Ray

Department of Computer Science,
Colorado State University
{xin, zhuy, iray}@cs.colostate.edu

Abstract. The traditional transaction processing model is not suitable for many advanced applications, such as those having long duration or those consisting of co-operating activities. Researchers have addressed this problem by proposing various new transaction models capable of processing advanced transactions. Advanced transactions are characterized by having a number of component subtransactions whose execution is controlled by dependencies. The dependencies pose new challenges which must be addressed to ensure secure and reliable execution of advanced transactions. Violation of dependencies in advanced transactions could lead to unavailability of resources and information integrity problems. Although advanced transactions have received a lot of attention, not much work appears in addressing these issues. In this paper, we focus on the problem of scheduling advanced transactions. Specifically, we show how the different dependencies constrain the execution of the advanced transaction and give algorithms for scheduling advanced transactions that preserve the dependencies. Our scheduler is not confined to any specific advanced transaction processing model, but is capable of handling different kinds of advanced transactions, such as, Saga, Nested Transactions and Workflow.

1 Introduction

Driven by the need for designing high performance and non-traditional applications, a number of advanced transaction models [2,7,9,12,17,19] have been proposed in recent years as extensions to the traditional flat transaction model. These advanced transaction models, though differ in forms and applicable environments, have two common properties: made up of *long running activities* and containing *highly cooperative activities*. We refer to these activities as subtransactions in this paper. Subtransactions need to be coordinated to accomplish a specific task. The coordination among subtransactions is achieved through *dependencies*. Existing research work in advanced transactions, like ACTA [8] and ASSET [6], have discussed dependencies as means to characterize the semantics of interactions between subtransactions. Using these dependencies, different kinds of advanced transactions can be generated. Although a lot of research appears in advanced transactions, reliable scheduling and execution have not been adequately addressed.

Improper scheduling of subtransactions in an advanced transaction may result in integrity and availability problems. For instance, suppose there is a *begin on commit* dependency between subtransactions T_1 and T_2, which requires that T_2 cannot begin until T_1 commits. If the scheduler fails to enforce this dependency, then the integrity

S. Jajodia and D. Wijesekera (Eds.): Data and Applications Security 2005, LNCS 3654, pp. 124–138, 2005.

of the application may be compromised. As a second example, consider the existence of a strong commit dependency between subtransactions T_3 and T_4 that requires T_4 to commit if T_3 does so. Suppose the scheduler executes and commits T_3 before T_4. Later if T_4 needs to be aborted for some reason, then we have a complex situation: T_4 needs to abort as well as commit. In such a case, allowing T_4 to complete will cause integrity problems and keeping it incomplete raises issues pertaining to availability.

In this paper, we propose a solution that overcomes the problems mentioned above. We first evaluate the scheduling constraints imposed by each dependency. We discuss the data structures needed by the scheduler, and give the detailed algorithm. In some situations, each pair of subtransactions can be related by multiple dependencies. We show how our algorithm can be extended to handle such scenarios. Note that, our scheduler is extremely general – it can be used for processing any advanced transaction where the transaction can be decomposed into subtransactions that are co-ordinated through dependencies.

The rest of the paper is organized as follows. Section 2 defines our advanced transaction processing model and describes the different kinds of dependencies that may be associated with it. Section 3 describes the different data structures needed by our scheduler. Section 4 presents the details of how an advanced transaction is scheduled by our model. Section 5 discusses related work. Section 6 concludes the paper with pointers to future directions.

2   Our Model for Advanced Transactions

Our definition of advanced transaction is very general; it can be customized for different kinds of transaction models by restricting the type of dependencies that can exist among component subtransactions. An advanced transaction AT is specified by the set of subtransactions in AT, the dependencies between these subtransactions, and the completion sets to specify the complete execution states. All subtransactions specified in an advanced transaction may not execute or commit. A completion set gives the set of transactions that needs to be committed for successfully completing the advanced transaction. The application semantics decides which subtransactions constitute a completion set. The set of subtransactions that commit in an advanced transaction model may vary with different instantiations of the advanced transaction. Thus, an advanced transaction may have multiple completion sets. With this background, we are now ready to formally define our notion of advanced transaction.

Definition 1
[Advanced Transaction] An *advanced transaction* $AT = < S, D, C >$ is defined by S, which is the set of subtransactions in AT, D, which is the set of dependencies between the subtransactions in S, and C, which is the set of completion sets in AT. We assume that the set of dependencies in D do not conflict with each other.

Definition 2
[Subtransaction] A *subtransaction* T_i is the smallest logical unit of work in an advanced transaction. It consists of a set of data operations (read and write) and transac-

tion primitives; the begin, abort and commit primitives of subtransaction T_i are denoted by b_i, a_i and c_i respectively.

Definition 3
[Dependency] A *dependency* specified between a pair of subtransactions T_i and T_j expresses how the execution of a primitive (begin, commit, and abort) of T_i causes (or relates to) the execution of the primitives (begin, commit and abort) of another subtransaction T_j.

A set of dependencies has been defined in the work of ACTA [8]. A comprehensive list of transaction dependency definitions can be found in [3,6,8,14]. Summarizing all these dependencies in previous work, we collect a total of fourteen different types of dependencies. These are given below. In the following descriptions T_i and T_j refer to the transactions and b_i, c_i, a_i refer to the events of T_i that are present in some history H, and the notation $e_i \prec e_j$ denotes that event e_i precedes event e_j in the history H.

[Commit dependency] $(T_i \rightarrow_c T_j)$: If both T_i and T_j commit then the commitment of T_i precedes the commitment of T_j. Formally, $c_i \Rightarrow (c_j \Rightarrow (c_i \prec c_j))$.

[Strong commit dependency] $(T_i \rightarrow_{sc} T_j)$: If T_i commits then T_j also commits. Formally, $c_i \Rightarrow c_j$.

[Abort dependency] $(T_i \rightarrow_a T_j)$: If T_i aborts then T_j aborts. Formally, $a_i \Rightarrow a_j$.

[Termination dependency] $(T_i \rightarrow_t T_j)$: Subtransaction T_j cannot commit or abort until T_i either commits or aborts. Formally, $e_j \Rightarrow e_i \prec e_j$, where $e_i \in \{c_i, a_i\}$, $e_j \in \{c_j, a_j\}$.

[Exclusion dependency] $(T_i \rightarrow_{ex} T_j)$: If T_i commits and T_j has begun executing, then T_j aborts. Formally, $c_i \Rightarrow (b_j \Rightarrow a_j)$.

[Force-commit-on-abort dependency] $(T_i \rightarrow_{fca} T_j)$: If T_i aborts, T_j commits. Formally, $a_i \Rightarrow c_j$.

[Force-begin-on-commit/abort/begin/termination dependency] $(T_i \rightarrow_{fbc/fba/fbb/fbt} T_j)$: Subtransaction T_j must begin if T_i commits(aborts/begins/terminates). Formally, $c_i(a_i/b_i/T_i) \Rightarrow b_j$.

[Begin dependency] $(T_i \rightarrow_b T_j)$: Subtransaction T_j cannot begin execution until T_i has begun. Formally, $b_j \Rightarrow (b_i \prec b_j)$.

[Serial dependency] $(T_i \rightarrow_s T_j)$: Subtransaction T_j cannot begin execution until T_i either commits or aborts. Formally, $b_j \Rightarrow (e_i \prec b_j)$ where $e_i \in \{c_i, a_i\}$.

[Begin-on-commit dependency] $(T_i \rightarrow_{bc} T_j)$: Subtransaction T_j cannot begin until T_i commits. Formally, $b_j \Rightarrow (c_i \prec b_j)$.

[Begin-on-abort dependency] $(T_i \rightarrow_{ba} T_j)$: Subtransaction T_j cannot begin until T_i aborts. Formally, $b_j \Rightarrow (a_i \prec b_j)$.

Let's see an example of an advanced transaction below.

Example 1
Let $AT =< S, D, C >$ be an advanced transaction where $S = \{T_1, T_2, T_3, T_4\}$, $D = \{T_1 \rightarrow_{bc} T_2, T_1 \rightarrow_{bc} T_3, T_2 \rightarrow_{ex} T_3, T_2 \rightarrow_a T_4\}$, and $C = \{\{T_1, T_2, T_4\}, \{T_1, T_3\}\}$. Thus, this transaction has two complete execution states: $\{T_1, T_2, T_4\}$ and $\{T_1, T_3\}$. The advanced transaction can be represented graphically as shown in Figure 1.

A real world example of such a transaction may be a workflow associated with making travel arrangements: The subtransactions perform the following tasks. T_1 – Reserve a ticket on Airlines A; T_2 – Purchase the Airlines A ticket; T_3 – Cancels the reservation, and T_4 – Reserves a room in Resort C. There is a *begin-on-commit* dependency between T_1 and T_2 and also between T_1 and T_3. This means that neither T_2 or T_3 can start before T_1 has committed. This ensures that the airlines ticket cannot be purchased or canceled before a reservation has been made. The *exclusion* dependency between T_2 and T_3 ensures that either T_2 can commit or T_3 can commit but not both. In other words, either the airlines ticket must be purchased or the airlines reservation canceled, but not both. And, there is an *abort* dependency between T_4 and T_2 - This means that if T_2 aborts then T_4 must abort. In other words, if the resort room cannot be reserved, then the airlines ticket should not be purchased.

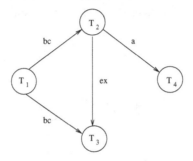

Fig. 1. Dependencies in the Advanced Transaction of Example 1

Sometimes one single dependency is not adequate for specifying the relationship between two subtransactions. For example, if we want to specify that (i) T_1 must begin after T_2 has committed and (ii) if T_2 aborts then T_1 must also abort. In such cases, a single dependency is not sufficient for expressing the co-ordination relationship between T_1 and T_2. A *composite dependency* is needed under this situation. A composite dependency contains two or more primitive dependencies which are applied towards the same pair of subtransactions. The single dependencies will be henceforth referred to as *primitive dependencies*. For example, the above two primitive could generate a composite dependency: $T_2 \rightarrow_{fbc,a} T_1$.

Definition 4
[**Composite Dependency**] A composite dependency between a pair of subtransactions T_i, T_j in an advanced transaction, denoted by $T_i \rightarrow_{d_1,d_2,...,d_n} T_j$, is obtained by combining two or more primitive dependencies $d_1, d_2, \ldots, d_n$. The effect of the composite dependency is the conjunction of the constraints imposed by the individual dependencies $d_1, d_2, \ldots, d_n$.

Note that, the constraints placed by the individual primitive dependencies might conflict with each other. In this paper, we assume that the advanced transaction specification does not have such conflicts.

2.1   Execution Model

Having presented the structural model of the advanced transaction, we now present our execution model. A subtransaction can be at different states during its lifetime. Rusinkiewicz and Sheth have discussed the states of workflow tasks in a similar manner [17]. In this paper, our approach will extend the their work. We will have the *unscheduled* state to identify that a subtransaction has not been submitted, and, we will require the subtransactions being hold in *prepare* state and cannot transit to final (commit or abort) state until the dependencies have been satisfied.

Definition 5

[State of a subtransaction] A subtransaction T_i can be in any of the following states: *unscheduled (un_i), initiation (in_i), execution (ex_i), prepare (pr_i)* (means prepare to commit), *committed (cm_i)* and *aborted (ab_i)*. Execution of subtransaction primitives causes a subtransaction to change its state. Detailed state transition diagrams are shown in figure 2.

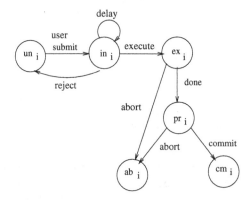

Fig. 2. States of subtransaction T_i

Below we formally define each state, and describe how and when state transitions take place.

- **unscheduled** (un_i), means a subtransaction (T_i) is not sent to a scheduler. At this point, a scheduler can do nothing about it.
- **initiation** (in_i), After subtransaction (T_i) is sent to the scheduler, its state changes to initiation. Now it is waiting to be executed. Later the scheduler can execute, delay or reject this subtransaction.
- **execution** (ex_i), a subtransaction (T_i) moves from initiation state to execution state by executing the begin primitive. When a subtransaction is in the execution state, the only way a scheduler can control it is by aborting the subtransaction.
- **prepare** (pr_i), After a subtransaction (T_i) finishes its execution and ready to commit, it is in the prepare state. At this point, a scheduler can determine whether the subtransaction should commit or abort.

- **committed** (cm_i), means a subtransaction (T_i) has committed.
- **aborted** (ab_i), means a subtransaction (T_i) has aborted. There are two ways to enter the aborted state. When a subtransaction is in the execution state, it may be aborted. Also when it is in the prepare state, the scheduler can abort it.

The aborted state and the committed states are called the final states. When a subtransaction has reached the final state, the scheduler can no longer change its state.

A reliable scheduler of an advanced transaction must be able to complete all the necessary subtransactions in an advanced transaction and not cause any dependency violation. A subtransaction that is never terminated but remains active even after the transaction has terminated is called an orphan subtransaction.

Definition 6

[Reliable Scheduling] The scheduling of an advanced transaction is *reliable* if it satisfies the following constraints.

1. all dependency constraints of the advanced transaction must be satisfied;
2. when execution completes, each subtransaction must be in final state (a committed/aborted state) or unscheduled state. In other words, when execution of an advanced transaction completes, there should be no orphan subtransaction. Notice that an orphan subtransaction will hold resources and possibly cause availability problems.

The above conditions are necessary to avoid availability and integrity problems caused by the advanced transaction.

3   Data Structures Required by the Scheduler

Before giving the details of the algorithm, we describe the data structures needed by our algorithm.

3.1   Scheduling Action Table for Primitive Dependencies

The actions to be taken by the scheduler in order to correctly enforce a dependency of the form $T_i \rightarrow_x T_j$ depends on the type of dependency existing between T_i and T_j and the states of T_i and T_j. This information is stored in the *scheduling action table*. For each dependency of the form $T_i \rightarrow_x T_j$, we construct a scheduling action table TB_x. This table has six rows and six columns corresponding to the different states of T_i and T_j respectively. An entry in this table is denoted as $EN_x(i, j)$ where i represents a state of the subtransaction (T_i), and j represents a state of the subtransaction (T_j). The entry $EN_x(i, j)$ can have the following values:

1. *no restriction*, shown as '−' in the table, means that the scheduler need not impose any restriction for the state transitions of the two subtransactions T_i and T_j. The subtransactions T_i or T_j can go into the next state without any restriction.
2. *delay* $T_i(T_j)$ means that the subtransaction $T_i(T_j)$ cannot make a state transition at this stage. It must wait at the current state until the other subtransaction $T_j(T_i)$ has entered another state.

3. *execute* $T_i(T_j)$ means that the subtransaction $T_i(T_j)$ must be executed.
4. *abort* $T_i(T_j)$ means that the subtransaction $T_i(T_j)$ must be aborted.
5. *reject* $T_i(T_j)$ means that the subtransaction $T_i(T_j)$ will be rejected instead of being scheduled for execution. This entry is only possible when subtransaction $T_i(T_j)$ is in its initiation state.
6. *prohibited*, shown as '/' in the table, means it is not possible for the subtransactions to be in the corresponding states simultaneously because of this dependency.
7. *final states*, shown as 'final' in the table, means both the subtransactions are in the final state. No further state transitions are possible.

The dependency scheduling tables specify the necessary actions that must be taken by the scheduler to ensure the satisfaction of all dependencies. For lack of space, we do not give the tables for all the dependencies. Table 1 shows the scheduling action table for the strong commit dependency.

Table 1. Scheduling action table for *strong commit* dependency

action	un_j	in_j	ex_j	pr_j	cm_j	ab_j
un_i	–	–	–	–	–	–
in_i	–	–	–	–	–	–
ex_i	–	–	–	–	–	abort T_i
pr_i	delay T_i	delay T_i	delay T_i	delay T_i	–	abort T_i
cm_i	/	/	/	/	final	/
ab_i	–	–	–	–	final	final

The first row of the table specifies the actions to be taken when T_i is in the unscheduled state. In this row all the entries are marked with '–' indicating that the scheduler does not impose any constraint on T_i or T_j changing states. The entry in the third row, last column (that is, $EN(ex_i, ab_j)$) is an 'abort T_i'. This means that when T_i is in the execution state, and T_j is aborted, then T_i must be aborted as well. The entry in the fourth row, first column (that is, $EN(pr_i, un_j)$) is 'delay T_i'. This means that when T_i is in the prepare state and T_j is unscheduled, T_i must wait in the prepare stage. The entry in the fifth row, first column (that is, $EN(cm_i, un_j)$) is '/'. This means that the scheduler will not allow this to happen. The entry in the fifth row, fifth column (that is, $EN(cm_i, cm_j)$) is 'final'. This means that both the transactions have reached their final states, and the scheduler need not do anything more.

The following ensures the correctness of our scheduling action table. For lack of space, we omit the proof.

Lemma 1. *The scheduler by taking the actions listed in the scheduling action tables for the primitive dependencies can enforce the dependencies correctly.*

3.2   Scheduling Action Table for Composite Dependencies

Based on the dependency scheduling action tables for all primitive dependencies, we propose an algorithm to create scheduling table for composite dependencies. This table is called the *composite dependency scheduling table*. The composite dependency scheduling table for the composite dependency consisting of primitive dependencies x, y, and z is denoted by $TBC_{x,y,z}$.

In determining the proper actions for a composite dependency, we need to combine the entries from two or more scheduling action tables of the component primitive dependencies. To obtain the correct action from these different entry items, we need to define the *priority* for each type of scheduling actions in the primitive scheduling action table. The different actions are prioritized in the following order: "prohibited", "reject", "abort", "delay", "execute", and "no restriction", where "prohibited" signifies the highest priority and "no restriction" signifies the least priority. We use the notation $>$ to describe the priority ordering. For instance, "prohibited $>$ reject" means that "prohibited" has a higher priority than "reject". In combining the actions of two or more primitive dependency tables, the scheduler will choose the table entry with the highest priority, and set this entry as the action for the composite dependency. For example, when a scheduler finds "no restriction" in one execution table and a "delay" entry in other scheduling table, it will take the "delay" entry as the action for the composite dependency.

We next give the algorithm to combine the scheduling tables and determine the correct actions for the composite dependency. To combine the scheduling tables of two (or more) primitive dependencies, we compare the corresponding table entries and choose the action that satisfies the constraints of all component dependencies.

Algorithm 1
Creating Composite Dependency Scheduling Table

Input: (i) $T_i \rightarrow_{d_1, d_2, \dots, d_n} T_j$ – the composite dependency composed of the primitive dependencies $d_1, d_2, \dots, \dots d_n$ and (ii) **TB** $= \{TB_{d_1}, TB_{d_2}, \dots, TB_{d_n}\}$ – the scheduling action tables for the primitive dependencies

Output: Scheduling action table TBC for this composite dependency.

begin

    for each state (S_i) of subtransaction $(T_i) \in \{un_i, in_i, ex_i, pr_i, ab_i, cm_i\}$

        for each state (S_j) of subtransaction $(T_j) \in \{un_j, in_j, ex_j, pr_j, ab_j, cm_j\}$

        begin

            /* initialization */

            $EN_{TBC}(S_i, S_j) =$ "–"

            set $max_p =$ "–"

            /* get every component dependency's scheduling table entry */

            for every primitive dependency d_k in this composite dependency

            begin

                access the scheduling action table TB_k for this dependency d_k

                get the corresponding entry $EN_k(S_i, S_j)$

                /* finding the highest priority entry in these dependencies */

                if $EN_k(S_i, S_j) > max_p$

                    $max_p = EN_k(S_i, S_j)$

            end for

            $EN_{TBC}(S_i, S_j) = max_p$

        end for

end

We next show that, with the priority assignment, the above algorithm could be able to ensure the satisfaction of all primitive dependencies in a composite dependency.

Lemma 2. *The scheduler can enforce composite dependencies correctly.*

3.3 State Table and Job Queue

The scheduler during the execution of advanced transactions maintains some dynamic data structures called *state tables*. A state table is created for each advanced transaction that has been submitted by the user. The state table records the execution states of the subtransactions in an advanced transaction while it is being executed. Whenever a subtransaction of this advanced transaction changes state, the corresponding entry in the state table is updated. When the advanced transaction terminates, the state table is deleted.

The *job queue* is another dynamic data structure that is needed by the scheduler. The job queue holds subtransactions that have been submitted by the user but which are not being currently executed. The jobs submitted by a user is initially placed in the job queue. Also, when a subtransaction needs to wait before being processed further, it is placed in the job queue. In other words, subtransactions in the initiation state or prepare state are placed in this job queue. When the subtransaction in the initiation (prepare) state is ready to execute (commit), it is removed from this queue.

4   Execution of an Advanced Transaction

In this section we describe how an advanced transaction is executed. The advanced transaction is executed in three stages: (i) Preparation Stage, (ii) Execution Stage, and (iii) Termination Stage. These stages are described in the following subsections.

4.1   Preparation Stage

In this stage, the user submits the advanced transaction for execution. After receiving the input from the user, a state table is created for this advanced transaction. The entries for each subtransaction in this state table is initialized to *initiation*. The subtransactions are placed in the job queue for later execution. When the user has completed submitting subtransactions for the advanced transaction, the advanced transaction moves into the execution stage. The following algorithm summarizes the work done in the preparation stage.

Algorithm 2
InputAdvancedTransaction
Input: (i) $AT_t = < S, D, C >$ – the advanced transaction.

Procedure InputAdvancedTransaction(AT_t)
begin
      receive the input $AT_t = < S, D, C >$
      create $StateTable_t$
      for each $T_i \in S$

begin

      $StateTable_t[T_i] = initiation$ /* set initial states for subtransactions */

      enQueue(JobQueue, T_i)   /* insert in the job queue */

   end for

end

4.2   Execution Stage

In this stage, the subtransactions submitted by the user get executed. When the scheduler gets a subtransaction, it first looks into the advanced transaction specification to find out all dependencies associated with it. For each dependency, the scheduler identifies the states of the two involved subtransactions. The scheduler then accesses the dependency scheduling action table, and gets the required action for the subtransactions. The action can be one of the following: allow the subtransaction to commit/abort, send the subtransaction to execute, delay the subtransaction, or reject the subtransaction. If the action causes the subtransaction to change state, the state table entry corresponding to this subtransaction may need to be modified. The following algorithm formalizes the actions taken in this stage.

Algorithm 3

Execution Stage

Input: (i) $AT_t = < S, D, C >$ – the advanced transaction that must be executed and (ii) **TB** – the set of primitive and composite scheduling action tables associated with the dependencies of the advanced transaction AT_t.

Procedure ExecuteAdvancedTransaction(AT_t, **TB**)

begin

    while(TRUE)

    begin

        $T_i = $ deQueue(JobQueue)   /* get the job from the job queue */

        $Action = $ getAction(T_i, AT_t, **TB**)

        if $Action = wait$

          enQueue(JobQueue, T_i)   /* insert in queue */

        else if $Action = abort$

          abort T_i

          $StateTable_t[T_i] = aborted$

        else if $Action = reject$

          $StateTable_t[T_i] = unscheduled$

        else if $Action = -$ /* no restriction for T_i */

        begin

          if $StateTable_t[T_i] = initiation$

            send (T_i) to execute   /* execute the operations for T_i */

            $StateTable_t[T_i] = executing$

          else if $StateTable_t[T_i] = executing$

            get execution results

            if execution result is $completed$ /* operations completed */

$$StateTable_t[T_i] = prepare$$
$$enQueue(JobQueue, T_i)$$
                     else if execution failed   /* operations failed */
$$StateTable_t[T_i] = aborted$$
                else if $StateTable_t[T_i] = prepare$
                  commit T_i
$$StateTable_t[T_i] = committed$$

      end
    end while
end

The above algorithm makes a call *getAction* to get the action that must be taken by the scheduler. We next describe the algorithm *getAction* that describes how the scheduler determines an action for scheduling a submitted subtransaction (T_i), focusing on ensuring the dependency constrains associated with T_i. We assume that the primitive and composite dependency tables that will be needed by this advanced transaction have already been created.

Algorithm 4
Get Action From ActionTables
Input: (i) T_i – the subtransaction for which the action must be determined, and (ii) $AT_t = <S, D, C>$ – the advanced transaction whose subtransaction is T_i, and (iii) **TB** – the set of primitive and composite scheduling action tables associated with the dependencies of the advanced transaction AT_t.
Output: The action the scheduler should take to for subtransaction T_i

Procedure getAction(T_i, AT_t, **TB**)
begin
    $ACTION = '-'$ /* Initialize ACTION */
    /* find out all the dependencies associated with T_i */
    for every dependency $T_m \rightarrow_d T_n \in D$
    begin
        if $(T_i \neq T_m)$ **AND** $(T_i \neq T_n)$
            skip this round, and continue to next round
        else /* this dependency is associated with T_i */
        begin
            if $(T_i = T_n)$ /* d is a dependency pointed to T_i */
                /* get the state of the subtransactions */
                let $S_y = StateTable_t[T_i]$
                let $S_x = StateTable_t[T_m]$
            else if $(T_i = T_m)$ /* d is a dependency that T_i lead out */
                /* get the state of the subtransactions */
                let $S_x = StateTable_t[T_i]$
                let $S_y = StateTable_t[T_n]$
            access the corresponding dependency scheduling table TB_d
            locate the corresponding entry $EN_d(x, y)$ according to the states
            if $EN_d(x, y) > ACTION$ /* check the priority */

$$ACTION = EN_d(x, y);$$
   end
  end
  return *ACTION*;
end

4.3 Termination Stage

When all the subtransactions of an advanced transaction have completed execution, the advanced transaction must be terminated. From the state tables, we find out the set of executing, committed and prepared subtransactions. If the set of prepared or executing subtransactions is not empty, then we return the message not terminated. Otherwise, we check whether the set of committed transactions correspond to one of the completion sets specified in the advanced transaction. If so, we return a successful termination message, otherwise we return an unsuccessful termination message. Once the advanced transaction is terminated, the state table corresponding to the advanced transaction is deleted.

Algorithm 5
Termination Stage
Input: (i) $AT_t = < S, D, C >$ – the advanced transaction whose termination is being determined.
Output: (i) result indicating whether the advanced transaction terminated successfully or not.

Procedure TerminateAdvancedTransaction(AT_t)
begin
  executing = *prepared* = *committed* = $\{\}$
  for each subtransaction $T_i \in S$
  begin
    if $StateTable_t[T_i] = committed$
    committed = *committed* $\cup T_i$
    else if $StateTable_t[T_i] = executing$
    executing = *executing* $\cup T_i$
    else if $StateTable_t[T_i] = prepared$
    prepared = *prepared* $\cup T_i$
  end
  /* check whether there are active subtransactions for AT_t */
  if *prepared* $\neq \{\}$ OR *committed* $\neq \{\}$
   return 'not terminated'
  else /* all subtransactions are finished */
  begin
    Delete $StateTable_t$
    /* check whether it matches some completion set */
    for each $C_i \in C$
    begin

if $(C_i = committed)$
        return 'terminated successfully'
end
/* none of the termination states are satisfied */
return 'terminated unsuccessfully'
    end
end

The following theorem ensures the correctness of the mechanisms.

Theorem 1
The mechanism described above ensures reliable scheduling as per Definition 6.

5 Related Work

In the past two decades, a variety of transaction models and technologies supporting advanced transaction have been proposed. Examples are ACTA [8], ConTracts [16], nested transactions [12], ASSET [6], EJB and CORBA object transaction services [13], workflow management systems [1], concurrency control in advanced databases [5] etc. Chrysanthis and Ramamrithan introduce ACTA [8], as a formal framework for specifying extended transaction models. ACTA allows intuitive and precise specification of extended transaction models by characterizing the semantics of interactions between transactions in terms of different dependencies between transactions, and in terms of transaction's effects on data objects. However, impacts of dependencies on reliable execution of advanced transactions are not discussed in ACTA.

Mancini, Ray, Jajodia and Bertino have proposed the notion of multiform transactions [11]. A multiform transaction consists of a set of transactions and includes the definition of a set of termination dependencies among these transactions. The set of dependencies specifies the commit, abort relationship among the component transactions. The multiform transaction is organized as a set of coordinate blocks. The coordinate block, along with the corresponding coordinator module (CM) can manage the execution of the transactions.

A workflow involves different computational and business activities which are coordinated through dependencies. Thus, we can consider a workflow as a type of advanced transaction. The importance of workflow models is increasing rapidly due to its suitability in the business application. For these reasons, a lot of research appears in workflow management systems [1,3,10,15].

Singh has discussed the semantical inter-task dependencies on workflows [18]. The author used algebra format to express the dependencies and analyze their properties and semantics in workflow systems. Attie at el. [4] discussed means to specify and enforce intertask dependencies. They illustrate each task as a set of significant events (start, commit, rollback, abort). Intertask dependencies limit the occurrence of such events and specify a temporal order among them. In an earlier work, Rusinkiewicz and Sheth [17] have discussed the specification and execution issues of transactional workflows. They have described the different states of tasks in execution for a workflow system.

They also discussed different scheduling approaches, like: scheduler based on predicate Petri Nets models, scheduling using logically parallel language, or using temporal propositional logic. Another contribution of their paper is that they discussed the issues of concurrent execution of workflows - global serializability and global commitment of workflow systems. However, none of these papers address the scheduling actions needed to satisfy the dependency constraints.

6   Conclusion and Future Work

An advanced transaction is composed of a number of cooperating subtransactions that are coordinated by dependencies. The dependencies make the advanced transaction more flexible and powerful. However, incorrect enforcement of dependencies can lead to integrity and availability problems. In this paper, we looked at how the subtransactions of an advanced transaction can be scheduled, such that the dependencies are not violated.

The constraints between the subtransactions of an advanced transaction must be maintained during recovery as well. In future, we would like to investigate how the dependencies impact the recovery algorithms and design a mechanism that is suitable for the recovery of advanced transactions. In future, we also plan to design mechanisms that will allow advanced transactions to recover from malicious attacks.

Acknowledgment

This work is partially supported by National Science Foundation under grant number IIS 0242258.

References

1. Gustavo Alonso, Divyakant Agrawal, Amr El Abbadi, Mohan Kamath, Roger G., and C. Mohan. Advanced Transaction Models in Workflow Contexts. In *In Proceedings of ICDE 1996*, pages 574–581, 1996.
2. M. Ansari, L. Ness, M. Rusinkiewicz, and A. Sheth. Using Flexible Transactions to Support Multi-System Telecommunication Applications. In *Proceeding of the 18th International Conference on Very Large DataBases*, August 1992.
3. V. Atluri, W-K. Huang, and E. Bertino. An Execution Model for Multilevel Secure Workflows. In *11th IFIP Working Conference on Database Security and Database Security, XI: Status and Prospects*, pages 151–165, August 1997.
4. Paul C. Attie, Munindar P. Singh, Amit P. Sheth, and Marek Rusinkiewicz. Specifying and enforcing intertask dependencies. In *19th International Conference on Very Large Data Bases, August 24-27, 1993, Dublin, Ireland, Proceedings*, pages 134–145. Morgan Kaufmann, 1993.
5. Naser S. Barghouti and Gail E. Kaiser. Concurrency control in advanced database applications. *ACM Computing Surveys*, 23(3):269–317, September 1991.
6. A. Biliris, S. Dar, N. Gehani, H.V. Jagadish, and K. Ramamritham. ASSET: A System for Supporting Extended Transactions. In *Proceedings of ACM SIGMOD International Coference on Management of Data*, May 1994.

7. P. K. Chrysanthis and K. Ramamritham. Synthesis of Extended Transaction Models Using ACTA. *ACM Transactions on Database Systems*, 19:450–491, September 1994.
8. Panayiotis K. Chrysanthis. ACTA, A Framework for Modeling and Reasoning about Extended Transactions Models. Ph.D. Thesis, September 1991.
9. U. Dayal, M. Hsu, and R.Ladin. Organizing Long-Running Activities with Triggers and Transactions. In *Proceeding of the 17th International Conference on Very Large DataBases*, September 1991.
10. D. Hollingsworth. Workflow Reference Model. Technical report, Workflow Management Coalition, Brussels, Belgium, 1994.
11. L. V. Mancini, I. Ray, S. Jajodia, and E. Bertino. Flexible transaction dependencies in database systems. *Distributed and Parallel Databases*, 8:399–446, 2000.
12. J. E. Moss. Nested Transactions: an approach to reliable distributed computing. PhD Thesis 260, MIT, Cambridge, MA, April 1981.
13. OMG. Additional Structuring Mechanisms for the OTS Specification. OMG, Document ORBOS, 2000-04-02, Sept. 2000.
14. M. Prochazka. Extending transactions in enterprise javabeans. Tech. Report No. 2000/3, Dep. of SW Engineering, Charles University, Prague, January 2000.
15. Indrakshi Ray, Tai Xin, and Yajie Zhu. Ensuring Task Dependencies During Workflow Recovery. In *Proceedings of the Fifteenth International Conference on Database and Expert Systems*, Aug. 2004.
16. A. Reuter. Contracts: A means for extending control beyond transaction boundaries. In *3rd International Workshop on High Performance Transaction Systems*, Sept. 1989.
17. Marek Rusinkiewicz and Amit P. Sheth. Specification and execution of transactional workflows. In *Modern Database Systems 1995*, pages 592–620, 1995.
18. Munindar P. Singh. Semantical considerations on workflows: An algebra for intertask dependencies. In *Proceedings of the Fifth International Workshop on Database Programming Languages*, Electronic Workshops in Computing. Springer, 1995.
19. Helmut Wuchter and Andreas Reuter. The ConTract Model. In *Database Transaction Models for Advanced Applications, A. K. Elmagarmid Ed., Morgan Kaufmann Publishers*, pages 219–263, 1992.

Privacy-Preserving Decision Trees over Vertically Partitioned Data*

Jaideep Vaidya[1] and Chris Clifton[2]

[1] MSIS Department, Rutgers University, Newark, NJ 07102
jsvaidya@rbs.rutgers.edu
http://cimic.rutgers.edu/~jsvaidya
[2] Department of Computer Science, Purdue University,
West Lafayette, IN 47907
clifton@cs.purdue.edu
http://www.cs.purdue.edu/people/clifton

Abstract. Privacy and security concerns can prevent sharing of data, derailing data mining projects. Distributed knowledge discovery, if done correctly, can alleviate this problem. In this paper, we tackle the problem of classification. We introduce a generalized privacy preserving variant of the ID3 algorithm for vertically partitioned data distributed over two or more parties. Along with the algorithm, we give a complete proof of security that gives a tight bound on the information revealed.

1 Introduction

There has been growing interest in privacy-preserving data mining since the seminal papers in 2000 [1,2]. Classification is one of the most ubiquitous data mining problems found in real life. Decision tree classification is one of the best known solution approaches. ID3, first proposed by Quinlan[3] is a particularly elegant and intuitive solution. This paper presents an algorithm for privately building an ID3 decision tree. While this has been done for horizontally partitioned data [4], we present an algorithm for *vertically partitioned* data: a portion of each instance is present at each site, but no site contains complete information for any instance. This problem has been addressed[5], but the solution is limited to the case where both parties have the class attribute. In addition, both the previous methods are limited to two parties. The method presented here works for any number of parties, and the class attribute (or other attributes) need be known only to one party. Our method is trivially extendible to the simplified case where all parties know the class attribute.

There has been other work in privacy-preserving data mining. One approach is to add "noise" to the data before the data mining process, and using techniques that mitigate the impact of the noise from the data mining results[1,6,7,8]. However, recently there has been debate about the security properties of such algorithms [9].

---

* This material is based upon work supported by the National Science Foundation under Grant No. 0312357.

S. Jajodia and D. Wijesekera (Eds.): Data and Applications Security 2005, LNCS 3654, pp. 139–152, 2005.
© IFIP International Federation for Information Processing 2005

Other work follows the secure multiparty computation approach found in cryptography, achieving "perfect" privacy, i.e., nothing is learned that could not be deduced from one's own data and the results. This includes Lindell's work [2], as well as work on association rule mining [10,11,12,13], clustering [14,15], and some work on classification [16,5]. While some of this work makes trade-offs between efficiency and information disclosure, all maintain provable privacy of individual information and bounds on disclosure, and disclosure is limited to information that is unlikely to be of practical concern.

Privacy preservation can mean many things: Protecting specific individual values, breaking the link between values and the individual they apply to, protecting source, etc. This paper aims for a high standard of privacy: Not only individual entities are protected, but to the extent feasible even the schema (attributes and possible attribute values) are protected from disclosure. Our goal is for each site to disclose as little as possible, while still constructing a valid tree in a time suitable for practical application.

To this end, all that is revealed is the basic structure of the tree (e.g., the number of branches at each node, corresponding to the number of distinct values for an attribute; the depth of each subtree) and which site is responsible for the decision made at each node (i.e., which site possesses the attribute used to make the decision, but not what attribute is used, or even what attributes the site possesses.) This allows for efficient *use* of the tree to classify an object; otherwise using the tree would require a complex cryptographic protocol involving every party at every *possible* level to evaluate the class of an object without revealing who holds the attribute used at that level. Each site also learns the count of classes at some interior nodes (although only the class site knows the mapping to actual classes – other sites don't even know if a class with 30% distribution at one node is the same class as one with a 60% distribution at a lower node, except to the extent that this can be deduced from the tree and it's own attributes.) At the leaf nodes, this is desirable: one often wants probability estimates, not simply a predicted class. As knowing the count of transactions at each leaf node would enable computing distributions throughout the tree anyway, this really doesn't disclose much *new* information.

We now go directly into the algorithm for creating a tree. In Section 3 we describe how the tree (distributed between sites) is used to classify an instance, even though the attribute values of the instance to be classified are also private and distributed between sites. Section 4 formalizes what it means to be secure, and gives a proof that the algorithms presented are secure. Section 5 presents the computation and communication complexity of the algorithm. Section 6 discusses future work and concludes the paper.

2   Privacy-Preserving ID3: Creating the Tree

The basic ID3 algorithm[3] is given in Algorithm 1. We will introduce our distributed privacy-preserving version by running through this algorithm, describing pieces as appropriate. We then give the full algorithm in Algorithm 7. Note

---

Algorithm 1. ID3(R,C,T) tree learning algorithm

Require: R, the set of attributes
Require: C, the class attribute
Require: T, the set of transactions
1: **if** R is empty **then**
2:    return a leaf node, with class value assigned to most transactions in T
3: **else if** all transactions in T have the same class c **then**
4:    return a leaf node with the class c
5: **else**
6:    Determine the attribute A that best classifies the transactions in T
7:    Let $a_1, \ldots, a_m$ be the values of attribute A. Partition T into the m partitions
      $T(a_1), \ldots, T(a_m)$ such that every transaction in $T(a_i)$ has the attribute value a_i.
8:    Return a tree whose root is labeled A (this is the test attribute) and has m
      edges labeled $a_1, \ldots, a_m$ such that for every i, the edge a_i goes to the tree
      $ID3(R - A, C, T(a_i))$.
9: **end if**

---

that for our distributed algorithm, no site knows R, instead each site i knows its own attributes R_i. Only one site knows the class attribute C. In vertical partitioning, every site knows a *projection* of the transactions $\Pi_{R_i} T$. Each projection includes a transaction identifier that serves as a join key.

We first check if R is empty. This is based on Secure Sum[17,10], and is given in Algorithm 2. Basically, the first party adds a random r to its count of remaining items. This is passed to all sites, each adding its count. The last

---

Algorithm 2. IsREmpty(): Are any attributes left?

Require: k sites P_i (the site calling the function is P_1; any other site can be P_k), each with a flag $AR_i = 0$ if no remaining attributes, $AR_i = 1$ if P_i has attributes remaining.
Require: a commutative encryption function E with domain size $m > k$.
1: P_1 chooses a random integer r uniformly from $0 \ldots m - 1$.
2: P_1 sends $r + AR_1$ to P_2
3: **for** $i = 2..k - 1$ **do**
4:    Site P_i receives r' from P_{i-1}.
5:    P_i sends $r' + AR_i$ mod m to P_{i+1}
6: **end for**
7: Site P_k receives r' from P_{k-1}.
8: $r' \leftarrow r' + AR_k$ mod m
9: P_1 and P_k create secure keyed commutative hash keys E_1 and E_k
10: P_1 sends $E_1(r)$ to P_k
11: P_k receives $E_1(r)$ and sends $E_k(E_1(r))$ and $E_k(r')$ to P_1
12: P_1 returns $E_1(E_k(r')) = E_k(E_1(r))$ $\{\Leftrightarrow r' = r \Leftrightarrow \sum_{j=1}^{k} AR_i = 0 \Leftrightarrow 0$ attributes remain $\}$

---

site and first then use commutative encryption to compare the final value to r (without revealing either) – if they are the same, R is empty.

Line 2 requires determining the majority class for a node, when only one site knows the class. This is accomplished with a protocol for securely determining the cardinality of set intersection. Many protocols for doing so are known [13,18,19]. We assume that one of these protocols is used. Each site determines which of its transactions *might* reach that node of the tree. The intersection of these sets with the transactions in a particular class gives the number of transactions that reach that point in the tree, enabling the class site to determine the distribution and majority class; it returns a (leaf) node identifier that allows it to map back to this distribution.

To formalize this, we introduce the notion of a *Constraint Set*. As the tree is being built, each party i keeps track of the values of its attributes used to reach that point in the tree in a filter $Constraints_i$. Initially, this is all don't care values ('?'). However, when an attribute A_{ij} at site i is used (lines 6-7 of id3), entry j in $Constraints_i$ is set to the appropriate value before recursing to build the subtree. An example is given in Figure 1. The site has 6 attributes $A_1, \ldots, A_6$. The constraint tuple shows that the only transactions valid for this transaction are those with a value of 5 for A_1, *high* for A_2, and *warm* for A_5. The other attributes have a value of ? since they do not factor into the selection of an instance. Formally, we define the following functions:

A_1	A_2	A_3	A_4	A_5	A_6
5	high	?	?	warm	?

Fig. 1. A constraint tuple for a single site

Constraints.set($attr, val$): Set the value of attribute $attr$ to val in the local constraints set. The special value '?' signifies a don't-care condition.

satisfies: x *satisfies* $Constraints_i$ if and only if the attribute values of the instance are compatible with the constraint tuple: $\forall i, (A_i(x) = v \Leftrightarrow Constraints(A_i) = v) \vee Constraints(A_i) = $ '?'.

FormTransSet: *Function* $FormTransSet(Constraints)$: *Return local transactions meeting constraints*

1: $Y = \emptyset$
2: **for all** transaction id $i \in T$ **do**
3:    **if** t_i satisfies $Constraints$ **then**
4:        $Y \leftarrow Y \cup \{i\}$
5:    **end if**
6: **end for**
7: return Y

Now, we determine the majority class (and class distributions) by computing for each class $\bigcap_{i=1..k} Y_i$, where Y_k includes a constraint on the class value. This is given in Algorithm 3.

Algorithm 3. DistributionCounts(): Compute class distribution given current constraints

---

Require: k sites P_i with local constraint sets $Constraints_i$
1: **for all** sites P_i except P_k **do**
2:     at P_i: $Y_i \leftarrow FormTransSet(Constraints_i)$
3: **end for**
4: **for** each class $c_1, \ldots, c_p$ **do**
5:     at P_k: $Constraints_k.set(C, c_i)$ {To include the class restriction}
6:     at P_k: $Y_k \leftarrow FormTransSet(Constraints_k)$
7:     $cnt_i \leftarrow |Y_1 \cap \ldots \cap Y_k|$ using the cardinality of set intersection protocol ([13,18,19])
8: **end for**
9: **return** $(cnt_1, \ldots, cnt_p)$

The next issue is determining if all transactions have the same class (Algorithm 1 line 3). If all are not the same class, as little information as possible should be disclosed. For efficiency, we do allow the class site to learn the count of classes even if this is an interior node; since it could compute this from the counts at the leaves of the subtree below the node, this discloses no additional information. Algorithm 4 gives the details, it uses constraint sets and secure cardinality of set intersection in basically the manner described above for computing the majority class at a leaf node. If all transactions are in the same class,

---

Algorithm 4. IsSameClass(): Are all transactions of the same class?

Require: k sites P_i with local constraint sets $Constraints_i$
1: $(cnt_1, \ldots, cnt_p) \leftarrow DistributionCounts()$
2: **if** $\exists j$ s.t. $cnt_j \neq 0 \wedge \forall i \neq j$, $cnt_i = 0$ {only one of the counts is non-zero} **then**
3:     Build a leaf node with distribution $(cnt_1, \ldots, cnt_p)$ {Actually, 100% class j}
4:     **return** ID of the constructed node
5: **else**
6:     **return** $false$
7: **end if**

---

we construct a leaf node. The class site maintains a mapping from the ID of that node to the resulting class distribution.

The next problem is to compute the best attribute: that with the maximum information gain. The information gain when an attribute A is used to partition the data set S is:

$$Gain(S, A) = Entropy(S) - \sum_{v \in A} \left(\frac{|S_v|}{|S|} * Entropy(S_v) \right)$$

Algorithm 5. AttribMaxInfoGain(): return the site with the attribute having maximum information gain

---

1: **for all** sites P_i **do**
2:     $bestgain_i \leftarrow -1$
3:     **for** each attribute A_{ij} at site P_i **do**
4:         $gain \leftarrow ComputeInfoGain(A_{ij})$
5:         **if** $gain > bestgain_i$ **then**
6:             $bestgain_i \leftarrow gain$
7:             $BestAtt_i \leftarrow A_{ij}$
8:         **end if**
9:     **end for**
10: **end for**
11: **return** $argmax_j\ bestgain_j$ {Could implement using a set of secure comparisons}

Algorithm 6. ComputeInfoGain(A): Compute the Information Gain for attribute A

1: $S \leftarrow DistributionCounts()$ {Total number of transactions at this node}
2: $InfoGain \leftarrow Entropy(S)$
3: **for** each attribute value a_i **do**
4:     $Constraints.set(A, a_i)$ {Update local constraints tuple}
5:     $S_{a_i} \leftarrow DistributionCounts()$
6:     $Infogain \leftarrow Infogain - Entropy(S_{a_i}) * |S_{a_i}|/|S|$ {$|S|$ is $\sum_{i=1}^{p} cnt_i$}
7: **end for**
8: $Constraints.set(A, \text{'?'})$ {Update local constraints tuple}
9: **return** InfoGain

The entropy of a dataset S is given by:

$$Entropy(S) = -\sum_{j=1}^{p} \frac{N_j}{N} \log \frac{N_j}{N}$$

where N_j is the number of transactions having class c_j in S and N is the number of transactions in S. As we see, this again becomes a problem of counting transactions: the number of transactions that reach the node N, the number in each class N_j, and the same two after partitioning with each possible attribute value $v \in A$. Algorithm 6 details the process of computing these counts; Algorithm 5 captures the overall process.

Once the best attribute has been determined, execution proceeds at that site. It creates an interior node for the split, then recurses.

3   Using the Tree

Instance classification proceeds as in the original ID3 algorithm, except that the nodes (and attributes of the database) are distributed. The site requesting classification (e.g., a master site) knows the root node of the classification tree.

Algorithm 7. PPID3(): Privacy-Preserving Distributed ID3

Require: Transaction set T partitioned between sites $P_1, \ldots, P_k$
Require: p class values, $c_1, \ldots, c_p$, with P_k holding the class attribute
1: **if** $IsREmpty()$ **then**
2:    Continue at site P_k up to the return:
3:    $(cnt_1, \ldots, cnt_p) \leftarrow DistributionCounts()$
4:    Build a leaf node with distribution $(cnt_1, \ldots, cnt_p)$
5:    $\{class \leftarrow argmax_{i=1..p} \, cnt_i\}$
6:    return ID of the constructed node
7: **else if** $clsNode \leftarrow$ (at P_k :) $IsSameClass()$ **then**
8:    return leaf nodeId $clsNode$
9: **else**
10:    $BestSite \leftarrow AttribMaxInfoGain()$
11:    **Continue execution at** $BestSite$**:**
12:    Create Interior Node Nd with attribute $Nd.A \leftarrow BestAtt_{BestSite}$ {This is best locally (from $AttribMaxInfoGain()$), and globally from line 8}
13:    **for** each attribute value $a_i \in Nd.A$ **do**
14:       $Constraints.set(Nd.A, a_i)$ {Update local constraints tuple}
15:       $nodeId \leftarrow PPID3()$ {Recurse}
16:       $Nd.a_i \leftarrow nodeId$ {Add appropriate branch to interior node}
17:    **end for**
18:    $Constraints.set(A, '?')$ {Returning to parent: should no longer filter transactions with A}
19:    Store Nd locally keyed by Node ID
20:    return Node ID of interior node Nd {Execution continues at site owning parent node}
21: **end if**

The basic idea is that control passes from site to site, based on the decision made. Each site knows the transaction's attribute values for the nodes at its site (and can thus evaluate the branch), but knows nothing of the other attribute values. The complete algorithm is given in Algorithm 8, and is reasonably self-explanatory if viewed in conjunction with Algorithm 7.

We now give a demonstration of how instance classification would actually happen in this instance for the tree built with the UCI "weather" dataset[20]. Assume two sites: The weather observatory collects information about relative humidity and wind, a second collects temperature and cloud cover forecast as well as the class ("Yes" or "No"). Suppose we wish to know if it is a good day to play tennis. Neither sites wants to share their forecasts, but are willing to collaborate to offer a "good tennis day" service. The classification tree is shown in Figure 2, with S1 and S2 corresponding to the site having information on that node. The private information for each site is shown within italics. If today is sunny with normal humidity, high temperature, and weak wind; classification would proceed as follows: We know that Site 1 has the root node (we don't need to know anything else). Site 1 retrieves the attribute for from $S1L1$: Outlook. Since the classifying attribute is outlook, and Site 1 knows the forecast is sunny,

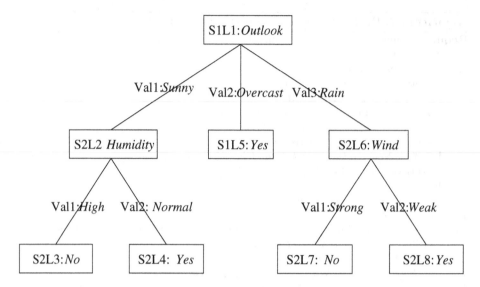

Fig. 2. The privacy preserving ID3 decision tree on the weather dataset (Mapping from identifiers to attributes and values is known only at the site holding attributes)

the token $S2L2$ is retrieved. This indicates that the next step is at Site 2. Site 2 is called with the token $S2L2$, and retrieves the attribute for $S2L2$: Humidity. The humidity forecast is normal, so the token $S2L4$ is retrieved. Since this token is also present at Site 2, it retrieves the class value for nodeId $S2L4$ and returns it: we receive our answer of "Yes".

4   Security Discussion

We evaluate the security of our algorithm under the basic framework of Secure Multiparty Computation [21]. As such, we assume the security of the underlying

---

Algorithm 8. classifyInstance(instId, nodeId): returns the class/distribution for the instance represented by instId

1: {The start site and ID of the root node is known}
2: **if** $nodeId$ is a LeafNode **then**
3:     return class/distribution saved in $nodeId$
4: **else** {$nodeId$ is an interior node}
5:     $Nd \leftarrow$ local node with id $nodeId$
6:     $value \leftarrow$ the value of attribute $Nd.A$ for transaction $instId$
7:     $childId \leftarrow Nd.value$
8:     return $childId.Site.classifyInstance(instId, childId)$ {Actually tail recursion: this site need never learn the class}
9: **end if**

---

set intersection algorithm, and then prove the security of our privacy-preserving ID3 algorithm.

The proof of security is given assuming semi-honest adversaries. A semi-honest party follows the rules of the protocol using its correct input, but is free to later use what it sees during execution of the protocol to compromise security. While this protocol provides somewhat strong guarantees in the absence of collusion, due to space constraints we will only prove security for the semi-honest case.

Privacy by Simulation. The basic proof style is to show that the view of each party during the execution of the protocol can be effectively simulated given the input and the output of that party. This is sufficient to prove that the protocol is secure [21]. Thus, in all of the following proofs of security, we show that we can simulate each message received. Once the received messages are simulated, the algorithm itself can be used to simulate the rest of the view. This does not quite guarantee that private information is protected. Whatever information can be deduced from the final result is not kept private. However, nothing *beyond* the results is learned.

4.1   Secure ID3

We first analyze the security of the constituent algorithms, then the security of the complete algorithm. Although it may seem that some of the constituent algorithms leak a large quantity of information, in the context of the full algorithm the leaked information can be simulated by knowing the distribution counts at each node, so overall privacy is maintained.

Lemma 1. *Algorithm 2 reveals nothing to any site except whether the total number of attributes left is* 0.

Proof. The algorithm has two basic phases: The sum (through P_k), and the comparison between P_k and P_1. First, the sum: simulating the messages received at lines 2 and 7. The value received by P_i at these steps is $r + \sum_{j=1}^{i-1} AR_j \bmod m$. We will simulate by choosing a random integer uniformly from $0 \ldots m-1$ for r'. We now show that the probability that the simulated $r' = x$ is the same as the probability that the messages received in the view $= x$.

$$Pr\{VIEW_i = x\} = Pr\{x = r + \sum_{j=1}^{i-1} AR_j \bmod m\}$$

$$= Pr\{r = x - \sum_{j=1}^{i-1} AR_j \bmod m\}$$

$$= \frac{1}{m}$$

$$= Pr\{Simulator_i r' = x\}$$

The key to the derivation is that arithmetic is mod m. r and r' are chosen uniformly from $0 \ldots m - 1$, so the probability of hitting any particular value in that range is $1/m$.

Simulating the message received by P_k at line 11 is simple: Secure encryption gives messages where the distribution is independent of the key/message, so a selection from this distribution of possible encrypted messages simulates what P_k receives.

The messages received by P_1 are more difficult. The problem is that if $r = r'$, $E_k(r')$ must be such that when encrypted with E_1 it is equal to $E_k(E_1(r))$. For this, the simulator requires the ability to decrypt. The simulator computes $m = D_1(E_k(E_1(r)) = E_k(r)$. If $r = r'$, this is the message used to simulate $E_k(r')$. If not, a random message $\neq m$ is chosen, as in the simulator for P_k. $\square$

Lemma 2. *Algorithm 3 reveals only the count of instances corresponding to all combinations of constraint sets for each class.*

Proof. The only communication occurs at line 7 which consists of a call to the Cardinality of Set Intersection algorithm. This reveals only the size of the intersection set for all subsets of Y_i, which are the counts revealed. Algorithm 3 is secure except for revealing this information. $\square$

Lemma 3. *Algorithm 4 finds if all transactions have the same class, revealing only the class distributions described in Lemma 2.*

Proof. Line 1 is an invocation of Algorithm 3; Everything else is computed locally, and can be simulated from the knowledge from Lemma 2. $\square$

Lemma 4. *Algorithm 6 reveals nothing except the counts S, S_{a_i}, and the constituent subcounts described in Lemma 2 for each attribute value a_i and class j, assuming the number of distinct class values is known.*

Proof. The only messages received are at lines 1 and 5, invocations of the $DistributionCounts()$ function. Since the underlying function is secure, Algorithm 6 is secure. $\square$

Lemma 5. *Algorithm 5 finds the site with the attribute having the maximum information gain while revealing only the best information gain at each site and the information discussed in Lemma 4.*

Proof. Communication occurs at lines 4 and 11. Line 4 consists of an invocation of Algorithm 6. Line 11 is implemented by letting the site compare all the values; revealing the value of the best information gain at each site. Assuming this is revealed (part of the input to the simulator), it is trivially simulated. $\square$

Further reduction of the information revealed is possible by using a secure protocol for finding the maximum among a set of numbers. This would reveal only the site having the attribute with the maximum information gain and nothing else.

Theorem 1. *Algorithm 7 computes the decision tree while revealing only:*

- *The distribution subcounts of each node, as described in Lemma 2. (The full counts, and some of the subcounts, can be computed knowing the distribution counts at the leaves.)*
- *The best information gain from each site at each interior node (as discussed above, this leak can be reduced.)*

Proof. Knowing the final tree, the simulator at each site can uniquely determine the sequence of node computations at a site and list the function calls occurring due to this. Given this function call list, if the messages received in each function call can be simulated, the entire algorithm can be proven to be secure.

Line 1 is an invocation of Algorithm 2. The result is simulated as either true or false depending on whether the node in question is a leaf node in the final tree or not.

Line 3 is an invocation of Algorithm 3. The actual counts are given by the counts *in* the leaf node, which are known to the site P_k that invoked the algorithm. The subcounts revealed by Algorithm 3 are presumed known.

Line 7 is an invocation of Algorithm 4. If the node in question is not a leaf node in the final tree, the result is false. Otherwise the result is the nodeId of the leaf node.

Line 10 consists of an invocation of Algorithm 5. The result is actually equal to the Site which will own the child node. This information is known from the tree structure. The subcounts and information gain values revealed during this step are presumed known.

Line 15 is a recursive invocation that returns a node identifier; a part of the tree structure.

Since all of the algorithms mentioned above have been proven secure, applying the composition theorem, Algorithm 7 is secure. The repeated invocations of the cardinality of set intersection protocol are valid because in each invocation, a new set of keys are chosen. This ensures that messages cannot be correlated across calls.   □

Theorem 2. *Algorithm 8 reveals nothing other than the leaf node classifying the instance.*

Proof. All the computations are local. The only information passed between various sites are node identifiers. This list of node identifiers can be easily simulated from the classification tree once the final leaf is known.   □

5   Computation and Communication Analysis

The communication/computation analysis depends on the number of transactions, number of parties, number of attributes, number of attribute values per attribute, number of classes and complexity of the tree. Assume that there are: n transactions, k parties, c classes, r attributes, p values per attribute (on average), and q nodes in final classification tree. We now give a rough analysis of the cost involved in terms of the number of set intersections required for building the tree (erring on the conservative side).

At each node in the tree the best classifying attribute needs to be determined. To do this, the entropy of the node needs to be computed as well as the information gain per attribute. Computing the entropy of the node requires c set intersections (1 per class). Computing the gain of one attribute requires cp set intersections (1 per attribute value and class). Thus, finding the best attribute requires cpr set intersections. Note that this analysis is rough and assumes that the number of attributes available at each node remains constant. In actuality, this number linearly decreases with the depth of the node in the tree (this has little effect on our analysis). In total, every node requires $c(1+pr)$ set intersections. Therefore, the total tree requires $cq(1+pr)$ set intersections.

The intersection protocol of [13] requires that the set of each party be encrypted by every other party. Since there are k parties, k^2 encryptions are required and k^2 sets are transferred. Since each set can have at most n transactions, the upper bound on computation is $O(nk^2)$ and the upper bound on communication cost is also $O(nk^2 * bitsize)$ bits.

Therefore, in total the entire classification process will require $O(cqnk^2(1 + pr))$ encryptions and $cqnk^2(1 + pr) * bitsize$ bits communication. Note that the encryption process can be completely parallelized reducing the required time by an order of k.

Once the tree is built, classifying an instance requires no extra overhead, and is comparable to the original $ID3$ algorithm.

6   Conclusions

It is possible to extend the protocols developed such that the class of each instance is learned only by the party holding the class attribute (nothing is learned by the remaining parties). In some cases, this might be preferable.

The major contributions of this paper are the following:

- It proposes a new protocol to construct a decision tree on vertically partitioned data with an arbitrary number of parties where only one party has the class attribute (The method is trivially extendible to the case where all parties have the class attribute, and in fact causes a significant increase in the efficiency of the protocol).
- The paper presents a general framework in which distributed classification would work and how such a system should be constructed.

As part of future work, we are actually implementing the entire protocol in JAVA, which should form the first working code in the area of PPDM. Our work provides an upper bound on the complexity of building privacy preserving decision trees. Significant work is required to propose more efficient solutions and/or to find a tight upper bound on the complexity. We leave this for the future.

References

1. Agrawal, R., Srikant, R.: Privacy-preserving data mining. In: Proceedings of the 2000 ACM SIGMOD Conference on Management of Data, Dallas, TX, ACM (2000) 439–450
2. Lindell, Y., Pinkas, B.: Privacy preserving data mining. In: Advances in Cryptology – CRYPTO 2000, Springer-Verlag (2000) 36–54
3. Quinlan, J.R.: Induction of decision trees. Machine Learning 1 (1986) 81–106
4. Lindell, Y., Pinkas, B.: Privacy preserving data mining. Journal of Cryptology 15 (2002) 177–206
5. Du, W., Zhan, Z.: Building decision tree classifier on private data. In Clifton, C., Estivill-Castro, V., eds.: IEEE International Conference on Data Mining Workshop on Privacy, Security, and Data Mining. Volume 14., Maebashi City, Japan, Australian Computer Society (2002) 1–8
6. Agrawal, D., Aggarwal, C.C.: On the design and quantification of privacy preserving data mining algorithms. In: Proceedings of the Twentieth ACM SIGACT-SIGMOD-SIGART Symposium on Principles of Database Systems, Santa Barbara, California, USA, ACM (2001) 247–255
7. Evfimievski, A., Srikant, R., Agrawal, R., Gehrke, J.: Privacy preserving mining of association rules. In: The Eighth ACM SIGKDD International Conference on Knowledge Discovery and Data Mining, Edmonton, Alberta, Canada (2002) 217–228
8. Rizvi, S.J., Haritsa, J.R.: Maintaining data privacy in association rule mining. In: Proceedings of 28th International Conference on Very Large Data Bases, Hong Kong, VLDB (2002) 682–693
9. Kargupta, H., Datta, S., Wang, Q., Sivakumar, K.: On the privacy preserving properties of random data perturbation techniques. In: Proceedings of the Third IEEE International Conference on Data Mining (ICDM'03), Melbourne, Florida (2003)
10. Kantarcıoğlu, M., Clifton, C.: Privacy-preserving distributed mining of association rules on horizontally partitioned data. IEEE Transactions on Knowledge and Data Engineering 16 (2004) 1026–1037
11. Rozenberg, B., Gudes, E.: Privacy preserving frequent item-set mining in vertically partitioned databases. In: Proceedings of the Seventeenth Annual IFIP WG 11.3 Working Conference on Data and Applications Security, Estes Park, Colorado, U.S.A. (2003)
12. Vaidya, J., Clifton, C.: Privacy preserving association rule mining in vertically partitioned data. In: The Eighth ACM SIGKDD International Conference on Knowledge Discovery and Data Mining, Edmonton, Alberta, Canada (2002) 639–644
13. Vaidya, J., Clifton, C.: Secure set intersection cardinality with application to association rule mining. Journal of Computer Security (to appear)
14. Lin, X., Clifton, C., Zhu, M.: Privacy preserving clustering with distributed EM mixture modeling. Knowledge and Information Systems (to appear 2004)
15. Vaidya, J., Clifton, C.: Privacy-preserving k-means clustering over vertically partitioned data. In: The Ninth ACM SIGKDD International Conference on Knowledge Discovery and Data Mining, Washington, DC (2003) 206–215
16. Vaidya, J., Clifton, C.: Privacy preserving naïve bayes classifier for vertically partitioned data. In: 2004 SIAM International Conference on Data Mining, Lake Buena Vista, Florida (2004) 522–526

17. Schneier, B.: Applied Cryptography. 2nd edn. John Wiley & Sons (1995)
18. Freedman, M.J., Nissim, K., Pinkas, B.: Efficient private matching and set inter-section. In: Eurocrypt 2004, Interlaken, Switzerland, International Association for Cryptologic Research (IACR) (2004)
19. Agrawal, R., Evfimievski, A., Srikant, R.: Information sharing across private databases. In: Proceedings of ACM SIGMOD International Conference on Management of Data, San Diego, California (2003)
20. Blake, C., Merz, C.: UCI repository of machine learning databases (1998)
21. Goldreich, O.: General Cryptographic Protocols. In: The Foundations of Cryptography. Volume 2. Cambridge University Press (2004)

Privacy-Preserving Collaborative Association Rule Mining

Justin Zhan, Stan Matwin, and LiWu Chang

[1] School of Information Technology & Engineering,
University of Ottawa, Canada
[2] School of Information Technology & Engineering,
University of Ottawa, Canada
Institute for Computer Science,
Polish Academy of Sciences, Warsaw, Poland
{zhizhan, stan}@site.uottawa.ca
[3] Center for High Assurance Computer Systems,
Naval Research Laboratory, USA
lchang@itd.nrl.navy.mil

Abstract. This paper introduces a new approach to a problem of data sharing among multiple parties, without disclosing the data between the parties. Our focus is data sharing among parties involved in a data mining task. We study how to share private or confidential data in the following scenario: multiple parties, each having a private data set, want to collaboratively conduct association rule mining without disclosing their private data to each other or any other parties. To tackle this demanding problem, we develop a secure protocol for multiple parties to conduct the desired computation. The solution is distributed, i.e., there is no central, trusted party having access to all the data. Instead, we define a protocol using homomorphic encryption techniques to exchange the data while keeping it private.

Keywords: Privacy, security, association rule mining.

1 Introduction

In this paper, we address the following problem: multiple parties are cooperating on a data-rich task. Each of the parties owns data pertinent to the aspect of the task addressed by this party. More specifically, the data consists of instances, all parties have data about all the instances involved, but each party has its own view of the instances - each party works with its own attribute set. The overall performance, or even solvability, of this task depends on the ability of performing data mining using all the attributes of all the parties. The parties, however, may be unwilling to release their attribute to other parties, due to privacy or confidentiality of the data. How can we structure information sharing between the parties so that the data will be shared for the purpose of data mining, while at the same time specific attribute values will be kept confidential by the

S. Jajodia and D. Wijesekera (Eds.): Data and Applications Security 2005, LNCS 3654, pp. 153–165, 2005.

parties to whom they belong? This is the task addressed in this paper. In the privacy-oriented data mining this task is known as data mining with vertically partitioned data (also known as heterogeneous collaboration [6].) Examples of such tasks abound in business, homeland security, coalition building, medical research, etc.

The following scenarios illustrate situations in which this type of collaboration is interesting: (1) Multiple competing supermarkets, each having an extra large set of data records of its customers' buying behaviors, want to conduct data mining on their joint data set for mutual benefit. Since these companies are competitors in the market, they do not want to disclose too much about their customers' information to each other, but they know the results obtained from this collaboration could bring them an advantage over other competitors. (2) Success of homeland security aiming to counter terrorism depends on combination of strength across different mission areas, effective international collaboration and information sharing to support coalition in which different organizations and nations must share some, but not all, information. Information privacy thus becomes extremely important: all the parties of the collaboration promise to provide their private data to the collaboration, but neither of them wants each other or any other party to learn much about their private data. (3) Vidya and Clifton [6] provide the following convincing example in the area of automotive safety: Ford Explorers with Firestone tires from a specific factory had tread separation problems in certain situations. Early identification of the real problem could have avoided at least some of the 800 injuries that occurred in accidents attributed to the faulty tires. Since the tires did not have problems on other vehicles, and other tires on Ford Explorers did not pose a problem, neither side felt responsible. Both manufacturers had their own data, but only early generation of association rules based on all of the data may have enabled Ford and Firestone to collaborate in resolving this safety problem.

Without privacy concerns, all parties can send their data to a trusted central place to conduct the mining. However, in situations with privacy concerns, the parties may not trust anyone. We call this type of problem the *Privacy-preserving Collaborative Data Mining problem*. Homogeneous collaboration means that each party has the same sets of attributes [7]. As stated above, in this paper we are interested in heterogeneous collaboration where each party has different sets of attributes [6].

Data mining includes a number of different tasks, such as association rule mining, classification, and clustering. This paper studies the association rule mining problem. The goal of association rule mining is to discover meaningful association rules among the attributes of a large quantity of data. For example, let us consider the database of a medical study, with each attribute representing a characteristic of a patient. A discovered association rule pattern could be "70% of patients who suffer from medical condition C have a gene G". This information can be useful for the development of a diagnostic test, for pharmaceutical research, etc. Based on the existing association rule mining technologies, we study the *Privacy-preserving Collaborative Association Rule Mining* problem defined as follows: multiple parties want to conduct association rule mining on a data set that consists of all the parties' private data, but neither party is willing to disclose her raw data to each other or any other parties. In this paper, we develop a protocol, based on homomorphic cryptography, to tackle the problem.

The paper is organized as follows: The related work is discussed in Section 2. We describe the association rule mining procedure in Section 3. We then present our proposed secure protocols in Section 4. We give our conclusion in Section 5.

2   Related Work

2.1   Secure Multi-party Computation

A Secure Multi-party Computation (SMC) problem deals with computing any function on any input, in a distributed network where each participant holds one of the inputs, while ensuring that no more information is revealed to a participant in the computation than can be inferred from that participant's input and output. The SMC problem literature was introduced by Yao [13]. It has been proved that for any polynomial function, there is a secure multi-party computation solution [5]. The approach used is as follows: the function F to be computed is firstly represented as a combinatorial circuit, and then the parties run a short protocol for every gate in the circuit. Every participant gets corresponding shares of the input wires and the output wires for every gate. This approach, though appealing in its generality and simplicity, is highly impractical for large datasets.

2.2   Privacy-Preserving Data Mining

In early work on privacy-preserving data mining, Lindell and Pinkas [8] propose a solution to privacy-preserving classification problem using oblivious transfer protocol, a powerful tool developed by secure multi-party computation (SMC) research. The techniques based on SMC for efficiently dealing with large data sets have been addressed in [6], where a solution to the association rule mining problem for the case of two parties was proposed.

Randomization approaches were firstly proposed by Agrawal and Srikant in [3] to solve privacy-preserving data mining problem. In addition to perturbation, aggregation of data values [11] provides another alternative to mask the actual data values. In [1], authors studied the problem of computing the kth-ranked element. Dwork and Nissim [4] showed how to learn certain types of boolean functions from statistical databases in terms of a measure of probability difference with respect to probabilistic implication, where data are perturbed with noise for the release of statistics. In this paper, we focus on privacy-preserving among the intra-party computation.

The work most related to ours is [12], where Wright and Yang applied homomorphic encryption [10] to the Bayesian networks induction for the case of *two* parties. However, the core protocol which is called *Scalar Product Protocol* can be easily attacked. In their protocol, since Bob knows the encryption key e, when Alice sends her encrypted vector $(e(a_1), \cdots, e(a_n))$ where a_is are Alice's vector elements, Bob can easily figure out whether a_i is 1 or 0 through the following attack: Bob computes $e(1)$, and then compares it with $e(a_i)$. If $e(1) = e(a_i)$, then $a_i = 1$, otherwise $a_i = 0$. In this paper, we develop a secure *two-party* protocol and a secure *multi-party* protocol based on homomorphic encryption. Our contribution not only overcomes the attacks which exist in [12], but more importantly, a general secure protocol involving multiple parties is provided.

3   Mining Association Rules on Private Data

Since its introduction in 1993 [2], the association rule mining has received a great deal of attention. It is still one of most popular pattern-discovery methods in the field of knowledge discovery. Briefly, an association rule is an expression $X \Rightarrow Y$, where X and Y are sets of items. The meaning of such rules is as follows: Given a database D of records, $X \Rightarrow Y$ means that whenever a record R contains X then R also contains Y with certain confidence. The rule confidence is defined as the percentage of records containing both X and Y with regard to the overall number of records containing X. The fraction of records R supporting an item X with respect to database D is called the support of X.

3.1   Problem Definition

We consider the scenario where multiple parties, each having a private data set (denoted by D_1, D_2, $\cdots$ and D_n respectively), want to collaboratively conduct association rule mining on the concatenation of their data sets. Because they are concerned about their data privacy, neither party is willing to disclose its raw data set to others. Without loss of generality, we make the following assumptions about the data sets (the assumptions can be achieved by pre-processing the data sets D_1, D_2, $\cdots$ and D_n, and such a pre-processing does not require one party to send her data set to other parties): (1) all the data sets contain the same number of transactions. Let N denote the total number of transactions for each data set. (2) The identities of the ith (for $i \in [1, N]$) transaction in all the data sets are the same.

Privacy-Preserving Collaborative Association Rule Mining problem: Party 1 has a private data set D_1, party 2 has a private data set D_2, $\cdots$ and party n has a private data set D_n. The data set $[D_1 \cup D_2 \cup \cdots \cup D_n]$ forms a database, which is actually the concatenation of D_1, D_2, $\cdots$ and D_n (by putting D_1, D_2, $\cdots$ and D_n together so that the concatenation of the ith row in D_1, D_2, $\cdots$ and D_n becomes the ith row in $[D_1 \cup D_2 \cup \cdots \cup D_n]$). The n parties want to conduct association rule mining on $[D_1 \cup D_2 \cup \cdots \cup D_n]$ and to find the association rules with support and confidence being greater than the given thresholds. We say an association rule (e.g., $x_i \Rightarrow y_j$) has confidence $c\%$ in the data set $[D_1 \cup D_2 \cup \cdots \cup D_n]$ if in $[D_1 \cup D_2 \cup \cdots \cup D_n]$ $c\%$ of the records which contain x_i also contain y_j

(namely, $c\% = P(y_j \mid x_i)$). We say that the association rule has support $s\%$ in $[D_1 \cup D_2 \cup \cdots \cup D_n]$ if $s\%$ of the records in $[D_1 \cup D_2 \cdots \cup D_n]$ contain both x_i and y_j (namely, $s\% = P(x_i \cap y_j)$). Consequently, in order to learn association rules, one must compute the candidate itemsets, and then prune those that do not meet the preset confidence and support thresholds. In order to compute confidence and support of a given candidate itemset, we must compute, for a given itemset C, the frequency of attributes (items) belonging to C in the entire database (i.e., we must count how many attributes in C are present in all records of the database, and divide the final count by the size of the database which is N.) Note that association rule mining works on binary data, representing presence or absence of items in transactions. However, the proposed approach is not limited to the assumption about the binary character of the data in the content of association rule mining since non-binary data can be transformed to binary data via discreterization.

3.2   Association Rule Mining Procedure

The following is the procedure for mining association rules on $[D_1 \cup D_2 \cdots \cup D_n]$.

1. $L_1 = $ large 1-itemsets
2. **for** (k = 2; $L_{k-1} \neq \phi$; k++) **do begin**
3. $C_k = $ **apriori-gen**(L_{k-1})
4.   **for** all candidates $c \in C_k$ **do begin**
5.   **Compute $c.count$** (*c.count divided by the total number of records is the support of a given item set. We will show how to compute it in Section 3.3.*)
6.   **end**
7. $L_k = \{c \in C_k \mid c.count \geq min\text{-}sup\}$
8. **end**
9. Return L = $\cup_k L_k$

The procedure **apriori-gen** is described in the following (please also see [2] for details).

apriori-gen(L_{k-1}: large (k-1)-itemsets)

1. insert into C_k
2. select $p.item_1, p.item_2, \cdots, p.item_{k-1}, q.item_{k-1}$
3. from L_{k-1} p, L_{k-1} q
4. where $p.item_1 = q.item_1, \cdots, p.item_{k-2} = q.item_{k-2}, p.item_{k-1} < q.item_{k-1}$;

Next, in the *prune* step, we delete all itemsets $c \in C_k$ such that some (k-1)-subset of c is not in L_{k-1}:

1. for all itemsets $c \in C_k$ do
2.   for all (k-1)-subsets s of c do
3.   if($s \notin L_{k-1}$) then
4.   delete c from C_k;

3.3   How to Compute *c.count*

In the procedure of association rule mining, the only steps accessing the actual data values are: (1) the initial step which computes large 1-itemsets, and (2) the computation of *c.count*. Other steps, particularly computing candidate itemsets, use merely attribute names. To compute large 1-itemsets, each party selects her own attributes that contribute to large 1-itemsets. As only a single attribute forms a large 1-itemset, there is no computation involving attributes of other parties. Therefore, no data disclosure across parties is necessary. However, to compute *c.count*, a computation accessing attributes belonging to different parties is necessary. How to conduct this computations across parties without compromising each party's data privacy is the challenge we address.

If all the attributes belong to the same party, then *c.count*, which refers to the frequency counts for candidates, can be computed by this party. If the attributes belong to different parties, they then construct vectors for their own attributes and apply our secure protocols, which will be discussed in Section 4, to obtain *c.count*. We use an example to illustrate how to compute *c.count* among two parties. Alice and Bob construct vectors C_{k1} and C_{k2} for their own attributes respectively. To obtain *c.count*, they need to compute $\sum_{i=1}^{N}(C_{k1}[i] \cdot C_{k2}[i])$ where N is the total number of values in each vector. For instance, if the vectors are as depicted in Fig.1, then $\sum_{i=1}^{N}(C_{k1}[i] \cdot C_{k2}[i]) = \sum_{i=1}^{5}(C_{k1}[i] \cdot C_{k2}[i]) = 3$. We provide a secure protocol in Section 4 for the two parties to compute this value without revealing their private data to each other.

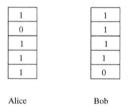

Alice   Bob

Fig. 1. Raw Data For Alice and Bob

4   Collaborative Association Rule Mining Protocol

How the collaborative parties jointly compute *c.count* without revealing their raw data to each other presents a great challenge. In this section, we develop two secure protocols to compute *c.count* for the case of two parties as well as the case of multiple parties, respectively.

4.1   Introducing Homomorphic Encryption

In our secure protocols, we use homomorphic encryption [10] keys to encrypt the parties' private data. In particular, we utilize the following characterizer of the homomorphic encryption functions: $e(a_1) \times e(a_2) = e(a_1 + a_2)$ where e is an encryption function; a_1 and a_2 are the data to be encrypted. Because of the property of associativity, $e(a_1 + a_2 + .. + a_n)$ can be computed as $e(a_1) \times e(a_2) \times \cdots \times e(a_n)$ where $e(a_i) \neq 0$. That is

$$e(a_1 + a_2 + \cdots + a_n) = e(a_1) \times e(a_2) \times \cdots \times e(a_n) \tag{1}$$

4.2   Secure Two-Party Protocol

Let us firstly consider the case of two parties $(n = 2)$. Alice has a vector A_1 and Bob has a vector A_2. Both vectors have N elements. We use A_{1i} to denote the ith element in vector A_1, and A_{2i} to denote the ith element in vector A_2. In order to compute the c.count of an itemset containing A_1 and A_2, Alice and Bob need to compute the scalar product between A_1 and A_2.

Firstly, one of parties is randomly chosen as a key generator. For simplicity, let's assume Alice is selected as the key generator. Alice generates an encryption key (e) and a decryption key (d). She applies the encryption key to the addition of each value of A_1 and $R_i * X$ (e.g., $e(A_{1i} + R_i * X)$), where R_i is a random integer and X is an integer which is greater than N. She then sends $e(A_{1i} + R_i * X)$s to Bob. Bob computes the multiplication $\prod_{j=1}^{n}[e(A_{1j} + R_i * X) \times A_{2j}]$ when $A_{2j} = 1$ (since when $A_{2j} = 0$, the result of multiplication doesn't contribute to the c.count). He sends the multiplication results to Alice who computes $[d(e(A_{11} + A_{12} + \cdots + A_{1j} + (R_1 + R_2 + \cdots + R_j) * X)])modX = (A_{11} + A_{12} + \cdots + A_{1j} + (R_1 + R_2 + \cdots + R_j) * X)modX$ and obtains the c.count. In more detail, Alice and Bob apply the following protocol:

Protocol 1. *(Secure Two-Party Protocol)*

1. Alice performs the following:
   (a) Alice generates a cryptographic key pair (d, e) of a homomorphic encryption scheme. Let's use $e(.)$ denote encryption and $d(.)$ denote decryption. Let X be an integer number which is chosen by Alice and greater than N (i.e., the number of transactions).
   (b) Alice randomly generates a set of integer numbers $R_1, R_2, \cdots, R_N$ and sends $e(A_{11} + R_1 * X)$, $e(A_{12} + R_2 * X)$, $\cdots$, and $e(A_{1N} + R_N * X)$ to Bob.
2. Bob performs the following:
   (a) Bob computes $E_1 = e(A_{11} + R_1 * X) * A_{21}$, $E_2 = e(A_{12} + R_2 * X) * A_{22}$, $\cdots$ and $E_N = e(A_{1N} + R_N * X) * A_{2N}$. Since A_{2i} is either 1 or 0, $e(A_{1i} + R_i * X) * A_{2i}$ is either $e(A_{1i} + R_i * X)$ or 0. Note that R_1, R_2, $\cdots$, and R_N are unrelated random numbers.
   (b) Bob multiplies all the E_is for those A_{2i}s that are not equal to 0. In other words, Bob computes the multiplication of all non-zero E_is, e.g., $E = \prod E_i$ where $E_i \neq 0$. Without loss of generality, let's assume only the first j elements are not equal to 0s. Bob then computes $E = E_1 * E_2 * \cdots * E_j = [e(A_{11}+R_1*X) \times A_{21}] \times [e(A_{12}+R_2*X) \times A_{22}] \times \cdots \times [e(A_{1j}+R_j*X) \times A_{2j}]$

$= [e(A_{11} + R_1 * X) \times 1] \times [e(A_{12} + R_2 * X) \times 1] \times \cdots \times [e(A_{1j} + R_j *$
$X) \times 1] = e(A_{11} + R_1 * X) \times e(A_{12} + R_2 * X) \times \cdots \times e(A_{1j} + R_j * X) =$
$e(A_{11} + A_{12} + \cdots + A_{1j} + (R_1 + R_2 + \cdots + R_j) * X)$ according to Eq. 1.
   (c) Bob sends E to Alice.
3. Alice computes $d(E) mod X$ which is equal to $c.count$.

4.3   Analysis of Two-Party Protocol

Correctness Analysis. Let us assume that both parties follow the protocol.
When Bob receives each encrypted element $e(A_{1i} + R_i * X)$, he computes $e(A_{1i} +$
$R_i) * A_{2i}$. If $A_{2i} = 0$, then $c.count$ does not change. Hence, Bob computes
the product of those elements whose A_{2i}s are 1s and obtains $\prod e(A_{1j} + R_j) =$
$e(A_{11} + A_{12} + \cdots + A_{1j} + (R_1 + R_2 + \cdots + R_j) * X)$ (note that the first j terms are
used for simplicity in explanation), then sends it to Alice. After Alice decrypts
it, she obtains $[d(e(A_{11} + A_{12} + \cdots + A_{1j} + (R_1 + R_2 + \cdots + R_j) * X))] mod X$
$= (A_{11} + A_{12} + \cdots + A_{1j} + (R_1 + R_2 + \cdots + R_j) * X) mod X$ which is equal to
the desired $c.count$. The reasons are as follows: when $A_{2i} = 1$ and $A_{1i} = 0$,
$c.count$ does not change; only if both A_{1i} and A_{2i} are 1s, $c.count$ changes. Since
$(A_{11} + A_{12} + \cdots + A_{1j}) \leq N < X$, $(A_{11} + A_{12} + \cdots + A_{1j} + (R_1 + R_2 +$
$\cdots + R_j) * X) mod X = (A_{11} + A_{12} + \cdots + A_{1j})$. In addition, when $A_{2i} = 1$,
$(A_{11} + A_{12} + \cdots + A_{1j})$ gives the total number of times that both A_{1i} and A_{2i}
are 1s. Therefore, $c.count$ is computed correctly.

Complexity Analysis. The bit-wise communication cost of this protocol is
$\alpha(N + 1)$ where α is the number of bits for each encrypted element. The cost
is approximately α times of the *optimal* cost of a two-party scalar product. The
optimal cost of a scalar product is defined as the cost of conducting the product
of A_1 and A_2 without privacy constraints, namely one party simply sends its
data in plaintext to the other party.

   The computational cost is caused by the following: (1) the generation of a
cryptographic key pair; (2) the total number of N encryptions, e.g., $e(A_{1i} + R_i * X)$
where $i \in [1, N]$; (3)at most 3N-1 multiplications; (4) one decryption; (5) one
modulo operation; (6) N additions.

Privacy Analysis. All the information that Bob obtains from Alice is $e(A_{11} +$
$R_1 * X)$, $e(A_{12} + R_2 * X)$, $\cdots$ and $e(A_{1N} + R_N * X)$. Bob does not know the
encryption key e, R_is, and X. Assuming the homomorphic encryption is secure,
he cannot know Alice's original element values. The information that Alice obtains from Bob is $\prod [e(A_{1i} + R_i * X) * A_{2i}]$ for those is that $A_{2i} = 1$. After
Alice computes $[d(\prod e(A_{1i} + R_i * X) * A_{2i})] mod X$ for those is that $A_{2i} = 1$,
she only obtains $c.count$, and can't exactly know Bob's original element values.
Note that the trouble with binary data presented in [6] does not exist for our
protocol. More importantly, [6] only deals with the case of two parties; however,
our protocol can cope with the case of two parties as well as the case of multiple
parties.

4.4   Secure Multi-party Protocol

We have discussed our secure protocol for two parties. In this section, we develop a protocol to deal with the case where more than two parties are involved. Without loss of generality, assuming Party 1 has a private vector A_1, Party 2 has a private vector A_2, $\cdots$ and Party n has a private vector A_n. For simplicity, we use P_i to denote Party i.

In our protocol, P_1, P_2, $\cdots$ and P_{n-1} share a cryptographic key pair (d, e) of a homomorphic encryption scheme and a large integer X which is greater than N. P_1 modifies every element of its private vectors with $R_{1i} * X$, where R_{1i} is a random integer number, then encrypts and sends them to P_n. Like P_1, all other parties send their encrypted values to P_n too. P_n will multiply received values with her own element, e.g., $E_i = e(A_{1i} + R_{1i} * X) * e(A_{2i} + R_{2i} * X) * \cdots * e(A_{(n-1)i} + R_{(n-1)i} * X) * A_{ni}$. P_n randomly permutes E_is and divides those non-zero E_is into n-1 parts with each part having approximately equal number of elements, and sends them to n-1 other parties who compute $[d(E_i)]modX = [d(e(A_{1i} + R_{1i} * X) * e(A_{2i} + R_{2i} * X) * \cdots * e(A_{(n-1)i} + R_{(n-1)i} * X))]modX = (A_{1i} + A_{2i} + \cdots + A_{(n-1)i} + (R_{1i} + R_{2i} + \cdots + R_{(n-1)i}) * X)modX = (A_{1i} + A_{2i} + \cdots + A_{(n-1)i})$. Suppose P_1 gets the above $[d(E_i)mod]X$. P_1 then compares whether $(A_{1i} + A_{2i} + \cdots + A_{(n-1)i}) = n - 1$. If it is true, then $c.count_1$ increases by 1. Consequently, P_1 gets $c.count_1$. Similarly, P_2 gets $c.count_2$, $\cdots$ and P_{n-1} gets $c.count_{n-1}$.

To avoid P_i knowing $c.count_j$, where $i \neq j$, we perform the following steps: P_n generates another cryptographic key pair (e_1, d_1) of a homomorphic encryption scheme and sends the encryption key e_1 to P_1, P_2, $\cdots$ and P_{n-1} who compute $e_1(c.count_1)$, $e_1(c.count_2)$, $\cdots$ and $e_1(c.count_{n-1})$ respectively. One of those n-1 parties (e.g., P_j) is randomly chosen. All other parties P_ks where $k \neq j$ send $e_1(c.count_k)$s to P_j. P_j multiplies all the encrypted counts and obtains the encrypted $c.count$. That is $e_1(c.count_1) * e_1(c.count_2) * \cdots * e_1(c.count_{n-1}) = e_1(c.count_1 + c.count_2 + \cdots + c.count_{n-1}) = e_1(c.count)$. P_j sends $e_1(c.count)$ to P_n who computes $d_1(e_1(c.count))$ and gets $c.count$.

Protocol 2. *(Secure Multi-Party Protocol)*

1. P_1, P_2, $\cdots$, and P_{n-1} perform the following:
   (a) P_1, P_2, $\cdots$ and P_{n-1} jointly generate a cryptographic key pair (d, e) of a homomorphic encryption scheme. Let's use $e(.)$ denote encryption and $d(.)$ denote decryption. They also generate the number, X, where X is an integer which is greater than N.
   (b) P_1 generates a set of random integers R_{11}, R_{12}, $\cdots$, R_{1N} and sends $e(A_{11} + R_{11} * X)$, $e(A_{12} + R_{12} * X)$, $\cdots$, and $e(A_{1N} + R_{1N} * X)$ to P_n; P_2 generates a set of random integers R_{21}, R_{22}, $\cdots$, R_{2N} and sends $e(A_{21} + R_{21} * X)$, $e(A_{22} + R_{22} * X)$, $\cdots$, and $e(A_{2N} + R_{2N} * X)$ to P_n, $\cdots$, P_{n-1} generates a set of random integers $R_{(n-1)1}$, $R_{(n-1)2}$, $\cdots$, $R_{(n-1)N}$ and sends $e(A_{(n-1)1} + R_{(n-1)1} * X)$, $e(A_{(n-1)2} + R_{(n-1)2} * X)$, $\cdots$, $e(A_{(n-1)N} + R_{(n-1)N} * X)$ to P_n.

2. P_n performs the following:

   (a) P_n computes $E_1 = e(A_{11}+R_{11}*X) * e(A_{21}+R_{21}*X) * \cdots * e(A_{(n-1)1}+R_{(n-1)1}) * A_{n1} = e(A_{11}+A_{21}+\cdots+A_{(n-1)1}+(R_{11}+R_{21}+\cdots+R_{(n-1)1})*X) * A_{n1}$,

   $E_2 = e(A_{12}+R_{12}*X) * e(A_{22}+R_{22}*X) * \cdots * e(A_{(n-1)2}+R_{(n-1)2}*X) * A_{n2} = e(A_{12}+A_{22}+\cdots+A_{(n-1)2}+(R_{12}+R_{22}+\cdots+R_{(n-1)2})*X)*A_{n2}$,

   $E_3 = e(A_{13}+R_{13}*X) * e(A_{23}+R_{23}*X) * \cdots * e(A_{(n-1)3}+R_{(n-1)3}*X) * A_{n3} = e(A_{13}+A_{23}+\cdots+A_{(n-1)3}+(R_{13}+R_{23}+\cdots+R_{(n-1)3})*X)*A_{n3}$,
   $\cdots$, and

   $E_N = e(A_{1N} + R_{1N} * X) * e(A_{2N} + R_{2N} * X) * \cdots * e(A_{(n-1)N} + R_{(n-1)N} * X) * A_{nN} = e(A_{1N} + A_{2N} + \cdots + A_{(n-1)N} + (R_{1N} + R_{2N} + \cdots + R_{(n-1)N}) * X) * A_{nN}$.

   Since A_{ni} is either 1 or 0, E_1 is either $e(A_{11} + A_{21} + \cdots + A_{(n-1)1} + (R_{11} + R_{21} + \cdots + R_{(n-1)1}) * X)$ or 0; E_2 is either $e(A_{12} + A_{22} + \cdots + A_{(n-1)2} + (R_{12} + R_{22} + \cdots + R_{(n-1)2}) * X)$ or 0; $\cdots$; and E_N is either $e(A_{1N} + A_{2N} + \cdots + A_{(n-1)N} + (R_{1N} + R_{2N} + \cdots + R_{(n-1)N}) * X)$ or 0.

   (b) P_n randomly permutes [9] the E_1, E_2, $\cdots$ and E_N, then obtains the permuted sequence D_1, D_2, $\cdots$ and D_N.

   (c) From computational balance point of view, we want each party among P_1, P_2, $\cdots$ and P_{n-1} to decrypt some of non-zero D_is. [1] Consequently, in our protocol P_n divides those non-zero elements from D_1, D_2, $\cdots$ and D_N into $n-1$ parts with each part having approximately equal number of elements.

   (d) P_n sends the $n-1$ parts to P_1, P_2, $\cdots$ and P_{n-1} respectively, so that P_1 gets the first part, P_2 gets the second part, $\cdots$ and P_{n-1} gets the $(n-1)th$ part.

3. Compute $c.count$

   (a) P_1, P_2, $\cdots$ and P_{n-1} decrypt the encrypted terms received from P_n, then modulo X. Due to the properties of homomorphic encryption, this gives them the correct value of $c.count$ for a candidate itemset consisting of attributes A_1, A_2, $\cdots$ and A_n. Note that if a decrypted term is equal to n-1 *mod* X, it means the values of P_1, P_2, $\cdots$, P_{n-1} and P_n are all 1s [2]. For example, if P_i obtains E_i, she then computes $d(E_i) \bmod X = (A_{1i} + A_{2i} + \cdots + A_{(n-1)i} + (R_{1i} + R_{2i} + \cdots + R_{(n-1)i}) * X) \bmod X = A_{1i} + A_{2i} + \cdots + A_{(n-1)i}$. Consequently, P_1, P_2, $\cdots$ and P_{n-1} compare whether each decrypted term is equal to $n - 1 \bmod X$. If yes, then each P_i ($i = 1, 2, \cdots$ and n-1) increases her $c.count_i$ by 1.

   (b) What remains is the computation of $c.count$ by adding the $c.count_i$s. Since we do not want a party P_i to know the $count_j$ for $j \neq i$, we use the following cryptographic scheme avoiding this disclosure: P_n generates

---

[1] We assume that the number of non-zero elements of D_is (Let's denote the number by ND) is $\geq$ n-1. If not, we randomly select the number of ND parties from P_1, P_2, $\cdots$ and P_{n-1}, and send each non-zero element to each of the selected parties. Moreover, in practice $N \gg n$.

[2] The value of P_n must be 1 because P_n doesn't send the D_is to those $n - 1$ parties if $D_i = 0$.

another cryptographic key pair (d_1, e_1) of a homomorphic encryption scheme[3]. She then sends e_1 to $P_1, P_2, \cdots$ and P_{n-1}. P_i $(i = 1, 2, \cdots, n-1)$ encrypts $c.count_i$ by using e_1. In other words, P_1 computes $e_1(c.count_1)$, P_2 computes $e_1(c.count_2)$, $\cdots$ and P_{n-1} computes $e_1(c.count_{n-1})$.

(c) One of parties among $P_1, P_2, \cdots$ and P_{n-1} (e.g., P_j) is randomly selected. Other parties P_ks among $P_1, P_2, \cdots$ and P_{n-1} $(k \neq j)$ send their encrypted $c.count_k$ to P_j, who then multiplies all the encrypted counts including her own $e_1(c.count_j)$ and obtains the encrypted $c.count$. That is, $e_1(c.count) = e_1(c.count_1) * e_1(c.count_2) * e_1(c.count_3) * \cdots * e_1(c.count_{n-1}) = e_1(c.count_1 + c.count_2 + \cdots + c.count_{n-1})$.

(d) P_j sends $e_1(c.count)$ to P_n.

(e) P_n computes $d_1(e_1(c.count)) = c.count$. Finally, P_n obtains $c.count$ and shares with $P_1, P_2, \cdots$ and P_{n-1}.

4.5   Analysis of Multi-party Protocol

Correctness Analysis. Assuming all of the parties follow the protocol, to show the $c.count$ is correct, we need to consider:

- If the element of P_n is 1 (e.g., $A_{ni} = 1$), and $A_{1i} + A_{2i} + \cdots + A_{(n-1)i} = n-1$, then $c.count$ increases by 1. Since $[d(e(A_{1i} + R_{1i} * X) * e(A_{2i} + R_{2i} * X) * \cdots * e(A_{(n-1)i} + R_{(n-1)i} * X))]$ mod $X = [d(e(A_{1i} + A_{2i} + \cdots + A_{(n-1)i} + (R_{1i} + R_{2i} + \cdots + R_{(n-1)i}) * X))]$ mod $X = A_{1i} + A_{2i} + \cdots + A_{(n-1)i}$, if $A_{ni} = 1$ and $A_{1i} + A_{2i} + \cdots + A_{(n-1)i} = n - 1$, that means $A_{1i}, A_{2i}, \cdots, A_{(n-1)i}$ and A_{ni} are all 1s, then $c.count$ should increase by 1. For other scenarios, either $A_{ni} = 0$ or $A_{1i} + A_{2i} + \cdots + A_{(n-1)i} \neq n - 1$ or both, $c.count$ doesn't change.
- In the protocol, P_n permutes E_is before sending them to $P_1, P_2, \cdots$ and P_{n-1}. Permutation does not affect $c.count$. We evaluate whether each element contributes to $c.count$, we then sum those that contribute. Summation is not affected by a permutation. Therefore, the final $c.count$ is correct.

Complexity Analysis. The bit-wise communication cost of this protocol is at most $2\alpha nN$ where α is the number of bits for each encrypted element. The following contributes to the computational cost: (1) the generation of two cryptographic key pairs; (2) the total number of $nN + (n-1)$ encryptions; (3) the total number of $n(N + 1) - 1$ multiplications; (4) the generation of permutation function; (5) the total number of N permutations; (6) at most N decryptions; (7) at most N modulo operations; (8) (n-1)N additions.

Privacy Analysis. P_n obtains all the encrypted terms from other parties. Since P_n does not know the encryption key, R_{ij}, and X, she cannot know the original values of other parties' elements. Each party of $P_1, P_2, \cdots$ and P_{n-1} obtains some of D_is. Since D_is are in permuted form and those n-1 parties don't know the permutation function, they cannot know the P_n's original values either.

---

[3] (d_1, e_1) is independent from (d, e).

In our protocol, those $n-1$ parties' *c.count*s are also preserved because of the encryption. What P_j receives from other $n-2$ parties is the encrypted counts. Since P_j doesn't know the encryption key e_1, P_j cannot know other $n-2$ parties' counts. What P_n receives from P_j is the multiplication of all *c.count$_i$*s. Therefore, she doesn't know each individual P_i's count (i = 1, 2, $\cdots$, n-1).

We also emphasis that Step (2b) are required, the goal is to prevent other parties from knowing P_n's values. Step (2c) is for the consideration of computational balance among P_1, P_2, $\cdots$, and P_{n-1}. Step (3b) to (3e) is to further prevent parties from knowing *c.count$_i$*s each other. If the collaborative parties allow sharing *c.count$_i$*s each other, some of steps can be removed and communication cost is saved.

5   Concluding Remarks

In this paper, we consider the problem of privacy-preserving collaborative association rule mining. In particular, we study how multiple parties can collaboratively conduct association rule mining on their joint private data. We develop a secure collaborative association rule mining protocol based on homomorphic encryption scheme. In our protocol, the parties do not send all their data to a central, trusted party. Instead, we use the homomorphic encryption techniques to conduct the computations across the parties without compromising their data privacy. Privacy analysis is provided. Correctness of our protocols is shown and complexity of the protocols is addressed as well. As future work, we will develop a privacy measure to quantitatively measure the privacy level achieved by our proposed secure protocols. We will also apply our technique to other data mining computations, such as secure collaborative clustering.

Acknowledgement

The first two authors acknowledge generous support of the Natural Sciences and Engineering Research Council of Canada, and the Communications and Information Technology Ontario for their research.

References

1. G. Aggarwal, N. Mishra, and B. Pinkas. Secure computation of the k th-ranked element. In *EUROCRYPT pp 40-55*, 2004.
2. R. Agrawal, T. Imielinski, and A. Swami. Mining association rules between sets of items in large databases. In P. Buneman and S. Jajodia, editors, *Proceedings of ACM SIGMOD Conference on Management of Data*, pages 207–216, Washington D.C., May 1993.
3. R. Agrawal and R. Srikant. Privacy-preserving data mining. In *Proceedings of the ACM SIGMOD Conference on Management of Data*, pages 439–450. ACM Press, May 2000.
4. C. Dwork and K. Nissim. Privacy-preserving datamining on vertically partitioned databases.

5. O. Goldreich. Secure multi-party computation (working draft). http://www.wisdom.weizmann.ac.il /home/oded/public_html/foc.html, 1998.
6. J.Vaidya and C.W.Clifton. Privacy preserving association rule mining in vertically partitioned data. In *Proceedings of the 8th ACM SIGKDD International Conference on Knowledge Discovery and Data Mining, July 23-26, 2002, Edmonton, Alberta, Canada.*
7. M. Kantarcioglu and C. Clifton. Privacy preserving data mining of association rules on horizontally partitioned data. In *Transactions on Knowledge and Data Engineering, IEEE Computer Society Press, Los Alamitos, CA, to appear.*
8. Y. Lindell and B. Pinkas. Privacy preserving data mining. In *Advances in Cryptology - Crypto2000, Lecture Notes in Computer Science,* volume 1880, 2000.
9. M. Luby. *Pseudorandomness and Cryptographic Applications.* Princeton University Press, January 1996.
10. P. Paillier. Public-key cryptosystems based on composite degree residuosity classes. In *Advances in Cryptography - EUROCRYPT '99, pp 223-238, Prague, Czech Republic,* May 1999.
11. L. Sweeney. k-anonymity: a model for protecting privacy. In *International Journal on Uncertainty, Fuzziness and Knowledge-based Systems 10 (5), pp 557–570.*
12. R. Wright and Z. Yang. Privacy-preserving bayesian network structure computation on distributed heterogeneous data. In *Proceedings of the 10th ACM SIGKDD International Conference on Knowledge Discovery and Data Mining (KDD),* 2004.
13. A. C. Yao. Protocols for secure computations. In *Proceedings of the 23rd Annual IEEE Symposium on Foundations of Computer Science,* 1982.

Privacy-Preserving Distributed k-Anonymity⋆

Wei Jiang and Chris Clifton

Department of Computer Science, Purdue University,
West Lafayette, IN 47907
{wjiang, clifton}@cs.purdue.edu
http://www.cs.purdue.edu/people/wjiang
http://www.cs.purdue.edu/people/clifton

Abstract. k-anonymity provides a measure of privacy protection by preventing re-identification of data to fewer than a group of k data items. While algorithms exist for producing k-anonymous data, the model has been that of a single source wanting to publish data. This paper presents a k-anonymity protocol when the data is vertically partitioned between sites. A key contribution is a proof that the protocol preserves k-anonymity between the sites: While one site may have individually identifiable data, it learns nothing that violates k-anonymity with respect to the data at the other site. This is a fundamentally different distributed privacy definition than that of Secure Multiparty Computation, and it provides a better match with both ethical and legal views of privacy.

Keywords: k-anonymity, privacy, security.

1 Introduction

Privacy is an important concept in our society, and has become very vulnerable in these technologically advanced times. Legislation has been proposed to protect individual privacy; a key component is the protection of *individually identifiable data*. Many techniques have been proposed to protect privacy, such as data perturbation [1], data swapping [2], query restriction [3], secure multiparty computation (SMC) [4,5,6], etc. One challenge is relating such techniques to a privacy definition that meets legal and societal norms. Anonymous data are generally considered to be exempt from privacy rules – but what does it mean for data to be anonymous? Census agencies, which have long dealt with private data, have generally found that as long as data are aggregated over a group of individuals, release does not violate privacy. k-anonymity provides a formal way of generalizing this concept. As stated in [7,8], a data record is k-anonymous if and only if it is indistinguishable in its identifying information from at least k specific records or entities. The key step in making data anonymous is to generalize a specific value. For example, the ages 18 and 21 could be generalized to

---

⋆ This material is based upon work supported by the National Science Foundation under Grant No. 0428168.

S. Jajodia and D. Wijesekera (Eds.): Data and Applications Security 2005, LNCS 3654, pp. 166–177, 2005.

an interval [16..25]. Details of the concept of k-anonymity and ways to generate k-anonymous data are provided in Section 2.

Generalized data can be beneficial in many situations. For instance, a car insurance company may want to build a model to estimate claims for use in pricing policies for new customers. To build this model, the company may wish to use state-wide driver's license records. Such records, even with name and ID numbers removed, are likely to contain sufficient information to link to an individual. However, by generalizing data (e.g., replacing a birth date with an age range [26..30]), it is possible to prevent linking a record to an individual. The generalized age range is likely to be sufficient for building the claim estimation model. Similar applications exist in many areas: medical research, education studies, targeted marketing, etc.

Due to vast improvements in networking and rapid increase of storage capacity, the full data about an individual are typically partitioned into several sub-data sets (credit history, medical records, earnings, ...), each stored at an independent site.[1] The distributed setting is likely to remain, partially because of performance and accessibility, but more importantly because of autonomy of the independent sites. This autonomy provides a measure of protection for the individual data. For instance, if two attributes in combination reveal private information (e.g., airline and train travel records indicating likely attendance at political rallies), but the attributes are stored at different sites, a lack of cooperation between the sites ensures that neither is able to violate privacy.

In this paper, data are assumed to be vertically partitioned and stored at two sites, and the original data could be reconstructed by a one-to-one join on a common key. The goal is to build a k-anonymous join of the datasets, so that the join key and any other candidate keys in the joined dataset are k-anonymized to prevent re-identification.

1.1   What Is a Privacy-Preserving Distributed Protocol?

A key question in this problem is the definition of privacy preservation. Simply stating that the result is k-anonymous is not enough, as this does not ensure that the participating sites do not violate privacy. However, since the sites already have individually identifiable information, we cannot fully extend the k-anonymity measure to them. We now give an informal definition for privacy preservation; the paper will then present an algorithm and show formally that it does not violate k-anonymity in the sense of the following definition.

Definition 1. *Let T_i be the input of party i, $\prod_i(f)$ be the party i's execution image of the protocol f, r be the result computed by f, and P be a set of privacy constraints. f is privacy-preserving if every inference induced from $< T_i, \prod_i(f), r >$ that violates any privacy constraint in P could also be induced from $< T_i >$.*

---

[1] In the context of this paper, assume data are represented by a relational table, where each row indicates an individual data record and each column represents an attribute of data records.

This definition has much in common with that of Secure Multiparty Computation (SMC) [9]. Both talk about a party's view during execution of a protocol, and what can be inferred from that view. The key distinction is the concept of privacy (and privacy constraints) versus security. An SMC protocol must reveal nothing except the final result, and what can be inferred from one's own input and the result. Definition 1 is weaker (giving greater flexibility): It allows inferences from the protocol that go beyond what can be inferred from the result, provided that such inferences do not violate the privacy constraints.

A more subtle distinction is that Definition 1 is also *stronger* than SMC. The above definition requires that the inferences from the result r and from one's own input combined with the result (and the protocol execution) do not violate the privacy constraints. The SMC definitions do not account for this.

For example, a privacy-preserving classification scheme meeting SMC definitions [10,11,12,13] ensures that nothing is disclosed but the resulting model. Assume that Party A holds input attributes, and B holds the (private) class attribute: B has committed to ensuring that the class is not revealed for the individuals that have given it data. An SMC protocol can generate a classifier without revealing the class of the individuals to A. Moreover, the classifier need not inherently violate privacy: A properly pruned decision tree, for example, will only contain paths corresponding to several data values. A, however, can use its input along with the classifier to learn (with high probability) the class values held by B. This clearly violates the commitment B has made, even if the protocol meets SMC definitions. More discussion of this specific problem can be found in [14].

Generally speaking, if the set of privacy constraints P can be easily incorporated into the functionality computed by a SMC protocol, a SMC protocol also preserves privacy. However, there is no obvious general framework that easily and correctly incorporates privacy constraints into part of the functionality computed by a SMC protocol.

This paper presents a privacy-preserving two-party protocol that generates k-anonymous data from two vertically partitioned sources such that the protocol does not violate k-anonymity of either site's data. While one site may already hold individually identifiable data, we show that the protocol prevents either site from linking its own individually identifiable data to specific values from the other site, except as permitted under k-anonymity. (This privacy constraint will be formally defined in Section 3.) Interestingly, one of distinctive characteristics of the proposed protocol is that it is not secure by SMC definitions; parties may learn more than they can infer from their own data and the final k-anonymous datset. Nevertheless, it preserves the privacy constraint.

The rest of the paper is organized as the following: Section 2 introduces the fundamental concepts of k-anonymity. Section 3 presents a generic two-party protocol, with proof of its correctness and privacy-preservation property. The paper concludes with some insights gained from the protocol and future research directions on achieving k-anonymity in a distributed environment.

2 Background

We now give key background on k-anonymity, including definitions, a single-site algorithm, and a relevant theorem, from [7,15,16]. The following notations are crucial for understanding the rest of the paper:

- Quasi-Identifier (QI): a set of attributes that can be used with certain external information to identify a specific individual.
- T, $T[\text{QI}]$: T is the original dataset represented in a relational form, $T[\text{QI}]$ is the projection of T to the set of attributes contained in QI.
- $T_k[\text{QI}]$: k-anonymous data generated from T with respect to the attributes in the Quasi-Identifier QI.

Definition 2. *$T_k[QI]$ satisfies k-anonymity if and only if each record in it appears at least k times.*

Let T be Table 1, T_k be Table 2 and QI = {AREA, POSITION, SALARY}. According to Definition 2, $T_k[\text{QI}]$ satisfies 3-anonymity.

Several algorithms have been proposed to generate k-anonymous data [17,8,18]. Datafly [8,18] is a simple and effective algorithm, so for demonstration of our protocol, Datafly is used to make local data k-anonymous. Algorithm 1 presents several key steps in Datafly (detailed explanations regarding this algorithm can be found in [8]). The main step in most k-anonymity protocols

---

Algorithm 1. Key Steps in Datafly

Require: T, QI$[A_1, \ldots, A_m]$, k, Hierarchies VGHs Assume $k \leq |T|$
 1: $freq \leftarrow$ a frequency list contains distinct sequences of values of $T[QI]$ along with the number of occurrences of each sequence.
 2: **while** (sequences $\in freq$ occurring less than k times that count for more than k tuples) **do**
 3:    $A_i \in QI$ having the most number of distinct values
 4:    $freq \leftarrow$ generalize the values of $A_i \in freq$
 5: **end while**
 6: $freq \leftarrow$ suppress sequences in $freq$ occurring less than k times
 7: $freq \leftarrow$ enforce k requirement on suppressed tuples in $freq$
 8: $T_k[\text{QI}] \leftarrow$ construct table from $freq$
 9: $return$ $T_k[\text{QI}]$

---

is to substitute a specific value with a more general value. For instance, Figure 1(a) contains a value generalization hierarchy (VGH) for attribute AREA, in which Database Systems is a more general value than Data Mining. Similarly, Figure 1(b) and Figure 1(c) present VGHs of attributes POSITION and SALARY contained in QI. Continuing from the previous example, $T_k[\text{QI}]$ satisfies 3-anonymity. According to the three VGHs and the original data represented by T, it is easily verified that Datafly can generate $T_k[\text{QI}]$ by generalizing the data on SALARY, then AREA, then SALARY again. Next, we present a useful theorem about k-anonymity.

Table 1. Original Dataset Before Partitioning

ID	AREA	POSITION	SALARY	SSN
1	Data Mining	Associate Professor	$90,000	708-79-1698
2	Intrusion Detection	Assistant Professor	$91,000	606-67-6789
3	Data Warehousing	Associate Professor	$95,000	626-23-1459
4	Intrusion Detection	Assistant Professor	$78,000	373-55-7788
5	Digital Forensics	Professor	$150,000	626-87-6503
6	Distributed Systems	Research Assistant	$15,000	708-66-1552
7	Handhold Systems	Research Assistant	$17,000	810-74-1079
8	Handhold Systems	Research Assistant	$15,500	606-37-7706
9	Query Processing	Associate Professor	$100,000	373-79-1698
10	Digital Forensics	Assistant Professor	$78,000	999-03-7892
11	Digital Forensics	Professor	$135,000	708-90-1976
12	Intrusion Detection	Professor	$145,000	606-17-6512

Table 2. Generalized Data with $k = 3$

ID	AREA	POSITION	SALARY	SSN
1	Database Systems	Associate Professor	[61k, 120k]	708-79-1698
2	Information Security	Assistant Professor	[61k, 120k]	606-67-6789
3	Database Systems	Associate Professor	[61k, 120k]	626-23-1459
4	Information Security	Assistant Professor	[61k, 120k]	373-55-7788
5	Information Security	Professor	[121k, 180k]	626-87-6503
6	Operating Systems	Research Assistant	[11k, 30k]	708-66-1552
7	Operating Systems	Research Assistant	[11k, 30k]	810-74-1079
8	Operation Systems	Research Assistant	[11k, 30k]	606-37-7706
9	Database Systems	Associate Professor	[61k, 120k]	373-79-1698
10	Information Security	Assistant Professor	[61k, 120k]	999-03-7892
11	Information Security	Professor	[121k, 180k]	708-90-1976
12	Information Security	Professor	[121k, 180k]	606-17-6512

Theorem 1. *If $T_k[QI]$ is k-anonymous, then $T_k[QI']$ is also k-anonymous, where $QI' \subseteq QI$ [8].*

Proof. Assume $T_k[QI]$ is being k-anonymous and $T_k[QI']$ does not satisfy k-anonymity. Then there exists a record $t(QI')$ that appears in $T_k[QI']$ less than k times. It is trivial to observe that $t(QI)$ also appears less than k times in $T_k[QI]$. That contradicts the assumption. Therefore, if $T_k[QI]$ satisfies k-anonymity, so does $T_k[QI']$. □

3   The Protocol: DPP$_2$GA

Before presenting the protocol, we present an alternative view of k-anonymity. Define T_k to be the k-anonymous data computed from T. Let $x \triangleright y$ denote that x is directly generalized from y. E.g., in Table 2 the Salary for ID 1: [61k, 120k] $\triangleright$ $90,000.

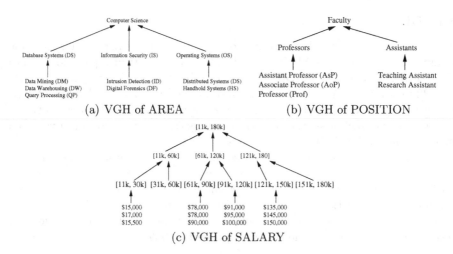

Fig. 1. Value Generalization Hierarchies

Theorem 2. T_k *achieved through generalization satisfies k-anonymity if and only if $\forall t' \in T_k, Prob[t' \rhd t \in T] \leq \frac{1}{k}$.*

Proof. $\Rightarrow$: Given generalized values t', if $t' \in T_k$ then there is a set S of identical $t'_i \in T_k$ s.t. $|S| \geq k$ and $t' = t'_i$ (by the definition of k-anonymity). Each $t'_i \in S \rhd t \in T$. Since we cannot distinguish between the t'_is, the probability that we have a particular $t'_i = \frac{1}{S} \leq \frac{1}{k}$. Thus the probability that t' is generalized from a particular t_i is $Prob[t' \rhd t_i] = Prob[t' = t'_i] \leq \frac{1}{k}$.

$\Leftarrow$: Let $Prob[t' \rhd t \in T] \leq \frac{1}{k}$, and t' be the record with the highest such probability for a generalization from t. Since the generalization is done according to a hierarchy, t must generalize to a (uniquely determined) single node in each hierarchy. This defines the only allowed values for t'. Thus all $t'_i \in T_k$ have $Prob[t'_i \rhd t] = 0$ or $Prob[t'_i \rhd t] = Prob[t' \rhd t] \leq \frac{1}{k}$. Since t must uniquely generalize to one of the t'_i, the sum of probabilities must be 1. Thus there must be at least k $t'_i \in T_k$ that are identical to t', so k-anonymity holds for t'. $\square$

From Theorem 2, the privacy constraint P in our application domain can be formally defined as: inferences from $< T_i, \prod_i(f), T_k >$ do not enable party i to conclude $\exists t' \in T_k$ (or a t' seen in $\prod_i(f)$) such that $Prob[t' \rhd t \in T] > \frac{1}{k}$. Informally, $< T_i, \prod_i(f), T_k >$ does not make T_k less k-anonymous. We will revisit this privacy constraint when proving that the proposed protocol is privacy-preserving.

Since the protocol can utilize any k-anonymity algorithm to compute locally anonymous data, we call the proposed approach Distributed Privacy-Preserving two-Party Generic Anonymizer (DPP$_2$GA). The protocol is presented in Section 3.1, Section 3.2 proves the correctness of the protocol and Section 3.3 proves the protocol satisfies the k-anonymity privacy constraint.

3.1   DPP$_2$GA

The protocol is executed between two parties: P1 and P2. Let T refer to Table 1 and QI = {AREA, POSITION, SALARY}. T is vertically partitioned into $T1 \equiv T$[ID, AREA, POSITION] and $T2 \equiv T$[ID, SALARY, SSN] stored at P1 and P2 respectively. Also, assume P1 and P2 are semi-honest in that they follow the execution of the protocol but may later use the information seen to try to violate privacy. (Discussion of the privacy properties under stronger adversarial models omitted due to space constraints.)

The key idea of the protocol is based on Theorem 1. Initially, each party Pi ($i = 1$ or 2) makes his data k-anonymous locally (for simplicity, Datafly is used for illustration). Based on this locally k-anonymous data, a set γ^i is produced containing IDs partitioned into subsets. Let $\gamma^i[p]$ indicates the pth subset in γ^i, then all records Pi whose keys are contained in $\gamma^i[p]$ have the same value with respect to QI. For any γ^i, the following properties hold:

– $\gamma^i[p] \cap \gamma^i[q] = \emptyset$, for any $1 \leq p, q \leq |\gamma^i|$ and $p \neq q$
– $\bigcup_p \gamma^i[p]$ is the same across all γ^is

Note that although each element $\gamma^i[p]$ in γ^i contains record keys, it does make sense to say that $\gamma^i[p]$ contains a subset of records or data tuples because each key is related to a single tuple. Define Ti_{γ^i} be the generalized data at Pi based on which γ^i is computed. For example, refer to Table 3, the columns [AREA^p, POSITION^q] indicate the generalized data of $T1$[AREA, POSITION], where $p+q$ indicates the number of times $T1$[AREA, POSITION] has been generalized (by Datafly). Also, the last generalization of $T1$[AREA, POSITION] was performed on the attribute whose superscript was incremented comparing to its previous value. $T2$[SALARY] can be interpreted similarly. According to Table 3, we have:

$$\gamma_1^1 = \{\{1, 3, 9\}, \{2, 4, 10\}, \{5, 11, 12\}, \{6, 7, 8\}\}$$
$$\gamma_1^2 = \{\{1, 4, 10\}, \{2, 3, 9\}, \{5, 11, 12\}, \{6, 7, 8\}\}$$

Table 3. P1 and P2 's Generalized Data (left and right respectively)

ID	AREA^1	POSITION^0	AREA^1	POSITION^1	ID	SALARY^1	SALARY^2
1	DB	AoP	DB	Professors	1	[61k, 90k]	[61k, 120k]
2	IS	AsP	IS	Professors	2	[91k, 120k]	[61k, 120k]
3	DB	AoP	DB	Professors	3	[91k, 120k]	[61k, 120k]
4	IS	AsP	IS	Professors	4	[61k, 90k]	[61k, 120k]
5	IS	Prof	IS	Professors	5	[121k, 150k]	[121k, 180k]
6	OS	RA	OS	Assistant	6	[11k, 30k]	[11k, 30k]
7	OS	RA	OS	Assistant	7	[11k, 30k]	[11k, 30k]
8	OS	RA	OS	Assistant	8	[11k, 30k]	[11k, 30k]
9	DB	AoP	DB	Professors	9	[91k, 120k]	[61k, 120k]
10	IS	AsP	IS	Professors	10	[61k, 90k]	[61k, 120k]
11	IS	Prof	IS	Professors	11	[121k, 150k]	[121k, 180k]
12	IS	Prof	IS	Professors	12	[121k, 150k]	[121k, 180k]

The two parties then compare γ_1^1 and γ_1^2. If they are *equal* (this notion of equality will be defined shortly), joining data $T1_{\gamma_1^1}$ and $T2_{\gamma_1^2}$ creates globally k-anonymous data. If γ_1^1 and γ_1^2 are not equal, each party generalizes his local data one step further and creates a new γ^i. Repeat the above steps until the two parties find a pair of equal γ^is. Let's define the notion of equality between any two γ^is.

Definition 3. *If $\gamma_\alpha^i \equiv \gamma_\beta^j$, then there are no p, q such that $0 < |\gamma_\alpha^i[p] \cap \gamma_\beta^j[q]| < k$.*

According to the above definition, $\gamma_1^1 \neq \gamma_1^2$ because $|\{1, 3, 9\} \in \gamma_1^1 \cap \{2, 3, 9\} \in \gamma_1^2| = 2 < k$ (where $k = 3$). Thus, P1 and P2 generalize their data one step further and compute two new γ^is:

$$\gamma_2^1 = \{\{1, 3, 9\}, \{2, 4, 5, 10, 11, 12\}, \{6, 7, 8\}\}$$
$$\gamma_2^2 = \{\{1, 2, 3, 4, 9, 10\}, \{5, 11, 12\}, \{6, 7, 8\}\}$$

Since $\gamma_2^1 \equiv \gamma_2^2$, the join of $T1_{\gamma_2^1}$ (columns [AREA^1, POSITION^1] in Table 3) and $T2_{\gamma_2^2}$ (column [SALARY^2] in Table 3) satisfies 3-anonymity.

Due to privacy issues, the comparison between γ^is are not performed directly. Instead, P1 encrypts γ^1 and sends $E_{K_{P1}}(\gamma^1)$ to P2. P2 then encrypts $E_{K_{P1}}(\gamma^1)$ and sends a copy of $E_{K_{P2}}(E_{K_{P1}}(\gamma^1))$ back to P1. γ^2 is treated similarly. After this exchange, both parties have copies of $\left[E_{K_{P2}}(E_{K_{P1}}(\gamma^1)), E_{K_{P1}}(E_{K_{P2}}(\gamma^2)) \right]$. Note that the encryption is applied to individual value, and we also adopt the commutative encryption scheme described in [19], but any other commutative encryption scheme can also be used. The key property of this scheme is that $E_{K_{P2}}(E_{K_{P1}}(v)) = E_{K_{P1}}(E_{K_{P2}}(v))$: encryption order does not matter.

Algorithm 2. DPP$_2$GA

Require: Private Data $T1$, $QI = (A_1, \ldots, A_n)$, Constraint k, Hierarchies VGH_{A_i}, where $i = 1, \ldots, n$, assume $k \leq |T1|$

1: P1 generalizes his data to be locally k-anonymous;
2: int $c \leftarrow 0$;
3: **repeat**
4:    $c = c + 1$;
5:    P1 computes γ_c^1;
6:    P1 computes $E_{K_{P1}}(\gamma_c^1)$ and sends it to P2;
7:    P1 receives $E_{K_{P2}}(\gamma_c^2)$ and computes $\Gamma_{P2} = E_{K_{P1}}(E_{K_{P2}}(\gamma_c^2))$;
8:    P1 receives $\Gamma_{P1} = E_{K_{P2}}(E_{K_{P1}}(\gamma_c^1))$;
9: **until** $\Gamma_{P1} \equiv \Gamma_{P2}$
10: *return* $T_k[QI] \leftarrow T1_{\gamma_c^1} \bowtie T2_{\gamma_c^2}$;

Key steps in our approach are highlighted in Algorithm 2. The algorithm is written as executed by P1. Note that synchronization is needed for the counter c, and the encryption keys are different for each round. When the *loop* is executed more than once, the algorithm requires local data to be generalized one step further before computing the next γ_c^1 at Step 5. At step 10, the symbol $\bowtie$ represents the one-to-one join operator on the ID attribute to create globally k-anonymous dataset from the two locally k-anonymous datasets.

3.2   Proof of Correctness

In this section, we prove Algorithm 2 achieves global k-anonymity. Refer to notations adopted in Section 3.1, let γ_c^1, γ_c^2 synchronously computed from P1 and P2's locally k-anonymous data and use the equality operator $\equiv$ defined in Definition 3. Define $T1_{\gamma_c^1}$ and $T2_{\gamma_c^2}$ as the locally k-anonymous data related to γ_c^1 and γ_c^2 respectively.

Theorem 3. *If* $\gamma_c^1 \equiv \gamma_c^2$, *then* $T_k[QI] \leftarrow T1_{\gamma_c^1} \bowtie T2_{\gamma_c^2}$ *satisfies global* k-*anonymity*.

Proof. Let's prove the above theorem by contrapositive. In other words, prove the following statement: If $T_k[QI]$ does not satisfy global k-anonymity, then $\gamma_c^1 \neq \gamma_c^2$. Suppose $T_k[QI]$ is not k-anonymous, then there exists a subset of records $S = \{t_1, \ldots, t_j\} \subset T_k[QI]$ such that $|S| < k$ or $j < k$. Let $t_j[\gamma_c^1]$ denote the portion of the record t_j related to γ_c^1 stored at P1 and $t_j[\gamma_c^2]$ denote the portion of the record related to γ_c^2 stored at P2. Then $\{t_1[\gamma_c^1], \ldots, t_j[\gamma_c^1]\}$ must be contained in some subset $\gamma_c^1[p]$, and $\{t_1[\gamma_c^2], \ldots, t_j[\gamma_c^2]\}$ must be contained in some subset $\gamma_c^2[q]$; as a result, $|\gamma_c^1[p] \cap \gamma_c^2[q]| < k$. According to Definition 3, the equality between γ_c^1 and γ_c^2 does not hold. Thus, the contrapositive statement is true, so Theorem 3 holds.   □

3.3   Proof of Privacy Preservation

Referring to Step 9 in Algorithm 2, although equality is tested on the encrypted version of γ_c^1 and γ_c^2, inference problems do exist.

For simplicity and consistency, let's use γ_c^1 and γ_c^2 instead of Γ_{P1} and Γ_{P2} for the following analysis. The inference problem exists only when $\gamma_c^1 \neq \gamma_c^2$. More specifically, we analyze the inference problem when $0 < |\gamma_c^1[p] \cap \gamma_c^2[q]| < k$ (for some p and q) because this inference seemingly violates global k-anonymity.

We classify inference problems into two types: final inference problem (FIP) and intermediate inference problem (IIP). FIP refers to the implication when the inequality occurs at Step 9 of Algorithm 2 only once. IIP refers to the implication when the inequality occurs multiple times. Let $T_k[QI]$ be the k-anonymous data computed by Algorithm 2.

Theorem 4. *FIP does not violate the privacy constraint P (previously stated in this section); in other words, FIP does not make* $T_k[QI]$ *less* k-*anonymous*.

Proof. If $\gamma_c^1 \neq \gamma_c^2$, then according to Definition 3, there must exist an intersection set $I_c = \gamma_c^1[p] \cap \gamma_c^2[q]$ such that $0 < |I_c| < k$. Since the equality test at Step 9 of Algorithm 2 is performed on the encrypted versions of γ_c^1 and γ_c^2, we are not able to know the exact records in I_c. Because of the definition of FIP, $\gamma_{c+1}^1 \equiv \gamma_{c+1}^2$ holds. Since γ_{c+1}^i computed from more generalized data than γ_c^i, the following conditions hold:

- $\gamma_c^1[p] \subseteq \gamma_{c+1}^1[p']$, where $1 \leq p' \leq |\gamma_{c+1}^1|$
- $\gamma_c^2[q] \subseteq \gamma_{c+1}^2[q']$, where $1 \leq q' \leq |\gamma_{c+1}^2|$

When the final generalized data released, for the worst case scenario, we may be able to identify unencrypted records related to $\gamma^1_{c+1}[p']$ and $\gamma^2_{c+1}[q']$. Define $I_{c+1} = \gamma^1_{c+1}[p'] \cap \gamma^2_{c+1}[q']$. According to the above conditions and $\gamma^1_{c+1} \equiv \gamma^2_{c+1}$, $I_c \subset I_{c+1}$ and $|I_{c+1}| \geq k$.

Since the equality test was performed on encrypted data, $Prob[x \triangleright y] = \frac{|I_c|}{|I_{c+1}|}$, where $x \in I_{c+1}$ and $y \in I_c$. If x is not directly generalized from y of any I_c, then $Prob[x \triangleright t \in T] \leq \frac{1}{k}$ because x is k-anonymous. If $x \triangleright y$, then $Prob[x \triangleright t \in T] = Prob[x \triangleright y] \cdot Prob[y \triangleright t]$. y is $|I_c|$-anonymous, so $Prob[y \triangleright t] = \frac{1}{|I_c|}$. Then we have $Prob[x \triangleright t \in T] = \frac{|I_c|}{|I_{c+1}|} \cdot \frac{1}{|I_c|} \leq \frac{1}{k}$. $\qquad\square$

Next, we show a concrete example that illustrates why FIP does not violate k-anonymity. Refer to $\gamma^1_1, \gamma^2_1, \gamma^1_2, \gamma^2_2$ in Section 3.1. Let $\gamma^i_c = \gamma^i_1$ and $\gamma^i_{c+1} = \gamma^i_2$ where $i \in \{1,2\}$. As stated previously, we have $\gamma^1_1 \neq \gamma^2_1$, so let $\gamma^1_c[p] = \{1,3,9\}$ and $\gamma^2_c[q] = \{2,3,9\}$. Then we have $I_c = \gamma^1_c[p] \cap \gamma^2_c[q] = \{3,9\}$, $\gamma^1_{c+1}[p'] = \{1,3,9\}$, $\gamma^2_{c+1}[q'] = \{1,2,3,4,9,10\}$ and $I_{c+1} = \gamma^1_{c+1}[p'] \cap \gamma^2_{c+1}[q'] = \{1,3,9\}$. Note that in this example, we can directly observe record IDs. However, in the real execution of the protocol, each party can only see the encrypted ID values. Now let's see if the data records contained in I_c violate the property stated in Theorem 2. Let $x \triangleright y \in I_c$, then $Prob[x \triangleright t \in T] = Prob[x \triangleright y] \cdot Prob[y \triangleright t] = \frac{|I_c|}{|I_{c+1}|} \cdot \frac{1}{|T|} = \frac{1}{3} = \frac{1}{k}$.

Theorem 5. *IIP does not violate the privacy constraint P; in other words, IIP does not make $T_k[QI]$ less k-anonymous.*

Proof. Use the notations defined in the proof of Theorem 4. According to the definition of IIP, $\gamma^1_c \neq \gamma^2_c$ and $\gamma^1_{c+1} \neq \gamma^2_{c+1}$. Define $I_c = \gamma^1_c[p] \cap \gamma^2_c[q]$ such that $0 < |I| < k$. Similar to the previous analysis, the following two conditions hold:

- $\gamma^1_c[p] \subseteq \gamma^1_{c+1}[p']$, where $1 \leq p' \leq |\gamma^1_{c+1}|$
- $\gamma^2_c[q] \subseteq \gamma^2_{c+1}[q']$, where $1 \leq q' \leq |\gamma^2_{c+1}|$

Define $I_{c+1} = \gamma^1_{c+1}[p'] \cap \gamma^2_{c+1}[q']$. If I_{c+1} is k-anonymous or $|I_{c+1}| \geq k$, then this inference problem caused by I_c is the same as FIP.

Now consider the case where $|I_{c+1}| < k$. Because γ^i_{c+1} computed from more generalized data than γ^i_c, $I_c \subseteq I_{c+1}$. If $|I_c| = |I_{c+1}|$, the inference effect caused by I_c does not propagate to the equality test between γ^1_{c+1} and γ^2_{c+1}. If $|I_c| < |I_{c+1}|$, define $x \in I_{c+1}$ and $y \in I_c$. If x is not directly generalized from y, then $Prob[x \triangleright t \in T] = \frac{1}{|I_{c+1}|}$ because x is $|I_{c+1}|$-anonymous. Nevertheless, if $x \triangleright y$, then $Prob[x \triangleright t \in T] = Prob[x \triangleright y] \cdot Prob[y \triangleright t] = \frac{|I_c|}{|I_{c+1}|} \cdot \frac{1}{|I_c|} = \frac{1}{|I_{c+1}|}$. As a result, $Prob[x \triangleright t \in T]$ is the same for all records in I_{c+1}. The inference effect caused by I_c is independent from one equality test to the next one. Consequently, the effect of IIP is the same as that of FIP. $\qquad\square$

The equality test between γ^1_c and γ^2_c is not the focal point of this paper. It is fairly simple to derive, so we do not provide any specifics about how to perform the equality test. In addition, we note that if $|I_c| \geq k$, the records in the I_c do not violate the privacy constraint due to the definition of k-anonymity.

4 Conclusion / Future Work

Privacy of information in databases is an increasingly visible issue. Partitioning data is effective at preventing misuse of data, but it also makes beneficial use more difficult. One way to preserve privacy while enabling beneficial use of data is to utilize k-anonymity for publishing data. Maintaining the benefits of partitioning while generating integrated k-anonymous data requires a protocol that does not violate the k-anonymity privacy constraint. In this paper, we have laid out this problem and presented a two-party protocol DPP_2GA that is proven to preserve the constraint. It is a generic protocol in a sense that any k-anonymity protocol can be used to compute locally k-anonymous data.

One disadvantage of DPP_2GA is that it may not produce as precise data (with respect to the precision metric defined in [8]) as other k-anonymity algorithms do when data are not partitioned. For instance, DPP_2GA could be modified to simulate Datafly. At Step 9 of Algorithm 2, when the equality does not hold, only the party with the attribute that has most distinct values globally should generalize the data. Then the equality test would be performed on the newly computed Γ_{c+1}^1 with previously used Γ_c^2. The data generated this way are the same as those computed by Datafly.

Even though this approach may produce more precise data, it does introduce additional inference problems because some Γ_{c+j}^i may be compared more than once. It is not obvious that this additional inference must (or can) violate k-anonymity with respect to individual parties, but proving this formally is not an easy task. One key design philosophy of DPP_2GA is to provably eliminate such inference problems, so DPP_2GA sacrifices a certain degree of precision. More precise protocols with fewer or no inference problems are a worthwhile challenge for future research. Another observation we have during the design of DPP_2GA is that more precise data can also be generated by removing already k-anonymous data at the end of each round (resulting in different data being generalized to different levels). Again, providing a formal method to analyze the inference problem might be very difficult, but this provides a valuable future research direction.

DPP_2GA is not a SMC protocol because it introduces certain inference problems, such as FIP and IIP. However, based on our analyses, both FIP and IIP do not violate the k-anonymity privacy constraint. Formally defining and understanding the differences between privacy-preserving and Secure Multiparty Computation may open up many new opportunities for designing protocols that preserve privacy.

Acknowledgements

We wish to thank Professor Elisa Bertino for comments and discussions that lead to this work.

References

1. Agrawal, R., Srikant, R.: Privacy-preserving data mining. In: Proceedings of the 2000 ACM SIGMOD Conference on Management of Data, Dallas, TX, ACM (2000) 439–450

2. Moore, Jr., R.A.: Controlled data-swapping techniques for masking public use microdata sets. Statistical Research Division Report Series RR 96-04, U.S. Bureau of the Census, Washington, DC. (1996)
3. Dobkin, D., Jones, A.K., Lipton, R.J.: Secure databases: Protection against user influence. ACM Transactions on Database Systems **4** (1979) 97–106
4. Yao, A.C.: Protocols for secure computation. In: Proceedings of the 23rd IEEE Symposium on Foundations of Computer Science, IEEE (1982) 160–164
5. Yao, A.C.: How to generate and exchange secrets. In: Proceedings of the 27th IEEE Symposium on Foundations of Computer Science, IEEE (1986) 162–167
6. Goldreich, O., Micali, S., Wigderson, A.: How to play any mental game - a completeness theorem for protocols with honest majority. In: 19th ACM Symposium on the Theory of Computing. (1987) 218–229
7. Sweeney, L.: k-anonymity: a model for protecting privacy. International Journal on Uncertainty, Fuzziness and Knowledge-based Systems **10** (2002) 557–570
8. Sweeney, L.: Achieving k-anonymity privacy protection using generalization and suppression. International Journal on Uncertainty, Fuzziness and Knowledge-based Systems **10** (2002) 571–588
9. Goldreich, O.: General Cryptographic Protocols. In: The Foundations of Cryptography. Volume 2. Cambridge University Press (2004)
10. Lindell, Y., Pinkas, B.: Privacy preserving data mining. Journal of Cryptology **15** (2002) 177–206
11. Du, W., Zhan, Z.: Building decision tree classifier on private data. In Clifton, C., Estivill-Castro, V., eds.: IEEE International Conference on Data Mining Workshop on Privacy, Security, and Data Mining. Volume 14., Maebashi City, Japan, Australian Computer Society (2002) 1–8
12. Vaidya, J., Clifton, C.: Privacy preserving naïve bayes classifier for vertically partitioned data. In: 2004 SIAM International Conference on Data Mining, Lake Buena Vista, Florida (2004) 522–526
13. Kantarcıoğlu, M., Clifton, C.: Privately computing a distributed k-nn classifier. In Boulicaut, J.F., Esposito, F., Giannotti, F., Pedreschi, D., eds.: PKDD2004: 8th European Conference on Principles and Practice of Knowledge Discovery in Databases, Pisa, Italy (2004) 279–290
14. Kantarcıoğlu, M., Jin, J., Clifton, C.: When do data mining results violate privacy? In: Proceedings of the 2004 ACM SIGKDD International Conference on Knowledge Discovery and Data Mining, Seattle, WA (2004) 599–604
15. Samarati, P., Sweeney, L.: Protecting privacy when disclosing information: k-anonymity and its enforcement through generalization and suppression. In: Proceedings of the IEEE Symposium on Research in Security and Privacy, Oakland, CA (1998)
16. Sweeney, L.: Computational Disclosure Control: A Primer on Data Privacy Protection. PhD thesis, Massachusetts Institute of Technology (2001)
17. Hundepool, A., Willenborg, L.: μ- and τ-argus: software for statistical disclosure control. Third International Seminar on Statistical Confidentiality (1996)
18. Sweeney, L.: Guaranteeing anonymity when sharing medical data, the datafly system. Proceedings, Journal of the American Medical Informatics Association (1997)
19. Pohlig, S.C., Hellman, M.E.: An improved algorithm for computing logarithms over GF(p) and its cryptographic significance. IEEE Transactions on Information Theory **IT-24** (1978) 106–110

Towards Database Firewalls*

Kun Bai, Hai Wang, and Peng Liu

The School of Information Science and Technology,
Pennsylvania State University,
University Park 16802 PA
{kbai, haiwang, pliu}@ist.psu.edu

Abstract. Authentication based access control and integrity constraints
are the major approaches applied in commercial database systems to
guarantee information and data integrity. However, due to operational
mistakes, malicious intent of insiders or identity fraud exploited by out-
siders, data secured in a database can still be corrupted. Once attacked,
database systems using current survivability technologies cannot continue providing satisfactory services according to differentiated information assurance requirements. In this paper, we present the innovative
idea of a database firewall, which can not only serve differentiated information assurance requirements in the face of attacks, but also guarantee
the availability and the integrity of data objects based on user requirements. Our approach provides a new strategy of integrity-aware data
access based on an on-the-fly iterative estimation of the integrity level
of data objects. Accordingly, a policy of transaction filtering will be dynamically enforced to significantly slow down damage propagation with
minimum availability loss.

1 Introduction

Data integrity, availability and confidentiality are the three major issues that
have been paid much attention in database security research. To protect the data
integrity, multi-layer approaches are proposed, from hardware, OS, DBMS to
transaction level. Mainly, there are two research focuses. One is *from-scratch*, the
other is *off-the-shelf*. Approaches presented in [1],[2],[3] are to close the security
holes on hardware, OS and DBMS, respectively, from the *from-scratch* direction.
[4] and [5] propose techniques to deal with data corruption and storage jamming
effectively on OS-level intrusions. Unfortunately, these technologies can not be
applied to handle authorized but malicious transaction.

[6] introduces an intrusion-tolerant database (ITDB) system architecture on
the transaction-level. It is noticeable that ITDB architecture is complicated because of the specific database vulnerability known as *damage spreading*. That is,
the result of a transaction can affect the execution of some later transactions,
directly or indirectly, through *read* and *write* operations.

* This work was supported by NSF CCR-0233324, NSF ANI-0335241, and Department
  of Energy Early Career PI Award.

S. Jajodia and D. Wijesekera (Eds.): Data and Applications Security 2005, LNCS 3654, pp. 178–192, 2005.

Since infected data objects can cause more damage through *read* and *write* operations, which, in turn, could lead to wrong decision and disastrous consequences, data corruption becomes a severe security problem in critical data applications, such as air traffic control, banking and combat-field decision making system. Furthermore, data corruption is not only an issue of data integrity issue, but also a concern of data availability. For example, in some cases, the purpose of an attack is just to deny the service. Generally, when the real-world database application is under an attack, the services the system provides have to be shut down to recover from the disaster. Thus, the system availability sacrificed in order to maintain the data integrity. A vast majority of research has been done on how to survive data corruption from malicious attacks and recover the data integrity and availability in an off-line manner. However, limited attention has been drawn to provide various database services in agreement with differentiated information assurance requirements while the system is being healed.

In this paper, we present a novel idea of database firewall that, in contrast to previous research, uses different strategies to prevent damage from spreading to other territories of the database in terms of tables, records and columns. The idea is to quickly estimate the integrity levels of data objects and use such integrity levels to smartly filter off the transactions that would spread damage according to a specific firewall policy upon the time a malicious transaction is detected. A unique feature of our approach is that transaction filtering is not universally enforced and the enforcement domain is dynamically adjusted so that maximum availability can be provided without jeopardizing integrity. According to a user requirement of quality of information assurance (QoIA), we not only provide a significant improvement of data availability, but also guarantee the integrity of data objects stored in the database. The database firewall framework is illustrated in the context of the transaction level in ITDB architecture.

The rest of this paper is organized as follows. In section (2), we review the background and related work. In section (3), we present the design issue of the database firewall. In section (4), we propose our naive estimator model and estimation algorithm. In section (5), we demonstrate some preliminary results. In section (6), we conclude the paper and future work.

2   Background and Related Work

Intrusion detection system (IDS) has attracted many researchers ([8],[9],[10]). In general, IDSs monitor system activities to discover attempts to gain illicit access to systems or corrupt data objects in systems. Roughly, the methodologies of IDS are in two categories, *statistical profile* and *known patterns of attacks*. However, intrusion detection systems have a few noticeable limitations: (1) Intrusion detection makes the system attack-aware but not attack-resistant. (2) Achieving accurate detection is usually difficult or expensive. (3) The average detection latency in many cases is too long to effectively confine the damage. To overcome these limitations, a broader perspective has been introduced, namely an intrusion tolerance database system [6].

Other than the ITDB approach, traditional recovery mechanisms execute complete rollbacks to undo the work of benign transactions as well as malicious ones when the malicious transactions are detected. Therefore, although rolling back a database to a previous checkpoint can remove all the corrupted data, the work of all the legitimate transactions which commit after the checkpoint is lost. This kind of approach would further exacerbate the situation of denial of service. [11] provides a recovery algorithm that, given a specification of malicious, unwinds not only the effects of each malicious transaction but also the effects of any innocent transaction that is directly or indirectly affected by a malicious transaction. A significant contribution of [11] is that the work of remaining benign transactions is saved. However, the fact is that transaction execution is much faster than detection and reparation. This indicates that the entire process of recovery could both take a relatively long time to finish and also repeat repairing certain data objects over and over again due to damage spreading. Thus, the data availability could be significantly lost due to this long latency.

[12] present an innovative idea known as multiphase damage containment. Upon the time a malicious transaction (denoted as B_i) is detected, in contrast to reactive damage containment, [12] uses one containing phase (denoted as initial containment) to proactively contain the data objects that might have been corrupted. In addition to this first phase, one or more later uncontaining phases (denoted as containment relaxation) will release the objects that are mistakenly contained during the first phase. This approach can guarantee that no damage caused by malicious transaction B_i will spread to any new update. However, an inherent limitation of multiphase containment is that this method could cost substantial data availability loss. Because the *initial containment* phase needs to instantly confine every data object possibly infected by B_i within a time window starting upon the commit of the malicious transaction B_i and ending at the detection of B_i, there is no time for the confining phase to precisely pinpoint the set of damaged data objects.

To overcome the limitations of the multiphase containment approach and to provide more data availability, delivering services by taking QoIA requirements into account seems to be a solution. In order to keep services available during attacks, it will be beneficial to continue allowing access to confined data objects during the repair time window. However, this needs to be conducted very carefully since a confined data object could have been corrupted. Thus, certain security rules and policies of access are required to achieve this original intention. [13] has taken the first step towards this goal. In this paper, we extend this topic and present database firewall technique as a solution to increase the data availability without imposing risks to applications users and degrading the system performance and data integrity.

3   Database Firewall Design

In this section, we first formalize several important concepts and the various problems studied in this paper, and then present the framework of database firewall. The idea of a database firewall can be better described in the context of an intrusion tolerant database system (ITDB) on the transaction level. Since this framework is an extension of the ITDB architecture, it inherits the features from ITDB that it could not directly defend against attacks from low level, such as OS and DBMS level attacks. However, when most attacks come from malicious transactions, our framework is effective. Moreover, the existing low level mechanisms can be easily integrated into our database firewall framework.

3.1 Theoretical Model

A *database* system is a set of data objects, denoted as DB=$\{o_1, o_2, \ldots, o_n\}$. A transaction G_i is a partial order with ordering relation $<_i$, where

1. $G_i \subseteq \{(r_i[o_x], w_i[o_x]) | o_x$ is a data object$\} \cup (a_i, c_i)$;
2. if $r_i[o_x], w_i[o_x] \in G_i$, then either $r_i[o_x] <_i w_i[o_x]$, or $w_i[o_x] <_i r_i[o_x]$;
3. $a_i \in G_i$ iff $c_i \notin G_i$.

and *r,w,a,c* relate to the operation of *read, write, abort,* and *commit,* respectively. The (usually concurrent) execution of a set of transactions is modeled by a structure called a history. Formally, let $G = \{G_1, G_2, \ldots, G_n\}$ be a set of transactions. A complete history H over G is a partial order with ordering relation $<_H$, where:

1. $H = \cup_{i=1}^{n} G_i$;
2. $<_H \supseteq \cup_{i=1}^{n} <_i$.

Since aborted transactions have nothing to do with database firewalls, for the sake of simplicity we assume every transaction commits. Two transactions conflict if they both have an operation on the same object, and one of them is *write*. Also, the correctness of a history is typically captured by the notion of *serializability*[14]. One assumption is that strict *two-phase locking* (2PL) is used to produce serializable histories where the commit order indicates the serial order among transactions.

First, how an object is damaged is defined in a conservative way. That is, every object updated by a malicious transaction is damaged, and that if a good transaction reads a damaged object, then every object updated by the good transaction is damaged. Next, a transaction dependent relation is denoted as follows. In a history composed of only committed transactions, a transaction G_i is *dependent upon* another transaction G_j if there exists an object o_x such that G_i reads o_x after G_j updates it, and there is no transaction that updates o_x between the time G_j updates o_x and G_j reads o_x. Finally, it is assumed that every data object modified by G_i will be read by G_i first. Thus, there is no *blind* writes.

3.2 Motivation and Challenges

As networks enable more and more applications and are available to more and more users, they become ever more vulnerable to a wider range of security threats. Thus, to combat those threats and ensure that applications are not compromised, security technologies such as network firewalls play a critical role in today's networks. Likewise, a broad span of research from authorization, to inference control, to multilevel secure database, and to multilevel secure transaction processing has addressed primarily on how to protect the security of a database. However, a very important vulnerability of database security, known as *damage spreading*, has been omitted by these researches. Database firewall technique is needed not only because malicious transactions can compromise data objects, but also because innocent transactions can accidentally spread the damage. Formally, *damage spreading* occurs because any good transaction reading a corrupted data object o_x can spread the damage on o_x to the data objects it updates. In this way, the spreading can be exponential. Still, the effect caused by a malicious transaction itself to a database is limited. Thus, it is the transactions that spread the effect that matter. Efforts have been made in existing data containment and damage assessment technologies to stop spreading and recover systems. However, data containment and damage assessment take a substantial amount of time. Thus, the loss of data availability is significant. Database firewall technique takes a step further to reinforce the above approaches by filtering the incoming transactions to simultaneously stop potential damage spreading at the doorway and to improve the data availability according to a certain security policy.

In sum, a database firewall should include at least three components: *Integrity Estimator, Firewall Manager* and *Access Policy Manager*. One of the challenges to guarantee the success of database firewalls is to design an efficient integrity level estimation algorithm, which can quickly and accurately estimate the data integrity without losing security. In this paper, a naive approach to achieve this goal is presented.

3.3   Architecture of Database Firewall

To develop the database firewall framework that can provide more data availability, there are several fundamental issues needed to be addressed and solved. First, how to formalize the integrity level model and estimate the data integrity during attacks. Second, how to constitute the security policy and access rulesets using estimated data integrity level. Third, how to manage the tradeoff between performance and security.

Database Firewall Components. As shown in *figure* (1), the database firewall architecture is built upon the top of a traditional "off-the-shelf" DBMS. Within the framework, *Intrusion Detector* (ID) identifies malicious transactions based on the operation records stored in the log. *Damage Assessor* (DA) locates the damage caused by the detected malicious transactions. *Damage Repairer* (DR) repairs the located damage using some specific *cleaning* transactions. *Integrity Estimator* (IE) estimates the integrity level of data objects. *Access Policy Manager* (APM) works as a *proxy* for decision making of data objects access. *Firewall Manager* (FM) functions when *Intrusion Detector* detects malicious

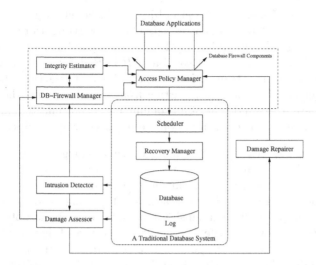

Fig. 1. Database Firewall Architecture

transactions. After the firewalls are built up, *Firewall Manager* triggers *Integrity Estimator* to start estimating the integrity of data objects and consequently force *Access Policy Manager* to set up access rulesets to restrict the access to the data items that are confined in firewalls according to a new policy. At each step of integrity estimation, the firewalls update themselves in co-response to the changes of data integrity level. Accordingly, any new transaction submitted by a user will comply with the new policy. Through several steps, *Integrity Estimator* will finally converge to the final solution, which has either a set of precise integrity of data objects or a set of approximate integrity of date objects.

3.4   Transaction Filtering Policies and Mechanism

In this section, an innovative mechanism for implementing security control which guards the door of database systems and prevents potential damage spreading from occurring is introduced. By conventional definition of firewall in network domain, a firewall is a system or group of systems that enforce an access control policy between two or more networks. Its operations are mainly based on three technologies: packet filtering, proxy server and stateful packet filtering. Similarly, in database security domain, particularly in our database firewall framework, a firewall operates based on transaction filtering technique. In addition, unlike a network firewall, which checks packet status, transaction filtering relies on the integrity level of data objects.

Integrity Level Model. When a malicious transaction B_i is detected, the data objects in the database could be in several different situations. In this section, an idea is presented to define the model illustrating the integrity of data objects.

1. **Data objects Integrity.** A data object could be either good or corrupted after the database system is attacked. Thus, it is straightforward to denote that the integrity of an object o_i $(1 \leq i \leq n)$ is good at particular time t as $I(o_i, t) \in \{G, B\}$, where G is *Good* and B is *Bad* for short. It is apparent that when a malicious transaction is captured, any transaction whose commit time is out of a time window, starting from the time point when B_i enters the database to the moment of its committing, is not infected, and the data objects belonging to the transaction are regarded as good objects.

   However, the status of those data objects that belong to transactions which commit within the time window are a little more complicated. It is difficult to attain such knowledge that data integrity can be precisely calculated in a short period of time. Methods, such as [12], mentioned in previous section (2), can precisely distinguish the integrity of each data object through several phases. However, safety comes at the sacrifice of significant data availability. This contradicts the goal of database firewall framework. Therefore, instead of deterministically marking the integrity of data objects, a practical integrity model that uses probabilistic estimation is favored. This model is applicable because the damage spreading is strongly related to the writeset of the malicious transaction B_i, denoted as W_{B_i}, and also relies on the transaction arrival and dependency patterns. For this reason, previous histories can be used to estimate the probability that a data object is good as the data integrity during an attack.

2. **Practical Integrity Model.** In this model, a data object o_i's integrity at a particular time t is shown in the equation.

$$I(o_i, t) = (1 - \frac{1}{R(t)}) \times 100\%, R(t) \geq 1 \qquad (1)$$

Where, R is the number of patterns matched with or similar to an attack pattern. We call $I(o_i, t)$ the data object o_i's *integrity level*, and $0 \leq I(o_i, t) \leq 1$. Integrity level of data object o_i indicates that the probability of o_i is good when a specific attack pattern occurs. For example, when $R(t) = 1, I(o_i, t) = 0$, it means the identical patterns are found, and the data object o_i is corrupted. Thus, the integrity of a data object o_i could be in one of the following three categories:

$$I(o_i, t) = \begin{cases} 100\% & t \notin [t_S^i, t_E^i] \quad \text{estimated} \\ 50\% & t \in [t_S^i, t_E^i] \quad \text{estimated} \\ 0\% & t \in [t_S^i, t_E^i] \quad \text{identified} \end{cases} \qquad (2)$$

Here, for the definition of t_S^i, t_E^i, please refer to section 3.4. With the above analysis about data integrity, in order to estimate the integrity of a data object, our research becomes to find answers to following three questions: What is an attack pattern? How does the integrity estimator use the patterns? How do we match two attack patterns? These concerns will be addressed in a later section (4).

Database Firewall Security Policy. A specific and strongly worded security policy is vital to the pursuit of internal data integrity. This policy is a subset of the database access contorl policy and never will rule over an access contorl policy, such as authorization, but should govern everything from acceptance of accessing data objects to response scenarios in the event a security incident should occur, such as policy updating upon a new attack.

Ideally, a database firewall security policy dictates how transactions traffic is handled and how filtering ruleset is managed and updated. Before a policy is created, a risk analysis on the database system must be performed to gain knowledge for the vulnerabilities associated with databases. For instance, we know one of the vulnerabilities in database security is the *damage spreading*. It is when a transaction, even if it is a legitimate one, accesses a corrupted data object that the damage will be spread to any other data object this transaction touches, directly or indirectly. Then, to limit the potential damage spreading, firewall policy needs to create a ruleset to restrict the entrance of transactions that could compromise other data objects while letting other transactions enter to achieve maximum throughput.

For example, suppose a transaction $G_1(t, tp) = r_1[o_x]r_1[o_y]w_1[o_y]$ requires to enter the database, where tp is transaction type. If it is known that the data object o_x has been corrupted at this momment, then our policy checker will screen the transaction and be aware if the request can be granted using the ruleset.

Definition 1 : Integrity Filtering List, $\hat{I} = \{i_1(o_{x_1}^{i_1}, o_{x_2}^{i_1}, .., o_{x_m}^{i_1}), i_2(o_{y_1}^{i_2}, o_{y_2}^{i_2}, .., o_{y_n}^{i_2}),$ ..}, where i is a set with data objects on same integrity level, and o_i is a data object associated with the integrity level i. The ruleset is defined as follows:
Rule 1 : $\forall$ transaction G, if $\exists$ data object $o_x \in R_G$, and $R_G \cap \hat{I} \neq \emptyset$, and if $W_G \neq \emptyset$, DENY;
Rule 2 : $\forall$ transaction G, if $\exists$ data object $o_x \in R_G$, and $R_G \cap \hat{I} \neq \emptyset$, and if $W_G = \emptyset$, and if $i < Q$ then DENY, otherwise GRANT;
Rule 3 : $\forall$ transaction G, if $\nexists$ data object $o_x \in R_G$, and $R_G \cap \hat{I} = \emptyset$, GRANT;
Here, Q is QoIA required by applications. R_G, W_G is the readset, writeset of a transaction, respectively. What we have presented here is a sample ruleset. We should be aware that firewall rulesets tend to become increasingly complicated with age.

Transaction Filtering Mechanism. In many cases when an attack is detected, not every data object in database is corrupted. Thus, simply applying the firewall ruleset to screen every incoming transactions is not wise. Here, we introduce a novel concept called *firewall time window*.

In the database firewall framework, for each detected attack, *Firewall Manager* has a life cycle with three different phases: *Firewall Generation*, *Firewall Mergence* and *Firewall Withdraw*. During the first phase, upon the time when a malicious transaction B_i is detected, *Firewall Manager* is notified to generate a firewall. A firewall time window $[t_S^i, t_E^i]$ is denoted as $\mathfrak{W}_i$. Here, the $[t_S^i, t_E^i]$ is defined as follows:

Definition 2 : Firewall Time Window $\mathfrak{W}_i$ of B_i, denoted as $[t_S^i, t_E^i]$, is defined as follows: t_S^i is the time when B_i starts; t_E^i is the time when malicious transaction B_i is detected.

For example, suppose a transaction $G_1(t, tp) = r_1[o_x]r_1[o_y]w_1[o_x]w_1[o_z]$ requires to enter a database, if it is found that $t_{o_x}^u$ is within the scope of firewall time window $[t_S, t_E]$, the ruleset is further checked for security concerns. Otherwise, the permission of entrance to the database can simply be granted. Here, $t_{o_x}^u$ is the time when data object o_x was updated.

Firewall Updating Mechanism. At phase two, if there are multiple malicious transactions detected during a period of time, there might exist multiple firewalls, and *Firewall Manager* will force the multiple firewalls to merge together according to certain rules. By doing this, *Access Policy Manager* can efficiently manage multiple versions of access policy. A set of malicious transactions is denoted as $B_{i1}, B_{i2}, ..., B_{ik}$. For each firewall time window, the mergence rules are defined as follows:

Mergence Rule 1 : Firewall time window $[t_S^i, t_E^i]$ is ahead of $[t_S^j, t_E^j]$ if $t_E^i < t_S^j$. Firewall time window $\mathfrak{W}_i$ and $\mathfrak{W}_j$ are *overlap* if no one is ahead of another. $\mathfrak{W}_i$ includes $\mathfrak{W}_j$ if $t_S^i < t_S^j$ and $t_E^i > t_E^j$.

The rule of firewall mergence is defined as follows:

Mergence Rule 2 : A set of firewall time windows can be merged as one if for any two time windows $\mathfrak{W}_{im}$ and $\mathfrak{W}_{in}$, $(m < n)$, there is a sequence of firewall time windows $\mathfrak{W}_{j_1}, \mathfrak{W}_{j_2}, ..., \mathfrak{W}_{j\ell}, ..., \mathfrak{W}_{jl}$, such that they are within the set where $\mathfrak{W}_{im}$ and $\mathfrak{W}_{j_1}$ overlap, $\mathfrak{W}_{j\ell}$ and $\mathfrak{W}_{j(\ell+1)}$ overlap, and $\mathfrak{W}_{j(\ell+1)}$ and $\mathfrak{W}_{jl}$ overlap.

By applying this firewall mergence ruleset, the framework dynamically adjusts the security policies and rulesets corresponding to the changes of firewalls.

In the third phase, there is a condition when it is satisfied, the *Firewall Manager* will stop restricting access to any data objects within the firewall time windows (That is, when *Damage Repairer* finishes repairing the located corrupted data objects). In response to the withdraw of firewall, *Access Policy Manager* will reset the access policy to the lowest level of restriction of data access, and the database system performs in the normal way until the next malicious transaction is detected.

4   Integrity Level Estimation

One critical issue to guarantee success of *Integrity Level Estimation* success is timing. The more time the estimation algorithm spends, the more accurate the estimation result can be, but the less data availability the database system can provide. Thus, instead of releasing a final solution of integrity estimation at the conclusion, the algorithm gives out several versions iteratively along the process.

Now, we propose our integrity estimator model and the first naive estimation algorithm (1) that balances the tradeoff between performance and security.

Integrity Estimator. *Figure* (2) illustrates the details of estimator component. Basically, there are two subcomponents: One is offline processor; the other

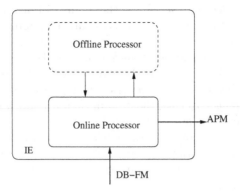

Fig. 2. Integrity Estimator Component

is online processor. Offline processor usually is executed after *Damage Repairer* finishes repairing and then triggers the *Database Firewall Manager* to withdraw the firewalls. In general, to gather knowledge about previous attacks and to save time for online processor to quickly and precisely estimate the data integrity, offline processor deals with all kinds of information it can obtain from history logs, IDS reports, customer profiles and database schemes. In this paper, it is assumed that offline processor only process the histories stored in database and subtracts valuable attributes from them, such as the transaction dependency graphes, attacking time and statistic data (the number of corrupted data objects, frequency of a data object being corrupted, the number of distinct values and transaction types, for example). The above information is called an *Attacking Pattern*, or *Fingerprint*. Once an attacking is detected, online processor in *Integrity Estimator* starts estimating data integrity based on both the knowledge the offline processor has obtained and the information of new attacking history. We define *Attacking Pattern* and *Spreading Pattern* as follows:

Definition 3 : *Attacking Pattern* $p = (R_j, W_j, a_j^1, a_j^2, \ldots, a_j^{m-1}, a_j^m, a_j^{m+1}, \ldots)$.

Definition 4 : *Spreading Pattern* P is a dependency related sequence of transactions, $P_i = \{p_{B_i}, p_1, p_2, \ldots, p_{n-1}, p_n, p_{n+1} \ldots\}$. Where, R_j, W_j is the readset, writeset of a transaction, respectively; B_i is a malicious transaction, and a_i is a valuable attribute that depicts a particular dimension of a transaction, such as occurrence frequency of a special value or the number of distinct values. And, $W_{n-1} \bigcap R_n \neq \emptyset$.

Algorithm (1) describes the naive approach of how to estimate data object integrity. In general, this algorithm is a pattern-match based approach. A vector containing spreading patterns is created by offline processor based on the histories it obtains. Basically, this algorithm scans the spreading patterns to compare the attacking pattern from a newly detected attack with the one in each spreading pattern in the vector. If a match is found, the R will be increased by one; otherwise, the unmatched spreading pattern is trimmed off the vector.

In addition, the confined data set C and the number of matched patterns R update correspondingly. Since this is a pattern-matched approach, an unavoidable problem is what to do in the absence of a matched pattern. From the mathematics perspective, R in equation 1 can not be zero. But, in the algorithm if R is equal to zero, it indicates the newly detected attacking pattern is one that had never occurred before. In this scenario, the algorithm stops estimating and notifies *Firewall Manager* to reset the firewall time window because damage had probably already been spread out by this moment. A possible solution to this problem is to apply a containment approach, such as multi-pahse containment method, to precisely distinguish the integrity of each data object, invoke the offline processor to consume the new attack and add this pattern to the vector.

Algorithm 1 Integrity Level Estimation Algorithm Pseudo Code

Require: $V[k]$: spreading pattern vector. P_{new}:newly detected attack   ▷ S is the corrupted data objects of spreading pattern i in V

1: **function** ILESTIMATOR(V, P_{new})
2:     $C = \emptyset, R = 0$ ▷ C → Confined data objects set
3:     **for** $i \leftarrow 1, n$ **do**   ▷ Scan the pattern vector
4:         $p \leftarrow P_{new}[i]$
5:         **for** $j \leftarrow 1, k$ **do**   ▷ Compare each spreading pattern
6:             $p_v \leftarrow V[j]$
7:             **if** $p_v \equiv p$ **then**
8:                 $R(t) \leftarrow (R(t) + 1)$
9:                 $C \leftarrow C \cup S_{V[j]}$
10:             **else**
11:                 $V \leftarrow V - V[j]$ ▷ Trim the unmatched pattern off the vector
12:                 $C \leftarrow \overline{C \cap S_{V[j]}}$
13:             **end if**
14:         **end for**
15:         **if** $R(t) = 0$ **then**
16:             break;
17:         **else**
18:             $\forall o_x \in C \leftarrow (1 - \frac{1}{R(t)})$ ▷ Set the integrity of data objects
19:         **end if**   ▷ Mark the integrity of data objects
20:         APM updates new policy
21:     **end for**
22: **end function**

---

5   Experiments and Results

In this section, the experiment results are demonstrated . In order to measure the effectiveness and performance of our proposed naive method, comprehensive experiments have been conducted on synthetic data sets generated according to a modified TPCC standard.

5.1   Generation of Experimental Data

For the experiment, synthetic data set has been used. All data are generated based on a modified TPCC dependency relationship, as shown in *figure* (3). Also, the data sets have $1M$ transactions history. 300 different patterns are summarized out of this history. For each pattern, the number of transactions varies in a range from 2000 to 3500. Furthermore, there are two possible consequences regarding an approaching attack. One, a new attack is a duplicate of a previous one, which implies that there is a previous version recorded in the history. Thus, it becomes a question whether or not identical twins can be found out of the previous patterns. Two, a new attack is a mutant of an existing version of attack. Thus, it becomes whether or not the similar ones can be distinguished. In addition, in these experiments, it is assumed there is only one malicious transaction B_i at each time. So, firewall mergence is not taken into consideration at current stage.

5.2   Experiment Results

Figure (4-[a,b,c].1) illustrates the results of the first possible attack pattern, which is a copy of a previous attack, from three different perspectives, objects integrity, system availability and estimation validation, respectively. *Figure* (4-a.1) presents the results of using our naive method. Obj_A, Obj_B and Obj_C are the representatives of three sets of data objects. Along the estimation process, data objects in set Obj_A are first marked as $I = \{1\}$ because they are those data objects that are not touched by transactions; thus, they do not belong to the patterns that are partials of or similar to the newly detected attack pattern. Those data objects in set Obj_B are assigned to be $I = \{1\}$ later than Obj_A because the estimator distinguishes that these objects do not belong to corrupted data set when more knowledge is obtained, and then remark their integrity. Obj_C is the data object set with all corrupted data objects, and it

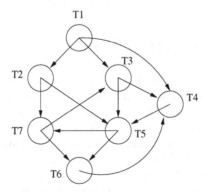

Fig. 3. Example Transaction Dependency Graph

shrinks because some objects are remarked and moved to Obj_A and Obj_B along the estimation process. *Figure* (4-b.1) shows the system availability in terms of the number of accessible data objects with a QOIA requirement of 100%. Corresponding to *Figure* (4-a.1), it can be seen the system availability increases as the integrity of data objects are remarked and moved to Obj_A and Obj_B. At step 11, the estimator finds the final solution of data integrity, and the availability reaches its highest level. Finally, when the system recovers itself from attacking, the availability goes back to normal level. In this experiment, it is assumed that applications only access data objects with marked integrity equal to $I = \{1\}$. For some applications that are aggressive and are willing to accept multiple levels quality of information assurance (QoIA), the system availability will be even higher. *Figure* (4-c.1) illustrates the progress of estimation validations. It can be seen that at the initial stage of estimation, because of limited knowledge about the newly detected attack, estimation has a relatively high estimation variance (normalized in the range of 0 to 1). However, it will quickly converge to zero (the diagonal denotes the actual errors, which is zero) as the procedure goes on.

Figure (4-[a,b,c].2) demonstrates the results of the second consequence of an attack from the same three aspects. Similarly, *Figure* (4-a.2) presents the results of data integrity using the naive method. In contrast to *Figure* (4-a.1), Obj_C does not drop down to zero because the estimator can only find out several similar patterns instead of one, which indicates that a new type of attack is found. Therefore, the estimator will be conservative and inform *Firewall Manager* to reset firewall time window to contain data objects in Obj_C in order to prevent damage leakage. Beyond the last step, the database will not continue rely on estimation. Instead, [12] can take over and continue the work. In *Figure* (4-b.2), corresponding to the changes of integrity of data objects, the system availability increases accordingly. *Figure* (4-c.2) demonstrates from another perspective that, unlike the convergence shown in *Figure* (4-c.1), the estimation error does not decline to zero beyond a certain time point when the estimator could not be more accurate on data object integrity. However, even this is a case, we still achieve the goal of improving the system availability.

6   Conclusion and Future Work

This paper presents an innovative idea of database firewall. Unlike the traditional recovery mechanisms, which shutdown the entire system and recovery itself in an offline manner, our framework can help a database system continue delivering services even when an attack is detected. We have developed a naive but effective approach to use histories and attacking patterns to probabilistically estimate the integrity level of data objects in the face of an attack, instead of deterministically finding the data integrity. However, this naive approach assumes a relative simple attacking pattern. In real world applications, this might be the case. In addition, efficient estimation of data object integrity is also a great challenge. A quick and accurate estimation algorithm is critical to the success of database firewalls.

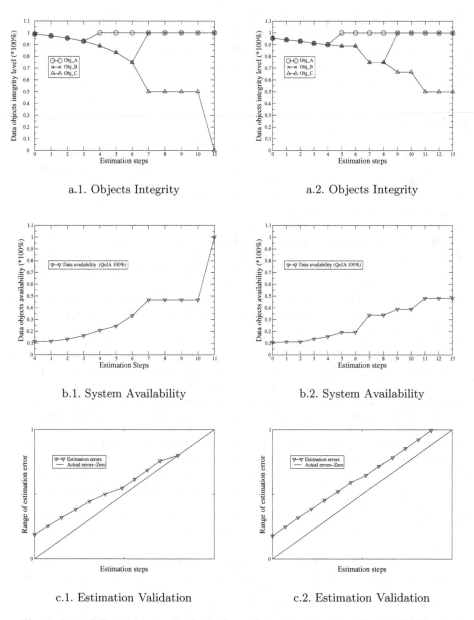

a.1. Objects Integrity   a.2. Objects Integrity

b.1. System Availability   b.2. System Availability

c.1. Estimation Validation   c.2. Estimation Validation

Fig. 4. Two different kinds of attacks from three aspects: integrity, availability, validation: 1. When a newly detected attack is matched with previous attacks. 2. When a newly detected attack is similar to the previous attacks

In future work, we plan to formalize the model of the attacking pattern and damage propagation, as well as redesign the integrity level estimation algorithm. A number of further SQL and DBMS enhancements are needed to fully exploit this interesting topic. We have found that the estimation approach we present may not work efficiently when there are several similar attack patterns or when a new type attack is detected. One possible solution to this problem could be, for example, using a sampling and similarity search technique to find out the final data object integrity solution.

References

1. S. Smith, E. Palmer, and S. Weingart, "Using a high-performance, programmable secure coprocessor," in Proc. International Conference on Financial Cryptography, Anguilla, British West Indies, 1998.
2. G. C. Necula, "Proof-carrying code," in Proc. 24th ACM Symposium on Principles of Programming Languages, 1997.
3. Z. Shao, B. Saha, and V. Trifonov, "A type system for certified binaries," in Proc. 29th ACM Symposium on Principles of Programming Languages, 2002.
4. D. Barbara, R. Goel, and S. Jajodia, "Using checksums to detect data corruption," in Proceedings of the 2000 International Conference on Extending Data Base Technology, Mar 2000.
5. J. McDermott and D. Goldschlag, "Towards a model of storage jamming," in Proceedings of the IEEE Computer Security Foundations Workshop, Kenmare, Ireland, June 1996, pp. 176–185.
6. P. Liu, "Architectures for intrusion tolerant database systems." in ACSAC, 2002, pp. 311–320.
7. P. W. P. J. Grefen and P. M. G. Apers, "Integrity control in relational database systems: an overview," Data Knowl. Eng., vol. 10, no. 2, pp. 187–223, 1993.
8. H. S. Javitz and A. Valdes, "The sri ides statistical anomaly detector," in Proceedings IEEE Computer Society Symposium on Security and Privacy, Oakland, CA, May 1991.
9. T. Garvey and T. Lunt, "Model-based intrusion detection," in Proceedings of the 14th National Computer Security Conference, Baltimore, MD, October 1991.
10. K. Ilgun, R. Kemmerer, and P. Porras, "State transition analysis: A rule-based intrusion detection approach," IEEE Transactions on Software Engineering, vol. 21, no. 3, pp. 181–199, 1995.
11. P. Ammann, S. Jajodia, and P. Liu, "Recovery from malicious transactions," IEEE Transactions on Knowledge and Data Engineering, vol. 15, no. 5, pp. 1167–1185, 2002.
12. P. Liu and S. Jajodia, "Multi-phase damage confinement in database systems for intrusion tolerance," in Proc. 14th IEEE Computer Security Foundations Workshop, Nova Scotia, Canada, June 2001.
13. J. Zhang and P. Liu, "Delivering services with integrity guarantees in survivable database systems," in IFIP WG 11.3 16th International Conference on Data and Applications Security, Cambridge, UK, vol. 256, July 28-31.
14. P. A. Bernstein, V. Hadzilacos, and N. Goodman, Concurrency Control and Recovery in Database Systems. Addison-Wesley, Reading, MA, 1987.

Complete Redundancy Detection in Firewalls

Alex X. Liu* and Mohamed G. Gouda

Department of Computer Sciences,
The University of Texas at Austin,
Austin, Texas 78712-0233, USA
{alex, gouda}@cs.utexas.edu

Abstract. Firewalls are safety-critical systems that secure most private networks. The function of a firewall is to examine each incoming and outgoing packet and decide whether to accept or to discard the packet. This decision is made according to a sequence of rules, where some rules may be redundant. Redundant rules significantly degrade the performance of firewalls. Previous work detects only two special types of redundant rules. In this paper, we solve the problem of how to detect all redundant rules. First, we give a necessary and sufficient condition for identifying all redundant rules. Based on this condition, we categorize redundant rules into upward redundant rules and downward redundant rules. Second, we present methods for detecting the two types of redundant rules respectively. Our methods make use of a tree representation of firewalls, which is called firewall decision trees.

Keywords: Firewall, Redundant Rules, Network Security.

1 Introduction

1.1 Firewall Basics

Serving as the first line of defense against malicious attacks and unauthorized traffic, firewalls are crucial elements in securing the private networks of most businesses, institutions, and even home networks. A firewall is placed at the point of entry between a private network and the outside Internet so that all incoming and outgoing packets have to pass through it. A packet can be viewed as a tuple with a finite number of fields; examples of these fields are source/destination IP address, source/destination port number, and protocol type. A firewall maps each incoming and outgoing packet to a decision according to its configuration. A firewall configuration defines which packets are legitimate and which are illegitimate by a sequence of rules. Each rule in a firewall configuration is of the form

$$\langle predicate \rangle \rightarrow \langle decision \rangle$$

The $\langle predicate \rangle$ in a rule is a boolean expression over some packet fields and the physical network interface on which a packet arrives. The $\langle decision \rangle$ of a rule can

---

* Corresponding author.

S. Jajodia and D. Wijesekera (Eds.): Data and Applications Security 2005, LNCS 3654, pp. 193–206, 2005.
© IFIP International Federation for Information Processing 2005

be *accept*, or *discard*, or a combination of one of these decisions with other options
such as a logging option. For simplicity, we assume that the ⟨*decision*⟩ in a rule
is either *accept* or *discard*. Since the focus of this paper is firewall configuration,
later we use "firewall" to mean "firewall configuration" if not otherwise specified.

A packet *matches* a rule if and only if (*iff*) the packet satisfies the predicate
of the rule. The predicate of the last rule in a firewall is usually a tautology to
ensure that every packet has at least one matching rule in the firewall. Firewall
rules often conflict. Two rules in a firewall *conflict* iff they not only overlap but
also have different decisions. Two rules overlap iff there is at least one packet that
can match both rules. Due to conflicts among rules, a packet may match more
than one rule in a firewall, and the rules that a packet matches may have different
decisions. To resolve conflicts among rules, for each incoming or outgoing packet,
a firewall maps it to the decision of the first (i.e., highest priority) rule that the
packet matches.

1.2   Redundant Rules

Firewalls often have redundant rules. A rule in a firewall is redundant iff removing
the rule does not change the function of the firewall, i.e., does not change the
decision of the firewall for every packet. For example, consider the firewall in
Figure 1, whose geometric representation is in Figure 2. This firewall consists of
four rules r_1 through r_4. The domain of field F_1 is $[1, 100]$.

We have the following two observations concerning the redundant rules in
the firewall in Figure 1.

1. Rule r_3 is redundant. This is because the first matching rule for all packets
   where $F_1 \in [30, 50]$ is r_1, and the first matching rule for all packets where
   $F_1 \in [51, 60]$ is r_2. Therefore, there are no packets whose first matching

$$r_1 : \ F_1 \in [1, \ \ 50] \ \rightarrow accept$$
$$r_2 : \ F_1 \in [40, \ 90] \ \rightarrow discard$$
$$r_3 : \ F_1 \in [30, \ 60] \ \rightarrow accept$$
$$r_4 : \ F_1 \in [51, 100] \rightarrow discard$$

Fig. 1. A simple firewall

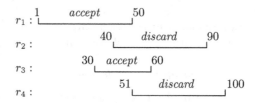

Fig. 2. Geometric representation of the firewall in Figure 1

rule is r_3. We call r_3 an upward redundant rule. A rule r in a firewall is *upward redundant* iff there are no packets whose first matching rule is r. Geometrically, a rule is upward redundant in a firewall iff the rule is overlayed by some rules listed above it.

2. Rule r_2 becomes redundant after r_3 is removed. Note that r_2 is the first matching rule for all packets where $F_1 \in [51, 90]$. However, if we remove r_2 (assuming that r_3 has been removed), the first matching rule for all those packets becomes r_4 instead of r_2. This does not change the function of the firewall since both r_2 and r_4 have the same decision. We call r_2 a downward redundant rule. A rule r in a firewall is *downward redundant* iff for each packet, whose first matching rule is r, the first matching rule below r has the same decision as r.

Redundant rules significantly degrade the performance of firewalls. A firewall maps a packet to the decision of the first rule that the packet matches using packet classification algorithms. A packet classification algorithm maps each packet to the right decision using an internal data structure built from a firewall of a sequence of rules. The fewer the rules in a firewall are, the faster a packet classification algorithm can map a packet to the right decision. To map a given packet to the decision of the first rule that the packet matches, according to the complexity bounds from computational geometry [15], the "best" software-based packet classification algorithm uses either $O(n^d)$ space and $O(\log n)$ time or $O(n)$ space and $O(\log^{d-1} n)$ time, where n is the total number of rules and d ($d > 3$) is the total number of fields that the firewall examines for every packet. Clearly, for software-based packet classification algorithms, either space or running time grows quickly as the number of rules increases. Reducing the space that a software-based packet classification algorithm needs also helps to reduce the running time of the algorithm because small space consumption could enable the use of very limited on-chip cache to store the data structure of the algorithm. All in all, for software-based packet classification algorithms, it is advantageous to reduce the number of rules in a firewall. For hardware-based packet classification algorithms, it is also advantageous to reduce the number of rules in a firewall. Consider the example of a TCAM (Ternary Content Addressable Memory). A TCAM uses $O(n)$ space and constant time in mapping a given packet to the decision of the first rule the packet matches. Moreover, TCAM consumes less power as the number of rules decreases.

1.3   Related Work

Previous work on firewalls has primarily focused on firewall design (see [5, 6, 10, 13, 8]) and firewall analysis (see [14, 16, 11, 12, 7]). None of these papers address the issue of redundant rules. The problem of detecting redundant rules only receives attention in [9, 2, 3, 4].

In [9], two special types of redundant rules are identified: backward redundant rules and forward redundant rules. A rule r in a firewall is backward redundant iff there exists another rule r' listed above r such that all packets that match r

also match r'. Clearly, a backward redundant rule is an upward redundant rule, but not vice versa. For example, rule r_3 in Figure 1 is upward redundant, but not backward redundant. A rule r in a firewall is forward redundant iff there exists another rule r' listed below r such that the following three conditions hold: (1) all packets that match r also match r', (2) r and r' have the same decision, (3) for each rule r'' listed between r and r', either r and r'' have the same decision, or no packet matches both r and r''. Clearly, a forward redundant rule is a downward redundant rule, but not vice versa. For example, rule r_2 in Figure 1, assuming r_3 has been removed previously, is downward redundant, but not forward redundant. It has been observed in [9] that 15% of the rules in real-life firewalls are backward redundant or forward redundant.

The redundant rules identified in [2,3,4] are similar to those identified in [9], except that for the case of backward redundant rules, they require that the two rules r and r' must have the same decision.

The bottom line is that the set of redundant rules identified by previous work is incomplete. In other words, given a firewall, after we remove the redundant rules identified in previous work, the firewall still possibly has redundant rules. So, how to detect all the redundant rules in a firewall? This is a hard problem and this problem has never been addressed previously.

1.4 Our Contribution

In this paper, we solve the problem of detecting all redundant rules in a firewall. First, we give a necessary and sufficient condition for identifying all redundant rules. Based on this condition, we categorize redundant rules into upward redundant rules and downward redundant rules. Second, we present methods for detecting the two types of redundant rules respectively. Our methods make use of a tree representation of firewalls, which is called firewall decision trees.

Note that removing redundant rules can be done by firewall software internally. Therefore, the external firewall configuration, i.e., the original sequence of rules which is viewed by firewall administrators, would remain the same. In other words, the procedure of removing redundant rules can be transparent to firewall administrators. Also note that applying our procedure of removing redundant rules does not prevent a firewall administrator from updating a firewall configuration. When the configuration of a firewall is changed due to some rules being inserted, deleted or modified, firewall software always needs to rebuild its internal data structure from the new sequence of rules.

2 Firewall Redundant Rules

We define a *packet* over the fields $F_1, \cdots, F_d$ as a d-tuple $(p_1, \cdots, p_d)$ where each p_i is a value in the domain $D(F_i)$ of field F_i, and each $D(F_i)$ is an interval of nonnegative integers. For example, the domain of the source address in an IP packet is $[0, 2^{32} - 1]$. We use Σ to denote the set of all packets over fields $F_1, \cdots, F_d$. It follows that Σ is a finite set and $|\Sigma| = |D(F_1)| \times \cdots \times |D(F_n)|$.

A *firewall* over the fields $F_1, \cdots, F_d$ is a sequence of rules, and each rule is of the following format:

$$(F_1 \in S_1) \wedge \cdots \wedge (F_d \in S_d) \rightarrow \langle decision \rangle$$

where each S_i is a nonempty subset of $D(F_i)$ and $\langle decision \rangle$ is either *accept* or *discard*. For simplicity, in the rest of this paper, we assume that all packets and all firewalls are over the fields $F_1, \cdots, F_d$, if not otherwise specified.

Some existing firewall products, such as Linux's ipchains [1], require each S_i in a rule to be represented in a prefix format. An example of a prefix is 192.168.0.0/16, where 16 means that the prefix is the first 16 bits of 192.168.0.0. In this paper we use "set", instead of "prefix", to describe firewall rules for two reasons. First, sets and prefixes are algorithmically interconvertible. For example, the set $\{2, 3, \cdots, 8\}$ can be converted to 3 prefixes: $001*, 01*, 1000$. Second, it is easier to argue the mathematical properties of sets than those of prefixes.

A packet $(p_1, \cdots, p_d)$ *matches* a rule $(F_1 \in S_1) \wedge \cdots \wedge (F_d \in S_d) \rightarrow \langle decision \rangle$ iff $(p_1 \in S_1) \wedge \cdots \wedge (p_d \in S_d)$ holds.

A sequence of rules $\langle r_1, \cdots, r_n \rangle$ is *comprehensive* iff for any packet p in Σ, there is at least one rule in $\langle r_1, \cdots, r_n \rangle$ that p matches. A sequence of rules needs to be comprehensive for it to serve as a firewall. From now on, we assume that each firewall is comprehensive. Henceforth, the predicate of the last rule in a firewall can always be replaced by $(F_1 \in D(F_1)) \wedge \cdots \wedge (F_d \in D(F_d))$ without changing the function of the firewall. In the rest of this paper, we assume that the predicate of the last rule in a firewall is $(F_1 \in D(F_1)) \wedge \cdots \wedge (F_d \in D(F_d))$. It follows from this assumption that any postfix of a firewall is comprehensive, i.e., given a firewall $\langle r_1, r_2, \cdots, r_n \rangle$, we know that $\langle r_i, r_{i+1}, \cdots, r_n \rangle$ is comprehensive for each i, $1 \leq i \leq n$.

We use $f(p)$ to denote the decision to which a firewall f maps a packet p. Two firewalls f and f' are equivalent, denoted $f \equiv f'$, iff for any packet p in Σ, $f(p) = f'(p)$ holds. This equivalence relation is symmetric, self-reflective, and transitive. Using the concept of equivalent firewalls, we define redundant rules as follows.

Definition 1 (Redundant Rule). A rule r is *redundant* in a firewall f iff the resulting firewall f' after removing rule r is equivalent to f.

Before introducing our redundancy theorem, we define two important concepts that are associated with each rule in a firewall: matching set and resolving set.

Definition 2 (Matching Set and Resolving Set). Consider a firewall f that consists of n rules $\langle r_1, r_2, \cdots, r_n \rangle$. The *matching set* of a rule r_i in this firewall is the set of all packets that match r_i. The *resolving set* of a rule r_i in this firewall is the set of all packets that match r_i, but do not match any r_j where $j < i$.

For example, consider rule r_2 in Figure 1: its matching set is the set of all the packets whose F_1 field is in $[40, 90]$; and its resolving set is the set of all the packets whose F_1 field is in $[51, 90]$.

The matching set of a rule r_i is denoted $M(r_i)$, and the resolving set of a rule r_i is denoted $R(r_i, f)$. Note that the matching set of a rule depends only on the rule itself, while the resolving set of a rule depends both on the rule and on all the rules listed above it in a firewall.

The following theorem states several important properties of matching sets and resolving sets.

Theorem 1 (Resolving Set Theorem). Let f be any firewall that consists of n rules: $\langle r_1, r_2, \cdots, r_n \rangle$. The following four conditions hold:

1. Equality: $\bigcup_{j=1}^{i} M(r_j) = \bigcup_{j=1}^{i} R(r_j, f)$ for each i, $1 \leq i \leq n$
2. Dependency: $R(r_i, f) = M(r_i) - \bigcup_{j=1}^{i-1} R(r_j, f)$ for each i, $1 \leq i \leq n$
3. Determinism: $R(r_i, f) \cap R(r_j, f) = \emptyset$ for each $i \neq j$
4. Comprehensiveness: $\bigcup_{i=1}^{n} R(r_i, f) = \Sigma$ □

The redundancy theorem below gives a necessary and sufficient condition for identifying redundant rules. Note that we use the notation $\langle r_{i+1}, r_{i+2}, \cdots, r_n \rangle(p)$ to denote the decision to which the firewall $\langle r_{i+1}, r_{i+2}, \cdots, r_n \rangle$ maps packet p.

Theorem 2 (Redundancy Theorem). Let f be any firewall that consists of n rules: $\langle r_1, r_2, \cdots, r_n \rangle$. A rule r_i is *redundant* in f iff one of the following two conditions holds:

1. $R(r_i, f) = \emptyset$,
2. $R(r_i, f) \neq \emptyset$, and for any p that $p \in R(r_i, f)$, $\langle r_{i+1}, r_{i+2}, \cdots, r_n \rangle(p)$ yields the same decision as that of r_i.   □

Note that removing rule r_i from firewall f only possibly affects the decision of the packets in $R(r_i, f)$. If $R(r_i, f) = \emptyset$, then r_i is clearly redundant. If $R(r_i, f) \neq \emptyset$, and for any p that $p \in R(r_i, f)$, $\langle r_{i+1}, r_{i+2}, \cdots, r_n \rangle(p)$ yields the same as that of r_i, then r_i is redundant because removing r_i does not affect the decision of the packets in $R(r_i, f)$.

The redundancy theorem allows us to categorize redundant rules into upward and downward redundant rules.

Definition 3. A rule that satisfies condition 1 in the redundancy theorem is called *upward redundant*. A rule that satisfies condition 2 in the redundancy theorem is called *downward redundant*.

Consider the example firewall f in Figure 1. Rule r_3 is an upward redundant rule because $R(r_3, f) = \emptyset$. Let f' be the resulting firewall by removing rule r_3 from f. Then rule r_2 is downward redundant in f'.

3   Firewall Decision Trees and Rules

In [8], Firewall Decision Diagrams are proposed as a useful notation for specifying firewalls. In this paper, we use a special type of firewall decision diagrams, called Firewall Decision Trees (FDTs), as the core data structure for detecting redundant rules.

Definition 4 (Firewall Decision Tree). A Firewall Decision Tree t over fields $F_1, \cdots, F_d$ is a directed tree that has the following four properties:

1. Each node v in t has a label, denoted $F(v)$, such that

$$F(v) \in \begin{cases} \{F_1, \cdots, F_d\} & \text{if } v \text{ is nonterminal,} \\ \{accept, discard\} & \text{if } v \text{ is terminal.} \end{cases}$$

2. Each edge e in t has a label, denoted $I(e)$, such that if e is an outgoing edge of node v, then $I(e)$ is a nonempty subset of $D(F(v))$.
3. A directed path in t from the root to a terminal node is called a *decision path* of t. Each decision path contains d nonterminal nodes, and the i-th node is labelled F_i for each i that $1 \le i \le d$.
4. The set of all outgoing edges of a node v in t, denoted $E(v)$, satisfies the following two conditions:
   (a) *Consistency*: $I(e) \cap I(e') = \emptyset$ for any two   distinct edges e and e' in $E(v)$,
   (b) *Completeness*: $\bigcup_{e \in E(v)} I(e) = D(F(v))$ □

Figure 3 shows an example of an FDT over the two fields F_1 and F_2, where $D(F_1) = D(F_2) = [1, 100]$. In the rest of this paper, including this example, we use "a" as a shorthand for *accept* and "d" as a shorthand for *discard*.

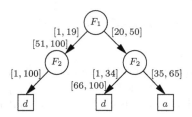

Fig. 3. An FDT

A decision path in an FDT t is represented by $(v_1 e_1 \cdots v_k e_k v_{k+1})$ where v_1 is the root of t, v_{k+1} is a terminal node of t, and each e_i is a directed edge from node v_i to node v_{i+1} in t. A decision path $(v_1 e_1 \cdots v_k e_k v_{k+1})$ in an FDT defines the following rule:

$$F_1 \in I(e_1) \wedge \cdots \wedge F_n \in I(e_n) \ \rightarrow \ F(v_{k+1})$$

For example, the leftmost path in Figure 3 defines the following rule:

$$F_1 \in [1, 19] \cup [51, 100] \wedge F_2 \in [1, 100] \rightarrow d$$

We use $\Gamma(t)$ to denote the set of all the rules defined by all the decision paths in FDT t. If we use t to denote the FDT in Figure 3, then $\Gamma(t) = \{(F_1 \in$

$[1, 19] \cup [51, 100]) \wedge (F_2 \in [1, 100]) \rightarrow d$, $(F_1 \in [20, 50]) \wedge (F_2 \in [1, 34] \cup [66, 100]) \rightarrow d$, $(F_1 \in [20, 50]) \wedge (F_2 \in [35, 65]) \rightarrow a\}$.

For any packet p, there is one and only one rule in $\Gamma(t)$ that p matches because of the consistency and completeness properties of FDT t. The semantics of an FDT t is that for any packet p in Σ, t maps p to the decision of the only rule that p matches in $\Gamma(t)$. We use $t(p)$ to denote the decision to which an FDT t maps a packet p. An FDT t and a sequence of rules f are equivalent, denoted $t \equiv f$, iff for any packet p, $t(p) = f(p)$ holds. Clearly, given an FDT t, any firewall that consists of all the rules in $\Gamma(t)$ is equivalent to t. The order of the rules in such a firewall is immaterial because there are no overlapping rules in $\Gamma(t)$.

In the process of checking upward redundant rules, the data structure that we maintain is called a partial FDT. A *partial* FDT is a tree that may not have the completeness property of an FDT, but has all the other properties of an FDT. For example, Figure 4 shows a partial FDT.

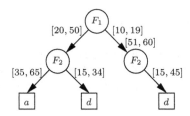

Fig. 4. A partial FDT

We use $\Gamma(t)$ to denote the set of all the rules defined by all the decision paths in a partial FDT t. For any packet p that $p \in \bigcup_{r \in \Gamma(t)} M(r)$, there is one and only one rule in $\Gamma(t)$ that p matches. We use $t(p)$ to denote the decision of the unique rule that p matches in $\Gamma(t)$.

Given a partial FDT t and a sequence of rules $\langle r_1, r_2, \cdots, r_k \rangle$ that may be not comprehensive, we say t is *equivalent* to $\langle r_1, r_2, \cdots, r_k \rangle$ iff the following two conditions hold:

1. $\bigcup_{r \in \Gamma(t)} M(r) = \bigcup_{i=1}^{k} M(r_i)$,
2. for any packet p that $p \in \bigcup_{r \in \Gamma(t)} M(r)$, $t(p)$ is the same as the decision of the first rule that p matches in the sequence $\langle r_1, r_2, \cdots, r_k \rangle$.

For example, the partial FDT in Figure 4 is equivalent to the sequence of rules $\langle (F_1 \in [20, 50]) \wedge (F_2 \in [35, 65]) \rightarrow a, \quad (F_1 \in [10, 60]) \wedge (F_2 \in [15, 45]) \rightarrow d \rangle$.

4   Removing Upward Redundancy

In this section, we discuss how to remove upward redundant rules. By definition, a rule is upward redundant iff its resolving set is empty. Therefore, in order to remove all upward redundant rules from a firewall, we need to calculate resolving set for each rule in the firewall. How to represent a resolving set? In this paper, we represent the resolving set of a rule by an effective rule set of the rule. An effective rule set of a rule r in a firewall f is a set of rules where the union of all the matching sets of these rules is exactly the resolving set of rule r in f. More precisely, an effective rule set of a rule r is defined as follows:

Definition 5. Let r be a rule in a firewall f. A set of rules $\{r'_1, r'_2, \cdots, r'_k\}$ is an *effective rule set* of r iff the following three conditions hold:

1. $R(r, f) = \bigcup_{i=1}^{k} M(r'_i)$,
2. r'_i and r have the same decision for $1 \leq i \leq k$. $\square$

For example, consider the firewall in Figure 1. Then, $\{F_1 \in [1, 50] \rightarrow accept\}$ is an effective rule set of rule r_1, $\{F_1 \in [51, 90] \rightarrow discard\}$ is an effective rule set of rule r_2, $\emptyset$ is an effective rule set of rule r_3, and $\{F_1 \in [91, 100] \rightarrow discard\}$ is an effective rule set of rule r_4. Clearly, once we obtain an effective rule set of a rule r in a firewall f, we know the resolving set of the rule r in f, and consequently know whether the rule r is upward redundant in f. Note that by the definition of an effective rule set, if one effective rule set of a rule r is empty, then any effective rule set of the rule r is empty. Based on the above discussion, we have the following upward redundancy theorem:

Theorem 3 (Upward Redundancy Theorem). A rule r is upward redundant in a firewall iff an effective rule set of r is empty. $\square$

Based on the above upward redundancy theorem, the basic idea of our upward redundancy removal method is as follows: given a firewall $\langle r_1, r_2, \cdots, r_n \rangle$, we calculate an effective rule set for each rule from r_1 to r_n. If the effective rule set calculated for a rule r_i is empty, then r_i is upward redundant and is removed. Now the problem is how to calculate an effective rule set for every rule in a firewall.

An effective rule set for each rule in a firewall is calculated with the help of partial FDTs. Consider a firewall that consists of n rules $\langle r_1, r_2, \cdots, r_n \rangle$. We first build a partial FDT, denoted t_1, that is equivalent to the sequence $\langle r_1 \rangle$, and calculates an effective rule set, denoted E_1, of rule r_1. Then we transform the partial FDT t_1 to another partial FDT, denoted t_2, that is equivalent to the sequence $\langle r_1, r_2 \rangle$, and during the transformation process, we calculate an effective rule set, denoted E_2, of rule r_2. The same transformation process continues until we reach r_n. When we finish, an effective rule set is calculated for every rule.

Here we use t_i to denote the partial FDT that we constructed from the rule sequence $\langle r_1, r_2, \cdots, r_i \rangle$, and E_i to denote the effective rule set that we calculated for rule r_i. By the following example, we show the process of transforming the partial FDT t_i to the partial FDT t_{i+1}, and the calculation of E_{i+1}. Consider the firewall in Figure 5 over fields F_1 and F_2, where $D(F_1) = D(F_2) = [1, 100]$. Figure 6 shows the geometric representation of this firewall, where each rule is represented by a rectangle. From Figure 6, we can see that rule r_3 is upward

$$r_1 : \ (F_1 \in [20, 50]) \wedge (F_2 \in [35, 65]) \rightarrow a$$
$$r_2 : \ (F_1 \in [10, 60]) \wedge (F_2 \in [15, 45]) \rightarrow d$$
$$r_3 : \ (F_1 \in [30, 40]) \wedge (F_2 \in [25, 55]) \rightarrow a$$
$$r_4 : \ (F_1 \in [1, 100]) \wedge (F_2 \in [1, 100]) \rightarrow d$$

Fig. 5. A firewall of 4 rules

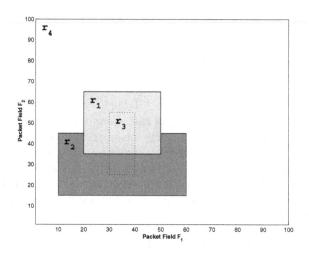

Fig. 6. Geometric representation of the rules in Figure 5

redundant because r_3, whose area is marked by dashed lines, is totally overlaid by rules r_1 and r_2. Later we will see that the effective rule set calculated by our upward redundancy removal method for rule r_3 is indeed an empty set.

Figure 7 shows a partial FDT t_1 that is equivalent to $\langle r_1 \rangle$ and the effective rule set E_1 calculated for rule r_1. In this figure, we use v_1 to denote the node with label F_1, e_1 to denote the edge with label $[20, 50]$, and v_2 to denote the node with label F_2.

Now we show how to append rule r_2 to t_1 in order to get a partial FDT t_2 that is equivalent to $\langle r_1, r_2 \rangle$, and how to calculate an effective rule set E_2 for rule r_2. Rule r_2 is $(F_1 \in [10, 60]) \wedge (F_2 \in [15, 45]) \rightarrow d$. We first compare the set $[10, 60]$ with the set $[20, 50]$ labelled on the outgoing edge of v_1. Since $[10, 60] - [20, 50] = [10, 19] \cup [51, 60]$, r_2 is the first matching rule for all the packets that satisfy $F_1 \in [10, 19] \cup [51, 60] \wedge F_2 \in [15, 45]$, so we add one outgoing edge e to v_1, where e is labeled $[10, 19] \cup [51, 60]$ and e points to the path built from $F_2 \in [15, 45] \rightarrow d$. The rule defined by the decision path containing e, i.e., $F_1 \in [10, 19] \cup [51, 60] \wedge F_2 \in [15, 45] \rightarrow d$, should be put in E_2 because for all packets that match this rule, r_2 is their first matching rule. Since $[20, 50] \subset [10, 60]$, r_2 is possibly the first matching rule for a packet that satisfies $F_1 \in [20, 50]$. So we further compare the set $[35, 65]$ labeled on the outgoing edge of v_2 with the set

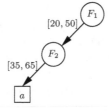

$$E_1 = \{F_1 \in [20, 50] \wedge F_2 \in [35, 65] \rightarrow a\}$$

Fig. 7. Partial FDT t_1 and the effective rule set E_1 calculated for rule r_1 in Figure 5

[15, 45]. Since $[15, 45] - [35, 65] = [15, 34]$, we add a new edge e' to v_2, where e' is labeled $[15, 34]$ and e' points to a terminal node labeled d. Similarly, we add the rule, $F_1 \in [20, 50] \wedge F_2 \in [15, 34] \rightarrow d$, defined by the decision path containing the new edge e' into E_2. The partial FDT t_2 and the effective rule set E_2 of rule r_2 is shown in Figure 8.

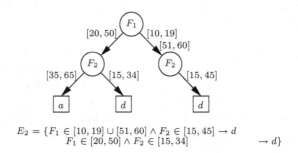

$$E_2 = \{F_1 \in [10, 19] \cup [51, 60] \wedge F_2 \in [15, 45] \rightarrow d$$
$$F_1 \in [20, 50] \wedge F_2 \in [15, 34] \qquad \rightarrow d\}$$

Fig. 8. Partial FDT t_2 and the effective rule set E_2 calculated for rule r_2 in Figure 5

Let f be any firewall that consists of n rules: $\langle r_1, r_2, \cdots, r_n \rangle$. The partial FDT that is equivalent to $\langle r_1 \rangle$ consists of only one decision path that defines the rule r_1.

Suppose that we have constructed a partial FDT t_i that is equivalent to the sequence $\langle r_1, r_2, \cdots, r_i \rangle$, and have calculated an effective rule set for each of these i rules. Let v be the root of t_i, and assume v has k outgoing edges $e_1, e_2, \cdots, e_k$. Let rule r_{i+1} be $(F_1 \in S_1) \wedge (F_2 \in S_2) \wedge \cdots \wedge (F_d \in S_d) \rightarrow \langle decision \rangle$. Next we consider how to transform the partial FDT t_i to a partial FDT, denoted t_{i+1}, that is equivalent to the sequence $\langle r_1, r_2, \cdots, r_i, r_{i+1} \rangle$, and during the transformation process, how to calculate an effective rule set, denoted E_{i+1}, for rule r_{i+1}.

First, we examine whether we need to add another outgoing edge to v. If $S_1 - (I(e_1) \cup I(e_2) \cup \cdots \cup I(e_k)) \neq \emptyset$, we need to add a new outgoing edge e_{k+1} with label $S_1 - (I(e_1) \cup I(e_2) \cup \cdots \cup I(e_k))$ to v. This is because any packet, whose F_1 field satisfies $S_1 - (I(e_1) \cup I(e_2) \cup \cdots \cup I(e_k))$, does not match any of the first i rules, but matches r_{i+1} provided that the packet also satisfies

$(F_2 \in S_2) \wedge (F_3 \in S_3) \wedge \cdots \wedge (F_d \in S_d)$. The new edge e_{k+1} points to the root of the path that is built from $(F_2 \in S_2) \wedge (F_3 \in S_3) \wedge \cdots \wedge (F_d \in S_d) \rightarrow \langle decision \rangle$. The rule r, $(F_1 \in S_1 - (I(e_1) \cup I(e_2) \cup \cdots \cup I(e_k))) \wedge (F_2 \in S_2) \wedge \cdots \wedge (F_d \in S_d) \rightarrow \langle decision \rangle$, defined by the decision path containing the new edge e_{k+1} has the property $M(r) \subseteq R(r_{i+1}, f)$. Therefore, we add rule r to E_i.

Second, we compare S_1 and $I(e_j)$ for each j $(1 \leq j \leq k)$ in the following three cases:

1. $S_1 \cap I(e_j) = \emptyset$: In this case, we skip edge e_j because any packet whose value of field F_1 is in set $I(e_j)$ doesn't match r_{i+1}.
2. $S_1 \cap I(e_j) = I(e_j)$: In this case, for a packet p whose value of field F_1 is in set $I(e_j)$, the first rule that p matches may be one of the first i rules, and may be rule r_{i+1}. So we append $(F_2 \in S_2) \wedge (F_3 \in S_3) \wedge \cdots \wedge (F_d \in S_d) \rightarrow \langle decision \rangle$ to the subtree rooted at the node that e_j points to in a similar fashion.
3. $S_1 \cap I(e_j) \neq \emptyset$ and $S_1 \cap I(e_j) \neq I(e_j)$: In this case, we split edge e into two edges: e' with label $I(e_j) - S_1$ and e'' with label $I(e_j) \cap S_1$. Then we make two copies of the subtree rooted at the node that e_j points to, and let e' and e'' point to one copy each. Thus we can deal with e' by the first case, and e'' by the second case.

In the process of appending rule r_{i+1} to partial FDT t_i, each time that we add a new edge to a node in t_i, the rule defined by the decision path containing the new edge is added to E_{i+1}. After the partial FDT t_i is transformed to t_{i+1}, according to the transformation process, the rules in E_{i+1} satisfy the following two conditions: (1) the union of all the matching sets of these rules is the resolving set of r_{i+1}, (2) all these rules have the same decision as r_{i+1}. Therefore, E_{i+1} is an effective rule set of rule r_{i+1}.

By applying our upward redundancy removal method to the firewall in Figure 5, we get an effective rule set for each rule as shown in Figure 9. Note that $E_3 = \emptyset$, which means that rule r_3 is upward redundant, therefore r_3 is removed.

$1 : E_1 = \{F_1 \in [20, 50] \wedge F_2 \in [35, 65] \qquad\qquad \rightarrow a\};$
$2 : E_2 = \{F_1 \in [10, 19] \cup [51, 60] \wedge F_2 \in [15, 45] \quad \rightarrow d$
$\qquad\quad F_1 \in [20, 50] \wedge F_2 \in [15, 34] \qquad\qquad \rightarrow d\};$
$3 : E_3 = \emptyset;$
$4 : E_4 = \{$
$\quad F_1 \in [1, 9] \cup [61, 100] \wedge F_2 \in [1, 100] \qquad\qquad \rightarrow d$
$\quad F_1 \in [20, 29] \cup [41, 50] \wedge F_2 \in [1, 14] \cup [66, 100] \rightarrow d$
$\quad F_1 \in [30, 40] \wedge F_2 \in [1, 14] \cup [66, 100] \qquad\quad \rightarrow d$
$\quad F_1 \in [10, 19] \cup [51, 60] \wedge F_2 \in [1, 14] \cup [46, 100] \rightarrow d\}$

Fig. 9. Effective rule sets calculated for the firewall in Figure 5

5   Removing Downward Redundancy

One particular advantage of detecting and removing upward redundant rules before detecting and removing downward redundant rules in a firewall is that an effective rule set for each rule is calculated by the upward redundancy removal method; therefore, we can use the effective rule set of a rule to check whether the rule is downward redundant. Note that knowing an effective rule set of a rule equals knowing the resolving set of the rule.

Our method for removing downward redundant rules is based on the following theorem.

Theorem 4. Let f be any firewall that consists of n rules: $\langle r_1, r_2, \cdots, r_n \rangle$. Let t'_i ($2 \leq i \leq n$) be an FDT that is equivalent to the sequence of rules $\langle r_i, r_{i+1}, \cdots, r_n \rangle$. The rule r_{i-1} with the effective rule set E_{i-1} is downward redundant in f iff for each rule r in E_{i-1} and for each decision path $(v_1 e_1 v_2 e_2 \cdots v_d e_d v_{d+1})$ in t'_i where rule r overlaps the rule that is defined by this decision path, the decision of r is the same as the label of the terminal node v_{d+1}.

Now we consider how to construct an FDT t'_i, $2 \leq i \leq n$, that is equivalent to the sequence of rules $\langle r_i, r_{i+1}, \cdots, r_n \rangle$. The FDT t'_n can be built from rule r_n in the same way that we build a path from a rule in the upward redundancy removal method.

Suppose we have constructed an FDT t'_i that is equivalent to the sequence of rules $\langle r_i, r_{i+1}, \cdots, r_n \rangle$. First, we check whether rule r_{i-1} is downward redundant by Theorem 4. If rule r_{i-1} is downward redundant, then we remove r_i, rename the FDT t'_i to be t'_{i-1}, and continue to check whether r_{i-2} is downward redundant. If rule r_{i-1} is not downward redundant, then we append rule r_{i-1} to the FDT t'_i such that the resulting tree is an FDT, denoted t'_{i-1}, that is equivalent to the sequence of rules $\langle r_{i-1}, r_i, \cdots, r_n \rangle$. This procedure of transforming an FDT by appending a rule is similar to the procedure of transforming a partial FDT in the upward redundancy removal method. The above process continues until we reach r_1; therefore, all downward redundant rules are detected and removed.

Applying our downward redundancy removal method to the firewall in Figure 5, assuming r_3 has been removed, rule r_2 is detected to be downward redundant, therefore r_2 is removed. The FDT in Figure 3 is the resulting FDT by appending rule r_1 to the FDT that is equivalent to $\langle r_4 \rangle$.

6   Concluding Remarks

We make two major contributions in this paper. First, we give a necessary and sufficient condition for identifying all redundant rules, based on which we categorize redundant rules into upward redundant rules and downward redundant rules. Second, we present methods for detecting the two types of redundant rules respectively. Our methods make use of a tree representation of firewalls, which is called firewall decision trees.

The results in this paper can be extended for use in many systems where a system can be represented by a sequence of rules. Examples of such systems are rule-based systems in the area of artificial intelligence and access control in the area of databases. In these systems, we can extend the results in this paper to remove redundant rules and thereby make the systems more efficient.

References

1. ipchains, http://www.tldp.org/howto/ipchains-howto.html.
2. E. Al-Shaer and H. Hamed. Firewall policy advisor for anomaly detection and rule editing. In *IEEE/IFIP Integrated Management IM'2003*, pages 17–30, March 2003.
3. E. Al-Shaer and H. Hamed. Management and translation of filtering security policies. In *IEEE International Conference on Communications*, pages 256–260, May 2003.
4. E. Al-Shaer and H. Hamed. Discovery of policy anomalies in distributed firewalls. In *IEEE INFOCOM'04*, pages 2605–2616, March 2004.
5. Y. Bartal, A. J. Mayer, K. Nissim, and A. Wool. Firmato: A novel firewall management toolkit. In *Proceeding of the IEEE Symposium on Security and Privacy*, pages 17–31, 1999.
6. Y. Bartal, A. J. Mayer, K. Nissim, and A. Wool. Firmato: A novel firewall management toolkit. *Technical Report EES2003-1, Dept. of Electrical Engineering Systems, Tel Aviv University*, 2003.
7. M. Frantzen, F. Kerschbaum, E. Schultz, and S. Fahmy. A framework for understanding vulnerabilities in firewalls using a dataflow model of firewall internals. *Computers and Security*, 20(3):263–270, 2001.
8. M. G. Gouda and A. X. Liu. Firewall design: consistency, completeness and compactness. In *Proceedings of the 24th IEEE International Conference on Distributed Computing Systems (ICDCS'04)*, pages 320–327.
9. P. Gupta. *Algorithms for Routing Lookups and Packet Classification*. PhD thesis, Stanford University, 2000.
10. J. D. Guttman. Filtering postures: Local enforcement for global policies. In *Proceedings of IEEE Symp. on Security and Privacy*, pages 120–129, 1997.
11. S. Hazelhurst, A. Attar, and R. Sinnappan. Algorithms for improving the dependability of firewall and filter rule lists. In *Proceedings of the International Conference on Dependable Systems and Networks (DSN'00)*, pages 576–585, 2000.
12. S. Kamara, S. Fahmy, E. Schultz, F. Kerschbaum, and M. Frantzen. Analysis of vulnerabilities in internet firewalls. *Computers and Security*, 22(3):214–232, 2003.
13. A. X. Liu and M. G. Gouda. Diverse firewall design. In *Proceedings of the International Conference on Dependable Systems and Networks (DSN'04)*, pages 595–604, June 2004.
14. A. Mayer, A. Wool, and E. Ziskind. Fang: A firewall analysis engine. In *Proceedings of IEEE Symp. on Security and Privacy*, pages 177–187, 2000.
15. M. H. Overmars and A. F. van der Stappen. Range searching and point location among fat objects. *Journal of Algorithms*, 21(3):629–656.
16. A. Wool. Architecting the lumeta firewall analyzer. In *Proceedings of the 10th USENIX Security Symposium*, pages 85–97, August 2001.

A Comprehensive Approach to Anomaly Detection in Relational Databases

Adrian Spalka[1] and Jan Lehnhardt[2]

[1] Dept of Computer Science III, University of Bonn
Römerstr. 164, 53117 Bonn, Germany
adrian@iai.uni-bonn.de
[2] NOVOTERGUM AG
Im Park 20, 50996 Köln, Germany
j.lehnhardt@novotergum.ag

Abstract. Anomaly detection systems assume that a certain deviation from the regular behaviour of a system can be an indicator for a security violation. They proved their usefulness to networks and operating systems for a long time, but are much less prominent in the field of databases. Relational databases operate on attributes within relations, ie, on data with a very uniform structure, which makes them a prime target for anomaly detection systems. This work presents such a system for the database extension and the user interaction with a DBMS; it also proposes a misuse detection system for the database scheme. In a comprehensive investigation we compare two approaches to deal with the database extension, one based on reference values and one based on Δ-relations, and show that already standard statistical functions yield good detection results. We then apply our methods to the user interaction, which is split into user input and DBMS behaviour. All methods have been implemented in a semi-automatic anomaly detection tool for the MS SQL Server 2000.

Keywords: Database security, anomaly detection, misuse detection, relational databases.

1 Introduction

Today's relational databases and database management systems (DBMS) offer a variety of protection mechanisms. As a prerequisite, users must pass the identification and authentication to obtain access to a DBMS. A user's powers at the DBMS-level, eg, the ability to perform data definition operations, to backup databases or to act as an administrator, are often constrained with privileges. Also at the DBMS-level is an access control system, which decides on a user's access to individual databases within the DBMS. Security at the database-level relies mostly on the mechanisms provided by SQL, the standard language for relational databases. Database developers are assumed to enforce confidentiality through authorisation, ie a restriction of access to relations and views with

S. Jajodia and D. Wijesekera (Eds.): Data and Applications Security 2005, LNCS 3654, pp. 207–221, 2005.

grant/revoke statements. The preservation of availability resorts to technical means, such as backups and execution time limits for queries.

Let us now turn our attention to the two concepts of integrity and accuracy. The (present) extension of a database, ie the data in its relations, should be an accurate image of the present state of the corresponding real-world section. A database supports accuracy by means of integrity, which is defined by a set of constraints. In SQL, data types and primary-key constraints are examples of declarative integrity constraints and triggers are used to specify operational integrity constraints.

From a database's viewpoint, integrity constraints separate the definitely inaccurate data sets from the possibly accurate data sets, which are admitted as extensions. In practice, the set of possible extensions of a database is very large. And thus, though we know that the extension is always possibly accurate, all its data can still be wrong. Well, every reasonably large database has a small fraction of inaccurate data – a well designed business process can cope with it. However, the larger this fraction grows the larger is its negative impact.

Anomaly detection is a technique that generates hints of probably wrong data and harmful operations. In a first step an anomaly detector examines the regular state and behaviour of a system and computes from them a set of reference data, which captures their characteristic properties. Then, the same computations are applied to the system in operation and the current set is compared with the reference set. Whenever the difference exceeds a specified threshold, the anomaly detector reports an anomaly, viz an unusual deviation.

Networks benefit from this idea for a long time. Intrusion detection systems (IDS) are the most popular type of anomaly detectors (there are countless references). But also operating systems are a prominent target for anomaly detectors (cf eg [2], [4] and [8]).

Anomaly detection works best, ie produces the fewest wrong hints and alarms, on systems with clear patterns of regularity. The identification or extraction of these patterns is the most difficult task in the design of an anomaly detection system (ADS) for networks and operating systems – with well designed relational databases many of them come for free.

Our ADS is based on the following facts and assumptions:

- An attribute in a relation has a simple data type. This guarantees a basic uniformity of its values, which can be exploited by specific functions.
- The extension of a database changes in a smooth way.
- A user executes syntactically related commands, which place a specific load on the DBMS.
- Some elements in a database scheme, eg integrity constraints and indexes, are particularly important for the security of the database.

Speaking in terms of operating systems, an ADS can operate in real-time or in batch-mode. A real-time operation depends mainly on three conditions:

- the ADS can monitor or collect system data at short time intervals
- the ADS can evaluate this data with a low overhead
- the ADS can make a decision on a possible anomaly based on this data

Our assumptions about a database do not meet these conditions. Long running transactions but also single SQL-statements, which affect a large number of tuples, obstruct a timely collection of data. The search for an anomaly can involve large parts of a database and, thus, may require a lot of time. And, lastly, many deviations from the assumed smoothness will only be caused by substantial amounts of data. We therefore design our ADS as a batch-mode system, which is executed at a time of low activity in the database, eg during night. The distance between two runs of the ADS is dictated by the environment in which the database is used. In general, once a day or once a week should be a good choice. We regard our ADS as an augmentation to preventive security systems for the ADS only checks if anomalies or misuse have occurred[1].

Our ADS is composed of three components:

- An anomaly detector for the database extension
- An anomaly detector for the user interaction
- A misuse detector for the database scheme

The main emphasis in the construction of the ADS is placed on the first component. Here we offer two approaches. The first one is based on the comparison of reference values, which are obtained with a combination of fairly basic statistical functions on the elements of single attributes. It yields surprisingly good results, so that we dropped – or at least postponed – the initial intention of applying data mining techniques to the extension. Although its time and space requirements are very modest, the detection process works best on databases in which deletions or updates of a large number of tuples occur only seldom. The second approach uses Δ-relations that record the history of changes of the values of the monitored attributes between two runs of the ADS. On the positive, it can be tuned to precisely detect every kind of misuse; on the negative, it can require considerable additional space.

The above-developed analysis techniques are then used in the second component for anomaly detection in the user interaction. It computes reference values from two sources: the user input, ie the SQL-command strings, and the resulting behaviour of the DBMS. This component can detect operations that are admitted by the authorisation controls of the DB/DBMS and yet violate a company's security policy, eg due to the abuse of rights by the legitimate user or masquerading by an intruder.

The third component should have become an ADS for the database scheme, but (according to [1]) it turned out to be a misuse detection system (MDS). Here we are interested in commands, in particular SQL data definition language (DDL) statements, that severely impair the security, including the availability, of a database. We store a list of possibly dangerous commands in a library of signatures and compare the current command to it. Each entry in the library is associated with a critical element in the schema and a possibly damaging

---

[1] We would like to mention that our ADS, like every threshold-based protection system, will raise a false alarm in case of an unusual normal change, and will fail to detect an attack that complies with our normality-rules.

command on it. This allows us, for example, to relate a performance degradation with a dropped index.

The first two components of the outlined ADS are implemented for the MS SQL Server 2000. Presented with a graphical user interface, a user can select relations or attributes that should be monitored. The ADS then generates the appropriate relations and monitoring routines. The derived reference values offer a guide to the user for the initial setting of alarm thresholds. At present, an email is sent to the administrator if the ADS detects a violation. But the ADS also provides a full graphical evaluation of its run or a history of runs.

The subsequent section comments on previous and related work in this area. The ADS component for database extension is presented in detail in section 3 and that for user interaction in section 4. Section 5 describes the approach to misuse detection for the database scheme. Section 6 illustrates the operation of our ADS on an example database. Lastly, a summary concludes this work.

2 Previous and Related Work

There are numerous works on IDS for operating systems and networks, but not on databases. And there are numerous works on database security, but not on anomaly detection. Hence, we are confronted with a fairly small group of works related to our approach.

The DEMIDS system presented in [3] uses anomaly detection methods for the detection of misuse. It focuses on the misuse of privileges. At the core are frequent item-sets, which are computed in the training phase of DEMIDS for each user. These sets comprise relations, attributes and values which a user most often uses in his SQL-commands. The authors develop a distance measure between such a set and a command. In the real-time monitoring stage DEMIDS uses this measure to compute the distance between a user's frequent item-set and his actual query. If a threshold is exceeded, the system raises an alarm.

Our work is influenced by some ideas of the DAS system described in [5]. In the training phase DAS computes data related to a database's extension. With a data centric-view, the authors concentrate on numerical data types. They use the min, max, avg and stddev SQL-functions during the monitoring phase to detect unusual changes in the extension. Our work extends this approach to derive a variant of the frequent item-sets.

We would also like to mention DIDAFIT, a system introduced by [6]. It deals with SQL injection attacks, in particular on web-applications, which construct SQL-commands from parameters supplied by the user. DIDAFIT can be applied to exisiting applications, which are prone to this type of attacks, without re-programming the input validation. It modifies the semantics of an SQL-command with random data, derives for a user a general form of his commands and checks the difference between this form and the current SQL-command.

Lastly, [7] consider temporal objects in databases that register sensor data and present a method for checking for anomalies in the registration intervals.

3   Anomaly Detection in the Database Extension

This section describes two approaches to the detection of anomalies in the database extension.

3.1   Anomaly Detection Based on Reference Values

The anomaly detection based on reference values uses the following method. In the first step the user specifies the attributes, which should be monitored for anomalies. Then our ADS computes for the data of each attribute a set of reference values. The number and type of the values depend on the data type of the attribute. Now the user can specify thresholds for each reference value. [2] When the ADS is executed again, eg a day later, it performs the same computations on the data in the database and compares the current values with the previously computed reference values. If the difference exceeds the threshold, the ADS raises an alert; otherwise we assume that the database has evolved in a regular fashion and the current values replace the old reference values.

We now identify for each data type the corresponding parameters that can be used to capture the behaviour of that data. The MS SQL Server 2000 supports the following six groups of data types:

- bit
- integer, floating point and money
- ascii strings
- unicode and binary strings
- date and time
- unique id

We exclude several data types from our consideration. The type timestamp/rowversion represents system-generated global identifiers and sql_variant is a generic data type, which expose no useful regularity; the types cursor and table are not used in relations (only in stored procedures).

We now describe all reference values; a suitable subset of these values is associated with each group of data types, which is summarised in a table at the end of this section.

- OC: Overall Count.
  It represents the number of tuples in a relation. It is the only value associated with relations; all other values are associated with attributes. Let OC_1 denote the old value and OC_2 the current value. Then OC raises an alarm if the absolute change in the number of tuples, $OC_1 - OC_2$, or the relative change, OC_1/OC_2, exceeds the bounds defined by the threshold.
- NNC: Non-NULL-Count.
  It holds the number of non NULL values in the extension of an attribute. Its alarm conditions are analogous to those of OC.

---

[2] We later address the problem of finding the *right* thresholds.

- NNR: Non-NULL-Ratio.
  It is defined as NNC/OC. It detects insertions of a large number of null values. Its alarm conditions are analogous to those of OC.
- MIN, MAX, AVG, $STDEV$ and $RANGE$.
  These values are the results of the SQL functions minimum, maximum, average and standard deviation, and $RANGE = MAX - MIN$ applied to the extension of an attribute. Their alarm conditions are analogous to those of OC. The thresholds for MIN, MAX and $RANGE$ are often set to zero.
- RC_i, $i = 1, \dots, 6$: Range Counters.
  The range counters monitor the distribution of the number of values of an attribute in the following six ranges:

  - RC_1: number of values below MIN
  - RC_2: number of values between MIN and $AVG - STDEV$
  - RC_3: number of values between $AVG - STDEV$ and AVG
  - RC_4: number of values between AVG and $AVG + STDEV$
  - RC_5: number of values between $AVG + STDEV$ and MAX
  - RC_6: number of values above MAX

  With these counters we can detect, eg, the insertion of an unusually large number of small values. Again, RC_i raises an alarm if the absolute or relative value changes too much.
- $CATC_i$: Category Counters.
  Defined analogously to RC_i, the category counters divide the extension of ASCII string-type and date/time-type attributes into several partitions and monitor the population in each partition. We use the following categories:

  - For date/time-type attributes: Month, day, weekday, hour, minute, second and millisecond
  - For ASCII string-type attributes: the fraction of letters, digits and other characters

  With these counters we can detect, eg, the insertion of an unusually large number of date data with the month January. An abnormal absolute or relative change results in an alarm.

- ZLC: Zero-Length String Count.
  It holds the number of non-NULL ASCII-strings with a length of zero. This is important because these instances have to be excluded from the computation of letter, digit and other character fractions. Again, an abnormal absolute or relative change results in an alarm.
- PBC: Positive Bit Count.
  It holds the number of non-NULL values in a bit-type attribute's extension with positive bit value. It reports an anomaly if the positive bit count increases or decreases absolutely or relatively too much.
- For each of the values RC_i, $CATC_i$, ZLC and PBC there is an additional value that describes the ratio of this value to NNC.

  - $RR_i = RC_i/NNC, i = 1, \dots, 6$: Range Ratios
  - $CATR_i = CATC_i/NNC$: Category Ratios

- $ZLR = ZLC/NNC$: Zero-Length String Ratio
- $PBR = PBC/NNC$: Positive Bit Ratio

An abnormal absolute or relative change results in an alarm.

There are a few subtleties in the computation of the deviations. The rule for NNC is simple:

$$\Delta NNC = NNC_2 - NNC_1$$

and

$$r\Delta NNC = \frac{\Delta NNC}{NNC_1}$$

But an analogous computation of the relative change of the MIN value does not yield the expected result. Consider an attribute that stores the year of birth of students. Suppose that the minimum value is 1972 and maximum is 1982. If a senior student born in 1932 joins the group, then $(1932 - 1972)/1972 = -0,02$, which is negligible. More important and really anomalous is the fact that the new minimum extended the range of this attribute by 400%. Thus, we here use the formula $(1932 - 1972)/(1982 - 1972) = -4$, ie:

$$-r\Delta MIN = -\frac{MIN_2 - MIN_1}{MAX_1 - MIN_1}$$

Finally, let us take a look at the average. A comparison of the old and new average values does not reveal an important anomaly. Suppose that a small number of anomalous tuples is inserted. Then $AVG_1 - AVG_2$ is likely to remain inconspicuous. To detect this anomaly we must compare AVG_1 with the average of these new tuples, ie with

$$\frac{1}{\Delta NNC} \sum_{i=NNC_1+1}^{NNC_2} x_i$$

These observations apply also to the standard deviation (but yield a much more complex formula).

The subsequent table summarises the use of the various parameters for the data types.

	OC	NNC	NNR	MIN,MAX	RANGE	AVG,STDEV	RC_i	RR_i
Numeric		X	X	X	X	X	X	X
ASCII string		X	X	X	X	X	X	X
Binary		X	X	X	X	X	X	X
Date and Time		X	X	X	X	X	X	X
Bit		X	X					
Unique ID		X	X					
Relation	X							

This approach yields the best results with growing-only relations. If updates and deletions of a large number of tuples are permitted, anomalous operations may remain undetected. To give an example, let us monitor only the number

	CATC	CATR	PBC	PBR	ZLC	ZLR
Numeric						
ASCII string	X	X			X	X
Binary					X	X
Date and Time	X	X				
Bit			X	X		
Unique ID						
Relation						

of tuples in a relation, and suppose that the normal behaviour of this relation is a growth of ten tuples between two runs of the ADS. Here we cannot detect an insertion of a million of tuples that is followed by a deletion of a million of tuples.

3.2   Anomaly Detection Based on Δ-Relations

The concept of Δ-relations is an extension to our approach that can detect various anomalies on relations regardless of the number of inserted, updated or deleted tuples. The Δ-relations record all changes to a relation, including old values of updated tuples and deleted tuples. Δ-relations can require a lot of storage, but they provide a precise and comfortable means to discover several anomalies. For example, an unusually high number of inserted tuples followed by a similar number of deleted tuples can now be detected. Moreover, we can identify the tuples that exceed a threshold.

Anomaly detection with the support of Δ-relations works as follows. For every relation that should be monitored four Δ-relations are created:

- INS: stores inserted tuples
- DEL: stores deleted tuples
- UPB: stores updated tuples before the update
- UPA: stores updated tuples after the update

There are two ways of using the data in the Δ-relations.

The first way computes a fictitious 'After'-state. Here we take all tuples from one Δ-relation, eg INS, and assume that only changes to these tuples have been made to the relation in its state before the current run of the ADS. This gives us a fictitious relation state after the run, which then can be compared to the before-state with the methods described in the previous section.

Δ-relations require some modifications to the way of detecting anomalies. On the one hand, it is now very simple to deal with values that record numbers of tuples, since we can directly compare the numbers in the relations. For example, we can count the number of deleted tuples by counting the number of tuples in the DEL relation (and omit a comparison of old and new states). The computation of MIN, MAX and $RANGE$ remains unaltered, and that of AVG and

$STDEV$ is straight forward. On the other hand, the computation of ratios is more complex. For example, we now have

$$|\Delta O| = |NNC_2/OC_2 - NNC_1/OC_1|$$

All the reference values can now be computed also for the Δ-relations and used in the anomaly detection.

The second way of using the data in the Δ-relations is direct comparison. Here the reference values for a Δ-relation are directly compared to the reference values of the associated relation in the state before the changes. Unfortunately, this approach is much too prone for erroneous alarms, in particular, if the Δ-relations are small. To give an example, consider an attribute of type bit. Suppose that 60% of values in its extension are 1 and that only a single element with the value 1 is inserted. This results in value of $PBR = 100\%$ for Δ-relation INS, which deviates by 40% absolutely from the value of PBR for the associated relation in its state before the change and by 66.7% relatively. Both deviations are like to raise a false alarm.

3.3 The Determination of Threshold Values

We suggest three ways for the determination of suitable thresholds.

We can set all thresholds manually to values that are dictated by our experience with the database. While it may be easy to decide on the relative thresholds, eg 5% or 10%, a careful determination of absolute thresholds can be very labour intensive – our system may require far more than 100 such values.

Secondly, we can assume that the initial database state, viz the state that is given to our anomaly detector for the first time, is normal. Then compute all reference values for the first time and derive the thresholds from them.

And, lastly, we can conduct a training phase with presumably regular activities and compute all reference values several times. Then consider the development of the reference values and determine the thresholds on these grounds. Still, we recommend a manual graphical analysis of this development to verify the plausibility of the thresholds.

4 Anomaly Detection in the User Interaction

Anomaly detection in the user interaction can make use of the same methods as anomaly detection in the database extension for the following reasons.

During the analysis cycle the ADS collects user interaction data with the auditing tools of the DBMS. This audit data consists of several sets of values that can be stored as tuples in a database table; we call this table the TraceTable. A single tuple represents a single user operation. Since the TraceTable is an ordinary relation with several attributes, the extension of which grows between two runs of the ADS, we can apply the analysis methods for the database extension to it. Note that we do not need to use Δ-relations.

In the auditing phase the following elements of a user operation are audited and stored in TraceTable:

- the user name
- the SQL command string
- the command's start time
- the command's duration
- the CPU time used by the command
- the number of affected tuples
- SQLCommandClass, a special attribute that classifies the SQL command with one of the follwing values:ADMIN, DDL, PRIVILEGE, DML, READ, EXEC and NULL.

During each run of the ADS all reference values are computed for this relation and compared in the familiar fashion with the corresponding old values.

The SQLCommandClass and the start time represent the part of the user interaction that is controlled by the user. Thus, these attributes reveal an anomaly in the user input.

SQLCommandClass is of type ASCII string and all applicable reference values are computed for it. However, this attribute can take only one of seven values and, therefore, $CATC_i$ and $CATR_i$ provide the most valuable hints to an anomaly. The attribute start time is of type datetime and is treated accordingly. An example of easily detectable anomalies are: a user submitted today too many DDL-commands or at an unusual time of day.

The system behaviour is the DBMS reaction to the user input. To check it for anomalies, we must analyse the duration, CPU time and number of affected tuples. All of them are of a numerical data type; thus, the reference values for anomaly detection in numerical attributes are applied to them.

5   Misuse Detection in the Database Scheme

To develop a comprehensive ADS for relational databases, we must also consider anomalies in the database scheme. Our approach relies on a library of attack signatures and is in fact a misuse detection system.

We first examine all database objects (MS SQL Server has 12: database, default, function, index, privilege, procedure, rule, schema, statistics, table, trigger and view) and all operations on them. Then we classify them with respect to the threat that they pose to a database and store a list of dangerous commands. The commands issued by users are compared to this list.

Let us take a look at a few dangerous commands. The database object is clearly critical. The drop database command is dangerous, for it does not only deletes the database from the system catalog but also the database files stored on disk. We do not consider the alter database command dangerous, because it can delete only empty database files. An index for a table is critical. A single drop index command can severely degrade availability, but also a large number of create index commands can affect performance.

6 A Brief Example of Anomaly Detection in a Database

We now present some screen shots of our ADS. It is applied to an example database, which is populated with data of about 300 CDs with their 4000 songs.

Figure 1 shows data that relate to the length of the songs' titles. The diagram visualises the distribution of the lengths. The Overall Watch section shows reference data for the old extension. The Delta Watch section shows the changes that occurred to the database in the meantime. We see that the standard deviation has increased by nearly 5%, which is due to an increase of the population in the R5-area by nearly 27%. In Figure 2, the Overall Watch section shows the data of the current extension. Note the dotted line in the R5-area, it depicts the value of the old extension. Figure 3 compares in the diagram the old values, represented by the dotted lines, to the new values, shown in solid colours. Here we can easily spot changes to the MIN, MAX, AVG and $STDEV$ values, as well as changes in the numbers of tuples in the respective areas. This provides a visual indication of anomalies.

Figure 4 analyses the fraction of letters in the songs' titles. We see that the numbers remained fairly the same and give no reason for a concern.

Figure 5 shows an analysis of the distribution of months in a date type attribute.

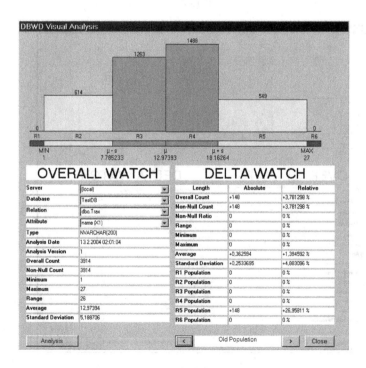

Fig. 1.

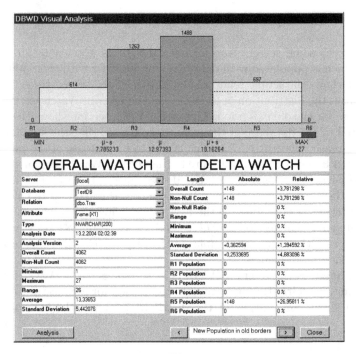

Fig. 2.

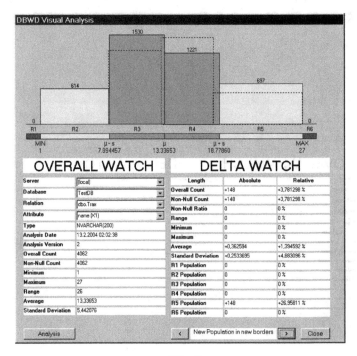

Fig. 3.

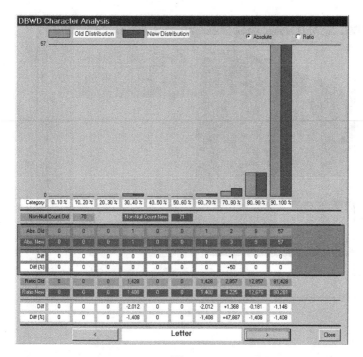

Fig. 4.

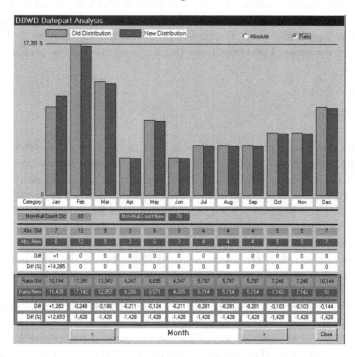

Fig. 5.

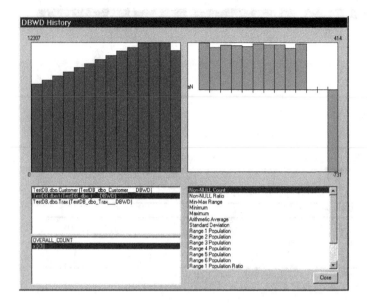

Fig. 6.

And, lastly, Figure 6 shows a longer history of a reference value, the non-Null count. We see in the left panel the absolute numbers and in the right panel the corresponding differences. We note that a continuous increase is followed by an abrupt decrease. The lower right panel allows the selection of numerous parameters.

7 Conclusion

In this work we have presented an anomaly/misuse detection system for relational databases. It can monitor the extension, the user interaction and the scheme. For each data type of the attributes there are numerous values which capture characteristic properties of the attribute's extension. For predominantly growing relations these reference values can help to detect a variety of anomalies. This technique can be applied to Δ-relations to detect even more anomalies in arbitrary relations, however, their space requirements must be carefully calculated. Reference values are also the key to anomaly detection in the user interaction. The ADS can detect many anomalies in the user input and in the reaction of the DBMS. Lastly, we sketched a misuse detector for the database scheme.

The ADS is implemented for the MS SQL Server 2000 and can be applied to any existing database.

On the conceptual side, we would like to examine in future the analysis of groups of attributes with data mining techniques and the suitability of our ADS for real-time detection.

References

1. Axelsson, Stefan. 'Intrusion Detection Systems: A Survey and Taxonomy'. *Technical Report 99.15* Dept. of Computer Engineering, Chalmers University of Technology, Sweden, 2000.
2. Burgess, Mark, Hårek Haugerud, Sigmund Straumsnes and Trond Reitan. 'Measuring system normality'. *ACM Transactions on Computer Systems* 20.2(2002):125-160.
3. Chung, Christina Yip, Michael Gertz, and Karl Levitt. 'DEMIDS: A misuse detection system for database systems'. *IFIP WG11.5 3rd Working Conference on Integrity and Internal Control in Information Systems*, pp 159-178. Kluwer Academic Publishers, 1999.
4. Gao, Debin, Michael K. Reiter and Dawn Song. 'Gray-box extraction of execution graphs for anomaly detection'. *11th ACM Conference on Computer and Communications Security*, pp 318-329. ACM Computer Press, 2004.
5. Gertz, Michael. 'Data Content Monitoring for Security, Integrity and Availability: A Mission-Critical Line of Defense'. *IICIS 2002: IFIP WG11.5 5th Working Conference on Integrity and Internal Control in Information Systems*, pp 189-201. Kluwer Academic Publishers, 2003.
6. Lee, Sin Yeung, Wai Lup Low, Pei Yuen Wong. 'Learning Fingerprints for a Database Intrusion Detection System'. *ESORICS 2002: 7th European Symposium on Research in Computer Security*. LNCS vol 2502, pp 264 - 279. Springer-Verlag, 2002.
7. Lee, Victor C.S., John A. Stankovic, Sang H. Son. 'Intrusion Detection in Realtime Database Systems Via Time Signatures'. *RTAS 2000: 6th IEEE Real Time Technology and Applications Symposium*, pp 124-133. IEEE Computer Society Press, 2000.
8. Michael, C.C., and Anup Ghosh. 'Simple, state-based approaches to program-based anomaly detection'. *ACM Transactions on Information and System Security* 5.3(2002):203-237.

An Authorization Architecture for Web Services

Sarath Indrakanti and Vijay Varadharajan

Information and Networked Systems Security Research,
Department of Computing, Macquarie University,
Sydney, NSW, 2109, Australia
{sindraka, vijay}@ics.mq.edu.au

Abstract. This paper considers the authorization service requirements
for the service oriented architecture and proposes an authorization architecture for Web services. It describes the architectural framework, the
administration and runtime aspects of our architecture and its components for secure authorization of Web services as well as the support
for the management of authorization information. The proposed architecture has several benefits. It is able to support legacy applications
exposed as Web services as well as new Web service based applications
built to leverage the benefits offered by the service oriented architecture; it can support multiple access control models and mechanisms and
is decentralized and distributed and provides flexible management and
administration of Web services and related authorization information.
The proposed architecture can be integrated into existing middleware
platforms to provide enhanced security to exposed Web services. The architecture is currently being implemented within the .NET framework.

1 Introduction

In general, security for the Service Oriented Architecture (SOA) [1] is a broad and
complex area covering a range of technologies. At present, there are several efforts
underway that are striving to provide security services such as authentication
between participating entities, confidentiality and integrity of communications.
A variety of existing technologies can contribute to this area such as TLS/SSL
and IPSec. There are also related security functionalities such as XML Signature
and XML Encryption and their natural extensions to integrate these security
features into technologies such as SOAP and WSDL.

WS-Security specification [2] describes enhancements to SOAP messaging to
provide message integrity, confidentiality and authentication. There is also work
on XKMS defining interfaces to key management and trust services based on
SOAP and WSDL. However, while there is a large amount of work on general
access control and more recently on distributed authorization [3][4] research in
the area of authorization for Web services is still at an early stage. There is
not yet a specification or a standard for Web services authorization. There are
attempts by different research groups to define authorization frameworks and
policies for Web services [5][6][7][8][9]. Currently most Web service based applications, having gone through the authentication process, make authorization

S. Jajodia and D. Wijesekera (Eds.): Data and Applications Security 2005, LNCS 3654, pp. 222–236, 2005.

decisions using application specific access control functions. This results in the practice of frequently re-inventing the wheel and motivates us to have a closer look at authorization requirements for the SOA.

1.1   Authorization Requirements for the SOA

Broadly speaking, the SOA is made up of Web services and business workflows built using Web services. These workflows are called business processes [10]. Figure 1 shows the layers comprising the SOA. In general, Web services and business processes have different authorization requirements. Authorization services for business processes must provide orchestration services to coordinate the authorization decisions from individual partner's authorization policy evaluators. Each partner must be allowed to control its own authorization policies and also not require disclosing them to all the partners. Even in cases where the binding to actual end-points of partner services happens dynamically at runtime, the authorization architecture must be able to orchestrate the partners' authorization policy evaluators and arrive at an authorization decision.

Authorization services for the Web services layer have different design requirements as Web services present a complex layered system. For instance, a service could be a front-end to an enterprise system and the enterprise system accesses information stored in databases and files. Web services may be used by enterprises to expose the functionality of legacy applications to users in a heterogeneous environment. Or new business applications could be written to leverage benefits offered by the SOA.

A Web service's method may invoke one or more abstract operations, each operation having its own responsible Authorization Policy Evaluator (APE). For instance, a purchase order service may have three methods – submit order, cancel order and confirm order as shown in Figure 2. Submit order and cancel order methods perform two operations say a Web operation and a mail operation,

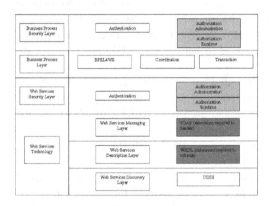

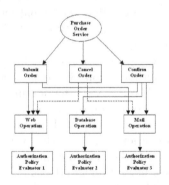

Fig. 1. Layers in the Service Oriented Architecture

Fig. 2. WS operations and Authorization Policy Evaluators

and confirm order performs say three operations a Web operation, a database operation and a mail operation. Each operation may have its own responsible APE to control access to the operation.

We envisage an authorization architecture for the SOA to provide extensions to both the security layers of Web services as well as business processes as indicated by the grey colored boxes in Figure 1. In this paper, we propose our Web Services Authorization Architecture (WSAA). WSAA provides authorization services for Web services. It extends the Web services security layer in the SOA. We also extend the Web services description and messaging layers (indicated by dark-grey colored boxes in Figure 1) to provide authorization support for Web services. We will describe our authorization services for the business process layer in a separate paper.

In section 2, we outline our design principles and goals underlying the design of WSAA. In Section 3, we give an overview of WSAA and discuss the design of our architecture. In Section 4, we briefly describe the extensions required to the Web service Description and Messaging Layers. We briefly describe the authorization algorithms used by WSAA in Section 5 and give a brief introduction to our implementation work in Section 6. We highlight the benefits of our architecture in Section 7 and discuss some related work in Section 8. Finally, we give some concluding remarks in Section 9.

2   Design Principles

In this section, we outline some of the key design principles and goals behind our proposed architecture.

(a) Different Access Control (AC) Models: WSAA should be able to support a range of AC models. This is necessary as it is not realistic to expect every Web service based application to use the same AC model. In fact, where Web services are used to expose the functionality of legacy enterprise applications, it is likely that organizations will prefer to use their currently existing AC mechanisms that they have been using before exposing them as Web services. Therefore, we believe an authorization architecture must be generic enough to support different AC models including traditional Discretionary Access Control (DAC), Mandatory Access Control (MAC), Role Based Access Control (RBAC), and Certificate based AC models.

(b) Authorization Architecture Design: Conceptually, there are two stages for authorization [3] namely the administration phase and the runtime or the evaluation phase. The administration phase involves facilities and services for the specification of authorization policies, updating and deleting of policies and their administration. The runtime phase is concerned with the use of these authorization policies in the evaluation of the access requests.

(c)Authentication: In WSAA, we assume that authentication is a prerequisite to authorization and that a principal (client) and its request has undergone some reliable authentication service before being subjected to the authorization service.

(d) Authorization Policy Evaluation: Every AC mechanism that is supported by WSAA defines an interface or end-point (defines the input parameters as well as the output result) to the Authorization Policy Evaluator (APE). APE is responsible for achieving end-point decisions on access control. An APE also defines a set of abstract operations such as Web operations, database operations or file operations to which it provides access control.

Note: A Web service method is a high-level task that the Web service exposes to its clients. WSAA provides access control indirectly to operations performed by a Web service method. We map each Web service method to a set of abstract operations. One or more of these operations are then mapped to an APE, which is responsible for controlling access to these operations. These abstract operations help security administrators and Web service developers have a common ground to map the resources (Web services themselves and any other resources such as databases, files, applications, etc.) to APEs and therefore to authorization policies.

e) Authorization Policies: Languages have long been recognized in computing as ideal vehicles for dealing with expression and structuring of complex and dynamic relationships. A language-based approach is helpful for not only supporting a range of AC policies but also in separating out the policy representation from policy enforcement. Hence one of our design principles is to enable the support of a range of policy languages for specifying AC policies. The policy language(s) used may support both fine-grained as well as coarse-grained policies depending on the requirement. The respective authorization policy administrators manage these policies.

(f) Authorization Credentials: WSAA provides support for defining what AC related credentials are required and how to collect them. Some AC mechanisms may pull the credentials from the respective authorities and send them to the responsible APEs. Other AC mechanisms may expect the principal to collect the credentials from the respective authorities and send them to the responsible APEs. WSAA supports both the push and pull model approaches to credentials collection and decision-making.

3   Design of the Proposed Architecture

3.1   Overview

Let us now first briefly describe an overview of the proposed architecture (refer to Figure 3). WSAA comprises of an administrative domain and a runtime domain. We manage Web services in the administration domain by arranging them into collections and the collections themselves into a hierarchy. We provide administration support to manage a collection of Web services. We also provide support for the arrangement (adding, removing) of Web services within the collections and the movement of Web services within collections. Authorization related components can be managed in the administration domain. Also security administrators can assign a set of APEs to authorize requests to Web services. To make the authorization process efficient, we have a runtime domain where the authorization related information such as what credentials are required to

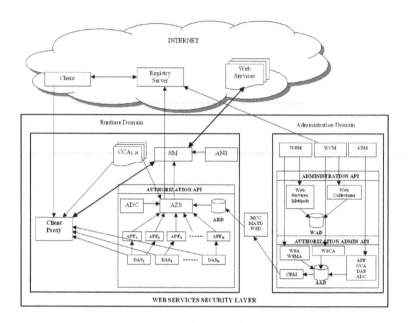

Fig. 3. Web Services Authorization Architecture (WSAA)

invoke a particular Web service and how to collect those credentials, is compiled and stored. This information is automatically compiled from time to time when necessary using the information from the administration domain and it can be readily used by components in the runtime domain.

The Registry Server located anywhere in the Internet is responsible for maintaining relations between services and their service providers. When a client requests the Registry Server (UDDI directory for instance) for a specific service, the latter responds with a list of Web services that implement the requested service.

3.2   System Components

We define the set of *Certificate and Credential Authorities, Dynamic Attribute Services, Authorization Policy Evaluators* and *Authorization Decision Composers* as objects in our system. The *Authorization Manager* (AZM) for an organization is responsible to manage these components. S/he uses the Authorization Administration API (AA-API) to manage them and the related data is stored in the *Authorization Administration Database* (AAD). These objects are formally defined in definitions 1–4.

Certificate and Credential Authority (CCA) is responsible to provide authentication certificates and/or authorization credentials required to authenticate and/or authorize a client.
Dynamic Attribute Service (DAS) provides system and/or network attributes such as bandwidth usage and time of the day. A dynamic attribute

may also express properties of a subject that are not administered by security administrators. For example, a nurse may only access a patient's record if s/he is located within the hospital's boundary. A DAS may provide the nurse's "location status" attribute at the time of access control. Dynamic attributes' values change more frequently than traditional "static" authorization credentials. Unlike authorization credentials, dynamic attributes must be obtained at the time an access decision is required and their values may change within a session.

Authorization Policy Evaluator (APE) is responsible for making authorization decision on one or more abstract system operations. Every APE may use a different access control mechanism and a different policy language. However, it defines an interface for the set of input parameters it expects (such as subject (client) identification, object information, and the authorization credentials) and the output authorization result.

Authorization Decision Composer (ADC) combines the authorization decisions from APEs using an algorithm that resolves authorization decision conflicts and combines them into a final decision.

Definition 1. Certificate and Credential Authority (CCA)
We define Certificate and Credential Authority (CCA) as a tuple cca = {i, l, CR, pa, ra(pa)}, where i is a URN, l is a string over an alphabet Σ^* representing a network location of the CCA such as a URL, CR is the set of credentials cca provides, pa is an input parameter representing a subject, ra uses pa and gives out an output (result) that is the set of credentials for the subject.

Definition 2. Dynamic Attribute Service
We define Dynamic Attribute Service as a tuple das = {i, l, AT, pd, rd(pd)}, where i is a URN, l is a string over an alphabet Σ^* representing a network location of the DAS such as a URL, AT is the set of attributes that das provides, pd is input parameter(s) representing attribute(s) name, rd uses pd and gives out an output (result) that is the value of the attribute(s).

Definition 3. Authorization Policy Evaluator
We define Authorization Policy Evaluator as a tuple ape = {i, l, pe, re(pe), OP, DAS, CCA}, where i is a URN, l is a string over an alphabet Σ^* representing a network location of the APE such as a URL, pe is the set of input parameters such as subject and object details, re is a function that uses pe and gives out an output (result) of authorization decision. OP is the set of abstract system operations for which ape is responsible. DAS is the set of dynamic attribute services responsible for providing dynamic runtime attributes to ape. ape uses these attributes to make authorization decisions. CCA is the set of certificate and credential authorities that provide the credentials required by ape.

Definition 4. Authorization Decision Composer
We define Authorization Decision Composer as a tuple adc = {i, l, a, pc, rc(pc)}, where i is a URN, l is a string over an alphabet Σ^* representing a network location of the ADC such as a URL, a is the name of a pre-defined algorithm adc uses to combine the decisions from the individual authorization policy evaluators. pc is an input parameter representing the decisions from individual APEs, rc uses

pc and authorization decision composition algorithm a to combine the decisions and gives out an output (result) that is the value of the final authorization decision.

The runtime domain consists of the *Client Proxy, Security Manager, Authentication Server* and the *Authorization Server* components.

Client Proxy (CP) collects the required authentication and authorization credentials from the respective authorities on behalf of the client before sending a Web service request and handles the session on behalf of the client with a Web service's Security Manager component.

Security Manager (SM) is a runtime component responsible for both authentication and authorization of the client. A client's CP sends the necessary authentication and authorization credentials to the SM. It is responsible for managing all the interactions with a client's CP. It uses the Authorization API to invoke the Authorization Server.

Authentication Server (ANS) receives the authentication credentials from SM and uses some mechanism to authenticate the client. We treat ANS as a black box in our architecture as our focus in this paper is on authorization of the client. We included this component in the Web services security layer for completeness.

Authorization Server (AZS) decouples the authorization logic from application logic. It is responsible for locating all the APEs involved, sending the credentials to them and receiving the authorization decisions. Once all the decisions come back, it uses the responsible ADCs to combine the authorization decisions. Where required, AZS also collects the credentials and attributes on behalf of clients from the respective CCAs and DASs.

3.3   Web Services Model

We consider a Web service model based on the model discussed in [11] where Web Service, Web Service Method and Web Service Collection are viewed as objects (definitions 5–7). Web service collections are used to group together a set of possibly related Web service objects.

Definition 5. Web Service
We define a Web Service as a tuple ws = {i, b, l, S, OP_{ws}, M, MD, wsm, sm}, where i is a non-empty string over an alphabet Σ^* representing a globally unique identifier such as a URN, b is a string over an alphabet Σ^* representing a network protocol binding such as SOAP over HTTP, l is a string over an alphabet Σ^* representing a network location such as a URL, S is a finite set of states representing the internal state of the object at a given time, OP_{ws} is the set of abstract operations performed by the methods of the ws object. M is the set of supported Web service methods, MD is the set of metadata providing additional description for ws, wsm is the Web Service Manager responsible for managing ws object. sm is the Security Manager responsible for ws object. S, M, OP_{ws} or MD can be the empty set ϕ.

Definition 6. Web Service Method
We define a Web Service Method as a tuple m = {i, ws, OP_{wsm}, pm, rm(pm), MD}, where i is a URN, ws is the Web service object the method belongs to, OP_{wsm} is the set of abstract operations wsm performs. OP_{wsm} is a subset of the set OP_{ws} defined in the ws object. pm is the set of input parameters, string over an alphabet Σ *, rm is a function $\Sigma^* \rightarrow \Sigma^*$ that maps pm onto a result string over an alphabet Σ^* representing the output (result) or return value(s) of a computation. pm and rm(pm) may be the empty string ϵ. MD is a set of metadata providing additional description for wsm. OP_{wsm} or MD can be the empty set ϕ. A wsm has to be a member of exactly one ws.

Definition 7. Web Service Collection
We define a Web Service Collection (WSC) as a tuple wsc = {i, WS, $WSC_{CHILDREN}$, p, MD, wcm, sm}, where i is a URN, WS is a finite set of (possibly related) Web service objects in wsc, $WSC_{CHILDREN}$ is a finite set of Web service collections that are children of wsc, p is the parent WSC (a WSC can have only one parent collection), MD is a finite set of metadata providing additional description and semantics for wsc. sm is the security manager responsible for wsc. wcm is the Web service Collection Manager responsible for wsc. sm is null for all Web service collections in a hierarchy except for the root Web service collection, or the one without a parent p. A root wsc object's sm is responsible for authentication and authorization of requests to all the ws objects under its descendant collections. Figure 4 shows an example of a hierarchy of Web service collections.

3.4   Authorization Administration and Policy Evaluation

A *Web Service Manager* (WSM) is responsible to manage the authorization information for the Web services s/he is responsible for. We consider a Web service

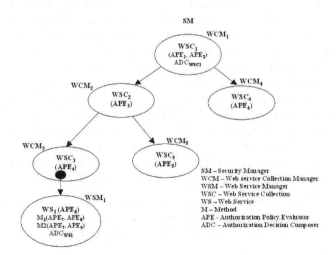

Fig. 4. Web Service Collection Hierarchy

method to be a high-level task that is exposed to clients. Each task (method) is made up of a number of system operations. These operations can be of different abstract types as shown in the example in Figure 2. It is reasonable to assume a WSM knows the set of tasks a Web service under his/her control performs. Similarly a WSM knows the set of operations each of these tasks (methods) perform. Using the APE definitions from AAD (database), WSM associates APEs to Web services and their methods. This association is made in the *Web Service Authorization* and the *Web Service Method Authorization* objects. WSM uses the AA-API to create and manage these objects. Similarly, a *Web service Collection Manager* (WCM) manages APE and authorization decision composer (ADC) information (using AA-API) in a separate tuple called *Web Services Collection Authorization* (WSCA) for all the collections s/he manages. We formally define these objects in definitions 8–10. These objects are stored in AAD.

Similar to Web service methods, a Web service can also have one or more APEs responsible for the Web service itself. Web service level policies are first evaluated before its method level authorization policies are evaluated. A Web service's APEs evaluate Web service level authorization policies. These policies will typically not be as fine-grained as method level policies. A WSM may choose to create a new ADC for one or more Web services s/he manages or may decide to use one from the set of existing ADCs from AAD if it serves the purpose.

Similar to Web services and their methods, a Web service collection can also have one or more APEs responsible for authorizing access to the collection itself. Collection level policies are first evaluated before a Web service's policies are evaluated. A Web service collection's APEs evaluate collection level policies. These policies will typically be course-grained when compared to the Web service and Web service method level policies. Every root Web service collection has an ADC associated with it responsible for combining the decisions from all APEs involved. The coarse-grained authorization policies for all the relevant ancestor Web service collections (of an invoked Web service) are first evaluated, followed by the Web service level policies and finally the fine-grained Web service method level policies are evaluated. For example (refer to Figure 4), when a client invokes WS_1's method M_1, WSC_1's authorization policies are first evaluated by APE_1 and APE_2, followed by WSC_2 (APE_3) and then WSC_3 (APE_4) policies. If APE_1, APE_2, APE_3 and APE_4 give out a positive decision, WS_1's authorization policies are evaluated by APE_6. If APE_6 gives out a positive decision, then finally M_1's authorization policies are evaluated by APE_7 and APE_8. WS_1's ADC, ADC_{WS_1} combines the decisions from APE_6, APE_7 and APE_8 and if the final decision is positive, WSC_1's ADC, ADC_{WSC_1} combines the decisions from APE_1, APE_2, APE_3, APE_4 and ADC_{WS_1}. If the final decision from ADC_{WSC_1} is positive, the client will be able to successfully invoke WS_1's method M_1.

Definition 8. Web Service Method Authorization
We define Web Service Method Authorization as a tuple wsma = {i, wsm, APE_{wsm}}, where i is a URN, wsm is the method to which wsma object is

defined. APE_{wsm} is the set of APEs responsible for authorizing requests from a client to wsm.

Definition 9. Web Service Authorization
We define Web Service Authorization as a tuple wsa $= \{i, ws, APE_{ws}, adc_{ws}\}$, where i is a URN, ws is the Web service to which wsa is defined. APE_{ws} is the set of APEs responsible for authorizing requests from a client to ws. adc_{ws} is an ADC for ws. It is responsible to combine the decisions from APEs (in the set APE_{ws}).

Definition 10. Web Service Collection Authorization
We define Web Service Collection Authorization as a tuple wsca $= \{i, wsc, APE_{wsc}, adc_{root}\}$, where i is a URN, wsc is the Web service collection for which wsca object is defined. APE_{wsc} is the set of APEs responsible for wsc. adc_{root} is an ADC for wsc. If wsc is not a root Web service collection, then adc_{root} is null. In other words, adc_{root} exists only for a root wsc.

3.5   Runtime Authorization Data

We addressed who assigns (and how) APEs and ADCs for Web services and Web service collections. The next question is, at runtime, how does a client know (where necessary) how to obtain the required authorization credentials and dynamic runtime attributes before invoking a Web service? What are the responsible APEs (and the credentials and attributes they require), CCAs (the credentials they provide) and DASs (the attributes they provide)? How does the Authorization Server (AZS) know what the set of responsible ADCs (adc_{ws} and adc_{root}) for a particular client request is?

To answer these questions, we have an Authorization Runtime Database (ARD) in the runtime domain. ARD consists of the runtime authorization related information required by clients and the Authorization Server. *Credential Manager* (CRM) is an automated component that creates and stores the authorization runtime information (using CRM algorithm) in ARD using the information from WAD (defined in section 3.6) and AAD. The runtime authorization information consists of three tuples defined in definitions 11–13. CRM is invoked from time to time, when a Web service object is added to or removed from a collection, moved within a hierarchy of collections or when the shape of the tree itself changes, to update these tuples in ARD. Refer to [12] for the CRM algorithm.

Definition 11. Method-Credential-CCA tuple
We define the Method-Credential-CCA tuple as mcc $= \{i, wsm, CR, cca, ape\}$, where i is a URN, wsm is a Web service method to which the tuple is defined, CR is the set of credentials to be obtained from the CCA cca to get authorized to invoke wsm. This means each wsm object can have one or more of these (tuple) entries in ARD. ape is the APE that requires these credentials.

Definition 12. Method-Attribute-DAS tuple
We define Method-Attribute-DAS tuple as matd $= \{i, wsm, AT, das, ape\}$, where i is a URN, wsm is a Web service method to which the tuple is defined, AT is

the set of attributes to be obtained from the DAS das. This means each wsm object can have one or more of these (tuple) entries in ARD. ape is the APE that requires these attributes.

Definition 13. WS-ADC tuple
We define WS-ADC tuple as wsd = $\{i, ws, adc_{ws}, adc_{root}\}$, where i is a URN, ws is a Web service, adc_{ws} is the ADC for ws. adc_{root} is the ADC for the root Web service collection in which ws is located.

3.6   Web Services Administration

A Web Service Manager (WSM) manages Web services and Web service methods and a Web service Collection Manager (WCM) manages Web service collections using the Administration API (see Figure 3). These objects are stored in the Web service Administration Database (WAD).

To effectively manage the collections, we arrange a set of related Web Service Collection (WSC) objects in a tree-shaped hierarchy as shown in Figure 4. Each WSC in the hierarchy has a responsible Web service Collection Manager (WCM). There is only one Security Manager for a hierarchy of WSCs. In a WSC hierarchy tree, the root WSC's manager is called the Root Web service Collection Manager (RWCM). A RWCM is responsible for providing the Security Manager details (such as its location) in the WSDL statement of every Web service located under the collections s/he manages.

Let us consider an organization with a single hierarchy (such as the one shown in Figure 4) of Web service collections. In Figure 4, the root WSC is WSC_1 and the RWCM is WCM_1. We can consider a newly initiated system to simply consist of the root WSC, WSC_1 and a few Web Service (WS) objects under it managed by WCM_1. WCM_1 can add new WS objects from WAD into WSC_1. S/he can delete or move WS objects within the collections s/he is responsible for. There are other issues to consider such as 1) Who decides the location of a WS object (and how is the location changed)? 2) Who decides the shape of the tree itself? There are various design choices to consider to answer these questions.

Due to space limitations, we have not included the discussion on such design choices in this paper. We refer the reader to [12] for a detailed discussion on Web services administration features provided by our architecture.

4   Extensions to the Description and Messaging Layers

WS-AuthorizationPolicy statement: We extend WSDL (description layer) to include a Web service's Authorization Policy as well as the location of its Security Manager. WS-SecurityPolicy [13] statement consists of a group of security policy "assertions", that represent a Web Service's security preference, requirement, capability or other property. Similarly, we define *WS-AuthorizationPolicy* as a statement that contains a list of authorization assertions. The assertions include which credentials (and from which CCA) and attributes (and from which DAS) a client's CP has to collect before invoking a Web Service. WS-PolicyAttachment [14] standard can be used to link the WS-AuthorizationPolicy to a Web Service's WSDL statement.

Security Manager Location: When a client wants to invoke a Web service WS_1, its Client Proxy requires its Security Manager's location. Therefore, we need to give this information in WS1's WSDL statement. We introduce a new element *SecurityManager* to the WSDL document that encapsulates the Security Manager location information required by the Client Proxies.

SOAP Header Extension: We provide extensions to the SOAP header (messaging layer) to carry authorization related credentials and attributes. WS-Security [2] enhancements for confidentiality, integrity and authentication of messages have extended SOAP header (SOAP-SEC element) to carry related information. Similarly we suggest extending SOAP header to carry authorization credentials and attributes to carry authorization related information. When a client wants to invoke a Web service object, its client proxy creates an authorization header object and adds it to SOAP Header before making a SOAP request.

Refer to [12] for XML schema skeletons for WS-AuthorizationPolicy, extended WSDL statement and extended SOAP Header. We have not included the schemas in this paper due to space restrictions.

5   Authorization Algorithms

WSAA supports three algorithms. The first, push-model algorithm supports authorizations where a client's Client Proxy, using WS-AuthorizationPolicy, collects and sends the required credentials (from CCAs) and attributes (from DASs) to a Web service's Security Manager. The second, pull-model algorithm supports authorizations where the AZS itself collects the required credentials and APEs collect the required attributes. The third, combination-model supports both the push and pull models of collecting the required credentials and attributes.

An organization must deploy one of these algorithms depending on the access control mechanisms used. If all the access control mechanisms used by the set of APEs are based on a pull model, then the organization must deploy the pull-model algorithm. If all the access control mechanisms used are based on a push model, then the organization must deploy the push-model algorithm. However, when some of an organization's APEs use the pull-model and others use the push-model, the combination-model algorithm must be deployed. The authorization algorithms along with their respective system sequence diagrams can be found in [12].

6   Implementation

We are currently implementing WSAA as a middleware layer within the .NET framework [15]. We have developed UML design specifications and specifed a case study in the healthcare domain to demonstrate the features proposed in this paper with an implementation. We will describe our design specifications and the implementation of WSAA along with the case study in detail in a separate paper.

7   Benefits of the Proposed Architecture

Some of the key advantages of the proposed architecture are as follows:

(a) Support for Various Access Control (AC) models: WSAA supports multiple AC models. The access policy requirements for each model can be specified using its own policy language. The policies used for authorization can be fine-grained or coarse-grained depending on the requirements. AC mechanisms may either use the push model or pull model or even a combination of both for collecting client credentials.

(b) Support for Legacy and New Web Service Based Applications: Existing legacy application systems can still function and use their current AC mechanisms when they are exposed as Web services to enable an interoperable heterogeneous environment. At the same time WSAA supports new Web service based applications built to leverage the benefits offered by the SOA. New AC mechanisms can be implemented and used by Web service applications. A new AC mechanism can itself be implemented as a Web service. All WSAA requires is an end-point URL and interface for the mechanism's APE.

(c) Decentralized and Distributed Architecture: A Web service can have one or more responsible APEs involved in making the authorization decision. The APEs themselves can be Web services specializing in authorization. This feature allows WSAA to be decentralized and distributed. Distributed authorization architecture such as ours provides many advantages such as fault tolerance and better scalability and outweighs its disadvantages such as more complexity and communication overhead.

(d) Flexibility in Management and Administration: Using the hierarchy approach of managing Web services and collections of Web services, authorization policies can be specified at each level making it convenient for Web service collection managers (WCM) and Web service managers (WSM) to manage their objects as well as their authorization related information.

(f) Ease of Integration into Platforms: Each of the entities involved both in administration and runtime domains is fairly generic and can be implemented in any middleware including the .NET platform as well as Java based platforms. The administration and runtime domain related APIs can be implemented in any of the available middleware.

(g) Enhanced Security: In our architecture, every client principal request passes through the Web service's security manager and then gets authenticated and authorized. The security manager can be placed in a firewall zone, which enhances security of collections of Web service objects placed behind an organization's firewall. This enables organizations to protect their Web service based applications from outside traffic. A firewall could be configured to accept and send only SOAP request messages with appropriate header and body to the responsible security manager to get authenticated and authorized.

8   Related Work

We briefly compare the related work in the area of design of authorization architecture for Web service layer (of the SOA) to WSAA.

Kraft [5] proposes an AC model based on a "distributed access control processor" for Web services. The model is generic enough to support different models of access control. This model however, does not provide support for administration of authorization related information. It also does not provide support to manage Web service collections and their authorization related information using standard APIs, which our architecture provides.

Yague and Troya [6] present a semantic approach for access control for Web services that is based on a Privilege Management Infrastructure (PMI). The authorization policies can only be written in the Semantic Policy Language (SPL). What is interesting in this model is that the authorization policies can be attached dynamically based on the metadata of the resource being accessed.

Agarwal et al [7] define an access control model that combines DAML-S , an ontology specification for describing Web services and SPKI/SDSI , used to specify access control policies and to produce name and authorization certificates for users. This is a certificate based AC model. The Access Control Lists (ACLs) in this model are simple and one cannot specify fine-grained and complex authorization policies using this model.

Ziebermayr and Probst propose an authorization framework [8] for "simple Web services". Their framework does not consider distributed authorization and assumes that Web services provide access to data or sensitive information located on one server and not distributed over the Web. This framework uses a simple rule based access control model. A disadvantage with this framework is that it cannot support authorizations for distributed Web services, which have access to data and/or information over a number of Web servers.

Unlike WSAA, the models [6][7][8] only support one model of AC and therefore legacy applications exposed as Web services cannot use different models of AC they have already been using. These models also do not provide management and administration support for Web service objects. There is also no abstraction of each Web service method's task into a set of operations in all these models [5][6][7][8]. This abstraction makes it easy to perform authorization administration as discussed earlier.

9   Concluding Remarks

We have proposed an authorization architecture for Web services that extends the Web services security layer in the Service Oriented Architecture (SOA). We have also provided extensions to the messaging and description layers to support the proposed architecture. We have described the architectural framework, the administration and runtime aspects of our architecture and its components for secure authorization of Web services as well as the support for the management of Web services as well as authorization related information. We are currently implementing the proposed architecture within the .NET framework.

The architecture supports legacy applications exposed as Web services as well as new Web service based applications built to leverage the benefits offered by the SOA; it supports old and new access control models and mechanisms; it is decentralized and distributed and provides flexible management and administration of Web service objects and authorization information. We believe that the proposed architecture is easy to integrate into existing platforms and provides enhanced security by protecting exposed Web services from outside traffic.

References

1. S. Wilkes and J. Harby. SOA Blueprints Concepts Draft v0.5. Technical report, The Middleware Research Company, June 2004.
2. B. Atkinson, G. Della-Libera, S. Hada, M. Hondo, et al. Web Services Security (WS-Security) Specification, http://www-106.ibm.com/developerworks/webservices/library/ws-secure/, 2002.
3. V. Varadharajan. Distributed Authorization: Principles and Practice. In *Coding Theory and Cryptology, Lecture Notes Series, Institute for Mathematical Sciences, National University of Singapore*. Singapore University Press, 2002.
4. K. Beznosov, Y. Deng, B. Blakley, and J. Barkley. A Resource Access Decision Service for CORBA-based Distributed Systems. In *Proceedings of the 15th Annual Computer Security Applications Conference*, page 310. IEEE Computer Society, 1999.
5. R. Kraft. Designing a Distributed Access Control Processor for Network Services on the Web. In *ACM Workshop on XML Security*, Fairfax, VA, USA, 2002.
6. M.I. Yague and J.M. Troya. A Semantic Approach for Access Control in Web Services. In *Euroweb 2002 Conference. The Web and the GRID: from e-science to e-business*, pages 483–494, Oxford, UK, 2002.
7. S. Agarwal, B. Sprick, and S. Wortmann. Credential Based Access Control for Semantic Web Services. *American Association for Artificial Intelligence*, 2004.
8. T. Ziebermayr and S. Probst. Web Service Authorization Framework. In *International Conference on Web Services (ICWS)*, San Diego, CA, USA, 2004.
9. S. Godik and T. Moses. eXtensible Access Control Markup Language v1.1 (XACML), 07 August, 2003.
10. T. Andrews, F. Curbera, H. Dholakia, Y. Goland, et al. Business Process Execution Language for Web Services v1.1 (BPEL4WS), http://www-128.ibm.com/developerworks/library/ws-bpel/, 2003.
11. R. Kraft. A Model for Network Services on the Web. In *The 3rd International Conference on Internet Computing (IC 2002)*, volume 3, pages 536–541, 2002.
12. S. Indrakanti. On the Design of an Authorization Architecture for Web Services. Technical report, Macquarie University, Sydney, Australia, January 2005.
13. G. Della-Libera, P. Hallam-Baker, M. Hondo, T. Janczuk, et al. Web Services Security Policy Language (WS-SecurityPolicy), http://www-106.ibm.com/developerworks/library/ws-secpol/. 2002.
14. S. Bajaj, D. Box, D. Chappell, F. Curbera, et al. Web Services Policy Attachment (WS-PolicyAttachment), http://www-106.ibm.com/developerworks/library/specification/ws-polatt/, September 2004.
15. Microsoft Corporation. .NET Framework, http://msdn.microsoft.com/netframework/. 2005.

Secure Model Management Operations for the Web

Guanglei Song, Kang Zhang, Bhavani Thuraisingham, and Jun Kong

University of Texas at Dallas, Richardson, Texas 75083-0688 USA
{gxs017800, kzhang, bhavani.thuraisingham, jxk019200}@utdallas.edu

Abstract. The interoperability among different data formats over the Internet has drawn increasing interest recently due to more and more heterogeneous data models are used in different Web services. In order to ease the manipulation of data models for heterogeneous data, generic model management has been intensively researched and also implemented in a prototype since its first introduction. Access control specifications attached to each individual data model require significant amount of efforts to manually specify. Based on a general security model for access control specifications on heterogeneous data models and its visual representation, we present secure model management operators for managing access control specifications.The secure model management operators disccussed in the paper include a secure match operator and a secure merge operator. We introduce a novel graphical schema matching algorithm and extend the algorithm to make a secure match operator. The paper also discusses secure merge principles for the integration of data models.

1 Introduction

The huge success of the Web as a platform for information dissemination has brought an increasing awareness of the fact that document exchange over the Internet should meet security requirements such as fine-grained authenticity and access control [24]. XML [4,5] and database [9] access control models have been a hot research topic. Recently, the continuing demand for information sharing has shifted interests from stand-alone XML repositories and databases to interconnected and large-scale cooperative systems [6].

Manually manipulating heterogeneous data models has been a time-consuming and error-prone process. Therefore a new approach to metadata management, i.e. Model Management, has been proposed [2]. Model management offers a high-level programming interface and avoids object-at-a-time primitives by manipulating models with generic operators. Our previous work provides a visual model management architecture, which eases the use of the generic operators [23]. The visual architecture, however, does not provide secure interfaces for managing access control specifications, which are associated with data models. These specifications can only be managed manually, and the procedure for managing secure models, therefore, cannot be fully realized by current model

S. Jajodia and D. Wijesekera (Eds.): Data and Applications Security 2005, LNCS 3654, pp. 237–251, 2005.
© IFIP International Federation for Information Processing 2005

management systems. This paper focuses on the security properties of model management, and explores various issues and solutions to achieve secure model management of data models.

One challenge of secure model management comes from the heterogeneity of data formats. Data encoded in different formats needs to be exchanged in cooperative systems, thus achieving interoperability. Even though every individual data model may have highly secure access control specifications and enforcement mechanism, the federation of data models is not necessarily secure. Security of a union of systems is determined by the weakest link. When information of different models is interchanging, it opens a window for attack. The security extensions presented in the paper ease the manipulation of models with access control specifications and provide a guidance for generating safe mappings and unions of models.

The remainder of the paper is organized as follows. Section 2 introduces a uniform access control model and an illustrative example. Section 3 proposes a graphical schema matching algorithm and the security extension to the algorithm. Section 4 presents security extensions to other model management operators. Section 5 discusses the future research directions. Section 6 compares related works and Section 7 concludes the paper.

2   A Uniform Access Control Model

Our uniform access control model consists of a set of rules, each being a tuple of five elements: *subject, object, action, authorization,* and *propagation* [24]. Access control regulates access to the data, such as XML documents, and databases called *objects*. Those who try to access these objects are called *subjects*. A subject is represented by a unique user-defined identifier called UPath [24], e.g. tables and columns of a relational schema, elements and attributes of an XML schema. Actions include *read, write, update,* and *delete*. An authorization specifies the negative or positive response to a request, i.e. *allow* or *deny*. The propagation can be either *local* or *recursive*, referring to the influence of the object locally or recursively to its child objects.

We visualize the access control rules by node-edge diagrams [24]. As shown in Figure 1, a rule is represented as a link and a subject is represented by a labeled rectangle connecting to objects (as labeled ellipses). A gray eclipse represents recursive access, and a white eclipse indicates local access. The label of each link, R or W, represents the activity. The circle and the cross on a link represent *allow* and *deny* of access respectively.

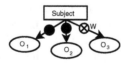

Fig. 1. Visual representation of access control

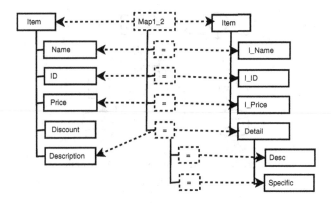

Fig. 2. Online shopping schemas for two companies

Table 1. Access Rules for Model A

	Subject	Object	Action	Authorization	Propagation
1	Customer	/Item/	Read	Allow	R
2	Vendor	/Item/	Read	Allow	R
3	Administrator	/Item/	Read	Allow	R
4	Administrator	/Item/Description	Write	Allow	L
5	Administrator	/Item/Discount	Write	Allow	L
6	Administrator	/Item/Price	Write	Allow	L

Table 2. Access Rules for Model B

	Subject	Object	Action	Authorization	Propagation
1	Cust	/Item/	Read	Allow	R
2	Provider	/Item/	Read	Allow	R
3	Admin	/Item/	Read	Allow	R
4	Admin	/Item/Detail	Write	Allow	R
5	Admin	/Item/Price	Write	Allow	L

Consider the following example. Two companies A_c and B_c want to offer a joint online solution for customers and vendors. Figure 2 shows the two schemas, A and B, for companies A_c and B_c.

Companies A_c and B_c have local access control rules as shown in Tables 1 and 2 respectively.

A model management system eases the process by providing generic operators like Match and Merge. Figure 3 shows the scenario of unifying the two models by the two operators [24]. ACR_A and ACR_B are access control rules for models M_A and M_B respectively. M_u is the unified model of M_A and M_B. ACR_u is a set of access control rules for model M_u. The system matches and merges M_A and M_B to generate M_u, but cannot automatically generate ACR_u. Users

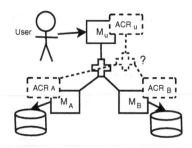

Fig. 3. Unified online shopping system

have to construct ACR_u manually from scratch. It is highly risky to manually manipulate access control rules in a large scale such as an online store site. To ease the process, a security extension for model management operators (like Match) is desirable for automatically managing access control rules.

3   Secure Schema Matching

This section introduces a new matching algorithm for graphical generation of schema mappings, and adapts the algorithm by adding a security extension.

3.1   A Graphical Schema Matching Algorithm

Schema matching is to find semantic correspondences among elements of two schemas. Most of the proposed approaches [20] concentrated on the similarity of individual elements or at most neighborhood information, rather than on the global semantics of the schemas. We propose a novel approach to the schema matching problem utilizing global semantics. A schema is represented by an acyclic directed graph, where nodes represent elements or attributes and links represent the containment relationships.

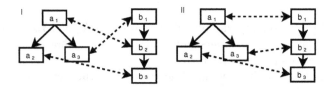

Fig. 4. I.A mapping with semantic contradiction; II. A harmonic mapping

Schemas are represented by acyclic graphs, which do not allow containment cycles that cause a *semantic contradiction*. If a semantic mapping between two schemas has no semantic contradiction, we call the mapping *harmonic*. Figure

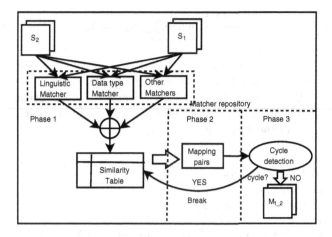

Fig. 5. Mapping generation process in GGS

4 shows an example of mapping with semantic contradiction and the other being harmonic. Figure 4.I includes mapping pairs (a_1, b_2) and (a_3, b_1), while a_1 contains a_3 and b_1 contains b_2. From the graphical representation of mapping, the relationships between (a_1, b_2) and (a_3, b_1) produce a non-harmonic crossing, which results in a semantic contradiction when applying the mapping. For example, in case of merging elements of the schemas based on the mapping in Figure 4.I, how can an algorithm decide whether the mapping (a_1, b_2) should contain the mapping (a_3, b_1) or the other way? Also the mapping pairs are self-contradictory due to $a_1 \rightarrow a_3 \leftrightarrow b_1 \rightarrow b_2 \rightarrow a_1$, i.e. a containment cycle, which is contradictory to the acyclic representation of schemas.

A harmonic mapping, such as the one in Figure 4.II, is desirable. We present a schema matching algorithm for producing harmonic mappings. Our schema matching algorithm proceeds in 3 phases as shown in Figure 5:

1. Use various types of matchers to compare element names and calculate similarity of data types and produce a similarity table for each pair of elements;
2. Produce an initial set of mapping pairs by selecting possible mappings from the initial similarity table;
3. Search and break cycles that exist, and go to Phase 1 for the next iteration until no cycle exists or when the number of iterations reaches a predefined upper bound (beyond which the computational cost is no longer worthwhile for users).

A single matcher generates a similarity table consisting of similarity values for any two input elements. A similarity value is a number between 0 (strong dissimilarity) and 1 (strong similarity). Our matching algorithm combines these similarity tables by computing weighted averages. Assume n single similarity tables, $table_1$ to $table_n$, each having a similarity value Sim_i (a, b), i =1..n, for any pair of elements (a, b). For each pair of elements (a, b) from schemas A and B, the overall similarity Sim (a, b) can be calculated by:

$$Sim(a,b) = \frac{\sum\limits_{i=1}^{n}(Sim_i(a,b) \times w_i)}{n}, \text{ where} \sum\limits_{i=1}^{n}(w_i) = 1, \text{ and } Sim_i \text{ is a similarity}$$

table produced by matcher i.

Phase 2 generates mapping pairs based on the combined similarity table by choosing the best match for each element in the table. Then in Phase 3, our matching algorithm, as shown in Algorithm 3.1, detects cycles by checking the decedents and ancestors of each element of a mapping pair to see if they contribute a pair in the mapping. If so, a cycle exits.

Algorithm 3.1 cycle detection

Require: Table table
  for each pair $p(a_i, b_j)$ in pairs; **do**
    Topsort(pairs);
    if $((\text{decedents}(a_i) \text{ X ancestors}(b_j)) \text{ U (ancestors } (a_i) \text{ X decedents } (b_j))) \cap$ pairs
    $\neq$ empty) **then**
      returntrue;
    end if
  end for

If a cycle exists in the mapping pairs, the algorithm needs to choose a mapping pair to adjust to remove the cycle. Conceptually, the pair that generates the most crossings should be removed, i.e. the key contradiction pair. For the example in Figure 4, the initial mapping pairs are produced from the similarity table as $\{(a_1, b_2), (a_2, b_3), (a_3, b_1)\}$. The algorithm detects that mapping pair (a_1, b_3) produces most contradictions with other mappings pairs, and therefore the pair as the key mapping pair needs to be adjusted. Then our algorithm breaks the cycle by finding the second most suitable mapping for the element in the table. Algorithm 3.2 describes the procedure: it finds the key contradiction by calculating the maximal intersection set between mapping pairs and decedents and ancestors of a mapping pair, and then chooses the second best mapping for the element.

Algorithm 3.2 breaking cycles

Require: Table table
  for each pair $p(a_i, b_j)$ in pairs; **do**
    Topsort(pairs);
    if $(|((\text{decedents}(a_i) \text{ X ancestors}(b_j)) \text{ U (ancestors } (a_i) \text{ X decedents } (b_j))) \cap$ pairs
    $|$ is max) **then**
      Choose the second biggest similarity for a_i
    end if
  end for

After breaking cycles, the algorithm generates mapping pairs based on the new similarity table and iteratively finds and breaks new crossings until no more

---

Algorithm 3.3 the matching algorithm

Require: Data models m1 and m2
  Table table = construct (m1, m2);
  Itno = 0;
  while into< bound **do**
    if (cycle (table) **then**
      Break(table);
    end if
    Into ++;
  end while
  Produce the mapping pairs from table;

---

crossing can be found or a threshold is reached. The pseudo code is described in Algorithm 3.3.

3.2 Schema Matching with Security Property

The Match operator takes models A and B as input, and produces mapping Map_{1_2}, called *object mapping*, but not mapping for access control rules. *Subject matching* matches the subjects of two access control rules. For example, "Cust" in Table 1 is mapped to "Customer" in Table 2. Match with a security extension takes two input models, each having a set of access control rules. The extended Match operator is defined as follows:

Definition 1: (Map_o, Map_s) = *Match* $((M_1, ACR_1), (M_2, ACR_2))$, where M_1 and M_2 are two data models, ACR_1 and ACR_2 are access control rules of models M_1 and M_2 respectively.

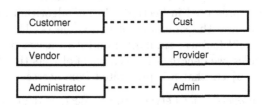

Fig. 6. The Maps example

The result (Map_o, Map_s) contains two mappings, Map_o between objects and Map_s between subjects. Figure 6 shows an example of subject mapping.

Object matching algorithms can be used for subject matching without considering security properties of access control rules, and thus may produce poor and even risky mappings. A security extension of match should avoid risky mappings and produce safe mappings defined as follows.

Assume models M_1 and M_2 have access control rules ACR_1 and ACR_2 respectively. S_1 and S_2 are subjects of ACR1 and ACR_2. Map_{1_2} is the object mapping between M_1 and M_2. Map_s is a subject mapping between S_1 and S_2.

Definition 2: Map_s is *safe* if and only if $(\forall~ (s_1, s_2)~ \in Map_s~ \forall~ (o_1, o_2)~ \in Map_{1\_2}$ a $\in A$ (allow (s_1, o_1, a) *if f* allow $(s_2, o_2, a)))$, where s_1 and s_2 are subjects of S_1 and S_2, o_1 and o_2 are objects of M_1 and M_2, a is an action in set A (all actions), allow (s_1, o_1, a) means that s_1 is allowed to perform action a on o_1.

To produce safe subject mappings, three options can be considered:

1. Security filter: The most straightforward approach is to transplant an object matching algorithm to match subjects with a security filter attached to the back end. Once the filter finds a violation, it removes the mapping pair. The approach is safe, but may impair effectiveness of the matching algorithm. For example, as described in Section 2, if another element called Supervisor in model B has full access to model B like Administrator of model A, and security filter cannot match Supervisor with Administrator, since Administrator is chosen to match Admin in the first place.

2. Security dimension: The approach provides security as another dimension of similarity. Careful scrutiny of this approach shows that violating mappings may be produced due to the influence of the other dimensions of similarity (e.g. data type or naming similarity).

3. Security isomorphism: The approach calculates the similarity of subjects based on not only subject names but also semantics of access control rules. It compares the access control rules of every pair of subjects from the graphical representation and generates subject mapping based on the isomorphism of ACRs.

Among the above three options, the security isomorphism algorithm generates more accurate mappings than security filter does, and can also be proved to be safe. Therefore we choose the third approach as the security extension to our matching algorithm presented in Section 3.1. The algorithm matches subjects' access rules to calculate the similarity of two subjects. The similarity of two subjects consists of SS (subject similarity) and AS (access similarity). If s is a subject of access rules, we denote G (s) as a set of objects that S has access and D (s) as the set of objects that S is prohibited from access.

Definition 3: The *overlap set* between two subjects is defined as: O $(s_1, s_2) = \{(o_1, o_2)|~ o_1 \in G~ (s_1)$ and $o_2~ \in G~ (s_2)$, and s_1 and s_2 are two subjects, and (o_1, o_2) is a mapping$\}$.

Definition 4: *The access similarity* between two subject nodes is defined as: $AS(s_1, s_2) = |O~ (s_1, s_2)|/~ N$, where $N = |G(s_1)| + |G(s_2)| - |O~ (s_1, s_2)|$, and no mapping (o, p) exists such that $o \in G(s_1)$ and $p \in D(s_2)$ or $o \in G(s_2)$ and $p \in D(s_1)$. Otherwise, $AS(s_1, s_2) = -1$.

As shown in Figure 7, the overlap set O (Vendor, Provider) = $\{(1, a)\}$. We use Algorithm 3.4 to compute the similarity of two subjects, and then match subjects by choosing the best match in the similarity table.

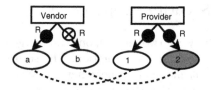

Fig. 7. Matching for access control rules

Algorithm 3.4 Subject matching

Require: Data models o1, o2, subjects s1, s2

Use graphical global schema matching algorithm to produce subject similarity table $SS(s_1, s_2)$ and mapping M;

$AS(s_1, s_2) = 0$;

for each pair of subjects **do**

  for every rule in ACR **do**

    if allow(s_1, o_1, a) and allow(s_2, o_2, a) and (o_1, o_2) $\in$ M **then**

      $O(s_1, s_2)$ $\Downarrow (o_1, o_2)$;

    end if

    if violation exists **then**

      $AS(s_1, s_2)$=-1; break;

    end if

    if $(AS(s_1, s_2)$!= -1 **then**

      $AS(s_1, s_2) = | O(s_1, s_2)|/ N$;

    end if

    if $AS(s_1, s_2)$ >=0 **then**

      $SIM(s_1, s_2) = w* AS(s_1, s_2) + (1-w) * SS(s_1, s_2)$;

    else

      $SIM(s_1, s_2) = -1$;

    end if

  end for

end for

for each subject s_1 in S_1 **do**

  if Max ($SIM(s_1, s_2)$) and $SIM(s_1, s_2)$ >0 **then**

    $ap_s \Downarrow (s_1, s_2)$;

  end if

end for

Theorem 1: Algorithm 3.4 generates safe mappings.

Proof: The algorithm computes the similarity between any pair of subjects in two input models based on the object mapping. Any possible violation will be identified by marking the semantic similarity as -1. The AS value will finally prevent mapping between any two violating subjects. Hence the algorithm generates the mapping between those pairs of subjects that have no possible violation of access control rules. According to Definition 2, the generated mapping is safe.

4   Merge with Security Property

Having the mapping between two models, one can merge the two models to generate a federation and exchange information. The security extension of Merge eases the process by automatically generating access control rules for the output data model. We define the Merge operator with security extension as the following:

Definition 5: $(M_3, ACR_3, Map_{1\_3}, Map_{2\_3}) = Merge$ $(M_1, M_2, Map_{1\_2}, ACR_1,$ $ACR_2, Map_a)$, where M_1 and M_2 are input data models, and Map_{1_2} represents the mapping between M_1 and M_2. Map_a represents the mapping between two access control rules ACR_1 and ACR_2. A Merge operator generates M_3, Map_{1_3},

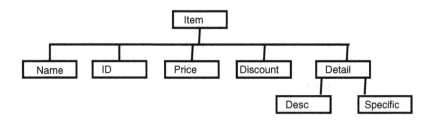

Fig. 8. Result merged schema

and Map_{2_3}. The result model M_3 for the previous example is shown in Figure 8. Mapped elements in M_1 and M_2 are collapsed into one element in the new model, such as Name and C_Name into Name. Other than object merge, the security extension of the Merge operator merges access control rules into a new set of access control rules, i.e. ACR_3. The process of merging two access control rules is called *access merge*.

Access merge is based on subject mappings. As shown in Figure 6, Map_a denotes the relationship between all possible subjects of two input access control rules. The two mapped subjects should be collapsed into one subject, such as Customer and Cust into Customer, and share the same access authorization. The access merge is represented by graph transformation as in visual model management [23], and should ensure a safe output by preventing violating accesses while keeping maximum access for subjects.

Suppose the Merge operator takes input models M_1 and M_2. If the mapped subjects have the same access to the same mapped objects in both models, then the related two rules can be merged into one output rule, e.g. Rule 1 of ACR_1 (in Table 1) and Rule 1 of ACR_2 (in Table 2).

Apart from the above case, three other cases need to be handled carefully as follows:

1. Unmapped subjects, subject S_1 for M_1 is not mapped and is a new subject to M_2. Since it is only effective on the elements in M_1, we simply add the related access control rules to the result.

2. Unmapped objects, object O_1 for M_1 is not mapped and is a new object to M_2. We simply add the two rules to the result.

3. Conflict, conflict occurs when a prohibited access is allowed. The following three access conflicts are discussed and corresponding solutions are presented.

a. Allow vs. Deny

Suppose Rule 1 allows subject S_1 the access to object O_1 in model M_1 and Rule 2 denies the access of S_2 to O_2, where S_1 mapped to S_2, O_1 mapped to O_2. Conflict arises when two subjects and their respective objects are merged, i.e. S_1 and S_2 into one subject (called S_3) and O_1 and O_2 into one object (O_3). Whether to allow the access of S_3 to O_3 would be a delicate issue. Possible solutions include:

(1) Deny the subject's access in the resulting rule;

(2) Allow the subject's access in the resulting rule;

(3) Separately create two rules for each subject, and remove the mapping between the two subjects;

(4) Request a user intervention.

Allowing all the access will break the access control rule for M_2. Solution (3) separates mapped objects thus breaks the mapping. Solution (4) requires users' intervention and will produce a result depending on the policy. Users' intervention requires a user interface with the security extension for model management to be user friendly, i.e. a visual environment. Our solution is a hybrid of solutions (1) and (4), i.e. denies the subject's access and requests users' intervention, thus provides safe suggestions that are customizable.

b. Local vs. Recursive

The mapped subjects may have different propagations, e.g. Rule 1 allows access of S_1 to O_1 locally while Rule 2 allows access of S_2 to O_2 recursively. Possible solutions to the conflict include:

(1) Restrict the access to be local in the resulting rule;

(2) Allow the access to be recursive.

Solution (2) gives more access to users than solution (1) does, but can produce possible violation. It would be safe to provide only local access with solution (1).

c. Read vs. Write

A conflict arises if a rule of mapped subjects has different actions to mapped objects, e.g. Rule 1 allows read access of S_1 to O_1 while Rule 2 allows write access of S_2 to O_2. Possible solutions include:

(1) Give only read access in the resulting rule;

(2) Allow write access.

For the similar reason as above, we choose solution (1) as the result.

Overall, our solution assures the maximum safe access for users, and prevents security violation caused by Merge while still being flexible and adjustable by security officers according to the application domains. Table 3 shows the resulting access rules for merged models.

Table 3. Access Control Rules for Merged Model

	Subject	Object	Action	Authorization	Propagation
1	Customer	/Item/	Read	Allow	R
2	Vendor	/Item/	Read	Allow	R
3	Administrator	/Item/	Read	Allow	R
4	Administrator	/Item/Detail	Write	Allow	R
5	Administrator	/Item/Price	Write	Allow	L

5 Discussion and Directions for Future Research

We have discussed access control for model management, and have essentially provided the foundation for work on secure model management.

5.1 Formalization and Other Operators

The access control models discussed here are somewhat informal. The next step is to expand on the work proposed here and develop a formal model and prove that security properties are maintained during the mappings. The access control rules essentially control access that a user can have to the various documents. However a user can receive legitimate responses and subsequently make sensitive associations. Such a problem has come to be known as the inference problem. Extensive work has been carried out on applying security constraint processing for the inference problem [26]. We need to apply intelligent inference to the access rules to achieve more personalized model management.

Other operators also need to extend with security properties, such as Model-Gen. After the ModelGen operation, some objects of the original model may be removed, and the security extension of the ModelGen operator needs to adjust the access control rules for the generated model. We will extend other visual model management operators with security properties as our future work.

5.2 Future Work

Future work will proceed in three directions. One is to apply the secure model management for RDF (Resource Description Framework) document. RDF is a critical part of the semantic web. The RDF data model is a syntax-neutral way of rep-resenting RDF expressions. The basic data model consists of three object types, resources, properties, and statements. A RDF model can be rep-resented by a directed graph. Therefore, any node in the RDF model can have multiple children and multiple parents. RDF is a foundation for processing meta-data; it provides interoperability between applications that exchange machine-understandable information on the Web. RDF emphasizes facilities which enable the automated processing of Web resources. Since RDF is designed to describe the re-sources and the relationship among them without assumption, the definition mechanism should be domain neutral, and can be applied to any domain.

RDF essentially utilizes XML syntax. Therefore, we need to extend the model driven operators for RDF syntax as well as semantics.

The second direction is to extend the concepts for secure information sharing in heterogeneous and federated environments. Organizations are forming coalitions to share data but at the same time maintain security and privacy. We need to integrate the heterogeneous data sources and at the same time enforce the various security policies. The model management approach needs to be examined for secure heterogeneous and federated data integration.

The third direction is to examine other access control policies and models. Notable among them are role based access control (RBAC) and Usage control (UCON) models [21] and [18]. RBAC is about users being allowed aces to object depending on other roles. Usage control model proposed recently subsumes several others models proposed in the literature. UCON consists of six components: subjects and their attributes, objects and their attributes, rights, authorizations, obligations and conditions. Subject must possess rights to access objects. In addition certain obligations have to be met and conditions have to be satisfied. Applying model management for RBAC and UCON needs to be examined.

6   Related Work

Since its first introduction in a vision paper [2], many implementations model management have been presented, such as Cupid [14,15] and SFA [16] as match operator implementations, Merge operator presented by Pottinger *et al* [19]. While most of the approaches only concentrate on individual operators of the model management, Rondo [17] is the first prototype of the generic model management system. None of these proposals addresses security extensions for any model management operators.

Many proposals on access control mechanisms have been presented in both database literature [9,11,10,12,22] and XML area [3,5,7]. There are however few proposals on access controls across heterogeneous data models, and the most related works are those on secure XML federations [27] and XML security models using relational databases [13]. Tan also proposed an idea of using RDBMS to handle access controls for XML documents, in a rather limited setting [25]. Farkas *et al.* developed algorithms to automate the access control rules transformation process, while preserving the Access Control requirements of the original systems [8]. They studied and developed methods for automatically translating Access Control Lists and Bell-LaPadula models to ASL. They concentrated only on the access control rules while our system can manipulate the related schemas at the same time.

In addition, there has been lot of work on access control on temporal models, multimedia models, geospatial information systems and multimedia systems [1]. While these works concentrate on domain-specific access controls, our approach provides security extensions to generic systems and can be applied to virtually any data models.

7 Conclusion

This paper has discussed uniform access control rules for heterogeneous data models and a visual representation of the access control model. We presented approaches for automatic generation of subject matching. We proved that the security isomorphism algorithm generates safe mappings. The paper also discussed the security issues involved in the Merge operator and other operators, and addressed the principles of a secure Merge operator. The security extensions to our previous work on visual model management operators provides automatic generation mechanism for managing access control specifications to allow heterogeneous Web data models to exchange information over public networks.

Model management is becoming an important technology for Web information management. It is critical that security be incorporated into the process at the beginning and not as an afterthought. The major contribution of this paper is attempting to incorporate security into the model management process.

References

1. V. Atluri and S. Chun, An Authiruization, Model for Geospatial Data, *IEEE Transactions on Depoendable and Secure Computing*, Volume 1, #4, 2005.
2. P.A.Bernstein, A. Halevy, and R.A. Pottinger, A Vision for Management of Complex Models, *SIGMOD Record*, 29(4), 55-63, 2000.
3. E. Bertino and E. Ferrari. Secure and Selective Dissemination of XML Documents, *IEEE Trans. Information and System Security (TISSEC)*, 5(3): 290 – 331, Aug. 2002.
4. Bray, T., Paoli, J., Sperberg-Mcqueen, C., and Maler, E. Extensible Markup Language (XML) 1.0 (2nd Edition), *World Wide Web Consortium (W3C)*, http://www.w3.org/TR/REC-xml, 2000.
5. E. Damiani, S. De Capitani di Vimercati, S. Paraboschi, P. Samarati, Securing XML Documents. *Proc. EDBT 2000 Konstanz, Germany, Lecture Notes in Computer Science*, Vol. 1777, Springer, New York, March, 2000, 121–135.
6. E. Damiani, S. De Capitani di Vimercati, S. Paraboschi, P. Samarati, Fine Grained Access Control for SOAP E-Services, *Proc. 10th Int. World Wide Web Conference*, Hong Kong, China, May, 2001.
7. E. Damiani, S. De Capitani di Vimercati, S. Paraboschi, P. Samarati, A Fine-Grained Access Control System for XML Documents, *ACM Trans. Information and System Security (TISSEC)*, 5(2)169-202, May 2002.
8. C. Farkas, A. Stoica, P. Talekar, APTA: an Automated Policy Translation Architecture, *Int. Conf. Computer, Communication and Control Technologies*, 2003.
9. P. P. Griffiths and B. W. Wade, An Authorization Mechanism for a Relational Database System, *ACM Trans. Database System (TODS)*, 1(3): 242 – 255, Sep. 1976.
10. S. Jajodia and R. Sanhu, "Toward a Multilevel Secure Relational Data Model", *ACM SIGMOD*, May 1990.
11. S. Jajodia, P. Samarati, V. S. Subrahmanian, and E. Bertino, A Unified Framework for Enforcing Multiple Access Control Policies, *ACM SIGMOD*, 474 – 485, May 1997.

12. S. Jajodia, P. Samarati, M. L. Sapino, and V. S. Subrahmanian, Flexible Support for Multiple Access Control Policies, *ACM Trans. Database Systems (TODS)*, 26 (2): 214 – 260, June, 2001.

13. B. Luo, D. Lee, W. Lee, P. Liu, A Flexible Framework for Architecting XML Access Control Enforcement Mechanisms, Proc. *VLDB Workshop on Secure Data Management in a Connected World (SDM)*, Toronto, Canada, August 2004.

14. J. Madhavan, P. A. Bernstein, and E. Rahm, Generic Schema Matching Using Cupid, *Proc. 27th VLDB Conf.*, Roma, Italy, Sep, 2001, 49-58.

15. J. Madhavan and A. Y. Halevy, Composing Mappings Among Data Sources, *Proc. 29th VLDB Conf.*, Berlin, German, Sep 2003, 572-583.

16. S. Melnik, H. Garcia-Molina and E. Rahm: Similarity Flooding: A Versatile Graph Matching Algorithm and its Application to Schema Matching, *Proc. 18th ICDE*, San Jose CA, Feb 2002.

17. S. Melnik, E. Rahm, and P. A. Bernstein, Rondo: A Programming Platform for Generic Model Management, *Proc. SIGMOD 2003 Conf.*, San Dieago, CA, June 2003, 193-204.

18. J. Park and R. Sandhu, The UCONABC Usage Control Model, *ACM Transactions on Information and System Security*, Volume 7, Number 1, February 2004.

19. R. A. Pottinger and P. A. Bernstein, Merging Models Based on Given Correspondences, *Proc. 29th VLDB Conf.*, Berlin, Germany, 2003, 826-873.

20. Rahm, Erhard and P. A. Bernstein. A Survey of Approaches to Automatic Schema Matching, *VLDB Journal*, 10(4): 334-350, 2001.

21. R. Sandhu, E. Coyne, H. Feinstein and C. Youman, Role-Based Access Control Models, *IEEE Computer*, Volume 29, Number 2, February 1996.

22. R. Sandhu, F. Chen, The Multilevel Relational (MLR) Data Model, *IEEE Trans. Information and System Security (TISSEC)*, 1 (1), 1998.

23. G.L. Song, K. Zhang, and J. Kong, Model Management Through Graph Transformations, *Proc. 2004 IEEE Symp. Visual Languages and Human-Centric Computing*, IEEE CS Press, Rome, Italy, September 2004, 75-82.

24. G.L. Song, K. Zhang, B. Thuraisingham, J. Cao, Towards Access Control of Visual Web Model Management, *Proc. 2005 IEEE International Conf. on e-Technology, e-Commerce and e-Service (EEE-05)*, IEEE CS Press, Hong Kong, March 2005.

25. K.-L. Tan, M. L. Lee, and Y. Wang. Access Control of XML Documents in Relational Database Systems, *Proc. Int. Conf. on Internet Computing (IC)*, Las Vegas, NV, Jun. 2001.

26. B. Thuraisingham. Security Constraint Processing in Multilevel Secure Distributed Systems, *IEEE Transaction on Knowledge and Data Engineering*, Vol. 7, #2, April 1995.

27. L. Wang, D. Wijesekera and S. Jajodia., Towards Secure XML Federations, *Proc. 16th IFIP WG11.3 Working Conference on Database and Application Security*, July 28-31, 2002.

A Credential-Based Approach for Facilitating Automatic Resource Sharing Among Ad-Hoc Dynamic Coalitions*

Janice Warner[1], Vijayalakshmi Atluri[1], and Ravi Mukkamala[2]

[1] Rutgers University, Newark NJ 07012, USA
{janice, atluri}@cimic.rutgers.edu
[2] Old Dominion University, Norfolk, VA 23529, USA
mukka@cs.odu.edu

Abstract. Today, there is an increasing need for dynamic, efficient and secure sharing of resources among organizations. In a dynamic coalition environment, participants (including users and systems) of an organization may need to gain access quickly to resources of other organizations in an unplanned manner to accomplish the task at hand. Typically, when entities agree to share their information resources, the access control policies are agreed upon at the coalition level. These coalition level agreements are not at the level of fine-grained policies, in the sense that they do not specify which specific users can access which data object. In this paper, we propose a *dynamic coalition-based access control* (DCBAC) model that allows automatic access to resources of one coalition entity by users from another coalition entity. To make the model applicable to true ad-hoc dynamic coalitions, we employ a *coalition service registry*, where coalition entities publicize their coalition level access policies. Any coalition entity wishing to access a specific resource of another coalition entity can obtain a *ticket* by submitting its entity credentials which are subsequently evaluated by the coalition service registry. DCBAC employs a policy mapper layer that computes the exact credentials required by remote users that are comparable to those required by local users. We demonstrate how the coalition and resource level access policies can be specified in XML-based languages and evaluated.

1 Introduction

Today, there is an increasing need for dynamic, efficient and secure sharing of resources among organizations. This is driven by a number of applications including emergency and disaster management, peace keeping, humanitarian operations, or simply virtual enterprises. Typically, resource sharing is done by establishing alliances and collaborations, also known as *coalitions*. Due to the nature of the applications, the coalitions are often *dynamic* where entities may join or leave the coalition in an ad-hoc manner.

In a dynamic coalition environment, participants (e.g. users, systems) of an organization may need to gain access to resources (both data and services) of other organizations to accomplish the task at hand. As an example, in a natural disaster scenario, such as the earth quake in Turkey on May 1, 2003 and the Tsunami in Asia on December 26, 2004, government agencies (e.g., FEMA, local police and fire departments),

---

* The work of Warner and Atluri is supported in part by the NSF under grant IIS-0306838.

S. Jajodia and D. Wijesekera (Eds.): Data and Applications Security 2005, LNCS 3654, pp. 252–266, 2005.

non-government organizations (e.g., Red Cross) and private organizations (e.g., Doctors without Borders, suppliers of emergency provisions) needed to share information about victims, supplies and logistics[10]. Similar examples include homeland security applications where sharing of information across different organizations is needed for identifying criminal and terrorist behavior, illegal shipments, and the like. In a commercial setting, organizations may share resources and information in order to provide comprehensive services drawing from unique skills of diverse participating entities.

Typically, when coalition entities agree to share their information resources, the access control policies are agreed upon at the coalition level. For example, an agreement between government entities A and B might be that they will share resources to aid in a smuggling investigation. These coalition level agreements are not at the level of fine-grained policies, in the sense that they do not specify which subjects are allowed to access which specific resources.

The security policy needed for allowing access would be "user Alice of entity A can access the *immigration* file of entity B." Enforcing the coalition-level security policies requires transforming the high-level policies to implementation level.

Current approaches to facilitate resource sharing resort to one of the following methods: (i) Users from one coalition entity are explicitly given permission to access resources from another coalition entity. This approach is administratively time consuming and requires explicit revocation after the coalition is disbanded or when a user is no longer affiliated with the coalition entity. (ii) A single access id is provided to all of the users of the coalition entity. While this simplifies administrative effort, it makes fine-grained access control impossible. (iii) The resources are copied to the coalition entity that requires access to them. Updates are difficult and may result in uncontrolled sharing. In addition, all the above approaches are not suitable for dynamic and ad-hoc coalitions, and are only feasible among entities that have pre-established partnerships.

Access control research in the area of dynamic coalitions is relatively new. Philips et al. [10] have described the dynamic coalition problem by providing several motivating scenarios in a defense and disaster recovery settings. They have developed a prototype that controls access to APIs and software artifacts [9]. Cohen et al. [3] have proposed a model that captures the entities involved in coalition resource sharing and identifies the interrelationships among them. In [2,5], the researchers have addressed the issue of automating the negotiation of policy between coalition members in a dynamic coalition. Finally, in [13], Yu et.al propose automated mechanisms for trust building between entities using digital credentials Our research complements these works by addressing the issue of automatic translation of coalition level policies to the implementation level policies, and vice versa.

Our approach is a coalition-based access control (CBAC) model that allows automatic access to resources of one coalition entity by users from another coalition entity[1] by employing three layers (coalition, role and user-object). A user's request for a specific remote object is first translated into a role level request, and then into a coalition level request before being sent to the remote coalition entity. At the remote coalition entity, the coalition level request is trickled down through the three layers and translated into an user-object access request. The information appended at each layer at the requesting coalition entity is understood and dealt with by the corresponding layer at the other coalition entity, much like the TCP/IP network protocol.

In this paper, we propose *dynamic coalition-based access control* (DCBAC) model that is specified based on the credentials possessed by coalitions as well as subjects. DCBAC extends CBAC in several directions in order to eliminate its inherent limitations. First, CBAC assumes that every pair of coalition entities have to agree on the coalition policies in advance in order to allow access to data from one entity to subjects[1] of the other entity. As a result, this model cannot entertain a "truly dynamic coalition", where entities of the coalition join or leave in an ad-hoc manner. To cater to true ad-hoc dynamic coalitions, we employ a *coalition service registry* (CSR) where coalition entities publicize their coalition level access policies. Any coalition entity wishing to access a specific resource of another coalition entity can obtain a *ticket* by submitting its entity credentials which are subsequently evaluated by the CSR. Second, CBAC computes the credentials required by a user wishing to access a remote object as a union of all the credentials possessed by all users playing a role, which has privileges to access that object. This is a very conservative approach, and requires a large number of unneeded credentials from a requesting user. Our DCBAC employs a *mapper layer* that accurately computes the credentials required by a user to access a resource. Third, we demonstrate how the access policies, at the coalition level and resource level, can be specified in XML and be evaluated.

Our DCBAC system comprises of four layers – (i) *coalition level*, which interacts with other coalition entities and is responsible for ensuring the authenticity of the coalition entity requesting access to its resources, (ii) *credential filter*, which is responsible for examining incoming credentials and attaching appropriate credentials to outgoing requests, (iii) *credential ⟺ local access control mapper*, which converts local access control rules to policies concerning credentials for outgoing requests and vice versa for incoming requests, and (iv) *local access control* layer, responsible for uniformly serving the both local and external access requests.

While facilitating automatic access, we ensure that the following requirements are met: (i) The existing access control mechanisms within each coalition entity remain intact. Our approach does not require any changes to the existing local access control mechanisms. (ii) Access is granted to subjects only if they belong to an organization recognized by the coalition, adhering to the coalition level access policies. (iii) Subjects of a coalition entity must have credentials with attribute values comparable to the values of those of the local subjects.

For example, in an emergency management scenario, the International Red Cross decides to make available its Emergency Response Information System to other relief organizations. However, it has three access requirements: (i) individuals who wish to access these resources must belong to an organization recognized by the International Red Cross as a reliable relief organization; (ii) they are allowed to only access information related to the emergency site in which they are currently operating; and (iii) they must possess credentials with attribute values comparable to the values of internal users of the resources. As an example, Dr. Roberts, a member of Doctors Without Borders, wishes to access data on infectious diseases in the area of an earthquake in Turkey,

---

[1] In this paper, we use subjects and users alternatively.

an emergency scenario that he is currently working on. Clearly, he meets the first two requirements as long as he can present the appropriate organizational credentials and proof that he is operating in Turkey. Whether or not he meets the third requirement, depends upon the credentials determined to be needed and the credentials he presents.

This paper is organized as follows. Section 2 presents required preliminaries to introduce our DCBAC system. Section 3 presents our DCBAC system. Section 4 demonstrates how the coalition and resource level policies can be specified in XACML specification language. Section 5 shows how access requests can be specified and evaluated. Finally, Section 6 summarizes our conclusions and outlines future research in this area.

2   The Preliminaries

We briefly present the necessary formalism required to describe our DCBAC model. Specifically, we review the formalism for resources and credentials.

Each organizational entity maintains a set of resources, RES, that can be shared with other organizational entities within a coalition. Resources may include data objects as well as services offered by the coalition entity. Each resource belongs to a resource-type, organized as a resource-type hierarchy.

Definition 1. [Resource-type] An resource-type rt is a pair (rt_id, RA), where $rt\_id \in RT$ is a unique resource-type identifier; and RA is the set of attributes associated with rt_id. Each $ra_i \in RA$ is denoted by an attribute name.

Definition 2. [Resource] A resource res is a triple $(rt\_id, res\_id, res\_attr\_values)$, where $rt\_id \in RT$, $res\_id \in RES$, $res\_attr\_values = (ra : v_1, \ldots, ra : v_n)$, where $\{ra_1, \ldots, ra_n\} \subseteq RA(rt)$. $RA(rt)$ denotes the set of attributes associated with rt.

We use $res(res\_id)$, $res(res\_id)$ and $res(res\_attr\_values)$ to denote the resource id, the resource-type id, and the set of attribute values of the resource res, respectively. The set of resource attributes describe the resource such as keywords or concepts.

We assume that each subject is associated with one or more *credentials*. Credentials are assigned when a subject is created and are updated according to the profile of the subject. To make the task of credential specifications easier, credentials with similar structures are grouped into *credential-types*. Credential-types are typically organized as *credential-type hierarchy*. We denote the set of credential-type identifiers with CT, the set of credential identifiers with CI, and the set of subject identifiers with U. A credential-type can be formally defined as follows.

Definition 3. [Credential-type] A credential-type ct is a pair (ct_id, A), where $ct\_id \in CT$ is a unique identifier and A is the set of attributes belonging to ct_id. Each $a_i \in A$ has an attribute name and $A(ct)$ is the set of attributes belonging to ct.

Definition 4. [Credential] A credential c, an instance of a credential-type ct, is a 4-tuple $(ct\_id, c\_id, subject\_id, subject\_profile)$, where $ct\_id \in CT, c\_id \in CI, subject\_id \in U$ and $subject\_profile = (a_1 : v_1, \ldots, a_n : v_n)$, where $\{a_1, \ldots a_n\} \subseteq A(ct)$.

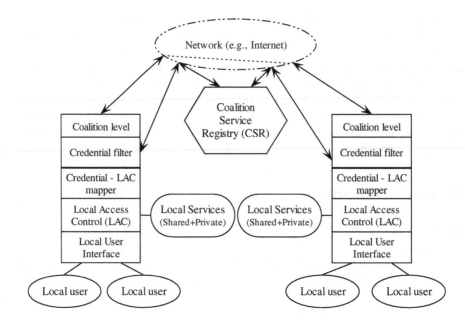

Fig. 1. Proposed Coalition Architecture

The set of credentials associated with subjects in the system is denoted by the credential base (CB). We use $c(c\_id)$, $c(subject\_id)$, $c(ct\_id)$ and $c(subject\_profile)$ to denote the credential id of c, the subject to which c is assigned, the credential type id of c and the set of attribute values of the subject u (the $subject\_profile$) for c, respectively.

Example 1. An example of a credential for credential type "doctor" is as follows: (doctor,045-999, (affiliation: Doctors-without-Borders, Specialty: immunology)). An example of a credential for an organizational level credential type "organization" is as follows: (organization, 943-777, CareNow, (headquarters: New York, NY, tax-status:non-profit)). It has two attributes - headquarters and tax-status.

3   The DCBAC System

Our DCBAC system is comprised of a four layered architecture as depicted in Figure 1. In this section, we briefly describe the functionalities of each of the components.

3.1   Coalition Service Registry

In order to facilitate dynamic and ad-hoc collaboration, we employ a registry service similar to the model adopted for web services through which resources are offered to potential collaborators. Such a model mitigates the need to negotiate and establish collaboration policies among coalition entities. Any entity can set its own sharing policies, describe the types of resources that it is willing to share, and specify the required organizational credentials needed to access these resources. Adopting a model similar to that of Web services is attractive in that it offers a readily available access interface.

We propose the use of a collaborative registry, called the *coalition service registry* (CSR), similar to the UDDI Web Service registry[7]. It is used to define the set of resources that coalition entities will make available and to describe the interfaces and credentials used to access those resources. Our CSR will also verify organization-level credentials and issue a "ticket" which can be submitted by individuals in the organization when submitting an access request for the advertised resources. This "ticket" is nothing but a SAML assertion.

UDDI offers a standard way for potential collaborators to search registries for resources based on a classification scheme or keyword. Queries for these resources can be modulated with acceptable security and transport protocols. These searches are performed against the information provided by the entity detailing to the desired extent who the entity is (using the "BusinessEntity" structure), what resources are being provided (using the "businessService" structure), and the details on how to request access to the resources (using the "binding template"). The binding template would indicate the network address of the *Coalition Access Point* (CAP) for the resource publishing entity. The CAP is able to interpret the requests and make access decisions. Specifics about the access requests would be posted in the binding template as well, including the format of credentials accepted, the format of the request and security requirements (i.e., digital signatures, encryption).

While publishing resources in a public registry would allow the potential collaborators to learn about offered resources, public announcement of shared resources is not desirable. The CSR is expected to be hosted at one or more secure sites for a community of interest. For our example, the Red Cross may state a coalition level policy by registering their service at a registry and make their service only accessible to reliable relief organizations through membership.

To gain access to a desired resource, a user (or an organization on behalf of its user) submits the requested organizational level credentials to the CSR. The registry validates the credentials and issues a SAML assertion. This is the "ticket" that a user from the authenticated coalition entity must present to attempt to access the specific resources being made available. Note that receipt of the ticket is not sufficient for access to the resources. Instead, the assertion merely confirms that the user is from an organization that matches the organizational level policy of the organization offering the resources.

Coalition entities may be permitted to join a coalition for a specific period of time. Of course, revocation may be desirable at any time. Revocation procedures may be performed at each individual CAP by implementing a function that follows decision rules on whether a given assertion is accepted at a given time.

3.2 The DCBAC Layers

Additional specification of the layers are given in the following.

Coalition level. The top layer is the coalition level. It interacts with the coalition level at other coalition entities. For simplicity, in this paper, we are considering only a single coalition (in which an entity participates). When a entity participates in multiple coalitions, there would be multiple interfaces at this level (similar to a virtual machine model that supports multiple virtual machine interfaces to its processes [11]). In that case, we can perceive this layer as having multiple coalition level software all existing simultaneously at an entity's CAP. This layer receives service requests from other coalition entity CAPs. The exact components of this request are presented later in Section 3.3.

On receiving an external service request, the top layer authenticates the requesting coalition entity by validating the "ticket" received with the request. It checks if the coalition policy has changed since the ticket was issued. If so, the request is rejected by this level. The authentication is for the coalition entity that is sending the request rather than for the individual user who may have initiated the request. The ticket is stripped off and the request is then forwarded to the credential filter.

Credential Filter. The credential filter layer is responsible for filtering incoming and outgoing requests and their associated user credentials. When this layer receives a service request from the coalition level layer, it checks whether or not the service is made available to the coalition (i.e., registered in CSR). It then checks whether or not the provided credentials are adequate to execute the request. If they are not adequate, it rejects the request and sends an exception to its coalition level. In addition, depending on its own organizational policies, it may downgrade or upgrade the credentials of a specific entity in the coalition. For example, if a coalition consists of 10 entities, and entity A has less trust on specific credentials offered by entity B, then it could downgrade them.

If one entity, for example, is suspected of revealing private information, another entity could downgrade the credentials from this entity. After such filtering/transformation of credentials, it forwards the request with credentials to its lower layer. It should be noted that the credential layer has access to both the CSR and the local policies (if any) regarding exception polices with regard to coalition entities. Below this layer, there is no distinction between local and non-local user requests.

Let us now consider its handling of requests made by a local user to access non-local services of the coalition. When its lower layer hands it a request and the associated user credentials, it accesses the CSR to check: (i) If the service is registered at the registry; (ii) If the provided credentials are adequate to provide the service. If both checks are positive, it filters out the credentials to be sent so that only the needed credentials ($required\_subject\_credentials$) are provided to the service provider. For example, if the requester is a PhD, an MD, and the director of a research institute, and if the service only requires MD as a credential, the credential filter would filter out the PhD and director credentials. This is in line with the need-to-know principle adopted in operating systems to provide resource protection and privacy [11]. It then sends up the request and filtered credentials to the coalition level.

Credential$\Longleftrightarrow$LAC Mapper. The credential$\Longleftrightarrow$LAC mapper is responsible for mapping the requestor's credentials to the local access control terminology and vice versa. It takes the local access control rules and converts them into a policy based on credential attributes and resource attributes.

When the mapper receives a request with credentials from the credential layer, it looks at its map and determines the possible local access controls that may be attributed to that request. For example, when it receives the credentials of ⟨Location: Turkey, Specialty: infectious disease, Education: MD⟩, and if the local access control policy is RBAC, then the mapper would search its local map to determine possible roles that may be assigned to the request. The map would specify required credentials derived from those credentials that internal users in a role have minus the set that are either individual attributes (e.g., name, e-mail address) or internal organizational attributes (e.g., department, project). The local map, for example, may associate the received credentials with the local roles of ⟨Doctor⟩ and ⟨Intern⟩. If two roles are in a single hierarchy, then the map identifies only the highest role among them. Otherwise, it will form a union of the roles and forwards this to the LAC layer along with the request. In other words, if the hierarchy consists of doctor and intern, only doctor will be forwarded.

For outgoing requests, the mapper receives determines the role of the requestor and computes the union of all credentials ($subject\_credentials$) associated with the associated roles. It forwards the request and credentials to its credential filter layer.

Local Access Control (LAC) Layer. The local access control layer enforces control on local services for both local and non-local requests. As shown in Figure 1, the local requests are received through the Local-user-Interface (LUI). The non-local requests are received through its upper layer. To understand its functionality, let us assume a specific LAC such as RBAC. Since both local and non-local requests are accompanied by the appropriate set of applicable roles, RBAC checks whether or not the service is permitted for any of those roles. Of course, problems may arise when the requested service is permitted for one of the roles and explicitly denied for some other role. Since this is not specific to coalitions, we do not handle this problem here.

If a service request passes the access control, it is forwarded to the local services module which executes the request and returns the result to the LAC. If the request came from the local user, the results are returned through LUI. For non-local requests, the results are forwarded to its upper layer.

3.3   The Request-Response Protocol

In the following, we present the detailed steps of how an access request is processed and give an example using an access request by Dr. Roberts of Doctors Without Borders for an object (RID_730) at the International Red Cross:

1. At the LAC Layer of the Requesting Entity: At the requesting coalition entity, a user requests an resource by specifying the user request for a specific resource type, which is as follows: ⟨$request\_id, subject\_id, rt\_id$⟩.
   For example, ⟨ 744, roberts, Red_Cross_RID_730 ⟩.

2. At the credential⟺LAC Mapper Layer of the Requesting Entity:
   ⟨$request\_id, subject\_credentials, rt\_id$⟩. For example, ⟨ 744, (degree:MD, gender:M, location:Turkey, specialty: infectious disease), Red_Cross_RID_730 ⟩.

3. At the credential filter layer of the Requesting Entity:
   ⟨$request\_id, required\_subject\_credentials, rt\_id$⟩. For example, ⟨ 744, (location:Turkey, specialty: infectious disease), Red_Cross_RID_730 ⟩.

4. At the coalition layer of the requesting entity: ⟨$request\_id, (requesting)entity\_id, (resourceprovider)entity\_id, organizational\_credential\_assertion, rt\_id, required\_subject\_credentials$⟩. For example, ⟨ 744,Doctors Without Borders, Red Cross, SAML Assertion, Red_Cross_RID_730, (location:Turkey, specialty: infectious disease) ⟩.

The message is sent to the service provider coalition entity.

1. At the Coalition Level Layer of the source entity, it validates the *organizational_credential_assertion* and sends the following to the credential filter layer. ⟨*request_id, required_subject_credentials, rt_id*⟩. For example, ⟨ 744, (location:Turkey, specialty: infectious disease), RID_730 ⟩.
2. At the credential filter layer of the requesting entity, it verifies that the *required_subject_credentials* are included in the request. It then passes ⟨*request_id, required_subject_credentials, rt_id*⟩ to the mapper layer. For example, ⟨ 744, (location:Turkey, specialty: infectious disease), RID_730 ⟩.
3. At the credential⟺LAC mapper layer of the source entity, it compares the credentials of remote subjects to the determined equivalent of the local access control. If they are acceptable, the mapper layer requests access from the LAC layer ⟨*rt_id*⟩. For example, ⟨ 744, RID_730 ⟩.
4. At the LAC layer of the source entity: This layer serves the access request. It identifies the requested resource or set of resources and makes them available to the requesting coalition entity.

4   Policy Specification

In this section, we present our approach to specifying coalition based access control policies. These policies are specified at two levels – coalition level and resource level. The coalition level policies state the high level access control rules of coalition entities on sharing resources among themselves that are publicized in the CSR.

The resource level policies state the access control rules on accessing a specific resource by a user belonging to a coalition entity. These policies are stored and maintained at the resource owners. We use XACML [6] policy language to specify both the coalition level and resource level policies. Finally, as noted in Section 3 we use SAML for specifying organizational tickets.

We have chosen to use XML-based specifications for realizing our model. This is because, using XML-standards, specifically UDDI, SAML and XACML provides many benefits. Standards exist through the OASIS organization, the protocols are being implemented, and parsers exist that can be readily used. The standards are extensible, allowing the addition of functions and labels as needed. In addition, since collaboration clearly involves multiple distributed parties, use of namespaces and semantics that have already been defined for credentials and resources can speed implementation due to re-use and can facilitate dynamic interoperability though common definitions.

4.1   Coalition Level Policies

The coalition level access policy specification can be compactly represented as follows: ⟨*entity_id, credential_set, rt_id*⟩. The e policy states that only organizations that possess the credentials specified in the *credenial_set* are allowed to access the resources belonging to the *rt_id* owned by the coalition entity with the specified *entity_id*. These organizational level policies are specified at the CSR. This coalition level policy represents only the organizational level credentials that must be provided by an individual who requires access.

```
01 XACML HEADER
02 <Policy>
03  <PolicyId=1>
04  <RuleCombiningAlgId= "deny-overrides">
05 <Description>
06  read access to emergency archives with non-profit
    relief organizations who are listed as ReliefWeb members
07 </Description>
09  <Subjects>
10      <Subject>
11         <SubjectMatch MatchId="name-match">
12              <Attribute Value DataType=string "www.reliefweb.org/~orglist">
13            <SubjectAttributeDesignator
14              AttributeId=organization_id
15                      DataType=string/>
16         </SubjectMatch>
17         <Subject Match matchId="string-match">
18              <Attribute Value DataType=string "non-profit">
19              <SubjectAttributeDesignator
20                      AttributeId=tax-status
21                      DataType=string/>
22         </SubjectMatch>
23      </Subject>
24  </Subjects>
25   <Resources>
26      <Resource>
27              <Attribute AttributeId=resource_type>
28              <AttributeValue>
29              emergency-archive
30              </AttributeValue>
31      </Resource>
32    </Resources/>
33 </Policy>
```

Fig. 2. An Example of the Coalition Level Policy

XACML [6] provides a way to describe the above policy. We have adopted XACML to specify this policy because of the following capabilities critical to our approach: (i) It provides a method for basing an authorization decision on attributes of the subject (e.g., subject credentials) and resource (e.g., resource type).(ii) It provides a method for combining individual rules and policies into a single policy set. This helps in combining rules applicable to one coalition into a policy set. (iii) XACML was written explicitly to provide a common way to express policies and ensure enforcement in a distributed environment, making it appropriate for a coalition based environment. (iv) Although not explicitly used in our example, the logical and mathematical operators on attributes of the subject, resource and environment will aid in flexible policy descriptions.

Example 2. Returning to our example, assume that the Coalition Level Policy for the Red Cross is as follows: "Allow read access on emergency archives to non-profit relief organizations who are listed as ReliefWeb members". This policy can be stated as ⟨RedCross, {ReliefWeb-member, non-profit}, emergency-archives⟩.

The example coalition level policy can be expressed in XACML-like specification, as shown in Figure 2, in which lines 1-7 introduce the policy and 8-23 indicate the subject attributes that must be matched. There are two attributes to be matched. The first, as specified in lines 11 - 16 is a name-match of the organization to names listed at "www.reliefweb.org/~orglist". The second, as specified in lines 17 - 22, is a string-match for tax-status which must equal non-profit. Lines 25-32 provide the resource attributes for the resources that are made available.

4.2 Resource Level Policies

The resource level access policy specification can be specified as: $\langle credential\_set, rt\_id \rangle$. This policy states that only the subjects who possess the credentials specified by the $credential\_set$ are authorized to access the resources of type specified in the rt_id. These policies are specified within the coalition entity organization, and are maintained in the local policy base. These are nothing but the local policies translated into this form by the credential$\Longleftrightarrow$LAC Mapper.

Example 3. Let us consider the following two resource level policies: (1) External individuals may only access information related to the emergency site in which they are currently operating. (2) Individuals must have credentials with attribute values comparable to the values of internal users of the resources.

The first policy serves as a filter, specifying that there must be a match between the subject's location and the location for which the resource is concerned. Specification of this policy using XACML requires that a variable be defined based on the credential attribute "location". This variable is then used to match resource attribute values. To specify the second policy in XACML is more straightforward. The required credentials generated by the mapper are specified in XACML as attributes of the subject to match.

Assume that Dr. Roberts, a member of Doctors Without Borders, wishes to access data on infectious diseases in the area of an earthquake in Turkey, an emergency on which he is currently working. The requested resources are distributed in two parts of our resource hierarchy, RID 517 and 730. To access these resources, the resource policy specifies that the subject must be a doctor with the specialty of infectious diseases to access RID 517, but there are no specialty restrictions for RID 730. Internally, the access control policy is that the subject must also be assigned to at least one of a set of specific projects. However, since this is an internal attribute, it would not be included in the attribute requirements for external users. This policy can be specified in XACML as shown in Figure 3, where it consists of a target (lines 2 - 9) and a rule for each resource type. The target is used to (1) check that the user has a location credential and (2) to store the value of the location attribute in a variable "LOC". The rules for each resource type match (1) the variable "location" to the resource attribute "theater-of-operation" (lines 21 to 24 for the first policy, and 41 to 44 for the second policy, (2) match the subject attributes presented by Dr. Roberts to the requirements for the requested resource. In the first policy, the credentials needed are specified in lines 13 to 15. In the second policy, there are no subject credentials matches to be found.

Note that there would be policies associated with all other shared resources, which are not illustrated here. Note also that the policy is specified on the highest resource of the hierarchy. For example, a policy is specified over resource 510 rather than resource 517 because the same policy applies to all of the children of 510.

```
01 XACML HEADER
02 <Target>
03  <VariableDefinition VariableId="LOC">
04          <Apply Function-Id="string-equal">
05          <SubjectAttributeDesignator AttributeId="location"
06          DataType=string/>
07               </Apply>
08  </VariableDefinition>
09 </Target>
10 <Rule RuleId=1 Effect=permit>
11    <Description>
12 Read  access is provided to users who present credentials showing a
   specialty of "infectious disease" and location credentials that
   match the "theater-of-operations" attribute of the requested
   resource.
13 </Description>
14    <Subjects>
15      <Subject>
16        <SubjectMatch>
17                    <AttributeValue ="infectious disease"
18                    Datatype = specialty>
19      </Subject>
20    </Subjects>
21    <Resources>
22      <Resource>
23         RID 510
24         <ResourceMatch>
25                    <AttributeValue = LOC
26             Datatype = theater-of-operation>
27          </ResourceMatch>
28      </Resource>
29      </Resources/>
30  <Actions>
31     <ActionMatch matchId=string-equal>
32        <AttributeValue DataType=string> read
33     </ActionMatch>
34 </Rule>
35 <Rule RuleId=2 Effect=permit>
36  <Description>
37 Read access is provided to users who present location credentials that
   match the "theater-of-operations" attribute of the requested resource.
38    </Description>
39    <Subjects>
40          <Subject>
41        <AnySubject>
42          </Subject>
43      </Subjects>
44    <Resources>
45        <Resource>
46             RID 730
47           <ResourceMatch>
48              <AttributeValue = LOC
49               Datatype = theater-of-operation>
50            </ResourceMatch>
51        </Resource>
52    </Resources/>
53    <Actions>
54     <ActionMatch matchId=string-equal>
55        <AttributeValue DataType=string> read
56     </ActionMatch>
57    </Actions>
58  </Rule>
```

Fig. 3. An Example of the Resource Level Policy

```
<saml:Assertion
xmlns:saml="urn:oasis:names:tc:SAML:1.0:assertion"//
    MajorVersion="1" MinorVersion="1"
    AssertionID="buGxcG4gILg5NlocyLccDz6iXrUa"
    Issuer="Coalition-service-registry095
    IssueInstant="2005-02-28T12:24:37">
    Recipient="Red Cross"
        <saml:Conditions NotBefore="2005-03-01T01:00:00"
            NotOnOrAfter="2006-06-15T01:00:00"/>
        <saml:AuthenticationStatement
            <saml:Subject>
                Doctors-without-Borders
            </saml:Subject>
        </saml:AuthenticationStatement>
</saml:Assertion>
```

Fig. 4. SAML Assertion

5   Access Request Evaluation

In this section, we describe how an access request is evaluated. In order to send an access request for a resource, the coalition entity of the requesting subject should first have the required credentials to access the resource. This verification is done at the CSR and a ticket to access the resource is issued to the requesting entity. In Section 5.1, we describe how such assertions are generated and their format. A user of a requesting entity then sends an access request to a coalition entity by appending this ticket. In Section 5.2, we discuss how this access request is specified in XML specification language and how it is evaluated.

5.1   SAML Assertion

In order to gain access to a CAP, a user must submit the SAML assertion generated by the CSR. The SAML assertion consists of a header, an assertion id, the Issuer element containing the identifier for the specific CSR, the issue instant element providing the date and time when issued, the recipient for the assertion, conditions for when the assertion can be applied and the assertion itself which consists of the subject, indicating the organization identity for which the assertion applies and any optional attributes.

In our example, Dr. Roberts' organization, Doctors without Borders, would have obtained a SAML assertion from the CSR, specified as shown in Figure 4.

5.2   Access Request Specification and Evaluation

XACML defines several functional components that work together to perform access control. We make use of the following components at the CAP. The functionalities supported by our CAP include: (i) a XACML Policy Enforcement Point (PEP), which assesses external resource requests and enforces authorization decisions (ii) a Policy Decision Point (PDP), which evaluates applicable policy and makes authorization decisions, and (iii) a Policy Information Point (PIP), which provides attribute values for outgoing requests as well as environmental attribute values such as time and date as necessary. Not included in our CAP is the Policy Administration Point functionality (PAP) which is the system used to create policies. A common policy system for all

```
<Request>
    <Subject>
        <SubjectAttribute>
            specialty = cr:doctor.specialty
        </SubjectAttribute>
        <SubjectAttribute>
            location = cr:work.site
        </SubjectAttribute>
    </Subject>
    <Resource>
        <ResourceAttribute>
            RID = 517 AND RID = 730
        </ResourceAttribute>
    </Resource>
    <Action>
        Read
    </Action>
</Request>
```

Fig. 5. Access Request

policies (local and external) is important to ensure that policies are not conflicting and carefully administered. This is out of scope of this paper.

Looking at our example again from end-to-end, Dr. Roberts would first search the CSR and find information that could be useful to him relevant to his relief work in Turkey is available from the Red Cross CAP. Triggered by his request, his organization submits its organizational level credentials to the registry, which verifies the credentials and then returns a signed SAML assertion to be used at the Red Cross CAP. The request can be expressed as: Request = ⟨SAML Assertion, Credential-set, Resource, Action⟩. It consists of the SAML Assertion from the CSR, a credential set associated with Dr. Roberts that meets the requirements of the access control rules for the requested resources, the resources and finally the action requested. The last two items as well as a reference to the portions of the submitted credentials that are applicable will be referred to as the "Req". The "Req" can be expressed in XACML with the ⟨SubjectAttribute⟩ tags referring to the portions of the submitted credentials that apply.

For example, Dr. Robert's request would consist of
⟨SAML-Assertion-for-Doctors-without-Borders, doctor-credential, work-credential, Req⟩ where Req would be formatted in XACML policy language as shown in Figure 5. The Red Cross CAP would match the request with the associated policy for the requested resources and validate the credentials if necessary. If there is a match, access is allowed. If not, access is denied.

6   Conclusions and Future Work

In this paper, we have presented a coalition-based access control system designed to automatically translate coalition level policies into subject-resource level policies by employing an attribute-based approach. It considers the attributes associated with user credentials and those associated with resources, making the formation of specific groups of subjects and resources unnecessary. Our system extends the original model proposed [1] in the following three directions: First, our system is capable of catering to "true" ad-hoc dynamic coalition by facilitating a coalition service registry where resources to be shared among potential coalition entities are advertised. Organizations can obtain tickets to access the resources if they satisfy the required organizational-level credentials. Second, our system is capable of assessing the exact credentials necessary by a remote user and be able to map the access request as if it was an access request from a local user. Finally, we have demonstrated how our CBAC system can be implemented using OASIS XML-based standards, including XACML, UDDI, and SAML.

Our DCBAC model assumes that the local policies are mapped to credential-based to facilitate external users to access the local resources. However, we have not addressed how this mapping can be accomplished. Our future work includes mapping of different types of local policies, including DAC, MAC, RBAC, etc., into credential based policies. Moreover, CSR and ticket issuing function could become a performance bottleneck. We are exploring the issue of distributing/replicating the CSR so that some of the functionalities of the CSR can be accomplished by the coalition entities themselves. The challenge is to accomplish this without having to have a trusted coalition entity. We are also exploring the case where resources are not owned by only one entity in the coalition, but instead are shared by several entities. We intend to extend our approach to facilitate such cooperative environments similar to the work on cooperative role-based administration in [12]. Finally, we believe that delegation is an important feature, which must be supported in coalition-based systems [4] and we intend to include this support as well.

References

1. V. Atluri and J. Warner. Automatic enforcement of access control policies among dynamic coalitions. In *International Conference on Distributed Computing and Internet Technology (ICDCIT) 2004*, December 2004.
2. V. Bharadwaj and J. Baras. A framework for automated negotiation of access control policies. *Proceedings of DISCEX III*, 2003.
3. E. Cohen, W. Winsborough, R. Thomas, and D. Shands. Models for coalition-based access control (cbac). *SACMAT*, 2002.
4. P. Freudenthal, K. Pesin, Keenan Port, and Karamcheti. drbac: Distributed role-based access control for dynamic coalition environments. *ICDCS*, July 2002.
5. H. Khurana, S. Gavrila, R. Bobba, R. Koleva, A. Sonalker, E. Dinu, V. Gligor, and J. Baras. Integrated security services for dynamic coalitions. *Proc. of the DISCEX III*, 2003.
6. OASIS. extensible access control markup language (XACML), version 2. *OASIS Standard*, February 2005.
7. OASIS. Universal description discovery and integration (UDDI), version 3.0.2. *OASIS Standard*, February 2005.
8. OASIS. Assertions and protocols for the oasis security assertion markup language (saml), version 2. *OASIS Standard*, January 2005.
9. C. Philips, E. Charles, T. Ting, and S. Demurjian. Towards information assurance in dynamic coalitions. *IEEE IAW, USMA*, February 2002.
10. C. Philips, T.C. Ting, , and S. Demurjian. Information sharing and security in dynamic coalitions. *SACMAT*, 2002.
11. A. Silberschatz, P. Galvin, and G. Gagne. *Operating System Concepts with Java*. John Wiley and Sons, 6 edition, 2004.
12. H. F. Wedde and M. Lischka. Cooperative role-based administration. *SACMAT*, 2003.
13. T. Yu, M. Winslett, and K.E. Seamons. Supporting structured credentials and sensitive policies through interoperable strategies for automated trust negotiation. *ACM Transactions on Information and System Security*, 6(1):1–42, February 2003.

Secure Mediation with Mobile Code[*]

Joachim Biskup, Barbara Sprick, and Lena Wiese

Universität Dortmund, D-44221 Dortmund, Germany
{biskup, sprick, wiese}@ls6.cs.uni-dortmund.de
http://ls6-www.cs.uni-dortmund.de/issi/

Abstract. A mediator helps a client of a distributed information system to acquire data without contacting each datasource. We show how mobile code can be used to ensure confidentiality of data in a secure mediation system. We analyze what advantages mobile code has over mobile data for secure mediation. We present a Java implementation of a system that mediates SQL queries. Security risks for the client and the mobile code are delineated; offending the integrity of its own data is identified as a special type of attack of mobile code in a mediation system. We name appropriate countermeasures and describe the amount of trust needed in our system. As an extension, we consider security in a hierarchy of mediators. Finally, we combine mobile code with mobile agent technology.

1 Introduction

In a world with a growing amount of digitalized information, finding relevant data is a tedious task – and it gets even more difficult if the information is distributed on several different host systems (the "datasources"). Wiederhold and Genesereth (cf. [13,14]) introduced the concept of mediation to support the client of a distributed information system: The client directs a query to a so-called mediator; the mediator tries to gather the data best fitting the client's interests by sending partial queries to datasources; finally, the mediator constructs a global result out of the partial results and sends it back to the client. See Figure 1 for a basic mediated system.

This basic system does not consider security aspects. However, participants may require some security demands to be fulfilled:

1. Anonymity of participants: Clients may wish to stay anonymous to the datasources.
2. Confidentiality of data: Datasources may wish to be sure that the requesting client is eligible to access the requested data; i.e., datasources have to perform some kind of access control.

---

[*] This work was funded by the German Research Council (DFG) under grant number BI 311/11-1.

S. Jajodia and D. Wijesekera (Eds.): Data and Applications Security 2005, LNCS 3654, pp. 267–280, 2005.

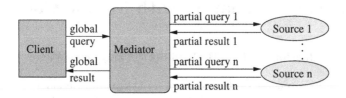

Fig. 1. A basic mediated information system

Altenschmidt et al. (cf. [2]) designed a system for secure mediation. Its general design is shown in Figure 2 and outlined in the following. Given that not revealing a client's identity is one precondition to ensure anonymity for the client (Point 1), in the secure mediated system a client attaches a credential to her global query; the mediator forwards the credential with the partial queries to the datasources. This credential is issued by a trusted certification authority (see Section 5 for a description of our trust model); it links properties of the client to her public encryption key but does not contain details of her identity. The client keeps another certificate linking her identity to her public key in a safe place. Instead of specifying just one key, the client can also attach a set of credentials (containing different properties linked with possibly different public keys of hers) and therefore combine multiple properties.

Datasources base their access control decisions only on the properties presented in the credentials. To keep the data confidential each datasource applies a hybrid encryption scheme to its partial result: A session key used to encrypt the partial result is itself encrypted with the client's public keys in the credentials. Assuming a reliable public key infrastructure and adequate encryption techniques, only the person who possesses the private decryption keys should be

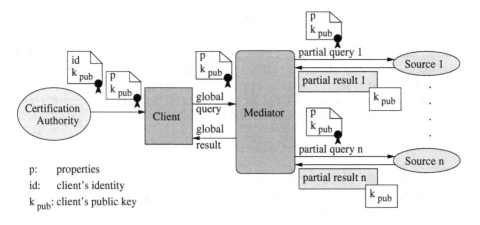

Fig. 2. A credential-based secure mediated information system

able to decrypt the session key and therefore the partial results and to access the returned data (i.e., Point 2 is fulfilled).

By encrypting the partial results we face the following problem that will be treated in this paper:

Given encrypted partial results, the mediator has to supply the client with a global result to her global query. However, the mediator may not be eligible to access the datasources' unencrypted data.

Unfortunately, there does not exist a general "privacy homomorphism" (as introduced in [11]) to solve the problem of "computing with encrypted data" (cf. [12]) where all data are encrypted with the same key. Furthermore, there are no approaches known to us that cover the problem of computing with data encrypted with different session keys; this is the case if the datasources apply a hybrid encryption scheme. So, up to now the mediator is not able to compute an encrypted global result from encrypted partial results. Moreover, the client should better not give away her private decryption keys as she cannot control what other parties use them for. Thus we have to impose the additional work of computing the global result on the client.

Section 2 introduces mobile data and mobile code as possible solutions to our problem and lists advantages of mobile code. Section 3 presents our Java implementation of the secure mediated system with mobile code. In Section 4 possible attacks by mobile code are depicted and a number of protection mechanisms are explained; attacks on the code are considered as well. Section 5 describes the model of trust we assume in our system. Section 6 covers additional security aspects in a hierarchy of mediators. We conclude the paper with an outline of another application area for a secure mediated system with mobile code. More details on our mediation system can be found in [16]; our Java implementation can be downloaded from [15].

2   Communication Between Mediator and Client

The basic idea to solve our problem is that the client gets the encrypted partial results from the mediator and additionally an instruction how to combine the partial results. We call the set of unencrypted partial results $\mathcal{R}$, the set of encrypted partial results $\mathcal{R}_{enc}$, and the combination instruction i. The client first decrypts the partial results and then computes the global result according to i; she uses a program for this computation. We distinguish two possible origins of this program:

1. A general program p was on the client's computer beforehand. The mediator specifies a format for i and $\mathcal{R}_{enc}$ and sends $d = (i, \mathcal{R}_{enc})$. On client side $\mathcal{R}_{enc}$ is decrypted to $\mathcal{R}$; then, i and $\mathcal{R}$ are used as inputs to compute the global result $p(i, \mathcal{R})$.
2. The mediator constructs a specialized program $p(i)$ based on i containing libraries that are necessary to compute the global result. The mediator then

sends $c = (p(i), \mathcal{R}_{enc})$. On client side $\mathcal{R}_{enc}$ is decrypted; the execution of $p(i)(\mathcal{R})$ yields the global result.

In general, the first approach corresponds to the concept of "mobile data", the second one to the concept of "mobile code"[1]. Similar to [1] and [10] we use the following definitions in this paper:

Definition 1. *Mobile data, data processor:*
A mobile data system comprises a client requesting information and a server supplying this information. Communication between client and server is merely an exchange of data without program code. Processing the data on client side is solely done by a program already residing on the client's computer; this program is called a data processor. The server has to transmit the data in a predefined format.

Definition 2. *Mobile code, execution environment:*
Mobile code consists of an executable program; there may also be a set of data included that the program operates on. An installation of the program is not needed; i.e., it can be executed immediately. A mobile code instance is sent to one single recipient only. To control mobile code, it should be run in an execution environment that shields the operating system from the mobile code. There is no need for a common data format. However, the mobile code has to provide a public execution interface to the recipient.

A pre-installed data processor on the client's computer is indispensable in the concept of *mobile data*. But also if we want to impose security settings on *mobile code*, a pre-installed execution environment is necessary. We opted for the mobile code approach as it offers some advantages that are described in the following.

In general, Fong [5] and Peine [10] consider mobile code advantageous over mobile data. Yet, their conclusions do not entirely apply to secure mediation. We now give just a short overview of our reasoning; see Table 1 for a summary and [16] for a detailed analysis.

In secure mediation, there is no difference between mobile code and mobile data considering **Distribution of state** and **Reliability of network**: Only one transmission from mediator to client is necessary, because the mediator collects all partial results; that is why inconsistencies in the distributed computation state or communication problems due to an unstable communication link hardly occur – be it with mobile data or mobile code. As for **Network traffic**, mobile code even increases the amount of transmitted data due to its additional libraries. However, mobile code offers the following advantages for secure mediation:

– **Locality:** Local interaction with resources (like the decryption keys for partial results) without further installation of libraries can only be guaranteed with mobile code.

---

[1] We also use the term "mobile code" in contrast to "mobile agents". The most distinctive feature of mobile agents is their ability to deliberately change their location in a network of host computers.

Table 1. Mobile code versus mobile data; gen. = general, med. = mediated, + = mobile code better than mobile data, 0 = equal, − = mobile code worse

Comparison	gen.	med.	Reason
Avoiding distribution of state	+	0	No inconsistency: Serial computation between mediator and client
Decoupling from network	+	0	Only one transmission: Mediator collects all partial results
Reduction of network traffic	+	−	Additional program binaries (e.g. class files)
Local interaction with resources	+	+	Computation at client without further installation
Footprint size	+	+	Small execution environment
Extensibility	+	+	Libraries are included in mobile code

- **Size:** The execution environment of mobile code may be considerably smaller than a data processor of mobile data as all necessary libraries are sent along with the code; those libraries occupy space on the client computer only while being used.
- **Extensibility:** The mobile code can use its up-to-date libraries without further need for action of the client.

3   Our Solution: Mobile Java Code

The Java implementation of our secure mediation system processes queries in the Structured Query Language (SQL). It comprises a client module (the execution environment for mobile code), a mediator module and a datasource module. The modules communicate via RMI calls. We describe each module in detail in the following subsections.

3.1   Datasource Module

The datasource module needs access to an appropriate Java database driver. When the datasource module receives a partial query, it opens a SQL connection to a database with the database driver to get the partial results. The datasource module encrypts a partial result with hybrid encryption. This has two advantages:

- Each partial result is encrypted with a newly generated symmetrical session key; this makes cyphertext-attacks aimed at recovering the client's private decryption keys more difficult.
- The possibly large set of data in the partial result is encrypted with the faster symmetrical encryption and only the small-sized session key is encrypted asymmetrically.

The default Java packages do not support asymmetrical encryption. However, it is possible to integrate so-called "cryptography providers". We used the "Bouncy Castle Provider" (BCP; see [4]). The session key is encrypted with the Bouncy Castle RSA algorithm (in Electronic Code Book mode and with Optimal Asymmetric Encryption Padding). Both asymmetrical encryption of the session key (with possibly a set of different public keys extracted from the client's credentials) and symmetrical encryption of the partial result are both carried out by the class `javax.crypto.Cipher`. The parameters for symmetrical encryption (algorithm and keylength) can be set in the GUI by a datasource administrator.

On client side, Java class definitions can be integrated at runtime. That is why datasources are not restricted in what data formats they use to represent their partial results. Their formats just have to implement the interface `Result` that is known to the client module; any format implementing `Result` can be processed on client side if the class definitions are sent within the mobile code.

3.2 Mediator Module

The mediator module uses the "SQL2Algebra" library developed at our department to process a client's SQL query. The library takes the query as input and outputs a so-called algebra tree. The leaves of this algebra tree contain the partial SQL queries that are forwarded to the datasources. Each inner node represents one of the algebraic operators *selection*, *projection*, *union*, *join* and *complement*; only queries representable with these operators can be processed by the library. This is an examplary SQL2Algebra transformation:

SQL query	Algebra tree

`Select distinct tv1.A`
`  from TABLE1 tv1`
`  union (select`
`  distinct tv2.A`
`  from TABLE2 tv2);`
	`UNION`
	`|_ PROJECT{A}`
	`|  |_ "Select * from TABLE1;"`
	`|_ PROJECT{A}`
	`   |_ "Select * from TABLE2;"`

Based on the algebra tree, the mediator module constructs the so-called "answer tree" – the executable that is returned to the client. Each inner node of the answer tree is an operator object; it provides a method that executes the respective operation on its child nodes. Similar to the data format of the datasources, the mediator can use operator classes unknown to the client as long as they implement the interface `ResultOperator` and their class definitions are included in the mobile code. A leaf of the answer tree is an object of type `ResultProxy`; it has a reference to a `java.util.Hashtable` that stores all encrypted partial results returned by the datasources. Then the mediator module constructs the mobile code by joining the answer tree and the necessary class definitions (as one or more Java Archives (JARs)) in an object of type `ResultExtractor`.

The mediator module encrypts the mobile code hybridly using the public keys contained in the client's credentials. Finally the mediator module signs the mobile code using `java.security.Signature`. Encrypting and signing is done to secure the mobile code during transmission between mediator and client.

3.3 Client Module

A client enters a SQL query and the mediator name (or its IP address) in the client module. She loads her credentials from a Java KeyStore (JKS); at the same time, the client module verifies whether she knows the password that secures the corresponding private decryption keys. The client module sends the query together with the credentials to the indicated mediator module.

After receiving the mediator's answer, the client module checks the signature of the mobile code with the verification key of the mediator that the client loaded from a JKS. If the signature is correct, the client module decrypts the mobile code with the private keys specified when loading the credentials. Decryption leaves the answer tree and the JARs. For each mobile code the client module creates a uniquely named working directory, where it temporarily stores the JARs. Then the client module accesses the `Hashtable` of the mobile code that contains the encrypted partial results, decrypts each partial result and writes the decrypted partial result back to the `Hashtable`.

Before execution is started, the JARs have to be made available to the Java classloading mechanism. We replaced the default system classloader with a new classloader that allows to add filenames to its search path and remove them again. As our classloader replaces the system classloader, simply the `new`-operator can be used in the mobile code to instantiate an object. So, the client module adds the JARs to the classloader's search path and calls the calculation method of the root operator of the answer tree. Each operator recursively calls the calculation methods of its children and then processes their return values. If a child is a leaf (i.e., a `ResultProxy`-object), the calculation method accesses the `Hashtable` containing the decrypted partial results and returns the appropriate one. The client module presents the global result to the client. After this, it resets the classloader's search path and deletes the working directory.

4 Security Issues

In general, in a dynamic mediated system with constantly changing, unidentified participants there is no basis for mutual trust between the participants. The client can protect her computer against outside attacks from other participants by adequate means (e.g., firewalls or authentication mechanisms). The crucial point is that the client has to let code enter her computer to benefit from the code mobility.

In our system, we still rely on certain trust relations (see Section 5); however, our design goal was to minimize the amount of trust the client has to put in the mobile code (specifically the program $p(i)$ she receives). To achieve this, we use an execution environment that takes care of a secure execution of the code. This implies that the client has to check the small execution environment for correctness once before using it (or the client trusts the execution environment instead).

A feature that distinguishes a mediated system from other mobile code systems is that a mobile code instance does not have one unique producer. Instead, the program part of the mobile code is constructed by the mediator while data parts are supplied by different datasources. That leads to a consideration of the following principals:

- the mediator (as producer of program $p(i)$ and sender)
- the datasources (as suppliers of data $\mathcal{R}_{enc}$)
- the mobile code c
- the program $p(i)$ inside the mobile code
- the data $\mathcal{R}_{enc}$ inside the mobile code (or $\mathcal{R}$ after decryption)
- the client (and her computer)

In the following two subsections we explore in what ways mobile code and the mediator could attack the client and what the execution environment can do to protect the client. In the third subsection, mobile code is considered as the victim of attacks of the client.

4.1   Mobile Code Attacks the Client

The client wants security criteria for her computer to be met. The basic requirements are *confidentiality* (of the data and programs on the computer), *integrity* (of these data and programs) and *availability* (of hard- and software on the computer). That means mobile code should not be able to spy out or corrupt data and programs or monopolize resources on the client computer.

In addition to plain espionage, corruption or monopolization there are three special types of behaviour of mobile code that could potentially lead to one or more of these attacks. Mobile code could

- **conspire with other mobile codes on the client computer:** Single mobile codes may seem harmless; but if several different codes are allowed to communicate on the client computer, they could carry out an attack in combination. As an example, let c_1 be a mobile code that is allowed to read a decryption key (e.g. one to decrypt partial results) but may not use a network connection, and let c_2 be a mobile code that can open a network connection but cannot read any data. It is a case of espionage if now c_1 communicates the decryption key to c_2 and c_2 sends the key via the network connection to another computer.

  As a second example, consider two mobile codes that monopolize the processing unit by permanently alternating calling procedures of one another. This would be a denial of service attack on the availability of the client computer.

- **masquerade as another identity:** If a mobile code succeeds in convincing the client that it represents a trusted identity, it could misuse this trust for starting attacks. A mobile code could pretend to be sent by a trusted mediator although its real sender is an attacker unknown to the client. The client possibly would run such code with less restrictions.

  Mobile code could also masquerade as a part of another program. It could for example simulate belonging to the execution environment by opening a similar looking input dialog; in this dialog the mobile code could for instance ask the user to enter the password that secures a decryption key.

- **download other programs or program parts:** If a mobile code is allowed to receive data via a network connection, it could download additional programs or program parts that eventually attack the client. Young and Yung (cf. [18]) call this a "malware loader".

Literature on mobile code considers the following techniques to protect a client from those attacks (see e.g. [5,8]):

1. **Dynamic Access Control**
2. **Signed** or **Certified Programs** in combination with contracts
3. **Program Checking**; e.g. **Proof-Carrying Code** (see [9])
4. **Sandbox**

Which (or which combination) of these techniques is appropriate for a secure mediated system?

For the client, *proof-carrying code* would possibly be a good solution: She would have to check the proof for correctness before starting the code but would not have any performance loss due to dynamic checks. However, there is the difficulty that the mediator generates the code (e.g. the SQL algebra tree) at runtime and therefore also has to generate the proof at runtime. Since proof generation generally is more complex than proof validation, the client would have to wait quite a long time for the mediator's result.

Nevertheless there would be the following remedy if the code is constructed from modular building blocks – as for example the SQL algebra tree is constructed from only a small number of basic algebraic operators: The mediator could have the proofs for the building blocks ready and just prove that they are combined correctly for the particular query. Unfortunately, automated proof generation is still a field of intensive research; it is so far impossible to generate a proof for an arbitrary program. That is why we have chosen another strategy explained in the following.

As for the mobile Java code, some security-relevant operations have to be performed on client side:

- the secret decryption keys have to be accessed to decrypt the mobile code and the partial results
- a working directory for the mobile code has to be created and the JARs have to be saved there
- the filenames of the JARs have to be added to the system classloader's search path and removed again after execution

- the mobile code has to be started (i.e., system resources like the processing unit or memory have to be assigned to the code)
- the working directory has to be deleted after execution.

If the mobile code carried out all this operations, it probably would need a lot of changing permissions; i.e., *dynamic access control* had to be performed on client side. In our design however, we let the client module do all security-relevant operations and let the mobile code run in a *sandbox*. More precisely the mobile Java code does not need any Java permissions on the client computer; just the client module (as the execution environment) gets a minimal set of permissions to access the decryption keys, save the JARs etc.

The sandbox is a sufficient basis for execution of mobile code in our secure mediated system. However, a more advanced implementation could exploit advantages of dynamically associating different mobile codes to different Java protection domains (and by that assigning code different Java permissions). This would enable the client to give some codes a higher priority or let some codes communicate while others are not allowed to do this. Possibly execution of mobile code could also be based on time-dependent conditions. If the client performs some computations regularly, mobile code could be denied execution at that time to avoid denial of service attacks. Similarly, a context-based condition could take other running mobile codes into consideration and could prevent a conspiracy.

In the sandbox, code is not executed on contract basis, but rather technical protection mechanisms are employed. However, *signing the mobile code* by the mediator (i.e., the code producer) is additionally used to check integrity of the code after transmission to the client.

4.2   Mediator Attacks Client

The mediator takes a central position in a mediation system. It has access to the global query and all credentials in it and constructs the mobile code. It can abuse this positions to attack the *semantic correctness* of the result; i.e., it constructs a program $p(i)$ that computes a wrong global result.

We did not include a countermeasure for this attack in the implementation but we suggest the following adoption of the **proof-carrying code** technique to detect such an attack. While in the original application area (see [9]) the proof states that the code does not harm the client, now the proof attests that the mobile code contains a correct result to the client's query.

Take the SQL algebra tree as an example: The mediator could construct a forged algebra tree by exchanging algebraic operators (e.g. a *join* instead of a *union*). With code carrying a proof of correctness, the mediator has to prove that the algebra tree has been correctly derived from the query. This could be done by a proof that restores the query from the algebra tree.

Apart from that, a more subtle attack is possible: As mentioned before, in a secure mediation system the program $p(i)$ is produced by the mediator and the data $\mathcal{R}_{enc}$ are supplied by several datasources. On client side, $p(i)$ operates on the decrypted data $\mathcal{R}$. The program $p(i)$ could again attack the *semantic correctness* of the global result and also the *integrity* of $\mathcal{R}$ while being executed on the client computer. In the Java implementation e.g., the operator classes inside the mobile code are unknown to the client. They process decrypted partial results $r \in \mathcal{R}$. The mediator could construct operators that compute an incorrect global result by changing values in every r.

The mediator could use traditional proof-carrying code or a certified program to assure the client of the correct execution of $p(i)$.

4.3   Client Attacks Mobile Code

The mobile code producer makes program $p(i)$ available to the client so that she can receive the global result; yet, the code producer may want $p(i)$ to be secured from infringement of *copyright*.

Several approaches have been made to address this problem. Software mechanisms are **obfuscating** (treated theoretically in [3]) and **computing with encrypted functions** (cf. [12]). Copyright protection in these forms is contradictory to program checking approaches used to protect the client from attacks of the mobile code (see Section 4.1); even proof-carrying code has to be processed by the client in clear to deduce a safety predicate. Especially Java byte code is difficult to protect due to the existence of decompilers and code purifiers. To overcome this problem, hardware components could be used in combination with certified programs (or certified proofs) to build a **trusted computing platform** (cf. [17]) but we have not considered this in our implementation.

5   The Trust Model

Our aim was to reduce the necessity for trust to a minimum. Yet, some trust requirements remain. The certification authority (CA) has to be trusted by all other participants (clients, mediators, and datasources) because all of them depend on its impeccable behaviour:

- A datasource has to trust that the CA issues correct and valid credentials such that only eligible clients are able to decrypt its data.
- Similar to the datasources, a mediator has to trust that the CA issues correct and valid credentials such that its mobile code is protected from access by clients other than the eligible one (or from access by the CA itself).
- A client has to trust the CA that it keeps her identity a secret.

Additionally, as long as copyright protection (as described in Section 4.3) is not put into practice, the mediator has to trust the client, that she does not use the mobile code in other ways than the mediator intended her to do (e.g., that the client follows a licence that accompanies the mobile code).

Equivalently, a datasource has to trust the client that she does not pass data on to other, non-eligible participants. However, a datasource does not need to trust a mediator; a mediator cannot attack the confidentiality of partial results if an appropriate encryption is used.

The main point is that the client has to trust the datasources (as suppliers of data) and the mediator (as producer of program code) just as far as *semantic correctness* of the global result is concerned because the execution environment protects her computer from other attacks (see Section 4.1). So, there remain two possibilities of attacks on the correctness of the global result: The data inside the mobile code might be semantically wrong (i.e., the client has to trust that the datasources supplied correct information; however, this is the same with any traditional database query), or the mediator might construct a mobile code that computes an incorrect global result (see Section 4.2; however, in basic ("unsecure") mediation the mediator could also corrupt the data supplied by the datasources).

6   Hierarchy of Mediators

As an extension to our system, we considered a hierarchy of mediators. The client still sends her query to one mediator, but mediators are able to forward partial queries to other mediators. This technique offers increased flexibility and scalability: Specialization of mediators to certain topics is possible; a mediator can also decide whether it forwards partial queries to more specialized mediators or just gathers partial results from its own datasources. In a hierarchy of mediators the mobile code is built by different code producers: Each mediator constructs a partial code containing its own program part, encrypted partial results and possibly other partial codes.

Since the execution environment protects the client from attacks (except the semantic ones) by mobile code of a single mediator, mobile code of a hierarchy of mediators does not mean an increased risk to the client. However, signature checking becomes complex when each partial code has been signed by a different producer; likewise a safety proof for proof-carrying code has to be combined from several partial proofs.

With a mobile code composed of different partial codes, not only attacks on the integrity of the data $\mathcal{R}$ are possible (see Section 4.2), similarly the *integrity of execution* of a partial code could be endangered by other partial codes. This problem is e.g. inherent to the Java classloading mechanism: In the JARs brought along with the mobile code, overwriting of class definitions can occur. A class is loaded from the JAR that is searched first; if a second JAR contains a class with the same class name, this second class definition is ignored. In our Java implementation, JARs are scanned for duplicate class definitions.

7   Conclusion

With the adoption of mobile code for secure mediation we are able to transmit data from datasources to a client in encrypted form; the mediator does not process any clear-text data. That ensures confidentiality of the data and reduces the necessity for trust in the mediator. Our mobile code system is easily extensible and its execution environment is small.

Optimizing runtime performance was not in the main focus of this work. In comparison to basic ("unsecure") mediation, in our secure mediated system performance penalties occur mainly due to encryption on datasource side, mobile code generation (and again encryption) on mediator side and decryption and mobile code execution on client side. Due to a lack of time, runtime performance has not been investigated systematically. Nevertheless, test runs performed in an acceptable amount of time. One possibility of reducing both encryption time and execution time would be to improve the SQL2Algebra-library that generates the algebra trees on mediator side; algorithms that minimize the size of partial results and the depth of the tree could be included.

Our mediation system with mobile code could be combined with existing mobile agent systems (see e.g. [10,7]) to profit from both technologies: The client directs her query to a mediator; the mediator constructs an agent to collect the partial results from the datasources. This reduces communication overhead between mediator and datasources. Wrapping functions could be carried out by such an agent as well to convert partial results into a homogeneous format. The client, however, is not charged with agent creation, agent management etc., since the mediator takes care of all agent-related actions. Security considerations for mobile agent systems have been investigated profoundly (see e.g. [1,6]).

References

1. Joy Algesheimer, Christian Cachin, Jan Camenisch, and Günther Karjoth. Cryptographic security for mobile code. In *SP '01: Proceedings of the IEEE Symposium on Security and Privacy 2001*, pages 2–11. IEEE Computer Society, 2001.
2. Christian Altenschmidt, Joachim Biskup, Ulrich Flegel, and Yücel Karabulut. Secure mediation: Requirements, design and architecture. *Journal of Computer Security*, 11(3):365–398, June 2003.
3. Boaz Barak, Oded Goldreich, Rusell Impagliazzo, Steven Rudich, Amit Sahai, Salil Vadhan, and Ke Yang. *On the (Im)possibility of Obfuscating Programs*, volume 2139 of *Lecture Notes in Computer Science*, pages 1–19. Springer, Berlin, 2001.
4. The Legion of the Bouncy Castle. http://www.bouncycastle.org/.
5. Philip W.L. Fong. *Proof Linking: A Modular Verification Architecture for Mobile Code Systems*. Phd thesis, Simon Fraser University, Burnaby, Canada, January 2004. See http://www.cs.sfu.ca/research/publications/theses/.
6. Günther Karjoth, Nadarajah Asokan, and Ceki Gülcü. *Protecting the Computation Results of Free-Roaming Agents*, volume 1477 of *Lecture Notes in Computer Science*, pages 195–207. Springer, Berlin, 1998.
7. Günther Karjoth, Danny B. Lange, and Mitsuru Oshima. *A Security Model for Aglets*, volume 1419 of *Lecture Notes in Computer Science*, pages 188–205. Springer, Berlin, 1998.
8. Sergio Loureiro, Refik Molva, and Yves Roudier. Mobile code security. In *Proceedings of ISYPAR'2000 (4ème Ecole d'Informatique des Systèmes Parallèles et Répartis)*, pages 95–103, Toulouse, France, 2000.
9. George C. Necula and Peter Lee. *Safe, Untrusted Agents Using Proof-Carrying Code*, volume 1419 of *Lecture Notes in Computer Science*, pages 61–91. Springer, Berlin, 1998.

10. Holger Peine. *Run-Time Support for Mobile Code*. Dissertation, Universität Kaiserslautern, Fachbereich Informatik, October 2002.

11. Ron L. Rivest, Leonard Adleman, and Michael L. Dertouzos. On data banks and privacy homomorphisms. *Foundations of Secure Computation*, pages 169–179, 1978.

12. Tomas Sander and Christian F. Tschudin. *Protecting Mobile Agents Against Malicious Hosts*, volume 1419 of *Lecture Notes in Computer Science*, pages 44–60. Springer, Berlin, 1998.

13. Gio Wiederhold. Mediators in the architecture of future information systems. *IEEE Computer*, 25(3):38–49, 1992.

14. Gio Wiederhold and Michael Genesereth. The conceptual basis for mediation services. *IEEE Expert Intelligent Systems and their Applications*, 12(5):38–47, September/October 1997.

15. Lena Wiese. Mediator with mobile code support. `http://ls6-www.cs.uni-dortmund.de/issi/projects/DFG_Kompositionalitaet/mobilecode.html.en`.

16. Lena Wiese. *Sichere Mediation mit mobilem Code – Implementierung und Sicherheitsanalyse*. Diploma thesis (in German), Universität Dortmund, Dortmund, Germany, October 2004. See `http://ls6-www.cs.uni-dortmund.de/issi/archive/literature/2004/Wiese_2004.pdf`.

17. Bennet Yee and J. D. Tygar. Secure coprocessors in electronic commerce applications. In *Proceedings of the First USENIX Workshop of Electronic Commerce*, pages 155–170, Berkeley, CA, USA, 1995. USENIX Assoc.

18. Adam Young and Moti Yung. *Malicious Cryptography – Exposing Cryptovirology*. Wiley, Indianapolis, Ind., 2004.

Security Vulnerabilities in Software Systems: A Quantitative Perspective

Omar Alhazmi, Yashwant Malaiya, and Indrajit Ray

Department of Computer Science, Colorado State University, Fort Collins, CO 80523, USA
{omar, malaiya, indrajit}@cs.colostate.edu

Abstract. Security and reliability are important attributes of complex software systems. It is now common to use quantitative methods for evaluating and managing reliability. In this work we examine the feasibility of quantitatively characterizing some aspects of security.In particular, we investigate if it is possible to predict the number of vulnerabilities that can potentially be identified in a future release of a software system. We use several major operating systems as representatives of complex software systems. The data on vulnerabilities discovered in some of the popular operating systems is analyzed. We examine this data to determine if the density of vulnerabilities in a program is a useful measure. We try to identify what fraction of software defects are security related, i.e., are vulnerabilities. We examine the dynamics of vulnerability discovery hypothesizing that it may lead us to an estimate of the magnitude of the undiscovered vulnerabilities still present in the system. We consider the vulnerability-discovery rate to see if models can be developed to project future trends. Finally, we use the data for both commercial and open-source systems to determine whether the key observations are generally applicable. Our results indicate that the values of vulnerability densities fall within a range of values, just like the commonly used measure of defect density for general defects. Our examination also reveals that vulnerability discovery may be influenced by several factors including sharing of codes between successive versions of a software system.

1 Introduction

Reliance on networked systems has brought the security of software systems under considerable scrutiny. Much of the work on security has been qualitative, focused on detection and prevention of vulnerabilities in these systems. There is a need to develop a perspective on the problem so that methods can be developed to allow risks to be evaluated quantitatively. Quantitative methods can permit resource allocation for achieving a desired security level, as it is done for software or system reliability. Thus far, only limited attention has been paid to the quantitative aspects of security. To develop quantitative methods for characterizing and managing security, we need to identify metrics that can be evaluated in practice and have a clearly defined interpretation. In this work we examine the problem of quantifying vulnerabilities in a complex software system. Security vulnerabilities are " defect(s) which enables an attacker to bypass security measures" [1]. Malicious attackers seek to identify and exploit system vulnerabilities to cause security breaches. Reducing the number of vulnerabilities in a system is thus of utmost importance.

S. Jajodia and D. Wijesekera (Eds.): Data and Applications Security 2005, LNCS 3654, pp. 281–294, 2005.

Quantitative methods for general defects are now widely used to evaluate and manage overall software reliability. Since software system vulnerabilities – the faults associated with maintaining security requirements – can be considered a special case of software defect, a similar measure for estimating security vulnerabilities appears long overdue. In this paper, we quantitatively examine the number of vulnerabilities in several popular operating systems. Such quantitative characterization of vulnerabilities can be used to evaluate metrics that can guide the allocation of resources for security testing, development of security patches and scheduling their releases. It can also be used by end-users to assess risks and estimate the needed redundancy in resources and procedures for handling potential security breaches.

It is not possible to guarantee absence of defects in non-trivial sized programs like operating systems. While extensive testing can isolate a large fraction of the defects, it is impossible to eliminate them. This is because the effort needed to discover residual defects increases exponentially [2]. Nonetheless, examination of defect densities (that is the number of defects identified in the unit size of the software code) is still useful. It can lead to the identification of fault-prone modules that need special attention. Researchers have evaluated the ranges of defect densities typically encountered during different phases of the software life cycle using data from available sources [3]. This has led to industry wide standards for software defect densities. The information can be used for comparison with the defect density measured in a project at a specific phase. The result can identify if there is a need for further testing or process improvement. Similar methods for managing the security aspects of systems by considering their vulnerabilities, can potentially reduce the risk of adopting new software systems. Researchers in software reliability engineering have analyzed software defect finding rates. Software reliability growth models relate the number of defects found to the testing time [2,3,4]. Methods have been developed to project the mean time to failure (MTTF) or the failure rate that will occur after a specific period of testing . Software defect density [5,6,7] has been a widely used metric to measure the quality of a program and is often used as a release criterion for a software project. Very little quantitative work has been done to characterize security vulnerabilities along the same lines.

Security can be characterized by several possible metrics. Littlewood et al. [8,9] discuss some possible metrics to measure security based on dependability and reliability perspectives. They propose using effort rather than time to characterize the accumulation of vulnerabilities; however, they do not specify how to assess effort. An analysis of exploits for some specific vulnerabilities has been considered by Arbaugh [10] and Browne [11]. The security intrusion process has also been examined by Johnson and Olovsson [12] and Madan et al. [13]. Other researchers have focused on modeling and designing tools that make some security assessment possible [1]. Only a few studies have examined the number of vulnerabilities and their discovery rates. Rescorla [14] has examined vulnerability discovery rates to determine the impact of vulnerability disclosures. Anderson [15] has proposed a model for a vulnerability-finding rate using a thermodynamics analogy. Alhazmi and Malaiya [16] have presented two models for the process of vulnerabilities discovery using data for Windows 98 and NT 4.0. In the current work we focus on the density of defects in software that constitute vulnerabilities, using data from five versions of Windows and two versions of Red Hat Linux.

Vulnerability density is analogous to defect density. Vulnerability density may enable us to compare the maturity of the software and understand risks associated with its residual undiscovered vulnerabilities. We can presume that for systems that have been in deployment for a sufficient time, the vulnerabilities that have been discovered represent a major fraction of all vulnerabilities initially present. For relatively new systems, we would like to estimate the number of remaining vulnerabilities. This requires development and validation of appropriate vulnerability discovery models. Ounce Labs uses a metric termed V-density [17] which appears to be somewhat related. However, their definition and evaluation approach is proprietary and is thus not very useful to the general community. Unlike the data for general defects in a commercial operating system, which are usually hard to obtain, the actual data about known vulnerabilities found in major operating systems are available for analysis. We analyze this data to address a major question: *Do we observe any similarity in behavior for vulnerability discovery rates for various systems so that we can develop suitable models?*

We examine several software systems, which we group into related families after determining the cumulative number of their vulnerabilities. One of our objectives is to identify possible reasons for the changes in the vulnerability detection trends. One major difference makes interpreting the vulnerability discovery rate more difficult than the discovery rate of general defects in programs during testing. Throughout its lifetime after its release, an application program encounters changes in its usage environment. When a new version of a software is released, its installed base starts to grow. As the newer version of the software grows, the number of installations of the older version starts to decline. The extent of vulnerability finding effort by both "white hat" and "black hat" individuals is influenced by the number of installations; this is because the larger the installed base the more is the reward for the effort. Thus, the rates at which the vulnerabilities are discovered are influenced by this variation in usage.

The rest of the paper is organized as follows. In section 2 we introduce the major terms we use in this work. We analyze, in section 3, the data for some of the Windows operating systems to evaluate the densities of vulnerabilities that are known. We talk about the remaining vulnerabilities (yet to be discovered) in section 3.1. In section 3.2 we present a model for the vulnerability discovery process. We then examine in section 4 the applicability of our major observations for two version of Linux, an open-source operating system. Finally, we conclude the paper in section 5 by identifying future research that is needed.

2   Measuring Systems' Vulnerability Density

We begin by introducing a new metric, vulnerability density, that describes one of the major aspects of security. Vulnerability density is a normalized measure, given by the number of vulnerabilities per unit of code size. Vulnerability density can be used to compare software systems within the same category (e.g., operating systems, webservers, etc.). To measure the code size we have two options. First, we can use the size of the installed system in bytes; the advantage of this measure is that information is readily available. However, this measure will vary from one installation to another. The second measure is the number of source lines of code. Here, we chose this measure for its simplicity and its correspondence to defect density metric in the software engineering domain. Let us now present a definition of vulnerability density (VD):

Definition 1. *Vulnerability density is the number of vulnerabilities in the unit size of a code. It is given by*

$$V_d = \frac{V}{S} \tag{1}$$

where S is the size of the software and V is the number of vulnerabilities in the system.

Following the common practice in software engineering, we consider one thousand source lines as the unit code size. When two systems, one large and one small, have the same defect density, they can be regarded as having similar maturity with respect to dependability. In the same manner, vulnerability density allows us to compare the quality of programming in terms of how secure the code is. If the instruction execution rates and other system attributes are the same, a system with a higher defect or vulnerability density is likely to be compromised more often. Estimating the exact vulnerability density would require us to know the number of all the vulnerabilities of the system. Consequently, we define another measure in terms of the known vulnerabilities.

Definition 2. *The known vulnerability density is the number of known vulnerabilities in the unit size of a code. The known vulnerability density is given by*

$$V_{kd} = \frac{V_k}{S} \tag{2}$$

where is the number of known vulnerabilities in the system.

It is the residual vulnerability density (VRD) given by

$$V_{rd} = V_d - V_{kd} \tag{3}$$

that (depending on vulnerabilities not yet discovered) contributes to the risk of potential exploitation. Other aspects of the risk of exploitation include the time gap between the discovery of a vulnerability and the release and application of a patch. In this study we focus on vulnerabilities and their discovery. Recently there have been a number of comparisons between several attributes of open-source and commercial software [7,15]. This is not, however, the focus of this paper. Rather, we want to probe the suitability of vulnerability density and vulnerability as metrics that can be used to assess and manage components of the security risk.

3   The Windows Family of Operating Systems

Table 1 presents values of the known defect density D_{KD} and known vulnerability density V_{KD} based on data from several sources [18,19,20,21] as of January 2005. Windows 95, 98 and XP are three successive versions of the popular Windows client operating system. We also include Windows NT and Windows 2000, which are successive versions of the Windows server operating systems. The known defect density values for Windows 95 and Windows 98 client operating systems are 0.33 and 0.55 per thousand

Table 1. Vulnerability density vs. defect density measured for some software systems

Systems	Msloc	Known Defects	Known Defect Density (per Ksloc)	Known Vulnera-bilities	V_{KD} (per Ksloc)	V_{KD} / D_{KD} Ratio (%)	Release Date
Windows 95	15	5	0.3333	50	.0033	1.00%	Aug 1995
Windows 98	18	10	0.5556	66	.0037	0.66%	Jun 1998
Windows XP	40	106.5	2.6625	88	.0022	0.08%	Oct 2001
Windows NT 4.0	16	10	0.625	179	.0112	1.79%	Jul 1996
Windows 2000	35	63	1.80	170	.0049	0.27%	Feb 2000

lines of code, respectively. The higher defect density for Windows XP is due to the fact the data available is for the beta version. We can expect that the release version had significantly fewer defects. The defect density values for Windows NT and 2000 are 0.6 and 1.8, respectively. The Known Vulnerabilities column gives a recent count of the vulnerabilities found since the release date. We note that the vulnerability densities of Win 95 and 98 are quite close. The known vulnerability density for Win XP is 0.0020, much lower than the values for the two previous Windows versions. This is due to the fact that at this time V_{KD} represents only a fraction of the overall VD. We can expect the number to go up significantly, perhaps to a value more comparable to the two previous versions. We notice that the vulnerability density for Windows NT 4.0 is about three times that of Win 95 or Win 98. There are two possible reasons for this. Since NT is a server, a larger fraction of its code involved external access, resulting in about three times the number of vulnerabilities. In addition, as a server operating system, it must have gone through more thorough testing, resulting in the discovery of more vulnerabilities. Windows 2000 also demonstrates nearly as many vulnerabilities as NT, although due to its larger size, the vulnerability density is lower than that of NT.

One significant ratio to examine is, which gives the fraction of defects that are vulnerabilities. McGraw [19] hypothetically assumed that vulnerabilities might represent 5% of the total defects. Anderson assumed a value of 1% in [15]. Our results show that the values of the ratio are 1.00% and 0.66% for Win95 and Win98. For Windows XP, the number of known defects is given for the beta version, and is therefore higher than the actual number at release. In addition, since it was released last, smaller fractions of XP vulnerabilities have thus far been found. This explains why the ratio of 0.083% for XP is significantly lower. We believe that this should not be used in a comparison with other Windows versions. It is interesting to note that the ratio of 1% assumed by Anderson is within the range of values in Table 1. Windows 2000 was an update of NT, with a significant amount of code added, much of which did not deal with external access; thus accounting for its relatively low ratio. In systems that have been in use for a sufficient time, VKD is probably close to VD. However, for newer systems we can expect that a significant number of vulnerabilities will be found in the near future. For a complete picture, we need to understand the process that governs the discovery of the remaining vulnerabilities, as discussed in the next sub-section.

3.1 An Examination of the Remaining Vulnerabilities

We now examine the rate at which vulnerabilities were reported in the five operating systems, as shown in Figures 1-3. Some specific vulnerabilities are shared by successive versions of the system. Such shared vulnerabilities are shown using a separate plot. The data show that some vulnerabilities were reported even before the general release date of a particular version. For consistency, we omit vulnerabilities encountered before the release date of a particular version. Figure 1 gives the cumulative vulnerabilities for Windows 95 and 98 [18]. At the beginning, the curve for Windows 95 showed slow growth until about March 1998, after which it showed some saturation for several months. Windows 98 also showed relatively slow growth until about June 1998. After that, both Windows 95 and Windows 98 showed a faster rate of growth. The similarity of the plots in the later phase suggests that Windows 98 and Windows 95 shared a significant fraction of the code. The installed base of Windows 98 peaked during 1999-2000 [16]. At some time after this, the discovery rates of vulnerabilities in both versions slowed down.

The saturation is more apparent in Windows 95. Based on our observation of shared vulnerabilities, we believe that many of the Windows 95 vulnerabilities discovered later were actually detected in the Windows 98 release. The cumulative vulnerabilities in Windows 95 and Windows 98 appear to have reached a plateau. Some vulnerabilities in Windows 98 were discovered rather late. This is explained by the code shared between the 98 and XP versions, as discussed next. Figure 2 gives the cumulative vulnerabilities in Windows 98 and XP [18]. It demonstrates that Windows XP showed swift growth in vulnerabilities with respect to its release date. There were also many vulnerabilities shared with Windows 98. However, XP has its own unique vulnerabilities, and they

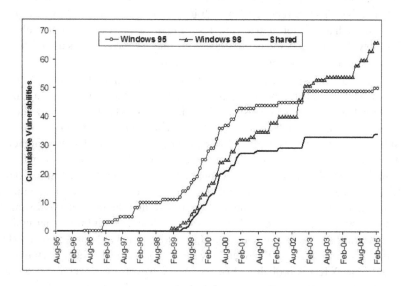

Fig. 1. Cumulative vulnerabilities in Windows 95 and Windows 98

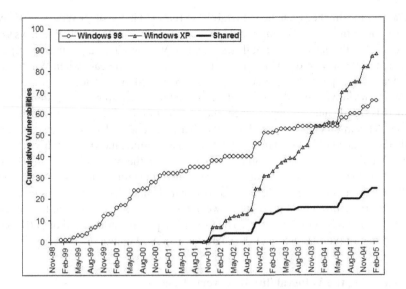

Fig. 2. Cumulative vulnerabilities in Windows 98 and its successor Windows XP

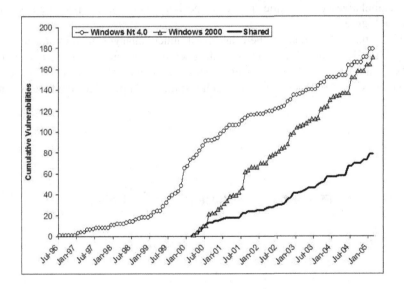

Fig. 3. Cumulative vulnerabilities of Windows NT and Windows 2000

form the majority. Windows XP shows practically no learning phase; rather, the plot shows a linear accumulation of vulnerabilities. The slope is significantly sharper than for Windows 98. The sharpness of the curve for XP is explained by its fast adoption rate [16], making finding vulnerabilities in XP more rewarding. Windows 98 has showed a longer learning phase followed by a linear accumulation, later followed by saturation.

The relationship between the vulnerabilities reported in the older Windows 95, Windows 98 and Windows XP is important. As we can observe in Figure 1, Windows 98 inherited most of the earlier vulnerabilities found in Windows 95. Vulnerabilities reported for Windows 98 slowed down at some point, only to pick up again when Windows XP was released. It appears that Windows XP has contributed to the detection of most of the later Windows 98 vulnerabilities. The data for the three operating systems demonstrates that there is significant interdependence among vulnerability discovery rates for the three versions. This interdependence is due to the sharing of codes. The shifting shares of the installed base need to be taken into account when examining the vulnerability discovery trends. Windows 98 represents a middle stage between the other two versions from the perspective of vulnerability detection. Figure 3 shows the vulnerabilities in Windows NT and 2000; the shared vulnerabilities are also shown. Unlike the two previous figures, we do not observe a prominent time-lag between the two. The reason is that both of them gained installed base gradually [16]. The use of NT peaked around end of 2001, but its share did not drop dramatically as the share for Win2000 grew.

3.2 Modeling the Vulnerability Discovery Process

From the data plotted in the figures above, we can see a common pattern of three phases in the cumulative vulnerabilities plot of a specific version of an operating system, as shown in Figure 4.

During these three phases, the usage environment changes, thereby impacting the vulnerability detection effort. In Phase 1, the operating system starts attracting attention and users start switching to it. The software testers (including hackers and crackers) begin to understand the target system and gather sufficient knowledge about the system to

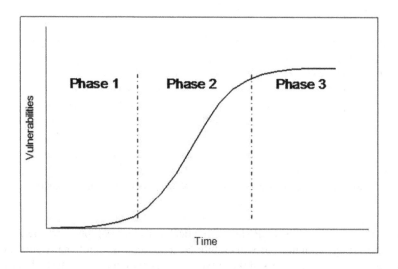

Fig. 4. The 3-phases of the vulnerability discovery process

break into it successfully. In Phase 2, the acceptance of the new system starts gathering momentum. It continues to increase until the operating system reaches the peak of its popularity. This is the period during which discovering its vulnerabilities will be most rewarding for both white hat and black hat finders. After a while, in Phase 3, the system starts to be replaced by a newer release. The vulnerability detection effort will then start shifting to the new version. The technical support for that version and hence the frequency of update patches will then begin to decline. This s-shaped behavior shown in Figure 4 can be described by a time-based model introduced earlier by Alhazmi and Malaiya [16]. Let y be the cumulative number of vulnerabilities. We assume that the vulnerability discovery rate is controlled by two factors. The first of these is due to the momentum gained by the market acceptance of the product; this is given by a factor Ay, where A is a constant of proportionality. The second factor is saturation due to a finite number of vulnerabilities and is proportional to (B - y), where B is the total number of vulnerabilities. The vulnerability discovery rate is then given by the following differential equation,

$$\frac{dy}{dt} = Ay(B - y) \tag{4}$$

where t is the calendar time. By solving the differential equation we obtain

$$y = \frac{B}{BCe^{-ABt} + 1} \tag{5}$$

where C is a constant introduced while solving Equation 4. It is thus a three-parameter model. In Equation 5, as t approaches infinity, y approaches B, as the model assumes. The constants A, B and C need to be determined empirically using the recorded data. An alternative effort-based model [16], which also fits well but requires extensive usage data collection was recently proposed by the authors. A time-based model was derived by Anderson [15]; however, its applicability to actual data has not yet been studied.

Figures 5 and 6 give the data for Windows 95 and NT 4.0 with a fitted plot according to the model given in Equation 5. The numerically obtained model parameters are given in Table 2. We have used chi-squared goodness of fit test to evaluate the applicability of the model. The fit is found be statistically significant, as indicated by a chi-squared value less than the critical value at the 95% significance level. A similar analysis for Windows 98, XP and 2000 also demonstrate a good fit of the model to the data.

Table 2. χ^2 goodness of fit test results

Systems	A	B	C	χ^2	$\chi^2_{critical}$ (5%)	P-value
Windows 95	0.001938	49.5	1.170154	40.72	119.87	0.9999998
Windows 98	0.001049031	66	0.140462	64.79	96.2	0.742
Windows XP	0.001391	88	0.190847	25.75	56.94	0.961
Windows NT 4.0	0.000584	153.62	0.47	82.3942	127.69	0.923
Windows 2000	0.000528	163.96	0.073187	60.91	80.23	0.444

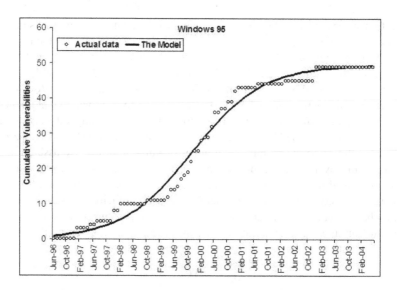

Fig. 5. Windows 95 data fitted to the model

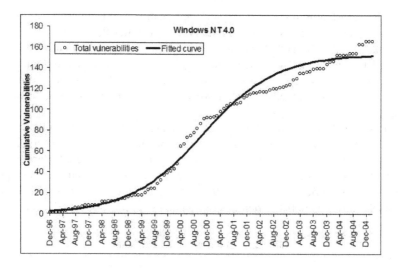

Fig. 6. Windows NT 4.0 data fitted to the model

4   Linux Operating System

We examine two versions of Red Hat Linux, versions 6.2 and 7.1, shown in Figure 7. In both, we observe saturation in the later period. We note that in the later duration, a majority of the vulnerabilities discovered in version 6.2 are in fact shared.

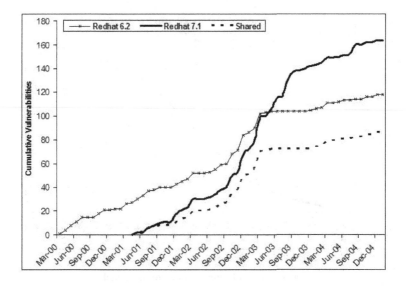

Fig. 7. Cumulative vulnerabilities of Red Hat Linux version 6.2 and 7.1

Table 3. Vulnerability density vs. defect density measured for Red Hat Linux 6.2 and 7.1

Systems	Msloc	Known Defects	Known Defect Density (per Ksloc)	Known Vulnera-bilities	V_{KD} (per Ksloc)	$V_{KD}/$ D_{KD} Ratio (%)	Release Date
R H Linux 6.2	17	2096	0.12329	118	.00694	5.63%	Mar 2000
R H Linux 7.1	30	3779	0.12597	164	.00547	4.34%	Apr 2001

In Table 3 [22,23], we observe that although the code size for Linux 7.1 is twice as big as Linux 6.2, the defect density and vulnerability density values are remarkably similar. We note that the VKD values for the two versions of Red Hat Linux are significantly higher than for Windows 95 and 98, and are approximately in the same range as for Windows 2000. However, VKD alone should not be used to compare of the two competing operating system families. It is not the discovered vulnerabilities but rather the vulnerabilities remaining undiscovered that form a significant component of the risk. In addition, the exploitation patterns and the timing of the patch releases also impact the risk. The VKD value for Red Hat Linux 7.1 can be expected to rise significantly in near future, just as those of Windows XP. It is interesting to note that ratio values for Linux are close to the value of 5% postulated by McGraw [19].

Figure 8 presents the raw data for 7.1, together with the fitted model. The model parameter values and the results of the chi-squared test are given in Table 4. Again, the application of the chi-squared test shows that the fit is significant.

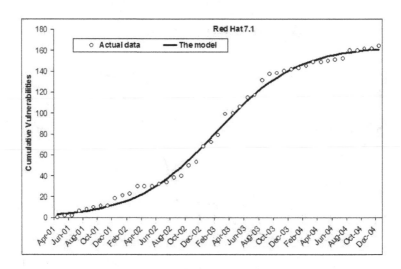

Fig. 8. Red Hat Linux 7.1 fitted to the model

Table 4. χ^2 goodness of fit test results

Systems	A	B	C	χ^2	$\chi^2_{critical}$ (5%)	P-value
Red Hat Linux 6.2	0.000829	123.9393	0.129678	34.62	76.78	0.999974
Red Hat Linux 7.1	0.001106	163.9996	0.379986	27.62715	61.65623	0.989

While the model of Equation 5 fits the data for all the operating systems examined here, some aspects of the process need further examination. There is often a significant overlap between two successive operating systems. The attention received by a version, n, results in detection of vulnerabilities not only in version n but also in the code shared between versions n and (n-1). This, in turn, results in a bump-up in the version (n-1) discovery rate, even though its installed base may be shrinking rapidly. This overlap causes some deviation for the model. Techniques need to be developed for modeling this overlap in order to achieve higher accuracy. We would like to be able to project the expected number of vulnerabilities that will be found during the major part of the lifetime of a release, using early data and a model like the one given in Equation 5. This would require an understanding of the three parameters involved and developing methods for robust estimation.

5 Conclusions

In this paper, we have explored the applicability of quantitative metrics describing vulnerabilities and the process that governs their discovery. We have examined the data for five of the most widely used operating systems, including three successive version of

Windows and two versions of Red Hat Linux. We have evaluated the known vulnerability densities in the five operating systems. The lower value for Win XP relative to Win 95 and 98 is attributable to the fact that a significant fraction of Win XP vulnerabilities have not yet been discovered. As has been observed for software defect densities, the values of vulnerability densities fall within a range, and for similar products they are closer together. We note that the ratio of vulnerabilities to the total number of defects is often in the range of 1% to 5%, as was speculated to be the case by some researchers. As we would expect, this ratio is often higher for operating systems intended to be servers. The results indicate that vulnerability density is a significant and useful metric. We can expect to gain further insight into vulnerability densities when additional data, together with suitable quantitative models, are available. Such models may allow empirical estimation of vulnerability densities along the lines of similar models for software cost estimation or software defect density estimation.

This paper has presented plots showing the cumulative number of vulnerabilities for the five operating systems. The vulnerabilities shared by successive versions are also given. These plots are analogous to reliability growth plots in software reliability. However, there are some significant differences. The initial growth rate at the release time is small but subsequently accelerates. Generally the plots show a linear trend for a significant period. These plots tend to show some saturation, often followed by abrupt increases later. This behavior is explained by the variability of the effort that goes into discovering the vulnerabilities. The model given by Equation 5 is fitted to vulnerability data for the seven operating systems and the fit is found to be statistically significant. We also observe that the code shared by a new and hence a competing version of the operating system can impact the vulnerability discovery rate in a previous version. Further research is needed to model the impact of the shared code. We expect that with further research and significant data collection and analysis, it will be possible to develop reliable quantitative methods for security akin to those used in the software and hardware reliability fields.

References

1. E. E. Schultz Jr., D. S. Brown and T. A. Longstaff, "Responding to Computer Security Incidents," Lawrence Livermore National Laboratory, ftp://ftp.cert.dfn.de/pub/docs/csir/ihg.ps.gz, July 23, 1990.
2. M. R. Lyu, editor., Handbook of Software Reliability Engineering, McGraw-Hill, 1995.
3. J. D. Musa, A. Ianino, K. Okumuto, Software Reliability Measurement Prediction Application, McGraw-Hill, 1987.
4. Y. K. Malaiya and J. Denton, "What Do the Software Reliability Growth Model Parameters Represent?" Proceedings IEEE International Symposium on Software Reliability Engineering, 1997, pp. 124-135.
5. Y. K. Malaiya and J. Denton, "Module Size Distribution and Defect Density," Proceedings IEEE International Symposium on Software Reliability Engineering, Oct. 2000, pp. 62-71.
6. P. Mohagheghi, R. Conradi, O.M. Killi and H. Schwarz, "An Empirical Study of Software Reuse vs. Defect-Density," Proceedings 26th International Conference on Software Engineering, 2004, May 2004, pp. 282-291.

7. A. Mockus, R.T. Fielding, and J. Herbsleb, "Two Case Studies of Open Source Software Development: Apache and Mozilla," ACM Transactions Software Engineering and Methodology, 11(3), 2002, pp. 309-346.

8. B. Littlewood, S. Brocklehurst, N. Fenton, P. Mellor, S. Page, D. Wright, "Towards Operational Measures of Computer Security," Journal of Computer Security, V. 2 (2/3), 1993, pp. 211-230.

9. S. Brocklehurst, B. Littlewood, T. Olovsson and E. Jonsson, "On Measurement of Operational Security," Proceedings of 9th Annual IEEE Conference on Computer Assurance, Gaithersburg, IEEE Computer Society, 1994, pp. 257-66.

10. W. A. Arbaugh, W. L. Fithen, J. McHugh, "Windows of Vulnerability: A Case Study Analysis," IEEE Computer, Vol. 33, No. 12, December 2000, pp. 52-59.

11. H. K. Browne, W. A. Arbaugh, J. McHugh, W.L. Fithen, "A Trend Analysis of Exploitation," Proceedings of IEEE Symposium on Security and Privacy, 2001, May 2001, pp. 214-229.

12. E. Jonsson, T. Olovsson, "A Quantitative Model of the Security Intrusion Process Based on Attacker Behavior," IEEE Transactions on Software Engineering, April 1997, pp. 235-245.

13. B.B.Madan, K.Goseva-Popstojanova, K.Vaidyanathan, K.S.Trivedi, "Modeling and Quantification of Security Attributes of Software Systems," Proceedings of IEEE International Performance and Dependability Symposium (IPDS 2002), June 2002.

14. Eric Rescorla, "Is Finding Security Holes a Good Idea?", Proceedings Third Annual Workshop on Economics and Information Security (WEIS04), May 2004, pp. 1-18, http://www.dtc.umn.edu/weis2004/rescorla.pdf

15. Ross Anderson, "Security in Open versus Closed Systems – The Dance of Boltzmann, Coase and Moore," Conf. on Open Source Software: Economics, Law and Policy, Toulouse, France, June 2002, pp. 1-15, http://www.ftp.cl.cam.ac.uk/ftp/users/rja14/toulouse.pdf

16. O. H. Alhazmi, Y. K. Malaiya, "Quantitative Vulnerability Assessment of Systems Software," Proceedings of International Symposium on Product Quality and Integrity (RAMS 2005), January 2005, pp. 14D3.1-6.

17. Ounce Labs, "Security by the Numbers: The Need for Metrics in Application Security," http://www.ouncelabs.com/library.asp, 2004.

18. ICAT Metabase, http://icat.nist.gov/icat.cfm, February 2004.

19. G. McGraw, "From the Ground Up: The DIMACS Software Security Workshop," IEEE Security and Privacy, March/April 2003. Volume 1, Number 2, pp. 59-66.

20. P. Rodrigues, "Windows XP Beta 02. Only 106,500 Bugs," http://www.lowendmac.com/tf/010401pf.html, Aug 2001.

21. O.S. Data, Windows 98, http://www.osdata.com/oses/win98.htm, March 2004.

22. The MITRE Corporation, http://www.mitre.org, February 2005.

23. Red Hat Bugzilla, https://bugzilla.redhat.com/bugzilla, January 2005.

Trading Off Security in a Service Oriented Architecture

G. Swart[*], Benjamin Aziz[†], Simon N. Foley[‡], and John Herbert[‡]

[*] IBM Almaden Research Center, 650 Harry Road, San Jose, CA, USA
gswart@us.ibm.com
[†] Department of Computing, Imperial College, London SW7 2AZ, UK
baziz@doc.ic.ac.uk
[‡] Department of Computer Science, University College Cork, Cork, Ireland
{sfoley, herbert}@cs.ucc.ie

Abstract. Service oriented architectures provide a simple yet flexible model of a computing system as a graph of services making requests and providing results to each other. In this paper we define a formal model of a service oriented architecture and using it, we define metrics for performance, for availability, and for various security properties. These metrics serve as the basis for expressing the business requirements. To make trade-offs possible we also define a set of cost metrics, denominated in a uniform currency, to measure the cost of not meeting a requirement. The model, the property metrics, and the cost metrics are then used to generate a Constraint Satisfaction Problem where the objective function is set to minimize the aggregate system cost. We have written these constraints and defined realistic requirements in OPL and we have used them to generate system configurations that minimize the overall cost by optimally trading off the business requirements.

Computing systems are designed to meet the security, performance availability, and economic requirements of the procurer. Sometimes not all of these requirements are simultaneously attainable to the maximum degree. In order to get as close as possible to meeting the requirements, trade-offs must sometimes be made between the individual requirements. In order to make these trade-offs in a sensible way and to find a system configuration that best meets our overall goals, we need a model of a system which can be evaluated quickly to determine how well the system is meeting its requirements and a uniform cost model that we can use to manage the trade-offs on the different requirements.

In this paper we use formal techniques to define a precise model of a service oriented architecture, a flexible yet simple computing model that underlies the Web Service standards so popular in data processing and integration applications. We argue that this model is close enough to the reality of such systems to be interesting. We then formally define various properties of the model that correspond to important properties in real systems. The properties that we define and optimize for are different aspects of data security, server throughput, service availability and network bandwidth. We do not claim that these are the

S. Jajodia and D. Wijesekera (Eds.): Data and Applications Security 2005, LNCS 3654, pp. 295–309, 2005.

only formal definitions of these properties that are sensible but that the ones we present are interesting and they capture important aspects of the system.

We then encode this model and properties into an Optimization Programming Language (OPL) application so that a combination of mathematical and constraint programming techniques that are part of the OPL implementation can be brought to bear on this problem to produce a set of optimal assignments of logical components to physical resources. Using the facilities of OPL, we write a system model that defines the data to be presented and its constraints. This model can be instantiated to represent any computing system that falls within the model. Once instantiated, the model can be solved by OPL to find the optimal configuration of resources that meets the requirements. This separation of the model, its instantiation and solution technique allow such systems to be used by systems administrators without a degree in operations research. Finally we show the results of this model when applied to a realistic system.

Novel aspects of this work include:

- The simultaneous modelling of important system metrics and the definition of a cost model that allows multiple business goals, defined in terms of these metrics, to be played off against each other.
- The careful definition of quantifiable security properties that correspond to properties that security experts attempt to optimize for. Security is often thought of as a binary property but the use of security metrics allows greater flexibility to the configuration process.

1   Modelling a Service-Oriented Architecture

In this section we define the components of our model and the information a user of the system has to provide about each component and the information that the optimizer needs to produce to specify a configuration of the system. In the next section we describe how we use this information to define properties of the system that meet the planning needs of system administrators. A UML class diagram showing the relationship between the components is shown in Figure 1.

Service. The fundamental system component in a service-oriented architecture is, of course, the service. We define a service to be an entity that can perform a set of operations on behalf of callers on a defined set of data. For example, Hertz may offer a car rental booking service that allows clients to book its cars. Avis may offer a distinct service that provides access to its cars. Travelocity and LastMinute may each run a travel agency that offers services that allow clients to book cars on either Hertz or Avis. These form four distinct services.

We denote the set of all services being modelled as a set named *Service*.

To specify the load generated by an invocation of a service on the server running the service we define a function *loadU* that defines the expected load units caused by a single invocation of the service.

$$loadU : Service \rightarrow \mathbb{R}^+$$

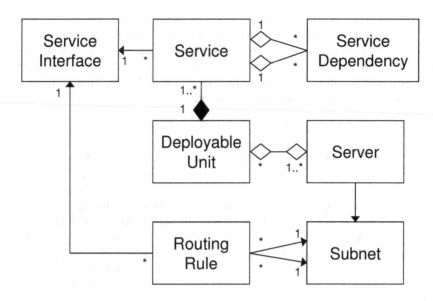

Fig. 1. A UML diagram of the service oriented model

Service Interface. Each service implements a certain protocol or language to fa-cilitate communication with it and its invokers. We call this protocol the interface to the service. To facilitate interoperability, many services may implement the same interfaces. In a Web Services infrastructure an interface may be specified as a WSDL object and identified by a URL. In a Corba infrastructure, an interface may be specified by an IDL file and identified by a UUID.

Formally we can represent this as a set *ServiceInterface* and an *implements* function that represents the relationship between the service interface and the services that implement it.

$$implements : Service \rightarrow ServiceInterface$$

Service dependencies. Services may be composed from other services. For each service we assume we have a set of services that are used in this service's imple-mentation and that we have determined the expected number of invocations of those subsidiary services for each invocation of the entry service. This can some-times be determined by code inspection and sometimes by measurement. Even if service binding is done dynamically, data can be collected on the long-term behaviour of a particular installation.

Each subsidiary service may be used by any number of layered service im-plementations. For simplicity, we assume that there are no cycles in the service implementation dependency directed graph. Since this information refers only to direct dependency we call the function representing this information *depen-dency1*.

$$dependency1 : Service \times Service \rightarrow \mathbb{R}^+$$

We use this information to estimate the complete dependency matrix, the number of calls generated, directly or indirectly, by a single call to a service on every other service. We estimate the complete dependency matrix by computing the transitive closure of the *dependency1* matrix. However if the complete graph has been measured, it should be used in preference to the estimate. This is the same approach used in gprof in estimating call graph values [1].

$$dependency : Service \times Service \rightarrow \mathbb{R}^+$$

Client Service. We define a distinguished client service whose function is to invoke the externally accessible services. The client service makes the correct mix of requests that match the expected calls from all the system's clients. The client service is special in that we do not attempt to model its internal behaviour or allocate resources to it. The distinguished client service gives us a single row of the dependency matrix to concentrate on that defines the expected call load that we are expecting for each service. Since there are no calls to the client service, one should think of the counts in the client row of the dependency matrix as representing the number of calls on the indicated services by external clients per unit time.

Formally, *client* is simply a distinguished element in *Service*.

$$client \in Service$$

In addition each service may have an availability requirement that defines the minimum probability that this service must be up and providing the needed service to the distinguished client service. We can define this requirement as a function that specifies the minimum probability that this service is allocated enough resources to perform its function. If there is no availability requirement on a particular service, the function may have value 0.

$$AvailableToClient : Service \rightarrow [0, 1]$$

Note that this function is used along with the dependency information to generate the complete service availability function in the next section.

Deployable unit. Each separate service is not typically deployable on a server independently. A developer or administrator will typically build or configure a set of services into a deployable unit that can be installed on one or more machines. The developer may decide services need to be collocated in the same process or on the same machine to maintain efficiency or to reduce development time. When services are combined into a deployable unit, we do not model the dependencies between these services; instead the load and dependencies are rolled up into the services that are invoked externally. The form a deployable unit takes depends on the system being used. In J2EE a deployable unit might be represented as a preconfigured WAR, or web application archive, on Linux a deployable unit might take the form of a preconfigured RPM [2] file. Unlike an unconfigured WAR or RPM file, which might contain a generic service implementation, a deployable unit contains all information to configure the implementation to take the role as a particular service, e.g., the data it will be accessing and the other services that it may need to contact.

Formally, the deployable units are just a set *Deployable* with a function *deploys* to represent the composition of a deployable unit out of its constituent services.

$$deploys : Service \rightarrow Deployable$$

Server. A server is an entity on which services can be executed. Servers are not referred to directly by applications; instead applications reference services that are automatically mapped to the servers on which they are deployed. Servers are typically hardware components, though servers can be constructed logically using virtual machine technology.

For each server we have a specified failure probability. This specifies the minimum long-term probability that the server is available and providing its full execution service. This is used in the next section to compute the probability that a service is available and providing service. We specify the server availability with a function:

$$ServerAvailability : Server \rightarrow [0, 1]$$

Associated with each server is a rate at which it can perform load units, expressed in the same time units that were used for the client counts in *dependency1* and the same load unit that was used for *loadU*. We specify the execution rate of a server with the function *powerU*:

$$powerU : Server \rightarrow \mathbb{R}^+$$

Resources on servers are assigned by the configuration system to deployable units. A deployable unit may not consume more resources on a server than it is assigned. A single deployable unit may be deployed on many different servers simultaneously, in which case the load on the component services is divided among the servers, according to the ratio of resources assigned by the server to the deployable unit. We define the number of load units per unit time allocated to a deployable unit on a server as:

$$allocU : Deployable \times Server \rightarrow \mathbb{R}^+$$

Unlike the functions defined so far, this function is not defined by the administrator, but is instead an output of the optimization process. It specifies what services a server should run and the amount of server resources that should be assigned to each deployable unit. In the next section we develop constraints that will ensure that the allocation of resources to deployable units satisfies the system requirements. The resulting allocation must not overload the server, that is the following constraint must hold:

$$\forall serv \in Server, \sum_{\forall d \in Deployable} allocU(d, serv) \leq powerU(serv)$$

Subnet. A subnet represents a portion of the network containing a set of servers. Servers on the same subnet can communicate more cheaply, but servers on different subnets can be protected from each other by router based filtering and firewalls. Formally, a subnet is just a set, *Subnet,* and a function *subnet* that assigns servers to subnets.

$$subnet : Server \rightarrow Subnet$$
$$clientSubnet \in Subnet$$

Routing rule. The filtering that can take place between subnets is represented as a set of allowable service interfaces whose messages may pass between the subnets. Typically a routing rule will be assigned to a router or firewall to ensure that only the required communication can be passed and that this required communication is safe. Like the allocation of deployable units to servers, the configuration optimization process produces the set of subnet rules.

Formally the set of filter rules is a function, *rules,* from pairs of subnets to a subset of allowable service interfaces whose messages are allowed to pass from one subnet to the other.

$$rules : Subnet \times Subnet \rightarrow \wp(ServiceInterface)$$

2   Properties of a Service-Oriented System

One measure of the usefulness of a model of a system is whether properties of the model can be defined that correspond to properties of the original system. In this section we present some interesting system properties that can be defined using our model and argue for their relevance.

Service Availability Requirement. A service's availability requirement is the probability that a service responds to a given request by one of its clients. A service's clients may include the distinguished *client* service as well as arbitrary other services that use this service. For a service to be available, in addition to the service itself being available all the service's dependencies must be available. Assuming that the availability of each request on each service is independent, we use the following constraint to define a *serviceAvailability* function that depends on the administrator-provided *availableToClient* as well as the *dependency1* function.

$$availableToClient(s1) \leq$$
$$serviceAvailability(s1) \leq \prod_{\substack{\forall s2 \in Service: \\ dependency1(s1,s2)>0}} serviceAvailability(s2)$$

Informally this says that the service can be no more available than its constituents, but that it must be at least as available as any clients need it to be.

These constraints can be solved by starting with the services called only by the distinguished *client* service. Such a service is likely to have a nonzero value for the *availableToClient* function. This value can be factored to determine availability requirements for each of the services it calls. This process can be repeated until service availability requirements are derived for all of the services. As might be expected this process causes lower level services to have higher availability requirements.

Availability with Throughput. We define execution throughput and availability constraints simultaneously, as for a service to be properly configured the probability that the service is meeting its throughput requirements must be as large as its availability requirement. An acceptable configuration must assign enough resources to each deployable unit so that with large enough probability all the services that are part of the deployable unit are getting enough execution resources to perform their function. We must also assign the resources in such a way that we never exceed the capacity of any server.

We can express the fact that a server may not be over allocated with the predicate:

$$\forall serv \in Server : \sum_{\forall d \in Deployable} allocU(d, serv) \leq powerU(serv)$$

This specifies that for all servers, that the sum of the load units allocated to each deployable is less than total load units provided by the server.

To form a predicate that insists that the needed throughput be provided with the required probability, consider a subset S of the *Server* set that represents the set of servers that are available at a moment in time. For each such subset $S \in Server$ there is a well defined probability that exactly those servers are available. Assuming that the availability of each server is independent, that probability is given by:

$$setProbability(S) = \prod_{\forall serv \in S} serverAvailability(serv) \times$$

$$\prod_{\forall serv \in Server-S} (1 - serverAvailability(serv))$$

That is, the probability that exactly the set of servers S is available is the probability that each server in S is available times the probability that each server not in S is not available. For each subset S, there is also an expression that represents the number of load units among the servers in S that are assigned to a given deployable unit, $d \in Deployable$. We compute this as a function *allocSU*:

$$allocSU(d, S) = \sum_{\forall serv \in S} allocU(d, serv)$$

For the set S to have adequate capacity to be classed as being available for d, the number of load units allocated to the unit d must be sufficient for performing the required load per unit time on the services making up d. We can compute this for a unit d by:

$$reqLoadU(d) = \sum_{\forall s \in Service:d=deploy(s)} dependency(client,s) \times loadU(s)$$

that is, the sum, over all services that are part of the deployable unit, of the number of invocations on that service per unit time multiplied by the number of load units consumed by each invocation. This gives us the load units required per unit time, the same units as the allocation units for server resources assigned to a deployable in *allocSU*.

The availability of a deployable unit d in a given configuration is the sum over all subsets S of *Server* where the load units allocated to the deployable unit is sufficient to meet the execution requirements of the services that are part of the deployable unit, of the probability that the server configuration S exists. We define the following.

$$deployAvailable(d) = \sum_{\substack{\forall S \subseteq Server: \\ allocSU(d,\bar{S}) \geq reqLoadU(d)}} setProbability(S)$$

If for each deployable unit this probability is larger than the maximum service availability requirement of all the services in the deployable unit, that is, when

$$\forall d \in Deployable : deployAvailable(d) \geq \max_{\forall s:d=deploy(s)} serviceAvailability(s)$$

then the allocation of resources meets the availability and throughput requirements.

Security Distance. One of the important security considerations that must be taken into account when building a service infrastructure is router and firewall configuration. There are some services in which considerable skill and attention have been lavished in making sure that the service is ready to withstand the slings and arrows of outrageous hackers and other services which, while nominally secure, had best not be accessible to outside users. There are also services that store such sensitive data that best practices dictate that they should be locked away behind many levels of firewall.

One simple way of rating network service security is by the minimum number of subnet hops needed to get from the attacker to the target service. Each step along such a shortest path represents a subnet that has to be traversed and presumably hacked, in order to reach the target service. For example, in many web application infrastructures the service network is divided into 5 successively deeper subnets as illustrated in Figure 2: a content subnet, a UI subnet, a business logic subnet, a database subnet and a SAN subnet. Each deeper level provides a lower level abstraction with less fine grain access checking and often less secure authentication. Accessing each successive subnet also requires hacking a different set of systems, typically using a different set of techniques.

When configuring routing rules it is important to allow communication between subnets where it is needed, e.g. services running on those subnets need direct communication, but at the same time we want to insist that certain services be run on servers that are deeply hidden from clients, that is there is a large security distance between the service and the attacker. Network subnet

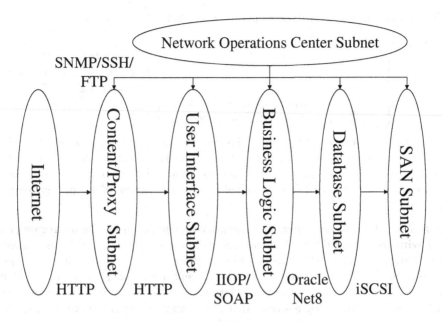

Fig. 2. A Typical Subnet Structure

distance is a simplification of the security restrictions one might contemplate, but it is a reasonable start and it mirrors current best practices [3].

The constraint on the existence of rules allowing all needed communication can be stated as:

$$\forall s1, s2 \in Service : dependency1(s1, s2) > 0 \Rightarrow$$
$$\forall serv1, serv2 \in Server :$$
$$(allocU(deploys(s1), serv1) > 0 \wedge$$
$$allocU(deploys(s2), serv2) > 0)$$
$$\Rightarrow interface(s2) \in rules(subnet(serv1), subnet(serv2))$$

which states that for all pairs of services that communicate, and all servers that are assigned to run those services, then the interface those services use to communicate must be present in the rules set of the router that connects the two subnets.

Given the rule above, the security distance between two services, which we will denote as $securityDistance(s1, s2)$, can be defined by the following recurrence.

First we define a predicate *connected* that determines whether there is a direct communications link between the two services, that is, whether any of the servers assigned to the services are on the same subnet.

$$connected(s1, s2) = \exists serv1, serv2 \in Server :$$
$$allocU(deploys(s1), serv1) > 0 \wedge$$
$$allocU(deploys(s2), serv2) > 0 \wedge$$
$$subnet(serv1) = subnet(serv2)$$

Then we define the security distance with the following recurrence.

$securityDistance(s1, s2) =$

$$\begin{cases} 0, & \text{if } connected(s1, s2) \\ 1, & \text{if } dependency(s1, s2) > 0 \\ & \land \neg connected(s1, s2) \\ \min_{\forall s3 \in Service} \left\{ \begin{array}{l} securityDistance(s1, s3) + \\ securityDistance(s3, s2) \} \end{array} \right. & \text{otherwise} \end{cases}$$

The security distance computed in this way can be used in constraints to insist that a sensitive service be a large distance from the client subnet. This can be used to restrict the optimizer from doing something silly like running a database service on the network DMZ in order to take advantage of its lightly loaded servers.

Data Risk. In another paper [4], a security metric based on the aggregate risk of having data from different customers make use of the same device is defined. For example, a storage service provider may decide to store data from a single commercial bank on a storage unit and to accept a level of risk r in making that assignment while adding an airline's data to that storage unit may increase the risk of the assignment by a small amount but adding a competitive bank to the same unit may raise the risk considerably.

In the service-oriented context, a similar measure of data risk can be defined that quantifies the risk of placing deployable units on the same server or on the same subnet. The risk depends on the assurance level or trust we have in the server or the subnet's ability to keep the data separate and the risk associated with the information being accessed from the dependent services.

This metric is not used in the OPL implementation described in this paper, but was used in a separate OPL model described in [4].

Network Bandwidth. The network bandwidth used in a system can sometimes be an important consideration in system design. The internal switching inside a subnet is generally implemented by high performance switching equipment that has been optimized for network performance. Communication between subnets is performed by routers that have been optimized for security and for implementing many hundreds of complex filtering rules. Limiting the load on these expensive routers can sometimes be an important consideration.

To help express constraints or optimizer objective functions dealing with bandwidth, we define a new *traffic* function. The value $traffic(sn1, sn2, interface)$ reports the number of invocations per unit time of the given interface that may travel between the given subnets. If the subnets are equal, the function gives the amount of intra-subnet traffic using the given interface. This function can be used to define constraints or minimize the usage of network traffic.

First we define the function *runsIn* that computes the set of subnets used for executing a given service:

$$runsIn(s) = \bigcup_{\substack{\forall serv \in Service: \\ allocU(deploys(s), serv) > 0}} subnet(serv)$$

Given this function we can define the traffic function as:

$$traffic(sn1, sn2, i) = \sum_{\substack{\forall s1,s2 \in Service: \\ i=implements(s2) \\ \wedge sn1 \in runsIn(s1) \\ \wedge sn2 \in runsIn(s2)}} dependency(client, s1) \times dependency1(s1, s2)$$

As can be seen this sums over all pairs of services where the second service implements the given interface and the services run on the given subnets. For each pair we look at the expected number of service invocations of the given type that will be requested per unit time. This is given by the expected number of invocations from the *client* to service $s1$ times the number of invocations that $s1$ makes directly to $s2$.

3   Optimizing a Service-Oriented System

In the previous sections we have seen how to describe a service-oriented system and how to define properties and constraints on a service-oriented system; we can now look at optimizing a service-oriented system. In mathematical programming, optimization is driven by an objective function.

The difference between an objective function and a constraint is that a constraint must hold in order to have a solution, while the objective function is merely optimized from among the solutions meeting all the constraints. While there can be many constraints in a constraint satisfaction problem, there can only be one objective function.

Some useful objective functions include those for:

- Minimizing the cost of the system. In this case the objective function may be the number of servers that have not been allocated to any deployable unit. That is to maximize:

$$| \{ serv \in Server \mid \forall d \in Deployable : allocU(serv, d) = 0 \} |$$

- Maximizing the security of a service. In addition to setting minimum security distance constraints, the administrator may be looking to maximize the minimum security distance from an attacker subnet to a given set of services. That is, given a priority set of services, *Protected*, we might want to maximize

$$\min_{s \in Protected} securityDistance(clientSubnet, s)$$

- Maximizing the capacity of a system. If the load on the services may grow unexpectedly, the administrator may wish to build a system out of an existing hardware base that can respond quickly to unexpected spikes in demand by spreading any extra capacity evenly throughout the service deployments. We can compute the percentage of over capacity allocated to a service and attempt to maximize the minimum level of over capacity over all the deployable units by maximizing:

$$\min_{d \in Deployable} \left(\frac{allocSU(d, Server)}{reqLoadU(d)} \right)$$

- Minimizing the number of routing rules. Routing rules consume resources on a router and having too many rules can cause the router to become overloaded, usually causing operators to ill advisedly remove rules. If an organization's routers are on the edge, minimizing this objective function could be important:

$$\max_{sn1, sn2 \in Subnet} \left| \bigcup_{i \in Interface} rules(sn1, sn2, i) \right|$$

There are many other objective functions that can be defined. This list is just meant to be illustrative.

4 Implementation Experience

To test the usefulness of this approach we wanted to apply the model to a realistic test case. In this test case we defined a configuration consisting of 26 services in 17 deployable units, with 8 different service interfaces, deployed on 160 servers in 8 different server classes running on 5 subnets. The availability of the servers varied from 3 nines of availability (i.e. 99.9%) to four nines. The service availability requirements of the top-level services varied from three to four nines. The derived service availabilities for the deeper services went up to five nines and these deeper services were constrained as needing a security distance from the client of at least 3. We set the objective function to maximize the minimum level of over capacity from among the 17 deployable units.

The services were designed to model a modern multi-tier web based system consisting of client accessible static content and reverse web proxy services fronting for an inner tier of application services providing the application UI control and page generation. The UI services were then built on a tier of business logic services. Unlike the other service layers, the business logic services are available both from the proxy layer, the UI layer and itself. The business logic services in turn build on a set of file and database services, which are in turn built on a set of virtual disk services implemented by a storage area network.

Considerable tuning in the search procedure was needed to order the configurations tested so that the progress towards a solution progressed at a reasonable rate. At this point, OPL is able to find acceptable solutions after running for several minutes on a single 1.5 GHz processor. Finding optimal solutions for nontrivial objective functions is more elusive as the entire solution space often has to be searched, taking over 10 hours for the sample problem. For many uses this performance is adequate, for example, in configuring an enterprise data center for a new application or an application service provider for a new customer. For other uses, such as online reconfiguration after a device failure or configuring a dynamic grid computer, this performance is not adequate.

Note that a numerical instability in the availability computations currently limits the number of servers per server class to 21. This result indicates that this approach to solving configuration problems is promising; though much more work remains to be done to show that it is practical and efficacious.

5   Related Work

A modelling based approach to quality of service prediction is standard fare in queuing theory, but the focus is generally on the much more difficult measure of response time, a measure we leave out of our analysis because of its complexity. However the typical server graph used in queuing theory carries over to the dependency graph used here.

Other attempts have been made to model quality of service properties of distributed systems, most recently in the context of a service grid [5], but many fewer properties are being optimized for. Other current work on service grids is focused on mechanism of configuration rather than the optimization of configurations [6].

The most closely related work to this has been done in the area of provisioning of storage in a storage network. Data storage and services are closely related, and in fact one can think of data access as a special case of service provisioning, where it happens that the services allow for data access. Work done in this area includes innovative work done at HP [6,7,8,9] in configuring storage systems. The authors have made their own forays into storage management in [4,10].

Other related work lies in network provisioning, where resources needed to provide the required quality of service are reserved in advance. In this work the model is more based on dynamic load rather than the static load model used in this work. Examples include [11,12].

A subset of the service provisioning problem being considered here was addressed using constraint satisfaction in [13], but the problem was simple enough that the big guns of constraint satisfaction was not necessary for the solution.

The SmartFrog [8] system from HP provides tools for describing and deploying configurations.

6   Conclusion and Future Plans

The approach of producing an abstract model of a complex system and reasoning about that abstract model is an oldie but a goodie. In this paper we have applied this technique to the problem of configuring a service oriented architecture. We have shown how to compute properties of the resulting network and to use those properties to drive the automatic optimization of that network to meet a set of requirements defined over those properties.

A necessary future step for this research is to experiment with configuring real systems to verify that the promised gains are actually achievable. This can also be used to determine if there are constraints missing in our model that allow the production of flawed configurations.

Another area for extension is the development of new types of security measures. Our security distance metric can be refined by allowing each routing rule to have a separate breakage cost, instead of the unit cost used here. The attacker would search for the lowest cost path to the inner systems. In addition the rules can be arranged in a partial order to represent which rules are implicitly broken when another rule is hacked. This can be used to model the fact that once a successful attack on a system is found, the same attack can be used against similar systems with no additional cost.

In this paper we define availability as a service having enough available resources to perform its function. This definition does not mean that the service has those resources for a long enough contiguous interval of time to actually *perform* its function. For example, a diabolical highly available server with a very short MTBF but an incredibly small MTTR, may provide high availability using our definition, but unacceptable performance in real situations. We would like to define service availability as the probability that a given request is successfully processed however, this doesn't easily match up with the definition of availability for a server, which is necessarily time based.

Acknowledgements

The authors would like to thank the anonymous referees for their helpful comments on this paper. This work was supported by the Boole Centre for Research in Informatics, University College Cork under the HEA-PRTLI scheme and by the Enterprise Ireland Basic Research Grant Scheme (SC/2003/007).

References

1. Graham, S.L., Kessler, P.B., McKusick, M.K.: gprof: A call graph execution profiler. In Thomas, W., ed.: Proceedings of the SIGPLAN '82 Symposium on Compiler Construction. Volume 17(6) of SIGPLAN Notices., Boston, MA, USA, ACM Press (1982) 120–126
2. Herrold, R.: Rpm package manager (2002) http://www.rpm.org.
3. Elizabeth D. Zwicky, Simon Cooper, D.B.C.: A Handbook of Process Algebra. 2 edn. O'Reilly (2000)
4. Aziz, B., Foley, S.N., Herbert, J., Swart, G.: Configuring storage area networks for mandatory security. In Farkas, C., Samarati, P., eds.: Proceedings of the 18th IFIP Annual Conference on Data and Applications Security, Sitges, Catalonia, Spain, Kluwer (2004) 357–370
5. Al-Ali, R., Hafid, A., Rana, O., Walker, D.: An approach for qos adaptation in service-oriented grids. Concurrency Computation: Practice and Experience **16** (2004)

6. Alvarez, G.A., Borowsky, E., Go, S., Romer, T.H., Becker-Szendy, R., Golding, R.A., Merchant, A., Spasojevic, M., Veitch, A.C., Wilkes, J.: Minerva: an automated resource provisioning tool for large-scale storage systems. ACM Transactions on Computer-Systems **19** (2001)

7. Anderson, E., Hobbs, M., Keeton, K., Spence, S., Uysal, M., Veitch, A.C.: Hippodrome: Running circles around storage administration. In Long, D.D.E., ed.: Proceedings of the FAST'02 Conference on File and Storage Technologies, Monterey, California, USA, USENIX (2002) 175–188

8. Goldsack, P., Guijarro, J., Lain, A., Mecheneau, G., Murray, P., Toft, P.: Smartfrog: Configuration and automatic ignition of distributed applications. In: Proceedings of the HP OpenView University Association 10th Workshop, University of Geneva, Switzerland (2003) http://www.smartfrog.org/papers/SmartFrog_Overview_HPOVA03.May.pdf.

9. Ward, J., O'Sullivan, M., Shahoumian, T., Wilkes, J.: Appia: automatic storage area network design. In Long, D.D.E., ed.: Proceedings of the FAST'02 Conference on File and Storage Technologies, Monterey, California, USA, USENIX (2002) 203–217

10. Swart, G.: Storage management by constraint satisfaction. In: Proceedings of the Workshop on Immediate Applications of Constraint Programming, Kinsale, Cork, Ireland (2003)

11. Balter, R., Bellissard, L., Boyer, F., Rivelli, M., Vion-Dury, J.: Architecting and configuring distributed applications with olan. In: Proceedings of the 1998 IFIP International Conference on Distributed Systems Platforms and Open Distributed Processing. Volume 1518 of Lecture Notes in Computer Science., The Lake district, UK, Springer Verlag (1998) 241–256

12. Chen, S., Nahrstedt, K.: An overview of quality-of-service routing for the next generation high-speed networks: Problems and solutions. IEEE Network Magazine **12** (1998) 64–79

13. Martín-Díaz, O., Cortés, A.R., Durán, A., Benavides, D., Toro, M.: Automating the procurement of web services. In Orlowska, M.E., Weerawarana, S., Papazoglou, M.P., Yang, J., eds.: Proceedings of the 1st International Conference on Service-Oriented Computing. Volume 2910 of Lecture Notes in Computer Science., Trento, Italy, Springer Verlag (2003) 91–103

Trusted Identity and Session Management Using Secure Cookies

Joon S. Park and Harish S. Krishnan

Laboratory for Applied Information Security Technology (LAIST),
Syracuse University, Syracuse, NY 13244-4100
{jspark, hskrishn}@syr.edu

Abstract. The concept of federated identity management is increasingly coming to use in order to bring Service Providers closer to customers. Users are being provided an enriched experience while carrying out business on the Web at reduced overhead and improved customer service. The idea of maintaining a single profile and gaining access to multiple services has been accepted well by the customers. However, the benefits of breaking through just one set of credentials to gain access to multiple services has made the concept of Federated Identity Management of high interest to malicious users. In this paper, we analyze the structure of a generic Federated Identity Management System and explore the .NET Passport framework in depth. We explore the current security mechanisms adopted by the .NET Passport and identify potential security weaknesses. We then propose our new approaches to enhance the security services in .NET Passport by using Secure Cookies. Our approaches are transparent to and compatible with the current .NET Passport server. Finally, we prove the feasibility by implementing our ideas in a real system.

Keywords: Cookies, Identity Management, .NET Passport.

1 Introduction

In the world of ever growing businesses it has become important to provide resources and services ubiquitously. This has lead to making businesses available through the Web. No doubt that the enabling of services or resources on the Web has opened up a gallery of opportunities, it has also brought along a wide range of security concerns. Providing services through the Web has enriched the experience of conducting business for the customers. However, this enriched experience is packaged with fears of compromising sensitive information to malicious subjects who intend to break through week security perimeters and gain access to unauthorized resources. One of the main security concerns while making businesses Web-enabled is Identity Management (IM [GC02, NRC02]). By Identity Management we mean capturing and storing of User identities, managing the identities of Users, and authenticating Users based on their identities. Once authenticated, the User has gained access into the system, but access control policies determine what parts of the system the User has access to. A strong and

S. Jajodia and D. Wijesekera (Eds.): Data and Applications Security 2005, LNCS 3654, pp. 310–324, 2005.
© IFIP International Federation for Information Processing 2005

effective access control mechanism should provide fine grained and scalable services [KPF01, PCZG04, PKF01]. Such mechanism can protect sensitive identity information from reaching malicious hands but still continue to provide Users with an enjoyable experience of conducting business on the Web [AAM, Cla94]. In this paper, we are first going to explore the ongoing efforts in Federated Identity Management. We examine the security strengths and potential weaknesses in one of the most popular IM models, namely .NET Passport [MNP04, Pass05]. We then go on to propose a possible solution to strengthen the current mechanism by extending our previous work, Secure Cookies [PSG99, PS00], within the .NET Passport framework. Our work is both transparent to and compatible with the current .NET Passport framework.

2   Related Work

In this section we discuss a generic identity management framework and explore the .NET Passport framework [MNP04, Pass05] and Liberty Alliance Project [ILAIA03, ISLSI03] in detail. In a later section we are going investigate the .NET Passport Service and explore the current security features of the framework. We go on to suggest mechanisms to improve on the exiting security features of .NET Passport. Although we have been working with the .NET Passport frame in this paper, we believe that our work can be applied to other Identity-Management systems including Liberty Alliance.

2.1   .NET Passport

Passport is a Web-based authentication service that helps Users and service provides use the Internet faster and easier. One of the largest online authentication systems in the world,.NET Passport provides Users with Single-Sign-in (SSI) services, reducing the amount of information the User needs to remember or resubmit to various sites. For businesses, Passport helps make their websites easier for visitors and customers to use and also helps reduce the costs associated with resetting forgotten User passwords. By helping Users to connect easily to websites, Passport also makes it easy for businesses to recognize their customers and deliver consistent, valuable services no matter how or where customers are connecting. Passport can help companies allow customers to easily identify themselves across all applications offered by a website, so that Users can go to the company website, interact with all of their account information, pay bills, and get the kind of experience they want. In this paper we first investigate the identity management capabilities of Passport and discuss the authentication mechanism used by it. We then investigate the impending threats in such form of authentication and propose feasible solutions.

2.2   Liberty Alliance

The Liberty Alliance Project aims at reducing the differences between various businesses of the networked world and providing a framework for different Web-enabled services and resources to interact across boundaries in way that respects privacy of the participating entities and enables security of shared identity information. The Liberty Alliance divides any Web-enabled business that requires authentication into 3 basic entities, namely - Identity Provider, Service Provider, and Principal. The Identity Provider is a Liberty-enabled entity that creates, maintains, and manages identity information or Users and provides Principal (User) Authentication to other Service Providers within a circle of trust. A Service Provider is an entity that provides different services to the Users. Finally, the Principal is an entity that can acquire a federated identity that is capable of making decisions and to which authenticated actions are done on its behalf. The Liberty-Alliance proposes the construction of a Circle-of-Trust between Service Providers (SP) and Identity Providers (IP), such that all authentications carried by the IP for a Principal is readily accepted by the SPs that require carrying out business with the Principal.

As it can be seen there are a number of similarities between the .NET Passport framework and the Liberty Alliance Project. Both of them have a single authority that provides authentication information based on which the other participating sites authenticate the User. Both IM systems provide capability for the User to login just once and access services across multiple providers who are all united in a circle of trust. Similarly, a single log-off request would invalidate the Users' identity across all partner Service Providers. The .NET Passport and the Liberty Alliance differ in the way they share the User authentication information within the circle of trust. The .NET Passport uses Cookie based authentication mechanisms that we explore in detail in later sections. The Passport Sign-in Server does not directly communicate with any of the other Passport-enabled sites to convey User authentication information. On the other hand, in the Liberty Alliance project, when a User authenticates with the Identity Provider, the Identity Provider federates the User Sign-in credentials with the Service Providers within the Circle of Trust. Here the User (actually the Web-Client) does not act as a medium to convey the authentication information.

3   Federated Identity Management (FIM)

A single customer may have transactions with many businesses that are Web-enabled and hence each business maintains the identity information of the User required to authenticate the User. The User has to also remember his/her authentication credentials (such as User-ID and Password) for each of the services/resources that are to be accessed through the Web. It is quite often the case that Users tend to forget their credentials and request for resetting this information. It lies in the interest of the service/resource providers to find a way to avoid the overhead and extra costs associated with resetting the authentication credentials frequently. In an attempt to address this issue, we look at the concept of Federated Identity Management. We investigate its use in the .NET Passport framework and in the Liberty Alliance Project.

By federation we mean the setting up of a trust relationship between two or more entities for a more tightly integrated approach to business. The members of one of the participating entities can freely access the resources or services provided by the other entities of the federation [PCND04]. Managing federations in essentially about a) Managing trust relationships between the participating entities and b) Managing identities of Users across the partners of the federation. Trust relationships between the participating entities of a federation can be achieved by pre-established legal agreements and implemented by the means by cryptographic techniques such as encryption/decryption and signatures. We discuss federated identity management in detail as below.

Federated Identity Management provides a mechanism for identity management across boundaries of the participating entities in the federation. One of the federation partners acts as an Identity Provider for all Users in the federation and other partners accept the authentication decisions made by the Identity Provider and allow authenticated Users to access the resources or services offered. The Identity Provider and other partners exchange User handles by means of a channel that is independent of the services offered by the partners, typically this is achieved through XML [XML] based SOAP [SOAP] messages. Once a circle of trust is established between a set of partners that includes at least one Identity Provider, the access of services or resources by a User can be carried out in two distinct ways. Firstly, the User creates an account with the Identity Provider and then goes on to access the services or resources offered by other partners of the federation. Alternatively, the User directly access any of the services or resources hosted on one of the Service Providers of the federation which directs the User to set up an account with the Identity Provider and then re-direct back the User to the Service Provider. Both of these scenarios are depicted in Figure 1 and Figure 2. The architecture for the Liberty Alliance is very similar to the described scenarios of Figure 1 and Figure 2. The User is termed as Principal and the federation of identities is achieved through the exchange of SOAP messages. The architecture of .NET Passport also resembles Figure 1 and Figure 2. However, the names by which Microsoft calls these entities of a circle of trust are Passport Sign-in Server (Identity Provider) and Service Providers configured with Passport Manager Objects (Service Providers). The .NET Passport has marked difference in the way it achieves federation of identities. Passport transfers it's identity management information via cookies [ES96, KM00]. The User sets up what is known as the Passport Profile with the Passport Sign-in Server. At this time the Sign-in Server creates a set of cookies. Using these cookies the User is authenticated at various Passport enabled Service Providers. By Passport-enabled we mean those Service Providers that have the Passport Manager installed on their systems that are responsible for authenticating Users based on Passport User-ID (PUID). In the Passport framework, the Passport Sign-in Server is essentially the Identity Provider and other Passport enabled sites are Service Providers and communication between the Identity Provider and Service Providers is achieved through exchange of cookies. Later on in this paper we discuss in detail the authentication mechanism adopted by Passport.

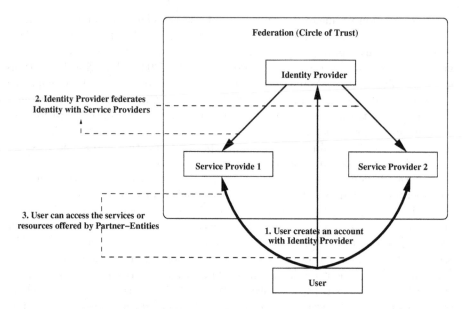

Fig. 1. User establishes Identity with Identity Provider before accessing services/resources of the federation

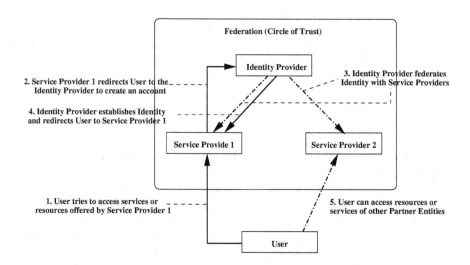

Fig. 2. User attempts to access services/resources of the federation and is directed to the Identity Provider to set up an account and then is allowed access

In the next section we look at the authentication activities involved when an existing User tries access a resource or service in the federation and how a single time signing-in provides access across the federation

4   Analyses of Authentication Mechanisms in .NET Passport

As we discussed briefly in the previous sections, the Passport framework uses "cookie-based authentication" mechanisms to convey identity related information to other Passport enabled sites and acquire service access for Users. This form of authentication is useful because, cookies are lightweight and convenient to store and forward. They involve very less processing overhead. In order to understand how .NET Passport uses cookies to authenticate Users with partner sites we analyze the mechanism in this section.

Figure 3 provides an overview of the authentication process. Before we dive into the details of the User authentication and service access mechanism, we briefly discuss the components of the Passport architecture. The Passport Sign-in Server provides authentication mechanism by which a User can be established as a trusted User among the Passport enabled sites. It takes the help of a User Authentication Database to authenticate any given User. On the other end, a Web-server serves the specific service that the User wants to access. The Service Provider is configured with a Passport Manager that is responsible for verifying the authenticity of the User.

The User starts by accessing the website that provides the desired service. It is assumed that the website is Passport enabled; by this we mean that the site has agreed to be a member of the federation of all Service Providers accepting the .NET Passport as a central identity manager and authenticator. The Web-server of the Service Provider, checks for available cookies issued by the Passport server, and if it cannot find any, it redirects the User to the Passport Sign-in server. (If Cookies are available on the Users system, probably saved from the previous access made to the Service Provider, then the process from step 7 of Figure 3 will be executed.) The User forwards his/her Sign-in credentials such as the email-address and password to the server. The server verifies these credentials of the User against the database and notifies the User of successful authentication. At this time the Passport login server places its cookies into the User's browser. Using these cookies the User is authenticated at various Passport enabled Service Providers. Having embedded the cookies in the browser the User is redirected to the Passport-enabled site where the Web-server extracts the cookies and forwards it to the Passport manager component. The Passport manager then verifies the User as already authenticated and signed-in and notifies the Web-server of the authenticity of the User. The Web-server then grants the User the permission to access the services provided. The site also records its URL in one of the cookies to reflect the visit of the User to that site. If the User goes on to access other Passport enabled sites, since he/she already has the required cookies embedded in the browser, the User can do so without any extra interaction either with the Passport Sign-in Server or the Service Provider.

It is however important to note here that, the Passport Manager on each Passport-enabled Service Provider only checks that the browser of the User accessing the website is embedded with the Passport Cookies. It does not in any way try to establish a link between the Cookies in the browser and the User

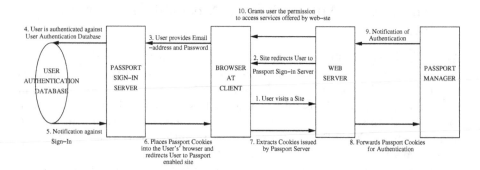

Fig. 3. Cookie-based authentication mechanism used by .NET Passport

whose browser is presenting the cookies to the Web-server. This is one of the main vulnerabilities in the current .NET Passport system that we discuss in the next sections.

5   Security Concerns in Conventional Cookies

Having stated that .NET Passport uses cookies for authentication, we briefly look at what cookies really are and discuss the security concerns associated with them.

Cookies are basically text files that were used to enhance stateless-HTTP by introducing what is known as a Session in HTTP. By this we mean that cookies are text files containing information that can be used to achieve continuity while surfing the internet. Cookies often contain information that was previously entered by a surfer, but they can also contain information added by Web-servers. A site stores cookies on the User's machine that it retrieves on subsequent visit to the site. The information contained in the cookies is what the User or the Web-server entered during the Users's previous visit to the site and the site extracts the corresponding cookies to obtain information.

There are no direct threats posed by cookies if they are used to store non-confidential User information. However, there are situations when a site might need to store some sensitive information such identity, passwords, etc. It is then that cookies become point of interest to malicious users. We now look at the possible security threats to cookies [PS00]. These threats can be classified into the following groups: Network Threats, End-System Threats, and Cookie-Harvesting Threats. As cookies are transmitted in clear text, Network Threats are implemented by snooping and replay with or without modification. One easy solution to thwarting Network-Threats on cookies is to use the "secure" flag field in the cookie. Setting the flag ensures that those cookies are transmitted only on SSL [WS96] so that the cookies are protected on the network. However, this does not mean that the cookies are protected in the end-systems, since SSL does not work in end-systems. The second type of threat is the End-System Threats. Cookies reside in the Users systems as plain text files. These cookies are open to be modified or copied to other systems with or without User consent. This gives rise to impersonation by identity forging. Actually, this is a serious drawback in the current .NET Passport authentication. One good example of the End-System Threat is the Cookie-Poisoning Attack [Kle]. In this form of attack, a malicious user modifies the contents of a Cookie to gain the identity of a genuine User and gain unauthorized access. The Cookie-Poisoning Attack is a Parameter Tampering Attack that involves the tampering of cookie parameters. Lastly, we have the Cookie-Harvesting Threat, where a malicious user collects User's cookies by claiming to be a site that accepts User cookies. The attacker then goes on to use these harvested cookies to gain access to the sites that actually accept these cookies. A good example of the Cookie-Harvesting threat is the Cross-Site Scripting attack. In this form of attack a malicious user can exploit the vulnerabilities of a Website that displays data, provided by a User, which has underlying malicious intent. For example, a malicious user could embed a script in a URL and place it in a Discussion Forum, Website, Web message board, or email. The underlying script could be activated when the User comes across the hyperlink and decides to follow it. The script would then copy all the cookies in the User's machine and relay they back to the malicious user for use with or without modification.

In all of the above cases it is seen that there is no means by which a site can establish a strong link between the cookies and the User providing the cookies. Furthermore, cookies do not provide confidentiality or integrity of their contents. All these attacks use the weak assumption made by a cookie-accepting site that the User providing the cookies is the actual owner of those cookies.

6   Security Vulnerabilities in .NET Passport Cookies

The .NET Passport uses a number of cookies that each carries state information for various tasks to be carried out by the Passport Sign-in Server and the participating Passport-enables sites. These cookies are divided into two groups, namely the "Domain Authority Cookies" and "Participating Site Cookies". Cookies that are written to the .Passport.com domain cannot be directly accessed by a participating site. On the other hand the Participating Site Cookies are written to the participating domain site and in path to which the participating site's Passport Manager Object is configured and enable the User to sign in at any Passport participating sites during a browser session. The cookies written in the passport.com domain are encrypted with the Passport key. The cookies written to the participating sites domain are encrypted with the participating sites' Passport key. Most of the Passport Cookies are temporary cookies and are not stored in the User's browser after each session. When a User signs out of either the Passport site or one of the participating sites, all Passport Cookies are deleted. By deleting the cookies at the end of each session, the possibility of end-system threats is thwarted. However, every session requires a new set of cookies from the User's browser, which is inconvenient to the User. It would make it much easier if the Users could preserve their cookies that provide automatic authentication each time the User uses the Passport site or any Passport-enabled site in the future. Technically, it should be possible to configure the Passport server to store its cookies in the User's browser after each session. However, this is not recommended because of the security vulnerabilities in the current Passport Cookies, although it could provide more transparent services to Users. We will discuss in the following sections how to solve this problem by using our Secure Cookies.

The Passport Cookies currently have two security features: namely the encryption using Passport Key and transmitting the cookies using SSL. The encryption provides protection against unauthorized disclosure. Setting the Secure flag in the cookie makes sure that it is transmitted over SSL thus giving away possibility of network-threats by malicious user. However, these features are not sufficient to protect the cookies in the User's machines(discussed in Section 5).

Furthermore, the current cookies don't have a mechanism to associate them with their actual owners. The cookies don't have a mechanism by which it can be established that the person forwarding the cookies is necessarily the owner of the cookies. This weakness can be exploited by steeling the cookies and reusing the cookies without modification before the cookies expire. In this way a malicious user pretends to be the cookie-owner and gains unauthorized access. Once any User signs in at the Passport Sign-in Server, that server places required cookies in the User's system to be used for authentication with Passport enabled sites. Any malicious user can carry out an end-system attack in order to obtain the cookies and use them as its owner. Therefore, we believe the current .NET Passport IM system shouldn't not store it's cookies in Users machines, even though it is technically possible and would be more convenient to Users.

7   Secure Cookies for .NET Passport Framework

We now look into the aspect of enhancing the security services in the Passport framework. We propose the use of Secure Cookies to improve the security of the cookies used in the current .NET Passport framework.

7.1   Cooking Secure Cookies

Secure Cookies provide three types of security services: authentication, integrity, and confidentiality. Authentication verifies the cookie's owner. Integrity protects cookies against unauthorized modification. Finally, confidentiality protects cookies against being revealed to an unauthorized entity. Detailed descriptions about Secure Cookies are available in [PS00].

Since typical cookies do not support authentication, a malicious user can simply snatch cookies from other Users and impersonate the real owner to the server that accepts those cookies. To solve this problem, we introduce three possible authentication methods for cookies. Authentication cookies can be address-based (IP_Cookie), password-based (Pswd_Cookie), or digital-signature-based

(Sign-Cookie). To prohibit individuals, perhaps even the cookie owner, from reading sensitive information in cookies, the Web-server can encrypt the contents of the cookies such as, names, roles [PSA01], credit card numbers, and so on. We use the Key-Cookie, to store an encrypted session key, which is used to encrypt sensitive information in other cookies. The session key can be encrypted either by the proper public or secret key. Finally, the Seal-Cookie determines if cookies have been altered. The Seal-Cookie's contents depend on the cryptographic technologies used - essentially, either a public- or secret-key-based solutions (e.g. digital signatures, message authentication codes).

As a result, Secure Cookies can be stored in the User's computer, even when it is off, after each session. This is possible because the Secure Cookies can be provided integrity and authentication services as well as encryption. Therefore, once the User obtains Secure Cookies, the information in the cookies can be used until the cookies expire. This approach completely solves the stateless problem of HTTP and security problems in typical cookies used in .NET Passport.

7.2   Enhanced Passport Architecture with Secure Cookies

Before we talk about the effect of using Secure Cookies, we describe the architecture that supports the use of Secure Cookies. In order to support the use of Secure Cookies we propose Proxy-Authentication architecture that is both transparent to and compatible with the current .NET Passport framework. Figure 4 is a schematic representation of the same. Figure 4 depicts the use of a Proxy-Authenticator to generate Secure Cookies from Passport Cookies. We have not shown the User Authentication Database and Passport Manager entities in Figure 4 as they do not form the core of the Proxy-Authentication architecture that we propose. However, these entities are required in the overall system. If this architecture is compared to the existing Passport architecture, we can clearly see that the User is no more talking directly to the Passport Sign-in Server. Instead the User provides the credentials to the Proxy and Proxy signs into Passport

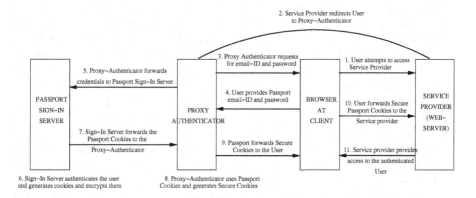

Fig. 4. Proxy Authenticator used to provide security to Passport Cookies by generating Secure Cookies

on the behalf of the User. The key role of the Proxy is to receive the post authentication Passport Cookies from Passport Sign-in Server, and to generate the Secure Cookies using them and forward them to the User. The Proxy thus wraps the less secure Passport Cookies in a secure envelop that is difficult to break. The User can then use these cookies for gaining access at each Passport partner site. The architecture also requires that the partner Service Providers possess the capability to unwrap the Passport Cookies from the Secure Cookie envelop. Hence each Service Provider needs to be configured not only with the Passport Manager Module but also a Secure Cookie Unwrapping module that extracts Passport Cookies and forwards them to the Passport Manager Module for verification. (This module is not shown in the architecture diagram presented in Figure 4). Furthermore, by using the proposed Proxy-Authenticator, our approach is still transparent to, and compatible with existing .NET Passport servers. Our approach does not require any change in the .NET servers. Instead, in our experimentation, we successfully changed the original content of the cookies issued by the Passport Server for our purposes. Actually, .NET Passport does not have any idea about the content change. Although changing the original cookie contents is not for a malicious purpose in this case, it clearly indicates that we can break the integrity of the original .NET Passport Cookies because they are insecure.

7.3   Operational Scenario

Having described the role of Proxy, we now present the detailed discussion on the sequence of the steps that take place for a User trying to gain access into a partner Service Provider that is Passport enabled. The User starts by trying to access the Service Provider and requests for the desired resource. The Service Provider does not find the required cookie in the User's Web-client and hence redirects the User to the Proxy to Sign-in to the Passport. At this time the User is interacting with the Proxy-Authenticator and not the Passport Sign-in server. However, this difference is transparent to the User. The User provides the Sign-in credentials just as he/she would interact with the Passport Sign-in server. The Proxy collects these credentials and forwards it to the Sign-in Server and signs in on behalf of the User. At this point a successful Sign-in would result in the User's Passport Cookies being written to the Proxy. The Proxy then generates a set of Secure Cookies for the User by wrapping all the Passport Cookies. These Secure Cookies are transferred to the User's Web-Client. The User is now redirected to the Service Provider that he/she initially tried to access. Now the Service Provider finds the valid cookies that it can use to verify the User and grant access. It is important to point out here that when the Secure Cookies are read by the service the User will be prompted for a password that is stored in the Hashed Format in the Authentication Cookie of the Secure Cookies (if the authentication mechanism in the Secure Cookie is implemented using Digital Signature or IP, then the verification mechanism is oblivious to the User). If the User provides the correct password then the Service Provider successfully verifies the User and strips the Passport Cookies from the Secure Cookies set and presents it to the Passport Manager Module. Based on the credentials in the Passport Cookies the Service Provider offers a range of services to the User.

7.4 Advantages

Having discussed the sequence of interactions in the new architecture we now shift our discussion towards the strengths of the proposed architecture. In spite of introducing a new component between the User and the Passport Sign-in Server, the amount of overhead is very little. In fact the overhead incurred is all on the Proxy and nothing on the User. The User still signs in at only one place. However there is one more level of communication behind the Proxy (between Proxy and Passport Sign-in Server) but this is transparent to the User. Again when the User's Web-client presents the Service Provider with the Secure Cookies (instead of the Passport Cookies as per the existing system) it is the Service Provider that first strips the outer Secure Cookie set and then the Passport Manager consumes the Passport Cookies. The Proxy based architecture is also robust as it does away with the Single-Point failure. The current Passport framework has a single Sign-in Server and can fall victim to single point failure. There could be multiple proxies thus eliminating single point failure for the signing-in part. The use of a Proxy is also secure in the sense that, the Proxy does not see the contents of the Passport Cookies as the cookies are already encrypted with the Passport Key when they arrive at the Proxy. It just adds another layer of security on the cookies making them more secure. Also the cookies are not stored at the Proxy, after creating them, the Proxy forwards them to the User. This eliminates any possibility of an end-system attack on the Proxy.

The use of Secure Cookies itself adds a number of advantages to the .NET Passport framework. Primarily the authentication cookie of the Secure Cookie set helps establishing a link between the Cookies and the Owner. If the authentication mechanism chosen is a Pswd_Cookie then the User incurs a minor overhead of having to remember a password to be provided at each Service Provider. Using Digital-Signature will also incur some amount of overhead as there needs to be a secure channel set up to exchange Security Keys and also each time the User needs to intervene in the process. However, if IP-based based authentication is used then there is no overhead for the User and the authentication mechanism is transparent to the User. Also we can incorporate access control mechanism by using the Secure Cookies. Secure Cookies can be stored on the User's system without concern of being tampered upon. Any unauthorized change to the contents of Secure Cookies would result in invalid cookies and denial of access. Also, if Secure Cookies comprising of Passport Cookies is stolen by a malicious user and used, the cookie will not be successfully validated as the malicious user has to know the password of the actual owner of the cookie. We can optionally add another cookie (e.g. Role_Cookie) to the Secure Cookie envelop that has defines access rights of the User. This concept can be further extended by using Role-Based Access Control (RBAC [PSA01, SCFY96]). We can include a Role_Cookie into the Secure Cookie envelop that caries the User's Role in it. This role information can be used by each of the Service Provider to make access decisions regarding User's request for services/resources. In such a scenario the Service Provider maintains a mapping between the defined Roles and corresponding access permissions. Thus Secure Cookies not only strengthen the existing Passport Cookies but also can provide a great deal of extended capability to them such as scalable access control.

7.5 Implementation

We carried out our implementation on Windows systems. We used the .NET platform for our development. We developed an initial version of Proxy Authenticator using ASPX and hosted it on IIS. We used the System.Security.Cryptography library to perform the necessary encryption, decryption and Digital Signing of the cookie contents. We use C# to implement the logic required by Proxy as well as the module on the Service Provider that performs the unwrapping of Secure Cookies to get the Passport Cookies.

In order to test the strength of the Passport Cookies we signed into Passport with the "sign me in automatically" option selected. This gave us access to the Passport Cookies that were written to the User's Web-client. We then accessed msn.com and selected the Passport "Sign-in" option and we were silently signed into the site. We then opened up the Passport Cookies stored on the system and modified a numerical value field in the MSPAuth cookie. We saved the changes and once again accessed the msn.com site. On clicking the Sign-in options for Users with Passport identities, we were silently authenticated and granted access to the site instead of being directed to the Passport Sign-in server for re-signing in. Keeping these changes intact we further modified the cookies by changing a similar numerical value field in the MSPProf cookie. We then accessed expedia.com (another Passport enabled site) and we were silently signed-in. Similar behaviors was seen when modifications were made to the MSPPre and MSPSec cookies. Hence this led us to conclude that there are points of vulnerabilities in the current Passport Cookies that can be exploited. It is this kind of attacks that the Secure Cookies look to thwart.

8 Conclusions and Future Work

In this paper, we analyze the structure of a generic Federated Identity Management System and explore .NET Passport framework in depth. We explore the current security mechanisms adopted by .NET Passport and identify potential security weaknesses. We then propose our new approaches to enhance the security services in .NET Passport by using Secure Cookies. Our approaches are transparent to and compatible with the current .NET Passport server. Finally, we prove the feasibility by implementing our ideas in a real system.

In our future work we intend to add a Role_Cookie in the set of cookies that forms a set of Secure Cookies to enable Role-Based Access Control that provides strong and scalable access control mechanisms. We intend to equip Proxy with capability to determine a role for the User who wants to Sign-in to Passport and add a Role-Cookie to reflect this information. We will be enabling the Service Providers with ability to map Roles to Permissions, so that on receiving the Secure Cookies from the User the Service Provider can not only get the Passport Cookies but also have access to a role cookie. This Role-Cookie can be used to determine the set of permissions that the User has while touring the Service Provider's website. The set of roles can be fixed but the access permissions associated to each role are flexible and the Service Providers can autonomously determine the set of permissions for each role. In this way we are able to embed RBAC mechanism into .NET Passport framework.

References

[AAM] American Association of Motor Vehicle Administrators (AAMVA). *Identification Security.* http://www.aamva.org/IDSecurity/

[Cla94] R. Clarke. *Human Identification in Information Systems: Management Challenges and Public Policy Issues.* Information Technology and People 7(4): 6-37, 1994.

[ES96] Easonn Sullivan. *Are Web-based cookies a treat or a recipe for trouble?* PC Week, June 26, 1996.

[GC02] Greenwood, D., D. Combs, et al. *Identity Management: A White Paper.* Lexington, KY, National Electronic Commerce Coordinating Council: 68, 2002.

[ILAIA03] Liberty Alliance Project. *Introduction to the Liberty Alliance Identity Architecture.* Identity Architecture Whitepaper. March, 2003. http://www.projectliberty.org/resources/whitepapers/LAP

[ISLSI03] Liberty Alliance Project. *Identity Systems and Liberty Specification Version 1.1 Interoperability.* February 14, 2003. https://www.projectliberty.org/resources/whitepapers/Liberty and 3rd Party Identity Systems White Paper.pdf

[Kle] A. Klein. *Hacking Web Applications Using Cookie Poisoning* Sanctum Inc. http://www.cgisecurity.com/lib/CookiePoisoningByline.pdf

[KM00] D. Kristol and L. Montulli. *RFC 2965, HTTP State Management Mechanism.* Network Working Group, October 2000.

[KPF01] Myong H. Kang, Joon S. Park, and Judith N. Froscher. *Access Control Mechanisms for Inter-Organization Workflow.* Proceedings of the 6th ACM Symposium on Access Control Model and Technologies (SACMAT), Chantilly, Virginia, May 3-4, 2001.

[MNP04] Microsoft .NET Passport. *Review Guide.* January 2004. http://www.microsoft.com/net/services/passport/review_guide.asp

[NRC02] Computer Science and Telecommunications Board, N. R. C. *IDs - Not That Easy: Questions about Nationwide Identity Systems.* Washington, DC, National Academy of Sciences, 2002.

[PCND04] Joon S. Park, Keith P. Costello, Teresa M. Neven, and Josh A. Diosomito. *A Composite RBAC Approach for Large, Complex Organizations.* Proceedings of the 9th ACM Symposium on Access Control Models and Technologies (SACMAT), Yorktown Heights, New York, June 2-4, 2004.

[PCZG04] Joon S. Park, Pratheep Chandramohan, Artur Zak, and Joseph Giordano. *Fine-Grained, Scalable, and Secure Key Management Scheme for Trusted Military Message Systems.* Proceedings of The Military Communications Conference (MILCOM), Monterey, CA, October 31-November 3, 2004.

[PKF01] Joon S. Park, Myong H. Kang, and Judith N. Froscher. *A Secure Workflow System for Dynamic Cooperation.* Proceedings of the 16th International Conference on Information Security (IFIP/SEC 2001), Paris, France, June 11-13, 2001.

[Pass05] .NET Passport. http://www.passport.NET

[PS00] Joon S. Park and Ravi Sandhu. *Secure Cookies on the Web.* IEEE Internet Computing, Volume 4, Number 4, July-August 2000.

[PSA01] Joon S. Park, Ravi Sandhu, and Gail-Joon Ahn. *Role-Based Access Control on the Web.* ACM Transactions on Information and System Security (TISSEC), Volume 4, Number 1, February 2001.

[PSG99] Joon S. Park, Ravi Sandhu, and SreeLatha Ghanta. *RBAC on the Web by Secure Cookies.* Proceedings of the 13th IFIP WG 11.3 Working Conference on Database Security, Seattle, Washington, July 26-28, 1999.

[SCFY96] R. Sandhu, E.J. Coyne, H.L. Feinstein, and C.E. Youman. *Role Based Access Control Models.* IEEE Computer 29 (2), February 1996.

[SOAP] Simple Object Access protocol. *Version 1.2 Specification.* June 24, 2003 http://www.w3.org/TR/soap/

[WS96] D. Wagner and B. Schneier. *Analysis of the SSL 3.0 Protocol.* Proc. Second Usenix Workshop on Electronic Commerce, Usenix Press, Berkeley, Calif., Nov. 1996, pp. 29-40.

[XML] Extensible Markup Language. www.w3.org/XML/

Security Issues in Querying Encrypted Data[*]

Murat Kantarcıoğlu[1] and Chris Clifton[2]

[1] Department of Computer Science, The University of Texas at Dallas,
Richardson, TX 75083
http://www.murat.kantarcioglu.net

[2] Department of Computer Science, Purdue University, West Lafayette, IN 47907
{kanmurat, clifton}@cs.purdue.edu,
http://www.cs.purdue.edu/people/clifton

Abstract. There has been considerable interest in querying encrypted data, allowing a "secure database server" model where the server does not know data values. This paper shows how results from cryptography prove the impossibility of developing a server that meets cryptographic-style definitions of security and is still efficient enough to be practical. The weaker definitions of security supported by previous secure database server proposals have the potential to reveal significant information. We propose a definition of a secure database server that provides probabilistic security guarantees, and sketch how a practical system meeting the definition could be built and proven secure. The primary goal of this paper is to provide a vision of how research in this area should proceed: efficient encrypted database and query processing with *provable* security properties.

1 Introduction

There is considerable interest in the notion of a "secure database service": A Database Management System that could manage a database without knowing the contents[1]. While the business model is compelling, such a system must be *provably* secure. Existing proposals have problems in this respect; the security provided leaves room for information leaks.

Any method for database encryption that does not meet rigorous cryptography-based security standards must be used carefully. For example, methods that quantize or "bin" values [1,2] reveal data distributions. Methods that hide distribution, but preserve relationships such as order [3,4], can also disclose information if used naïvely. While they may hide values in isolation, using such techniques on multiple attributes in a tuple can pose dangers.

Suppose a bank is trying to find who is responsible for missing money (e.g., fraud or embezzlement). They have gathered information on suspect employees and customers. Even though much of the information is publicly known (name, size of mortgage, age, postal code, ...), revealing *who* is being investigated is

---

[*] This material is based upon work supported by the National Science Foundation under Grant No. 0312357.

S. Jajodia and D. Wijesekera (Eds.): Data and Applications Security 2005, LNCS 3654, pp. 325–337, 2005.

sensitive: The appearance that they are accusing a customer of fraud could lead to a libel suit. Therefore they have encrypted each of the values using an order-preserving encryption scheme. Are they protected?

The answer is probably not. Assume a newspaper wants to know if an individual "Chris" is being investigated. They obtain the encrypted database. They know that the name "Chris" would rank at about 15% of all names – so if it appears in the encrypted database, it will be roughly in that position (the range for a given sample size and probability can be calculated using order statistics). The newspaper can do the same with size of mortgage, age, and other known data about Chris – and with the other employees/customers of the bank. If there is a tuple in the database whose rank on all attributes is close to the corresponding rank of Chris (in the overall dataset), and there is no other customer/employee tuple whose ranks are similar, then the newspaper knows that with high probability, Chris is being investigated.

The key problem is that while encrypting a single value using order preserving encryption or a binning scheme may reveal no information, supporting multiple search keys for each tuple reveals a surprising amount. While methods meeting cryptographic security standards have emerged for some types of queries (e.g., keyword equality [5,6], additive update [7]) they do not meet the need for general database queries. To protect against naïve misuse of order-preserving, homomorphic, or other such encryption techniques, we propose definitions for what it means for an encrypted database to be secure.

This paper presents a vision for how research enabling a secure database service should proceed: Establish solid definitions of "secure", develop encryption and query processing techniques that meet those definitions, demonstrate that such techniques have practical promise. Section 2 gives security definitions for database and query indistinguishability based on the cryptographic concept of *message indistinguishability*. This leads to a troubling result: prior work in cryptography shows that a secure DBMS server meeting these definitions requires that the cost of every query be linear in the size of the database, making a secure DBMS impractical for real-world use.

Section 3 begins the real contribution of this paper: a slightly relaxed definition that gives probabilistic guarantees of security. For the data itself, security is equivalent to strong cryptographic definitions. An adversary tracing query *execution* could conceivably infer information over many queries, but the quality of the information decays exponentially – before enough queries have been seen to infer anything, the relationship between early and late queries will have been broken, preventing the adversary from inferring sensitive data.

In Section 3.2 we show that for this definition, a secure DBMS server with reasonable performance could be constructed. The one caveat is that it requires the existence of a secure execution module: a way of running programs on the server that are hidden from the server. We show how basic query processing operations (select, join, indexed search) can be implemented with a simple secure execution module supporting encryption, decryption, pseudo-random number generation, and comparison. Fortunately, there is an efficient and practical way to achieve such a module: tamper-proof hardware [8]. We give sketches of how the operations could be proven to meet our definition of security. This paper addresses read-only queries (select-project-join); extension to insert/update is reasonable, but beyond the scope of the current work.

2   Implausibility of a Fully Secure Database Server

The cryptography community has developed solid and well-regarded definitions for securely encrypting a message. Encryption schemes are defined to be semantically secure if and only if the ciphertext reveals no information about the plaintext. We now use security definitions from cryptography to define what it means to "securely" encrypt and query a database.

2.1   Security Definitions for Encrypted Database Tables

Semantic security implies that, given any two pairs of ciphertexts and plaintexts of the same length, it must be infeasible to figure out which ciphertext goes with which plaintext. This means that any two database tables with the same schema and the same number of tuples must have indistinguishable encryptions. To be more precise, we now give a database-specific adaptation of the definitions stated in [9].

Definition 1. *An encryption scheme (G, E, D) for database tables; consisting of key generation scheme G, encryption function E, and decryption function D; has indistinguishable encryptions if for every polynomial-size circuit family $\{C_n\}$, every polynomial p, and all sufficiently large n, every database R_1 and $R_2 \in \{0, 1\}^{poly(n)}$ with the same schema and the same number of tuples (i.e., $|R_1| = |R_2|$): $|Pr\{C_n(E_{G(1^n)}(R_1)) = 1\} - Pr\{C_n(E_{G(1^n)}(R_2)) = 1\}| < \frac{1}{p(n)}$. The probability in the above terms is over the internal coin tosses of G and E.*

This definition says that if we try to construct a polynomial circuit for distinguishing any given encrypted database table R_1 (i.e., the circuit will output one if the encrypted form belongs to R_1, else it will output zero), the circuit will have a success probability that is at most slightly better than a random guess.

2.2   A Secure Method for Encryption of Database Tables

While one solution to the securely encrypting a database is to simply encrypt the entire database as a single message this would prevent any meaningful query processing (the entire encrypted database would have to be returned to the querier to enable decryption). Fortunately, we can use Counter (CTR) mode with a secure block cipher algorithm such as AES ([10], note that AES operates on 16 bytes blocks) to meet Definition 1 while still encrypting the individual fields in a tuple independently.

The idea in CTR mode is to choose a unique number (counter) for each block (a field of a tuple can be composed of multiple blocks but for simplicity and without loss of generality, we assume that each field corresponds to a block) and encrypt that unique number. The resulting encryption of the counter is then xor-ed with the actual message block. The counter is stored in plaintext with the encrypted message. For example, let T_i be the ith field of a tuple and C_i be the ith encrypted field. We can encrypt the ith field based on a counter value (ctr) that is incremented by n after encrypting a tuple with n fields. Encryption and decryption in CTR mode can be summarized as follows:

$$\text{CTR Encryption: } C_i = T_i \oplus E_K(ctr + i), i = 1..n$$
$$\text{CTR Decryption: } T_i = C_i \oplus E_K(ctr + i), i = 1..n$$

Since identical field values will now be xor-ed with different values, the fact that they are identical (or any other relationship between them) will be hidden.

2.3 Database Indistinguishability in the Presence of Queries

Database research has concentrated on efficient processing of queries. We would like to maintain this efficiency even if the data is encrypted. As examples in the introduction show, many prior proposals for querying encrypted data do not meet Definition 1 if an adversary is allowed to view data access patterns. This is not just a problem of poor use of encryption. What we really need to ensure is that not only is the encrypted database itself secure, but that the act of processing queries against the database does not reveal information. Unfortunately, achieving such security is at odds with efficient query processing. We now give a definition of secure database querying based on a model from the cryptography community, and show that the only way to meet this strict definitions is to access the entire database for each query. In Section 3.1 we will build on these definitions to give a slightly weaker (but still semantically meaningful) definition supporting more efficient queries. In our current discussion, we assume that data resides on single server and do not consider potential gains due to the replicated data.

Database Queries as a Special Case of Private Information Retrieval
We still require that tuples be indistinguishable (Definition 1), and also require that two *queries* be indistinguishable (e.g., the queries are encrypted). The idea is that if we can't tell tuples or queries apart, we don't really gain information from processing the queries. Unfortunately, this leads us to a result where full database scan is required.

The definition comes from Private Information Retrieval (PIR) [11], which protects the query from disclosure. The server knows the data, but should learn nothing about the query. A PIR server must protect query privacy, and ensure the correctness of the query result.

Why do we want the privacy of the user query be protected? The problem is that if the server knows the query, knowing just the size of the result reveals information about the database. For example, if server knows that $\sigma_{R.a1=300}(R)$ returns three tuples, then the server will have the knowledge of those tuples' $a1$ fields. Note that we only require query indistinguishability for queries that have the same result size. Otherwise we would need to set an upper bound on query result size (the entire database if we want to support full SQL), and transmit that much data for every query – the actual result size would distinguish queries. We now formally define the correctness and privacy requirements.

Definition 2. (Correctness)
Assume database D is stored securely on a server w.r.t Definition 1. Let $E(D)$ be the securely encrypted database and let Q be a query issued on the database. A query execution is said to be correct if given $(Q, E(D))$, an honest server provides a result enabling the query issuer to learn $Q(D)$.

The correctness definition implies that if the server follows the protocol, the query issuer will get the correct result. Also privacy must hold even for a dishonest server:

Definition 3. (Privacy)
For every query pair Q_i, Q_j that run on the same set of tables over D and have the same size results, the messages m_{Q_i}, m_{Q_j} sent for executing the queries are computationally indistinguishable if for every polynomial-size circuit family $\{C_n\}$, every polynomial p, all sufficiently large n, m_{Q_i} and $m_{Q_j} \in \{0,1\}^{poly(n)}$, $|Pr\{C_n(m_{Q_i}) = 1\} - Pr\{C_n(m_{Q_j}) = 1\}| < \frac{1}{p(n)}$. The probability in the previous terms is taken over the internal coin tosses of the query issuer and the server.

This privacy definition implies that whatever the server tries to do, it will not be able to distinguish between two different queries run on the same set of tables and returning the same size results. For example, if $Q1 = \sigma_{a1=300}(R)$ returns 100 tuples and $Q2 = \sigma_{a1=100}(R)$ returns 100 tuples, there is no way for the server to predict which of the two is executed more effectively than a random guess. This could hold for even distinctly different queries (queries can inexpensively be padded to hide the differences), provided the same tables are access and the results are the same size. (The requirement that results be the same size is because padding results to the "maximum possible" result size would impose unacceptable inefficiences.)

We can define a secure query execution as one that runs on securely encrypted data and satisfies Definitions 3 and 2. We can show that even for queries that are running on a single table, above definitions imply that we need to scan the entire table.

We first prove that given a set of queries on a particular table with t, if there exists a query that must access at least v tuples, then we can distinguish it from a query that occasionally accesses fewer than v tuples. Second, we show that for any admissible query result size t, there exists a query which requires the scan of the entire database.

Lemma 1. *Let S_t be queries that run on table R with result size t, and let us assume that there exists a query Q_1^t that needs to access at least v tuples for correct evaluation. Let Q_2^t be an element of S_t that needs to access at most $v-1$ tuples with probability greater than $\frac{1}{p(n)}$. Then there exists a polynomial-size circuit family C_n that can distinguish them with non-negligible probability.*

Proof. We define C_n as follows. Given the messages exchanged during the execution of the query, the circuit will count the number of the tuples accessed. If it is $\geq v$, C_n will output 1; otherwise it will output zero. Note that C_n only does a simple counting, therefore is polynomial in terms of the input size. Now let us calculate the probability $P =| \ Pr\{C_n(m_{Q_1^t}) = 1\} - Pr\{C_n(m_{Q_2^t}) = 1\} \ |$.

$$
\begin{aligned}
P &= | \ Pr\{C_n(m_{Q_1^t}) = 1\} - Pr\{C_n(m_{Q_2^t}) = 1\} \ | \\
&= | \ 1 - Pr\{C_n(m_{Q_2^t}) = 1\} \ | \\
&= | \ 1 - Pr\{\text{more than } v - 1 \text{ tuples accessed}\} \ | \\
&> | \ 1 - (1 - \frac{1}{p(n)}) \ | \\
&> \frac{1}{p(n)}
\end{aligned}
$$

Again, note that the probability is taken over the internal coin tosses of the query issuer and the server; it does not depend on the database values.

Since P is bigger then $\frac{1}{p(n)}$ we can conclude than C_n distinguishes the above queries with non-negligible probability. $\square$

We now show that the queries needed by the above definition exist.

Lemma 2. *For any given result size t, there exists a query that needs to access the entire table.*

Proof. Since the result must be encrypted to preserve security (otherwise all queries would have to return the same result to avoid being distinguished), the resulting set size must be a multiple of the cipher block size k of size, up to the size of the table. Let R have n tuples with a attributes blocked into u blocks of size k. Here without loss of generality, we assume that each attribute is k bits long, therefore u is equal to a.

Let assume that id field added to the database is also k bit long. So for each admissible size t where t is the multiple of k and less than $k * n * a$, we can define a query that needs to access the entire database as follows.

$$
Q_1^t = \bigcup_{i=1}^{\lfloor \frac{t}{kn} \rfloor} \pi_{a_i}(R)
$$
$$
\cup \pi_{a_1}(\sigma_{id < (t \bmod kn - 1)*a}(R))
$$
$$
\cup avg(\pi_{a_1}(R))
$$

The above query simply gets the average of a single attribute to make sure that query needs to access the entire table, and pads the result set to make sure that result size is t. (Since we have not specified a value for k, this generalizes to any block size, including 1.) $\square$

Using the above lemmas, we can now prove the following:

Theorem 1. *A query execution that is secure in the sense of Definitions 3 and 2, even for queries known to access a particular database table, must scan the entire database table non-negligibly often.*

Proof. For the set of queries returning a result of size t, at least one must require full table access (Lemma 2), if not then not all queries would satisfy the correctness Definition 2. We can now build a distinguisher for any query that requires less than full table access (Lemma 1). Since at least one query in t requires full table access, if any requires less than full access a non-negligible portion of the time, the distinguisher will be able to tell the two apart. Such a distinguisher contradicts Definition 3.   □

Database Queries as a Special Case of Software Protection. More generally, the cryptography community has produced the concept of *oblivious RAM*[12]: a method to obscure the program even to someone watching the memory access patterns during execution. They provide a solution such that the distribution of memory accesses does not depend on input. This implies that execution of queries can be made indistinguishable if they access the same number of tuples and have the same result size.

In their main result, they show that if a program and its input with total size y uses memory size m and has a running time t, then it can be simulated by using $m \cdot (\log_2 m)^2$ memory in running time $O(t(\log_2 t)^3)$ without revealing the memory access patterns of the original program (assuming $t > y$). Unfortunately, even under this relaxation, we will not achieve much improvement in terms of efficiency. They show that the lower bound on the oblivious simulation cost is $max\{y, \Omega(t \log t)\}$. In their model, the input y includes everything to be protected, including the program and data. The database would be modeled as part of the program, so the size of the database and the program will be a lower bound for number of memory access. This still implies a full database scan. At this point, we would like to stress that we are considering running a query in isolation – batching queries could improve throughput (a full scan for each batch), but would prevent effective ad-hoc or interactive querying.

3   Plausible Definition for a Secure Database Server

We have shown that any strict security and privacy requirement force us to scan entire databases. The previous definitions' main problems are that they try to preserve indistinguishability even if a server can look at tuple access patterns. What we need is a definition that allows revealing the access patterns for a tuple, enabling more efficient query processing.

3.1   Definition

If the data and queries are encrypted, and the encryption satisfies multiple-message indistinguishability (e.g., Definition 1), then the ability to distinguish between queries or tuples carries little information, especially if the ability to trace tuple access between queries is limited. Using this observation, we give a new definition that guarantees some level of privacy while allowing a higher degree of efficiency than the previous examples.

First, we define a minimum set of support tuples for each query: the tuples that must be accessed to compute the query results. We then only apply query indistinguishability to queries that have the same support tuple set.

Definition 4. (Min support set)
Let query Q be defined on tables $R_1, R_2, \ldots, R_n$. Let S be the set of elements in $R_1 \times R_2 \times \ldots \times R_n$. A set $S \subset (R_1 \times R_2 \times \ldots \times R_n)$ is a min support set for Q if $Q(S) = Q(R_1 \times R_2 \times \ldots \times R_n)$, and S is the smallest such set for which this is true.

We can now give a definition that ensures nothing is disclosed by watching query processing except the size of the result and what tuples were processed in arriving at the result.

Definition 5. (Query Indistinguishability)
For every query pair Q_i, Q_j on the same set of tables, with the same result size and min support set, the messages m_{Q_i}, m_{Q_j} sent for executing the queries are computationally indistinguishable if for every polynomial-size circuit family $\{C_n\}$, every polynomial p, all sufficiently large n, and m_{Q_i} and $m_{Q_j} \in \{0, 1\}^{poly(n)}$,

$$\mid Pr\{C_n(m_{Q_i}) = 1\} - Pr\{C_n(m_{Q_j}) = 1\} \mid < \frac{1}{p(n)}$$

This, combined with Definition 1, guarantees that all an adversary can do is to trace the tuples accessed during query execution, and possibly relate that to result size. As this could disclose information over the course of many queries, we also give the following definition, requiring that the confidence in tracing tuples drops over time:

Definition 6. (Three Card Monte Secure)
A database is c-secure if given a query Q with min support set T, the probability that a server trying to track $t \in T$ can do so correctly is $< \frac{1}{c(k+1)} + \frac{|T|}{|DB|}$, where k is the number of times the server has accessed t since completion of Q.

The key to this definition is that an adversary's confidence that they know which tuples Q accessed will decrease over time. (Formal proof of the efficacy of this definition of security is beyond the scope of this paper.) With high probability any useful information inferred from tracking tuple access will be incorrect.

Definition 7. *We consider a database to support secure query processing if it meets Definitions 1, 2, 5, and 6.*

We now describe how to construct a database server meeting these definitions.

3.2   Requirements for a Database Server

Methods that allow equality test of encrypted tuples, or field values in the tuples, violate Definition 7 because tuples can be distinguished. The problem is that if the tuples are truly indistinguishable, the server will be unable to do any query processing beyond "send the entire table to the client" – any meaningful query processing requires distinguishing between tuples. If the tuples can be distinguished, then they can be tracked over multiple queries, disclosing information in violation of Definition 6.

However, if we support a few simple operations that are "hidden" from the server, we can meet Definition 7. The key idea is that operations that must distinguish between tuples (e.g., comparing a tuple with a selection criteria) occur by decrypting and evaluating a tuple in a manner invisible to the server. The tuples accessed are then re-encrypted and written back to the database, but not necessarily in the same order. This prevents the server from reliably tracking the tuples accessed across multiple queries. To do this without sending tuples back to the querier we assume the existence of a module capable of the following:

1. decrypt tuples,
2. perform functions on two tuples,
3. maintain simple (constant-size) history for performing aggregate functions,
4. generate a new tuple as a function of the inputs, and
5. maintain a constant-size store of tuples, and
6. perform a counter-based CTR mode encryption of the new tuple.

The module may return an (encrypted) tuple to write back into the location most recently read from – but this is not necessarily the most recently read tuple (making tracking difficult). (Such swapping was proposed for PIR in [13], here we amortize the cost as opposed to periodically shuffling off-line.) It also optionally returns a tuple that becomes part of the result. The module also returns the address of the next tuple to be retrieved. Assuming such a module can perform these operations while obscuring its actions and intermediate results from the server, we can construct a machine meeting Definition 7.

The idea is that the database is encrypted as in Section 2.2. An encrypted catalog (in a known location) contains pointers to the first tuple in each table or index. The secure module decrypts the query, reads the catalog to get the location of the first tuple of the relevant tables/indexes, then begins processing. We first show how individual relational operations can be securely performed using the above module. We give a sketch of the proof of security of each using a simulation argument (as used in Secure Multiparty Computation[14]) – the idea is that given the results (min support set and result size), the server is able to simulate the actions of the secure module. If it is able to do so, then all queries on that set and result size must be indistinguishable from the simulator, and thus indistinguishable from each other. (These are sketches; full details require probabilistic simulation proofs to meet Definition 6.) We will then discuss composing operations to perform complex queries.

Selection makes use of the fact that we have some memory hidden from the server (adversary). The secure module keeps the results until the local memory is partially filled. At this point, after each new tuple is read, one of the cached result tuples *may* be output to the server. This decision is a random choice, with the probability based on the estimated size of the results relative to the estimated number of tuples read.

Formally, assume that the estimated number of tuples needed to execute the query is t, the estimated result size is r, and the local memory size is m. The secure module reads the first $(t/r) \cdot (m/2)$ tuples, caching the results in local memory. At this point, for every tuple read, with probability r/t one of the cached result tuples is given to the server. Finally, the remaining cached tuples are given to the server for delivery to the client.

Theorem 2. *Provided that tuples contributing to the result are (approximately) uniformly distributed across tuples read, this process meets Definition 7 for full table scan selections.*

Proof sketch. Using a simulation argument, we assume the simulator for the server is given t and r (since these will be known at the end of the query.) m is public knowledge. The simulator can thus compute $(t/r) \cdot (m/2)$. After this many tuples have been read, the simulator begins creating result tuples. Since the tuples are encrypted using pseudo-random encryption, the simulator just uses a counter and an appropriate length random string of bits to simulate a tuple. By arguments on the strength of encryption the simulated output tuples and re-encrypted tuples are computationally indistinguishable from the real execution. After each tuple is read, a simulated result tuple is created with probability t/r. When all tuples have been read, the simulator creates the remaining result tuples (so the total is r.)

Since the result tuples can be simulated using this approach, and the simulator decides when to create the result tuple in exactly the same fashion as the real algorithm decides when to output a result tuple, the simulator is (computationally) indistinguishable from the actual selection. This shows that it meets Definition 5.

Definition 6 is more difficult. This relies on the assumption of approximately uniform distribution. Because of this, the a-priori probability that a given tuple is in the first t/r tuples is high, so little information is revealed by disclosing that the first result occurs in the first $(t/r) \cdot (m/2)$ tuples. □

This approach does fail when the distribution of which tuples contribute to the result to all query tuples is skewed. For example, if none of the first $(t/r) \cdot (m/2)$ tuples cause a result tuple to be generated, the algorithm will be unable to begin outputting result tuples "on schedule". Thus the server can make an improved estimate of the probability that a tuple contributes to the result. In the worst case (e.g., only the last r tuples contribute to the result), this probability approaches 1.

Queries that generate most results based only on the first tuples read are unlikely. Queries that generate results only after reading most or all of the tuples are more common: aggregation, indexed search. However, these queries will generally return a small number of results. If $r \leq m/2$, the secure coprocessor will not be expected to produce results until all tuples are read, so Theorem 2 holds. Queries where the results are highly skewed should be processed using an indexed selection anyway (to efficiently access only the desired tuples.)

Indexed Selection can be done using a method developed for oblivious access to XML trees[15]. Nodes are swapped, re-encrypted, and written back to the tree. The key idea is that each time a node is read, $c - 1$ additional nodes are read – one of which is known to be empty. All the nodes are re-encrypted and written, with the target written into the empty node. When the nodes are written, the original is written into the empty. This proceeds in levels: The first two levels are read, the location of the second level empty node is determined, and the parent is updated to point to the previous empty node, and the first level written. The third level is read, second level parent updated, etc.

Theorem 3. *The algorithm of [15] satisfies Definition 7.*

Proof sketch. Definition 5 is satisfied because queries with the same min support set will follow the same path to the same leaf. The random choice of $c - 1$ additional nodes comes from the same distribution, and are thus indistinguishable. Likewise, encryption and rewriting is indistinguishable by arguments based on strength of encryption.

Definition 6 is satisfied because of the swapping. Each time a node is accessed, it is placed in a new location. However, since c locations have been read and written, and are indistinguishable to the server, the probability that the server can pick which of the c locations the node is in is $1/c$.

The next time the node is read, it is again placed in one of c locations, with which one unknown to the server. The best the server can now do is guess that it is in one of the $2c$ locations. (Access to other of the original $2c$ locations may confuse the server, causing it to guess more than $2c$ locations, but we are guaranteed at least $2c$.) This continues, with each access to the tuple causing an additional c decrease in the server's best guess, giving our $1/c(k + 1)$ target.

The only problem is that the randomly chosen set of "masking" locations may include locations previously used. This is inherent in a finite database - the best we can do is $1/|DB|$. This is the reasoning behind the $|T|/|DB|$ "floor" factor in Definition 6. □

This analysis is based on a single tuple result. Extension to range queries is straightforward.

Projection is straightforward. The comparison function simply returns $E(\Pi \ tuple)$ rather than $E(tuple)$. Knowing the length of a projection from the encrypted result, the simulator can randomly generate an equivalent-length string that is computationally indistinguishable from the real encrypted result.

Join can be either repeated full-table scan selection (nested loop join) or indexed selection (index join). To perform a join, the module first requests a tuple from one table, then from the second table. Both are decrypted, the join criteria is checked, and if met the joined tuple is stored for output. Assuming a reasonably uniform distribution of tuples meeting the join criteria, or a small number of tuples meeting the join criteria, the proof follows that of Theorem 2. A similar argument holds for an index join. Again, we need a reasonably uniform distribution of tuples meeting the join criteria. The swapping in the index search prevents too much tracking between tuples, and caching the results allows the resulting tuples to be output at a constant rate.

Set operations are straightforward, except for duplicate elimination. Union is simply two selections. Intersection is a join. Set difference is again similar to a join, but output only occurs if after completion of a loop (or index search), a joining tuple is not found.

Duplicate elimination could reveal equality of two tuples. This is more than simply "does it contribute to the result", and thus violates Definition 7. One solution is to replace duplicates with an encrypted dummy tuple. The client thus gets a correct result by ignoring the dummy tuples, at the cost of increased size of the result.

4   Conclusions

The idea of a database server operating on encrypted data is a nice one: It opens up new business models, protects against unauthorized access, allows remote database services, etc. Achieving this vision requires compromises between security and efficiency. We have shown that a server that would be considered secure by the cryptography community would be hopelessly inefficient by standards of the database community. Efficient methods (e.g., operations on encrypted data) can not meet cryptographic standards of security.

We have given a definition of security that is the best that can be achieved while maintaining reasonable levels of performance. We have shown that this definition can be realized using commercially available special-purpose hardware.

References

1. Hacigumus, H., Iyer, B.R., Li, C., Mehrotra, S.: Executing SQL over encrypted data in the database-service-provider model. In: Proceedings of the 2002 ACM SIGMOD International Conference on Management of Data, Madison, Wisconsin (2002) 216–227
2. Damiani, E., Vimercati, S.D.C., Jajodia, S., Paraboschi, S., Samarati, P.: Balancing confidentiality and efficiency in untrusted relational dbmss. In: Proceedings of the 10th ACM conference on Computer and communications security, Washington D.C., USA, ACM Press (2003) 93–102
3. Ozsoyoglu, G., Singer, D.A., Chung, S.S.: Anti-tamper databases: Querying encrypted databases. In: Proceedings of the 17th Annual IFIP WG 11.3 Working Conference on Database and Applications Security, Estes Park, Colorado (2003)
4. Agrawal, R., Kiernan, J., Srikant, R., Xu, Y.: Order-preserving encryption for numeric data. In: Proceedings of the 2004 ACM SIGMOD International Conference on Management of Data, Paris, France (2004)

5. Boneh, D., Boyen, X.: Efficient selective-id secure identity-based encryption without random oracles. In: EUROCRYPT. (2004) 223–238
6. Song, D., Wagner, D., Perrig, A.: Search on encrypted data. In: Procedings of IEEE SRSP, IEEE (2000)
7. Ahituv, N., Lapid, Y., Neumann, S.: Processing encrypted data. Communications of the ACM **20** (1987) 777–780
8. IBM: IBM PCI cryptographic coprocessor (2004) http://www.ibm.com/security/cryptocards/html/pcicc.shtml.
9. Goldreich, O.: Encryption Schemes. In: The Foundations of Cryptography. Volume 2. Cambridge University Press (2004)
10. NIST: Advanced encryption standard (aes). Technical Report NIST Special Publication FIPS-197, National Institute of Standards and Technology (2001) http://csrc.nist.gov/publications/fips/fips197/fips-197.pdf.
11. Chor, B., Kushilevitz, E., Goldreich, O., Sudan, M.: Private information retrieval. Journal of the ACM **45** (1998) 965–981
12. Goldreich, O., Ostrovsky, R.: Software protection and simulation on oblivious RAMs. Journal of the ACM **43** (1996) 431–473
13. Asonov, D., Freytag, J.C.: Almost optimal private information retrieval. In: Second International Workshop on Privacy Enhancing Technologies PET 2002, San Francisco, CA, USA, Springer-Verlag (2002) 209–223
14. Goldreich, O.: General Cryptographic Protocols. In: The Foundations of Cryptography. Volume 2. Cambridge University Press (2004)
15. Lin, P., Candan, K.S.: Hiding traversal of tree structured data from untrusted data stores. In: Proceedings of Intelligence and Security Informatics: First NSF/NIJ Symposium ISI 2003, Tucson, AZ, USA (2003) 385

Blind Custodians: A Database Service Architecture That Supports Privacy Without Encryption

Amihai Motro and Francesco Parisi-Presicce

Department of Information and Software Engineering,
George Mason University, Fairfax, VA, USA
{ami, fparisip}@gmu.edu

Abstract. We describe an architecture for a database service that does not assume that the service provider can be trusted. Unlike other architectures that address this problem, this architecture, which we call *blind custodians*, does not rely on encryption. Instead, it offers confidentiality by means of *information dissociation:* The server only stores "fragments" of information that are considered safe (i.e., each fragment does not violate privacy), while the client stores the associations between the fragments that are necessary to reconstruct the information. We argue that this architecture allows satisfactory confidentiality, while offering two important advantages: (1) It does not restrict the types of queries that can be submitted by clients (as encryption-based methods invariably do), and (2) it requires only light processing at the client, assigning the bulk of the processing to the server (as befits a true service). Moreover, the architecture permits flexible control over the level of confidentiality that should be maintained (at the cost of additional overhead).

1   Introduction

With the improvement of network availability, reliability, and speed, more and more information management tasks that traditionally have been performed on the computer of the data owner, are now being offered as *services*: the information is stored in the computer of the service provider, and can be managed remotely over the network. Primary examples include web hosting, the management of electronic mail, appointment calendars, address books, investment portfolios, and, more recently, general database management services. Such information management services provide clients with performance and features at a level often not available at their own enterprises. These include continuous availability, accessibility from virtually anywhere in the world, reliable data backup and prompt recovery, and protection from unauthorized or malicious access. In many cases, a remote information management service can prove to be more cost-effective than traditional, local processing.

The downside of such information management services is that *privacy* may have to be sacrificed. The operators of the service, the *custodians* of the information, may promise complete confidentiality, but they themselves may not be

S. Jajodia and D. Wijesekera (Eds.): Data and Applications Security 2005, LNCS 3654, pp. 338–352, 2005.
© IFIP International Federation for Information Processing 2005

entirely trustworthy. From the client's point of view, custodians should be *blind*; that is, they should perform the functionalities promised, but without being able to observe the data themselves. We shall refer to such information services as *blind custodians*. In a way, a bank that offers safe deposit boxes to its clients is serving as a blind custodian: It safekeeps the contents without knowing what they are. The complication in being the blind custodian of information is that you are also required to *manipulate* the information without knowing what it is.

There have been several recent works that address this or similar issues [9,8,5,6]. Invariably, these works describe architectures that protect the information by means of *encryption*. By encrypting the information, the client is guaranteed that it alone can observe the data. The problem, of course, is how to perform functions such as *selective retrieval* on encrypted information. Simply put, if the records of an employee file are stored encrypted, how does the client request to retrieve only the records of the engineers? This issue has led to solutions that are only partially successful. In a typical solution [8], the file is partitioned into "buckets", and each retrieval request is mapped (at the client's end) to a specification of buckets. Such an architecture has several weaknesses. It requires the predetermination of all columns for which selection is to be enabled (each column requires its own partitioning), it normally retrieves more records than requested, and it limits severely the selection comparisons that are feasible (for example, processing range queries is problematic).

In this paper we take the more general approach that regards information as an *association among values*. For instance, the information comprising the employee record (*Andrei, Engineer*, $75,000) is the three constituent values, as well as their mutual association. Consequently, hiding information is done both by hiding the values (e.g., by means of encryption) and by concealing the association. In our approach, the custodian might be able to observe data values (unless they are hidden by encryption), but would be denied knowledge of their association. In duality with encryption keys, the *cipher* for associating the disparate fragments would be available only to the client. Hence the objective of blind custodians is achieved by *information dissociation*.

The proposed architecture is described in Section 4 and preliminary discussion and assessment of this architecture are offered in Section 5. Section 6 concludes the paper with a brief summary and discussion of the considerable work that still remains to be done. We begin with a formal definition of the problem (Section 2), followed by a brief survey of related work (Section 3).

2   Formal Definition of the Problem

The general problem of a database service with privacy is formalized here abstractly. This abstraction allows us to position the works discussed in Section 3 in a unified framework.

Assume a database D and a query Q, and let $A = Q(D)$ denote the answer to the query Q in the database D. In a database service architecture, D is stored on the server, the client sends Q to the server, the server evaluates $A = Q(D)$ and returns A to the client.

Assume now that certain information in D must be kept confidential (it could be all or just part of D). A transformation T is then required, as follows:

1. T transforms the database into $D^* = T(D)$, and the query into $Q^* = T(Q)$.
2. Let $A^* = Q^*(D^*)$ denote the answer to Q^* in the transformed database D^*.
3. When the inverse transformation T^{-1} is applied to A^* it yields $T^{-1}(A^*) = A$.

In the database service architecture, the transformed database D^* is stored on the server. When the client needs to evaluate a query Q, it sends to the server its transformed version Q^*. The server evaluates Q^* on D^* and sends back the answer A^*. The client then transforms A^* into A. The transformation T should hide the confidential information in D, and should be such that knowledge of A^* would not be sufficient to determine the answer A. This discussion is illustrated in the following diagram:

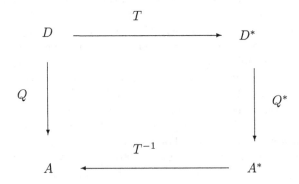

This simple formulation may be overly "tidy" to be sufficiently general, and we consider here several more elaborate variations.

First, we may allow a transformation T that does not satisfy $T^{-1}(A^*) = A$, as long as there exists another query that can extract the answer A from $T^{-1}(A^*)$. That is, there exists a query Q' such that $Q'(T^{-1}(A^*)) = A$. Second, we may divide the transformed database D^* into two parts, one to be stored at the server, the other at the client. The query Q^* is performed on the server's part only, yielding A^*. The client receives A^* and applies T^{-1} and Q' to both A^* and its part of the transformed database. Third, the computations done at the server and at the client may be *interleaved*, thus producing the final answer after a process of data exchange.

There are two trivial and impractical "solutions" to this problem:

- **Confidentiality without service.** In this solution, the transformation T is an encryption of the entire database, and the inverse transformation T^{-1} is simply decryption. Every query is translated to the trivial query Q^* that, when submitted to D^*, returns the entire database (i.e., $A^* = D^*$). The transformation T^{-1} converts A^* back to D and the additional query Q' is nothing more than the original query Q. In summary, the entire database is encrypted, and this encrypted database is retrieved in response to every query. Following decryption at the client, the query is processed locally. This "solution" obviously preserves the confidentiality of the information in the database, but is otherwise impractical, because no query processing is done on the server, and the client must have complete database management facilities. Indeed, the "server" does not deliver most of the functionalities or benefits of a Web service. Moreover, this solution requires the transmission of the entire database, an expensive, time-consuming operation.

– **Service without confidentiality**. At the opposite end of the spectrum, T is the identity transformation. Thus, $D^* = D$, $Q^* = Q$, $A^* = A$ (and Q' is unnecessary). In this case, all computations are performed at the server and only the exact answer A is transmitted back to the client. Obviously, this approach provides no confidentiality whatsoever.

These two extreme approaches demonstrate the tradeoffs involved: complete confidentiality, but no service (all work is done at the client), *vs.* complete service (all work is done at the server) but no confidentiality. The works discussed in the following section are positioned in-between these two extremes because they choose smaller granularities for their encrypted transformation T. This allows some queries to be performed on the encrypted version D^* which is on the server.

3   Related Work

Work on information management services is quite extensive, with focus on issues such as availability, anywhere accessibility and reliability. More recently, efforts have concentrated on the need for a particular form of confidentiality [9,8,5,6,1], intended to protect clients' information from the service provider itself. These works discuss just two basic approaches to achieving confidentiality, both relying exclusively on encryption (either at the tuple level or at the field level).

The overall goal in [8] is to develop techniques for querying an encrypted database. The approach is restricted to integer-valued attributes and encryption is at the *field* level. If the encryption function is monotonic with respect to a predefined partial order on the plaintext database D, then queries Q involving ranges, comparisons, maximal value, minimal value, and so on, can be translated to queries Q^* on D^*, for which the answer A^* contains all (and sometimes, as in the case of maximal value, only) the tuples sought. More generally, encryption can be tailored to be a homomorphism with respect to a restricted set S of allowable queries, so that the result of a query Q in the allowable set S on the plaintext database D is obtained by decrypting the result of the encrypted query Q^* on the encrypted database D^*. An advantage of this approach is that for any query Q in S, only a single encrypted query needs to be evaluated on the encrypted database and its output needs no additional processing except for decryption. The problem, however, is to maintain the requirement that the encryption function be a homomorphism, while still allowing a reasonably broad set of queries. For an encryption to be a homomorphism, restrictions are placed on the possible closed-form (i.e., definable by an expression) or open-form (i.e., definable via an algorithm) encryption functions. Among them are order-preservation and distance-preservation. Although effective and efficient in its restricted domain, the approach is limited by the requested properties on the encryption functions.

A different approach is offered in [9], where encryption is at the *tuple* level, and an *indexing* scheme is used. If A is an attribute of R on which the client may need to issue selection queries, then the values of this attribute are partitioned, and every tuple of R is assigned to a single partition based on its A value. This scheme amounts to an *index* on attribute A. The mapping ϕ_A from the values of A to the partition identifiers is available only to the client, whereas the association between the partition identifiers and the encrypted tuples is known to the server. The latter association can be implemented as an extra attribute in the encrypted relation R, in which the values of ϕ_A will be stored. Each query Q on attribute A is converted to a query Q^* on the new attribute ϕ_A, and evaluated on D^*. The result A^* is returned to the client and decrypted. The initial query Q is then evaluated on the decrypted version of A^*. If Q selects the tuples of R for which the attribute A has value a, then Q^* returns all the encrypted tuples with the index value $\phi_A(a)$. By the very nature of indexing, a statistical query that is derived from the entire set of A values (e.g., the average value or the most frequent value) requires that *all* the tuples of R be retrieved from the server. Another drawback of this approach is that it requires a separate indexing scheme for each attribute on which selection queries are to be enabled; moreover, the selection attributes must be anticipated ahead of querying: A query on any attribute not indexed cannot be properly evaluated and the client would need to retrieve the entire relation. As each index requires an additional attribute on the server, indexing every attribute would double the size of the relation.

This approach is adopted and extended in [5], where different possibilities for representing indexing (partitioning) information are discussed. The authors propose to compute the indexing information so that it relates to the data well enough to provide an effective query execution mechanism, without releasing information about the relationship between indexes and data. Their solution is to base the indexing on direct encryption and hashing. They provide a detailed analysis on the inference exposure of the encrypted/indexed data. The paper also describes an enhancement of the indexing information that supports range queries.

The authors of [6] too investigate the approach of [9], which they term *aggregate-then-encrypt*. They propose a formalization to assess the security of privacy-preserving database outsourcing schemes, and apply it to analyze the scheme in [9]. They identify weaknesses and suggest a number of improvements to strengthen the approach. In addition, their paper contains an interesting result on the *impossibility* of achieving complete security by means of *privacy homomorphisms* (encryption functions that allow limited processing of the encrypted data), which is essentially the technique used in [8]. A review of several solutions to the problem of using the services of a provider without giving unnecessary access to sensitive data is included in [3].

The work in [2] concerns outsourcing scientific computations, where the external agent should not learn the actual data or the result of the computation.

The client *disguises* the problem and data with local preprocessing before sending it to the agent, and obtains the true answer after further local post-processing of the result it receives. The major difference between that problem and the one addressed in this paper is that in [2] the client does not keep data permanently at the external agent. As in our approach, and unlike [10], the client's processing power is not limited to encryption and decryption.

The approach in [1] is to enforce privacy by replacing identifying information with values obtained through an anonymization process. It allows a choice of three basic properties of the anonymizing function: reversibility (by using encryption to allow the recovery of the original data if the appropriate key is known), irreversibility (by using one-way hash functions to prevent the recovery of the original information), and inversibility (pseudoanonymization, in Common Criteria terms, allowing the recovery by means of exceptional procedures to be applied by trusted parties only). The results of this anonymizing process are then used in different databases in place of the private information. Regardless of the anonymization objectives listed above, the "link" between random (anonymous) identities and actual identities is protected by encryption.

Two research areas that are somewhat related are privacy-preserving data mining [12] and secure multi-party computation [7, Chapter 7]. The blind custodian approach differs from these two areas in two important aspects: The secret data is not distributed among several parties (it could be physically distributed, but it is still controlled by a single client) and the client is expected to perform only minimal database work.

4   The Architecture

4.1   Information Dissociation

We have already observed that information is an *association among values*, and hence confidentiality may be achieved by hiding the association. The technique for hiding the *association*, which we term *information dissociation*, is discussed next.

Consider a database relation $R = (A_1, \ldots, A_m)$. Assume that it has been determined that while the tuples in this relation are confidential and should not be disclosed, subtuples with attributes $A_1, \ldots, A_i$ and subtuples with attributes $A_{i+1}, \ldots, A_m$ may be disclosed. For example, consider a table of employees with fields that concern employment (e.g., employee id, name, position and department), and fields that contain a home address (e.g., street, number, city, state and zip code; but not employee id). It may be considered acceptable to disclose each of these groups of fields separately, but not complete records (as they associate employees with their addresses).

Two views of R are defined (e.g., by appropriate SQL queries), and each of the resulting relations is augmented by an identifying field (an *index*) I_1 or I_2, thus obtaining new relations F_1 and F_2. The blind custodian is then entrusted with F_1 and F_2, while the client maintains the correspondence between I_1 and

I_2 which is necessary to recover the complete tuples of the original relation R. The latter information is referred to as the *cipher* of the dissociation. In general, the number of fragment views may be arbitrary (i.e., not limited to two).

The database transformation $D^* = T(D)$ described in Section 2 is the decomposition of each of the database relations into a set of fragment relations and a cipher. This decomposition is somewhat reminiscent of other decompositions known from database theory, such as lossless-join decompositions or dependency-preserving decompositions in normalization theory [11, pages 392–412], or file fragmentation and replication in distributed database design [4, pages 67–92]. To satisfy the requirement that T hide confidential information, this decomposition must be done judiciously. Presently, we observe two broad approaches towards this problem, one qualitative and one quantitative.

The qualitative approach uses external (subjective) judgment to determine that information, say, on an individual's employment, should not be associated with this individual's address. A simple way to annotate these constraints is to identify maximal sets of attributes that *may* be kept together (in the same fragment). Typically, several such safe fragments would be identified. ¿From these, a set of fragments should be chosen that is both *consistent* and *complete*. Consistency guarantees that the set would not include two fragments that overlap on an attribute that is a key for at least one of the fragments, as this would allow the construction of a larger (unsafe) fragment. Completeness guarantees that the fragments in the set are sufficient to reconstruct the original relation (using the cipher).

A second possible way to dissociate a relation is to use objective (quantitative) criteria. The intuition here is that decomposing a relation into F_1 and F_2 is not very useful if R contains most of the tuples of the Cartesian product of the two fragments. If the original relation R has n tuples and is split into fragments F_1 and F_2 with n_1 and n_2 tuples, respectively, with no attributes in common, then the probability that a random tuple from F_1 and a random tuple from F_2 are related (form a tuple in the original relation R) is $p = n/(n_1 * n_2)$. When p is small (its lower bound is 0), then it is difficult to guess the associations among the subtuples of F_1 and F_2 that are valid. When p is high (its upper bound is 1), then a random tuple of F_1 is more likely to be associated with a random tuple of F_2. In the latter case, the value of decomposing R into F_1 and F_2 is rather low. Hence, decompositions with low p values should be preferred.

A combination of the two approaches would call for an initial dissociation based on subjective criteria, followed by a quantitative approach to choose among the resulting alternatives.

4.2   Query Evaluation

We now turn to the issue of evaluating client queries in this architecture. For simplicity, we assume that the database D consists of a single relation R, and that queries are selection-projection expressions; the generalization to multi-relation databases and other types of queries will be discussed later.

Assume that R has been decomposed to the fragments $F_1, \ldots, F_k$. Let I_i denote the index field that was added to the fragment F_i $(i = 1, \ldots, k)$, and let $C = (I_1, \ldots, I_k)$ denote the new cipher relation. $F_1, \ldots, F_k$ are stored at the server, and C is stored at the client. In terms of the formal problem defined in Section 2, this decomposition is the transformation T, and $F_1, \ldots, F_k$ and C make up the new database $D^* = T(D)$.

Consider a query Q on R submitted at a client. First, Q is transformed into a query Q^* on the server's database $F_1, \ldots, F_k$. The evaluation of this query on the server's database is returned to the client (this result is denoted A^*). The client then transforms this result into a new relation using its cipher C (this result is denoted $T^{-1}(A^*)$). To this, the client applies final processing (Q') to obtain the answer A. We observe at least two possible implementations of this process, each based on a well-known query optimization technique.

To illustrate the two techniques, we describe a simple example, in which information on employees is dissociated, so as to separate employment-related information from personal information:

$$F_1 = (I_1, Eid, Ename, Salary, YearHired)$$
$$F_2 = (I_2, Gender, Nationality, YearBorn)$$

Assume that the cardinality of R is 1,000, the cardinality of F_1 is also 1,000, but the cardinality of F_2 is only 750. Since the number of possible matchings among tuples of F_1 and F_2 is $1,000 \cdot 750 = 75,000$, and since only 1,000 of these are valid tuples of R, it follows that the probability that a random tuple from F_1 and a random of F_2 form a tuple of R is $1/750 = 0.00133$. We may assume that this probability is low enough to provide confidentiality (i.e., to thwart guessing).

Frugal Join. The relation R is substituted in Q by an expression that joins the cipher and the relevant fragments, and the query's selection and projection operations are "pushed" to the individual fragments, as practicable. The evaluation of the transformed query proceeds as follows. First, the server performs selections and projections on its fragments and sends the results to the client. The client then joins the results using its cipher and applies the final selection and projection (which could not be pushed to the fragments).

Consider now a query about the id's of female employees who earn over $80,000 and have been in employment for more than half their lives:

Q :
select *Eid*
from *Employee*
where *Salary* $> 80,000$ **and** *Gender* $=$ 'female'
    and $(2005 - YearHired) > 0.5 * (2005 - YearBorn)$

The server performs this two-part query Q^*:

Q_1^* :
select I_1, *Eid*, *YearHired*
from F_1
where *Salary* $> 80,000$

Q_2^* :
select I_2, *YearBorn*
from F_2
where *Gender* $=$ 'female'

It sends the results, denoted A_1^* and A_2^* respectively, to the client, who then concludes the processing with a query that joins the answers through its cipher and then extracts the final tuples that constitute the answer A:

Q' :
select *Eid*
from A_1^*, A_2^*, C
where $A_1^*.I_1 = C.I_1$ **and** $A_2^*.I_2 = C.I_2$
     and $(2005 - YearHired) > 0.5 * (2005 - YearBorn)$

With respect to confidentiality, this process does not disclose to the server anything than it does not already know. From the request to deliver the two sets A_1^* and A_2^*, the server may be able to guess the client's query Q, but forming the two sets (something it could do all along, anyhow) does not increase its ability to match F_1 tuples with F_2 tuples. In other words, the probability of generating random R tuples through random guessing remains unchanged at 0.00133.

With respect to transmission costs, assume further that of the 1,000 employees 500 are females, 400 earn over \$80,000, and of the latter only 100 are females. The server sends to the client 400 tuples of three fields each and 500 tuples of two fields each, for a total of 2,200 fields.

Semi-join. Here, the joins among the fragments and the cipher are done in stages. Assume that m fragments are involved in the query, and let α_i denote the selection-projection query on the i'th fragment. The server begins by sending the client the result of performing α_1 on the first fragment. The client matches the id's of the tuples it received through its cipher, and sends to the server the corresponding tuple id's for the second fragment. The server then performs α_2 on the second fragment after it has been pruned with the id's it received, and sends the result to the client. The client matches the id's of the tuples it received through its cipher, and sends to the server the corresponding tuple id's for the third fragment. The process continues until the results from m'th fragment are sent to the client. The client then constructs the required answer from the data it has received. This version is often superior to the previous one because it reduces data transmission substantially (transmission can be further optimized by scheduling the order of fragments effectively).

In our two-fragment example, consider the same query. The server begins with a query on the first fragment

Q_1^* :
select I_1, *Eid*, *YearHired*
from F_1
where *Salary* $> 80,000$

and sends the result, denoted A_1^*, to the client. The client matches this information through its cipher

Q_1' :
select I_2
from A_1^*, C
where $A_1^*.I_1 = C.I_1$

and sends the resulting tuple id's, denoted A'_1, back to the server. The server then performs

$$Q^*_2:$$
select I_2, *YearBorn*
from F_2, A'_1
    where $F_2.I_2 = A'_1.I_2$
        and *Gender* = 'female'

and sends the result, denoted A^*_2, to the client. The client concludes the processing with the query

$$Q'_2:$$
select *Eid*
from A^*_1, A^*_2, C
where $A^*_1.I_1 = C.I_1$ **and** $A^*_2.I_2 = C.I_2$
    and $(2005 - YearHired) > 0.5 * (2005 - YearBorn)$

Assuming the cardinalities given above, transmission costs are reduced. The server sends to the client 400 tuples of 3 fields each, the client then sends to the server about 300 tuples of one field each,[1] and the server sends to the client only 100 tuples of two fields each, for a total of only 1,700 fields.

However, with respect to confidentiality, this strategy discloses information to the server. The server delivered a set of I_1 values and received in return a matching set of I_2 values. In our example, the cardinality of these sets are 400 and 300, respectively. Hence, the probability of reconstructing an employee tuple in this subset of high-salaried employees is $400/(400 \cdot 300) = 0.00333$. Confidentiality has thus been reduced by a factor of 2.5. This reduction in confidentiality can be seen as a result of providing the server with information that was cycled through the cipher. Care must be taken when using the semi-join strategy, to assure that a desirable level of confidentiality is maintained.

5   Discussion

5.1   Measuring and Maintaining Protection Levels

How much protection does the blind custodian architecture provide? Essentially, the challenge for the server is to recover protected information by finding associations among the fragments. Assume a relation R is dissociated into two fragments F_1 and F_2. Let n, n_1 and n_2 denote the cardinalities of R, F_1 and F_2, respectively. As already suggested in the previous section, confidentiality is provided by having large enough cardinalities n_1 and n_2 and a relatively smaller cardinality n. Specifically, the number of possible associations between tuples of F_1 and tuples of F_2 is $n_1 \cdot n_2$, of which only n are valid. Consequently, the probability that a random matching of a tuple of F_1 with a tuple of F_2 will coincide

---

[1] Since 1,000 employees share 750 personal records, we may assume that 400 employees share 300 personal records.

with an actual tuple of R is $n/(n_1 \cdot n_2)$. We adopt this probability of disclosure as a measure of the protection afforded to the fragments F_1 and F_2 (or to R itself). It quantifies the ability to associate information from the two fragments, and thus gain knowledge of protected information. Note that lower probabilities indicate better protection. So that higher values indicate better protection, we define the *protection level* of F_1 and F_2 as $1 - n/(n_1 \cdot n_2)$.

Each pair of fragments has its own level of protection. Protection levels can also be defined for sets of fragments larger than two. Assume R is dissociated into fragments $F_1, \ldots, F_k$. The protection level of $F_1, \ldots, F_k$ is $1 - n/(n_1 \cdots n_k)$. This number reflects the ability to create complete tuples of R.[2] Protection levels can also be defined for fragment subsets that do not "cover" all of R. In such cases the numerator cardinality is the number of tuples in the projection of R that corresponds to the attributes in the fragment subset. A definition of protection level in the general case follows.

Assume a relation R is dissociated into fragments $F_1, \ldots, F_k$. Let $F_{i_1}, \ldots, F_{i_p}$ be a subset of the fragments, and let n_{i_j} be the cardinality of F_{i_j} ($j = 1, \ldots, p$). The protection level of $F_{i_1}, \ldots, F_{i_p}$ is defined to be $1 - n'/(n_{i_1} \cdots n_{i_p})$, where n' is the cardinality of the projection of R onto the attributes of $F_{i_1}, \ldots, F_{i_p}$.

The protection level required for each subset of fragments may be defined by setting threshold values during the dissociation process sketched in Section 4.1. Or one may simply adopt a single threshold for all the possible combinations of fragments.

These thresholds must be upheld during both the initial design and in subsequent query processing. During the initial design, it must be ensured that for every subset of fragments the protection level exceeds the threshold. During query processing, when the semi-join strategy is used, care must be taken not to exchange subsets with small cardinalities, as this may result in decreased protection levels (as was illustrated in the example).[3]

In both the initial design and subsequent query processing, whenever protection levels fall below the threshold, cardinalities may be artificially increased by adding *spurious tuples*, thus improving protection levels. (1) In the initial design, spurious tuples may be added to fragments as necessary. The id's of these "bogus" tuples must be kept on the client, to ensure that this information is not included in the final answers. (2) During query processing, when the client receives a set of tuple id's from one fragment and responds with a corresponding set of tuple id's of another fragment, the outgoing set may be enlarged with additional tuple id's from the second fragment. These may be either "real" or "bogus" tuples; however, the client must log these additions, to ensure that they do not taint the final answers. Clearly, the use of spurious tuples increases the cost of query processing.

---

[2] Note that it may be misleadingly high, as just associating a few of the fragments may be worrisome.

[3] The frugal join strategy has no effect on the protection level.

5.2   Multi-relation Databases and Join Queries

The architecture we described assumed that the database has only one relation. However, the extension to several relations is relatively simple, and we sketch it here briefly. Each of the database relations is dissociated into a set a fragments and a cipher, and the client stores all the ciphers. However, extra care must be taken to protect key or foreign key relationships among the different relations, as necessary. For example, assume two database relations $Employee = (\underline{Eid}, Ename, Salary)$ and $Assignment = (\underline{Eid, Project}, Performance)$ with the requirement that performance information be kept separate from salary. If the two relations are considered individually, then it may appear that no dissociation is necessary; i.e., each relation will require a single fragment containing all its attributes. Yet, when considered together, the common attribute Eid allows performance and salary to be associated. A simple solution is to remove Eid from the relation in which it is a foreign key. Thus, the fragments would be $F_1 = (I_1, Eid, Ename, Salary)$, and $F_2 = (I_2, Project, Performance)$. This solution depends on the fact that all employee id's in $Assignment$ appear in $Employee$.

Consider now database queries that involve joins among relations. The techniques described in Section 4.2 are applicable without significant changes. A query that requires a join $R_1 \bowtie R_2$ will be decomposed into a query that joins fragments of R_1, fragments of R_2, and a fragment of R_1 with a fragment of R_2. The joins may be based on either the frugal or the semi-join approaches.

5.3   Comparison

How does the blind custodians architecture compare with other methods? In Section 3 we discussed the two main alternatives: field-level encryption that uses encryption functions with exacting properties [8], and a combination of tuple-level encryption with index-like structures [9]. Below, we briefly discuss the blind custodians architecture vis-a-vis these two alternatives

We observe two important performance criteria for a non-trusting database service: (1) the family of queries that can be processed should be as general as possible, and (2) the service provider should do as much of the work as possible, and the amount of data transmitted should be as small as possible.[4]

Clearly, a strong encryption function that is a homomorphism for general queries would provide an ideal solution, as it would fully satisfy both requirements. Note that because the encrypted answers sent to the client would be exact, all work (except for decryption) would done at the server, and data transmission would be minimal. Unfortunately, such ideal encryption functions are not available. Hence, the main disadvantage of the approach advocated in [8] is that it severely limits the generality of queries that can be processed. And if more general queries are attempted, then the burden of processing shifts drastically to the client.

---

[4] Note that the relative amount of work done at the server and the volume of data transmission are strongly related: More work accomplished at the server implies less data transmitted, and vice versa.

A similar disadvantage is also apparent in the index-based architecture [9]. To increase query processing capabilities, indexing structures must be devised for most every attribute; and even then some queries (e.g., certain statistical queries) may require the entire set of tuples to be sent to the client. Consequently, clients must have substantial database management capabilities to process the tuples they receive.

In contrast, the blind custodian architecture has a clear advantage in the first of the two criteria, as it places no restrictions on the types of queries allowed. It is difficult to estimate its relative performance with respect to the second criteria, as it depends strongly on the *profile* of the queries submitted, and the *implementation* of the other architectures (i.e., the types of encryption functions adopted in the first approach, and the extent of indexing performed in the second approach).

How much work is done at a blind custodian client? It can be described as a "light" database management system. Among other tasks, it should be able to convert queries to appropriate execution plans, join relations through their ciphers, and apply final extractions. Except for the ciphers, data is only cached temporarily at the client, and only limited storage capabilities are therefore necessary. Of course, the client system does not need to manage functions such as backup, recovery, or transaction synchronization.

6   Conclusion

We outlined an architecture for a database service that provides confidentiality by means of information dissociation. The essential paradigm of our architecture — decompose the database into fragments and then transform queries on the original database into queries on the fragments — is similar to that of *distributed databases*, with a notable difference: The *motivation* for the decomposition is different. In distributed databases decomposition is dictated by requirements such as (1) data must be stored only in the computers of their owners, (2) data is preferably stored in computers that access them frequently, and (3) data could be replicated to provide redundancy and to reduce transmission; whereas here, the decomposition is motivated by the need to protect the data from the server, while letting the server store as much information as possible.

The discussion in this paper is only preliminary and many issues still have to be addressed in appropriate detail. Several of these research issues have already been given limited treatment earlier, and we mention here three additional issues.

Queries. We considered at some detail queries that are join-selection-projection expressions. Other important query operations include set operations (e.g., union or difference) and statistical functions (e.g., count or average). We conjecture that these operations can be accommodated in the architecture without requiring any modifications. Indeed, as the architecture is analogous to a distributed database, every query should be feasible, the only constraint being that its execution plan should maintain the requisite level of protection.

Protection. We analyzed protection levels under the naive assumption that no external knowledge is used in attempts to gain hidden information, and our protection analysis assumed *uniform* probability distribution functions. In various circumstances, external information available to the server may allow it to infer a non-uniform probability distribution function that is much closer to the actual function. For example, there may be 40 different values of *YearBorn* and 20 different values of *YearHired*, but of the 800 combinations, some combinations may be known to have probabilities that are much higher than those of other combinations. Such knowledge may lower substantially the protection level. Additionally, the cardinalities of some domains may be misleadingly high. For example, there may be 3,000 different salary values in the database, yet for practical purposes one may consider similar all salaries that round to the same $1,000, resulting in a much smaller number of "significantly different" values. These and other issues require a more elaborate analysis of protection levels.

Encryption. A basic feature of the blind custodians architecture is that it does not involve encryption. The architecture attempts to protect relationships, while assuming that there is no harm in disclosing the values in the database. Yet there may be circumstances in which even the domain values should not be made public. This could be achieved by substituting the domain values with identifiers and associating the identifiers with the actual values by means of a new client relation. This solution is not attractive because it increases the storage requirements on clients beyond the essential ciphers. Alternatively, we could use field-level encryption to hide values when necessary.

References

1. A. Abou El Kalam, Y. Deswarte, G. Trouessin, and E. Cordonnier. A generic approach for healthcare data anonymization. In *Proceedings of WPES 04, the 2004 ACM Workshop on Privacy in the Electronic Society*, pp. 31–32, 2004.
2. M. J. Atallah, K. N. Pantazopoulos, J. R. Rice, and E. H. Spafford. *Secure Outsourcing of Scientific Computations*, Volume 54 in Advances in Computers, pp. 215–272. Elsevier, 2001.
3. C. Boyens and O. Gunther. Trust is not enough: Privacy and security in ASP and Web service environment. In *Proceedings of ADBIS 02, Advances in Database and Information Systems*, LNCS No. 2435, pp. 8–22. Springer, 2002.
4. S. Ceri and G. Pelagatti. *Distributed Databases: Principles and Systems*. McGraw-Hill, 1984.
5. E. Damiani, S. De Capitani di Vimercati, S. Jajodia, S. Paraboschi, and P. Samarati. Balancing confidentiality and efficiency in untrusted relational DBMSs. In *Proceedings of the 10th ACM Conference on Computer and Communication Security*, pp. 93–102, 2003.
6. M. Fischmann and O. Gunther. Privacy tradeoffs in database service architectures. In *Proceedings of BIZSEC 03, the First ACM Workshop on Business Driven Security Engineering*, 2003.
7. O. Goldreich. *Foundations of Cryptography, Volume II: Basic Applications*. Cambridge University Press, 2004.
8. G. Ozsoyoglu, D. A. Singer, and S. S. Chung. Anti-tamper databases: Querying encrypted databases. In *Proceedings of the 17th Annual IFIP WG11.3 Working Conference on Database and Application Security*, 2003.

9. H. Hacigumus, B. Iyer, C. Li, and S. Mehrotra. Executing SQL over encrypted data in the database-service-provider model. In *Proceedings SIGMOD 02, International Conference on Management of Data*, pp. 216–227, 2002.

10. R. L. Rivest, L. Adleman, and M. L. Dertouzos. On databanks and privacy homomorphisms. In R. D. DeMillo, editor, *Foundations of Secure Computations*, pp. 169–177. Academic Press, 1978.

11. J. D. Ullman. *Database and Knowledge-Base Systems, Volume I.* Computer Science Press, 1988.

12. Y. Lindell and B. Pinkas. Privacy preserving data mining. In *Proceedings of CRYPTO 00, 20th Annual International Cryptology Conference*, LNCS No. 1880, pp. 36–54. Springer, 2000.

Author Index

Lecture Notes in Computer Science

For information about Vols. 1–3514

please contact your bookseller or Springer